# The
# Post-Traumatic
# Stress Disorder
## SOURCEBOOK Second Edition

## A GUIDE TO HEALING, RECOVERY, AND GROWTH

### Glenn R. Schiraldi, Ph.D.

Mc
Graw
Hill

New York  Chicago  San Francisco  Lisbon  London  Madrid  Mexico City
Milan  New Delhi  San Juan  Seoul  Singapore  Sydney  Toronto

The **McGraw·Hill** Companies

**Library of Congress Cataloging-in-Publication Data**

Schiraldi, Glenn R., 1947–
   The post-traumatic stress disorder sourcebook / Glenn R. Schiraldi. — 2nd ed.
      p.    cm.
   Includes bibliographical references and index.
   ISBN 978-0-07-161494-8 (alk. paper)
   1. Post-traumatic stress disorder.    I. Title.

   RC552.P67S326    2009
   616.85′21—dc22                                               2008035964

The information contained in this book is intended to provide helpful and informative
material on the subject addressed. It is not intended to serve as a replacement for
professional medical or psychological advice. Any use of the information in this book
is at the reader's discretion. The author and publisher specifically disclaim any and
all liability arising directly or indirectly from the use or application of any information
contained in this book. A health-care professional should be consulted regarding your
specific situation.

This book is printed on acid-free paper.

# Contents

# *Acknowledgments*

In recent years, so much has been learned about post-traumatic stress disorder (PTSD). No one compiles a synthesis such as this one without relying on the cumulative efforts of many brilliant theorists, researchers, and clinicians who have advanced our understanding of PTSD and its treatment. I am grateful to dissociation pioneers Drs. Pierre Janet, Richard P. Kluft, Frank W. Putnam, and Richard J. Loewenstein. I am thankful to Dr. Bessel van der Kolk for his insights regarding the brain and trauma and to Drs. George S. Everly, Jr., Charles R. Figley, Edna B. Foa, Judith L. Herman, Mardi Horowitz, Donald Meichenbaum, James W. Pennebaker, Beverly Raphael, Francine Shapiro, John P. Wilson, and many others who have so diligently labored to further our knowledge.

I am most grateful for those who gave so generously of their time to review this book and suggest helpful improvements. These include Drs. Bethany Brand, George S. Everly, Jr., Charles R. Figley, David Keller, Donald Meichenbaum, Raymond M. Scurfield, Francine Shapiro, Mary Beth Williams, John P. Wilson; and Robert L. Bunnell, John W. Downs, Esther Giller, and Mary Beth Quist.

It is rare to find an editorial team that functions with such conscientious, thoughtful, and sensitive attention to detail; my thanks to Rachel Chance, Julia Anderson Bauer, and John Aherne.

Finally, I am exceedingly grateful to the survivors of trauma—in all walks of life—who have battled to overcome their symptoms and by their courage, inspired us all.

Portions of this book have been adapted from some of my previous works: *Conquer Anxiety, Worry and Nervous Fatigue: A Guide to Greater Peace*; *The Anger Management Sourcebook*; *The Self-Esteem Workbook*; *Facts to Relax By: A Guide to Relaxation and Stress Reduction*; *Hope and Help for Depression: A Practical Guide*; and *Stress Management Strategies*.

# Introduction

**We are never prepared for what we expect.**
—*James A. Michener,* Caravans

A firefighter cradles a lifeless little girl. Seven months later, he leaves his beloved profession because of post-traumatic stress disorder (PTSD). In a dimly lit campus parking lot, a bright coed is assaulted. Three weeks later she drops out of college. PTSD has claimed yet another victim.

Life doesn't prepare us for trauma. Following exposure to traumatic events, millions of people develop PTSD or lesser forms of this condition—with symptoms ranging from nightmares to headaches, flashbacks, withdrawing from people, profound sadness, anxiety, anger, guilt, fatigue, pessimism, sexual problems, and emotional numbing. Unless proper treatment is found, many, perhaps most, of these people will secretly and needlessly battle distressing symptoms for life. The good news, however, is that PTSD can be treated successfully. With the right treatment, victims can begin to heal and return to the journey of joyful living.

This book is written for all victims of trauma. You will find it useful if you are a survivor of rape, abuse of any kind, domestic violence, war, crime, natural disasters, industrial disasters, accidents, terrorism, and other traumatic events. It will also be helpful to those whose work exposes them to trauma. Such professions include police officers, firefighters, rescue and disaster workers, military service personnel, emergency medical service workers, paramedics, physicians, and nurses. The book will help you understand the changes that traumatic events cause in people, the process of recovery, and the full range of treatment options. In addition, this book will be of great use to concerned friends, family, and health professionals who associate with survivors of traumatic events.

If you are a survivor, the book will involve you in your own healing and help you to take control of your recovery process. It will also help you to recognize your limitations, determine if help is needed, and find the right help. Once you understand the promising range of treatment options available, you will be better able to choose the best ones for you and benefit from their use. Should you decide to seek the services of a mental health professional, this book will be a valuable resource to you both.

In one sense, PTSD is described by great emotional upheaval and the feeling that the soul is shattered. From another view, PTSD is also the story of courage, determination, resilience, and the ultimate triumph of the human spirit. Today there is much cause for hope. People with PTSD *can* be helped. We now know many ways to lessen the great suffering caused by traumatic events, to help victims deal more comfortably with lingering or recurrent symptoms, and to help them move beyond the trauma. It seems that these words apply especially to this book:

> Pain is a great teacher. Yet the greatest teacher imparts little wisdom if the student has not eyes to see and ears to hear. I write this so that we may benefit from our suffering and triumph over our pain . . . and in the process become better, stronger, warmer, more compassionate, deeper, happier human beings—realizing that the ultimate value of pain reduction is not comfort, but growth.[1]

The goal of this book, then, is to help you move beyond survival, toward the realm of living well. Because you are certainly more than a survivor . . . and much more than just a victim.

Pace yourself when reading this book so as not to become overwhelmed. The treatment approaches described herein can be very effective if properly timed, paced, and applied within the context of a sound working relationship with a skilled mental health professional. Conversely, some approaches (sometimes even certain symptom management approaches), when applied too early, too fast, or alone, might actually increase symptoms. A skilled therapist can help ensure that issues of pacing and safety are attended to, while helping to provide perspective amidst the complexities of recovery. If in doubt, discuss any questions you have with a mental health professional specializing in post-traumatic stress disorder before attempting any approach described herein.

Research regarding the treatment of PTSD is in its early stages. As yet, no one treatment approach has been shown to be superior to any other for all people. Thus, it is important that survivors and clinicians be informed about the range of treatment options so that they can make the best decisions possible about the treatment or combination of treatment approaches.

The book is organized as follows: Part I explains all about PTSD. You'll understand that the symptoms you are experiencing make sense and that you are not going crazy. You'll understand anxiety, dissociation, memory networks, and triggers. And you'll get answers to commonly asked questions.

Part II explains that healing, recovery, and growth are possible. You'll understand the principles of treatment and healing, and the broad types of treatment approaches that are available.

Part III prepares you for healing and recovery. You'll be guided to establish physical and emotional safety and to take care of important needs.

In Part IV, you will learn how to manage troubling symptoms of PTSD so that you can be more comfortable and progress more successfully and confidently in treatment.

Part V explains the broad range of treatment options that are available to you. Chapters 17 through 20 explain important basic principles and skills for neutralizing traumatic memories, including changing commonly held negative and guilt-promoting thoughts. You'll learn how confiding traumatic wounds begins the healing process. Tried and promising therapeutic approaches are described in Chapters 21 through 24. These are applied under the direction of a therapist; however, you'll know what to ask for and will tend to be more comfortable with these approaches once you've read about them. Chapters 25 through 36 describe other important approaches to healing. Some approaches, including those in Chapters 26 and 30, are applied under the direction of a therapist. Other chapters will be useful to discuss in a therapeutic setting and/or to try as homework under a therapist's direction. The reminder is constant: read for understanding—there is power in being informed. If there is any doubt about what to apply or when, discuss your questions with a trauma specialist before attempting anything in this book.

Part VI will help you move beyond PTSD and grow despite your experience with trauma. We'll explore positive aspects of living including intimacy, sexuality, meaning and purpose, spiritual and religious satisfaction, happiness, pleasure, and humor. And finally, you'll be shown how to plan for setbacks and cope with them confidently.

Finally, a range of appendices will direct you to additional important information. Also included is a very comprehensive resource list (see Additional Resources).

Read this book with hope, for indeed there is good reason to hope. Remain committed to your well-being and to the enjoyment of life, and you will become a more valuable resource to others and to yourself.

The

# Post-Traumatic
# Stress Disorder

SOURCEBOOK Second Edition

# PART I

# About PTSD

# CHAPTER 1

# PTSD Basics

Humpty Dumpty sat on a wall
Humpty Dumpty had a great fall
All the king's horses and all the king's men
Couldn't put Humpty Dumpty together again

Post-traumatic stress disorder (PTSD) results from exposure to an overwhelmingly stressful event or series of events, such as war, rape, or abuse. It is a normal response by normal people to an abnormal situation.

The traumatic events that lead to PTSD are typically so extraordinary or severe that they would distress almost anyone. These events are usually sudden. They are perceived as dangerous to self or others, and they overwhelm our ability to respond adequately.[1]

We say that PTSD is a normal response to an abnormal event because the condition is completely understandable and predictable. The symptoms make perfect sense because what happened has overwhelmed normal coping responses.

## THE HUMAN FACE

In another sense, however, the mental and physical suffering in PTSD is beyond the range of normalcy and indicates a need for assistance.[2] People with PTSD call to mind the Humpty Dumpty nursery rhyme. They often report feeling

- Shattered, broken, wounded, ripped, or torn apart
- Like they'll never get put back together
- Bruised to the soul, devastated, fallen apart, crushed
- Shut down, beaten down, beaten up
- Nothing seems sacred or special anymore
- As though they are in a deep black hole, damaged, ruined
- Different from everybody else
- As though they are losing their mind, going crazy, doomed
- Dead inside, "on the sidelines of life's games"[3]

Many PTSD sufferers also report feeling fundamentally changed by their traumatic experience: "I used to be happy-go-lucky, now I'm serious and quiet." "My life seems to be divided into two periods, before the trauma and after." "It really threw me." "My life was derailed."

## WHAT CAUSES PTSD?

As Table 1.1 indicates, PTSD could be caused by a wide range of events, grouped here into three categories. As a general rule, intentional human causes are the most difficult to recover from,[4] followed by unintentional human causes. Acts of nature are the least complex and typically resolve more quickly than the other categories.

## WHAT SPECIFICALLY IS PTSD?

A trauma is a wound. PTSD refers to deep emotional wounds. In 1980, following the Vietnam experience, the American Psychiatric Association formally defined PTSD, categorizing it as one of the anxiety disorders. Table 1.2 lists the diagnostic criteria, or requirements for determining if one has PTSD, as described in the *Diagnostic and Statistical Manual of Mental Disorders* (DSM) of the American Psychiatric Association.

## DSM CRITERIA EXPLAINED

At first, PTSD might seem quite confusing. However, you'll soon realize that the symptoms are very understandable. They make sense, and seeing this is, in itself, somewhat curative. The explanations that follow will help to clarify these criteria (see Table 1.2).

**Table 1.1**
## POTENTIALLY TRAUMATIC EVENTS AND STRESSORS

### Intentional Human (man-made, deliberate, malicious)

Combat, civil war, resistance fighting

Abuse
- Sexual—incest; rape; forced nudity, exhibitionism, or pornography; inappropriate touching, fondling, or kissing
- Physical—beating, kicking, battering, choking, tying up, stalking, forcing to eat/drink, threatening with weapon, elder abuse by own children
- Emotional—isolation, threats to leave or have affair, intimidation, degrading names, economic neglect, minimizing or denying abuse, taking away power/control, destroying property, torturing pets, physical neglect (leaving alone, not feeding or bathing)[5]

Torture (sexual being the worst because it combines physical, emotional, and spiritual cruelty)

Criminal assault, violent crime, robbery, mugging, family violence/battery

Being held hostage; imprisonment as a POW or in a concentration camp

Hijacking

Cult abuse

Terrorism

Bombing (e.g., Hiroshima, Oklahoma City)

Witnessing a homicide, sexual assault, battering, torture, etc.

Sniper attack

Kidnapping

Riot

Witnessing parents' fear reactions

Alcoholism (due to its effects on family members)

Participating in violence/atrocities (e.g., as Nazi doctors or as soldiers) or identifying with the aggressor/perpetrator

Suicide or other form of sudden death

Death threats

Damage to or loss of body part

### Unintentional Human (accidents, technological disasters)

Industrial (e.g., a crane crashes down)

Fire, burns (e.g., an oil rig catches fire)

Explosion

Motor vehicle accident, plane crash, train wreck, boating accident, shipwreck

Nuclear disaster (Chernobyl, Three Mile Island)

Collapse of sports stadium, building, dam, or skywalk

Surgical damage to body or loss of body part; botched anesthesia (especially when very young)

### Acts of Nature/Natural Disasters

Hurricane

Typhoon

Tornado

Flood

Earthquake

Avalanche

Volcanic eruption

Fire

Drought, famine

Attack by animal (such as a pit bull)

Sudden life-threatening illness (e.g., heart attack, severe burns)

Sudden death (e.g., loss of unborn child)*

---

*Although death from natural causes is generally not considered a traumatic stressor, clearly some people do develop PTSD after watching a loved one die from an illness.*

**Table 1.2**
**PTSD DIAGNOSTIC CRITERIA**

### Exposure to Stressor

A person must be exposed to a traumatic event involving both of the following:

1. Experiencing, seeing, or learning of event or events that involve actual or threatened death, serious injury, or violation of the body of self or others.
2. Responding to this event with intense fear, helplessness, or horror. In children, the response may involve disorganized or agitated behavior.

### Reexperiencing of Event

The trauma is persistently reexperienced in at least one of the following ways:

1. Recurrent, intrusive recollections (images, thoughts, or perceptions) of the event. In children, repetitive play may express themes or aspects of the event.
2. Recurrent, distressing dreams of the event. Children may have no content recognizably related to the trauma in dreams.
3. Acting or feeling as if the trauma were recurring (including feeling a sense of reliving the incident, experiencing illusions or hallucinations, and having dissociative flashback episodes, including those on awakening or when intoxicated). Children may reenact the trauma.
4. Intense psychological distress upon exposure to internal or external cues that symbolize or resemble an aspect of the trauma.
5. Reacting physiologically upon exposure to such cues.

### Avoidance

Persistent avoidance of stimuli associated with the trauma and numbing of general responsiveness that was not present before the trauma, as indicated by at least three of the following:

1. Making efforts to avoid thoughts, feelings, or conversations that remind one of the trauma.
2. Making efforts to avoid activities, places, or people that arouse recollections.
3. Inability to recall an important aspect of the trauma.
4. Markedly diminished interest or participation in significant activities that used to be pleasurable.
5. Experiencing a feeling of detachment or estrangement from others.
6. Restricted range of affect. For example, one might have a hard time having loving feelings, especially those associated with intimacy, tenderness, or sexuality.
7. A sense of foreshortened future. One may not expect to have a career, marriage, children, or normal life span.

### Arousal

Persistent symptoms of increased arousal that were not present before the trauma. At least two of the following occur:

1. Difficulty falling or staying asleep.
2. Irritability or outbursts of anger.
3. Difficulty concentrating.
4. Hypervigilance.
5. Exaggerated startle response.

### Duration

The symptomatic criteria described above (Reexperiencing of Event, Avoidance, and Arousal) lasts longer than one month.

### Life Disrupted

The disturbance causes clinically significant distress or impairment in social, occupational, or other important areas of functioning.

## Exposure to Stressor

PTSD is the only DSM condition for which the occurrence of a stressor is part of the diagnosis. Unlike other anxiety disorders that are simply described by their symptoms, PTSD requires the occurrence of a catastrophic event or events. You might wish to refer again to Table 1.1 for a listing of such events. PTSD can result from any severe stressor, and the symptoms are similar if the stressors are severe enough. Thus, the PTSD resulting from rape or violent crime is quite similar in appearance to the PTSD resulting from combat.

Of the three categories of stressors in Table 1.1, intentional human traumas are usually the worst. PTSD symptoms resulting from such stressors are usually more complex, are of longer duration, and are more difficult to treat for a number of reasons. Such traumas are typically the most degrading and cause the most shame. They often involve feelings of being stigmatized, marked, different, or an outcast (as in rape). Man-made traumas are also most likely to cause people to lose faith and trust in humanity, in love, and in themselves. By contrast, natural disasters are, typically, less difficult to recover from. Survivors often bond. Frequently, heroism and community support is evident. Survivors often feel a reverence or awe for nature that leaves faith in humanity intact.

Categories may be combined in traumatic stress. For example, a hurricane (a natural disaster) might cause the collapse of improperly built homes (unintentional or intentional trauma).

We shall discuss the next three PTSD symptom groups in the sequence in which they logically occur. That is, people reexperience the trauma in distressing ways and become very aroused as a result. They then make various attempts to avoid the PTSD symptoms.

## Event Reexperienced

In one sense, PTSD can be viewed as a fear of the unpleasant memories of the traumatic event that repeatedly intrude into one's awareness. Intrusive recollections can occur in the form of thoughts, images, or perceptions. These intrusions are unwelcome, uninvited, and painful, and the person experiencing them wishes that they could put a stop to them. They often elicit feelings of fear and vulnerability, rage at the cause, sadness, disgust, or guilt. Sometimes these intrusions break through when one is trying to relax and one's guard is down. Sometimes a trigger that reminds one of the trauma will start the intrusions. For example, a survivor of a Russian prisoner-of-war camp often daydreams, absorbed in unpleasant memories and out of touch with his surroundings. A number of cues can trigger this re-experience, including thin soup, walking in the woods, Russian music, a harsh rebuke by a supervisor, or any unpleasant confrontation.[6] Sometimes there is no apparent connection to the thoughts or feelings that are replayed.

Nightmares are a common form of reexperiencing the trauma. The nightmares might be fairly accurate replays of the traumatic event, or they might symbolically depict the trauma with themes of threats, rescuing self or others, being trapped or chased by monsters, or dying.

Flashbacks are a particularly upsetting form of reexperiencing the traumatic event. In flashbacks, we feel that we are going back in time and reliving the trauma. Typically, flashbacks are visual re-experiences. However, they can also involve sensations, behavior, or emotions. For example, a war veteran hits the ground when a car backfires, and sees a battle recurring, begins to hear sounds of battle, and feels hot, sweaty, and terrified. Later, he does not remember the incident. Flashbacks can last from seconds to hours, and even days. They are usually believed to be real and then forgotten, but sometimes the sufferer will realize that the flashback was not reality. Flashbacks are often triggered by insomnia, fatigue, stress, or drugs.[7]

Experiencing the intrusive memories is very distressful, both psychologically and physically. Although one might not realize that a cue triggers the distress that accompanies intrusive thoughts, some searching can usually find it. The trigger might be either a cue in the environment, such as the backfiring car that reminded the veteran of gunfire, or an internal trigger, such as a nauseous feeling that is similar to one experienced after a rape.

## Arousal

Like other anxiety disorders, PTSD is characterized by extreme general physical arousal and/or arousal following exposure to internal or external triggers. The nervous system has become *sensitized* by an overwhelming trauma. Thus, two things can happen. General arousal becomes elevated, while the nervous system overreacts to even smaller stressors. Signs of arousal include the following:

- **Troubled sleep** includes difficulty falling or staying asleep, twitching, moving, and/or awakening unrested. Awakenings may be due to nightmares. Fear of nightmares might then lead to fear of going to sleep, especially if one was violated in bed.[8]
- **Irritability or outbursts of anger** might be displayed as smashing things, heated arguing, flying off the handle, screaming, intense criticizing, or

impatience. Unresolved anger is fatiguing. It might be mixed with shame, frustration, betrayal, or other uncomfortable emotions that lead to moodiness and explosions of pent-up anger. One might then feel embarrassed or guilty.

- **Difficulty concentrating or remembering** can occur when one is still battling for control of intrusive memories.
- **Hypervigilance.** People who have endured a trauma will be on guard against intrusive memories. They are also likely to be unusually cautious to ensure that further injury does not occur. Hypervigilance might be demonstrated as
    Feeling vulnerable, fearful of lots of things, unable to feel calm in safe places
    Fear of repetition
    Anticipating disaster, such as needing to sit in the corner of a room with one's back to the wall while looking for exits or places to hide (one fireman carried around a fire extinguisher for a year after being burned by a petroleum ball)[9]
    Rapid scanning, looking over one's shoulder
    Keeping a weapon or several weapons
    Being overprotective or overcontrolling of loved ones
- **Exaggerated startle response** means you are easily frightened. A sensitized nervous system will overreact to frightening or even unusual stressors. Thus, you might jump, flinch, or tense when someone appears suddenly or from behind, when a sudden noise occurs, when someone wakes you up when sleeping, or when someone touches you. Eye blinking may become more rapid. One woman who was struck in a head-on car accident will now jerk the steering wheel when she sees another car approaching.[10]

In addition to the above symptoms, indications of a sensitized nervous system might include the following:

- Elevation of certain stress hormones in the blood[11]
- Elevated heart rate (either resting or in response to stress)
- Elevated blood pressure
- Hyperventilation (expelling $CO_2$ too quickly—usually caused by rapid, shallow "chest breathing" but could also result from deep breathing)

- Tight chest or stomach
- Light-headedness
- Sweating
- Tingling, cold, or sweaty hands

These might occur generally or in response to a trigger.

## Avoidance and Numbing

Because the intrusive thoughts and accompanying arousal are so unpleasant, people with PTSD desperately try to avoid all reminders of the trauma. They might refuse to talk about it. They might block from their mind thoughts, images, or feelings about the event. They might avoid activities, places, people, or keepsakes that arouse recollections. Some might become housebound in attempts to avoid fearful encounters. Some turn to drugs or overwork to avoid their painful feelings, while others simply shut down all feelings in order to avoid their pain. Some live in a fantasy world, trying to pretend that nothing bad happened.[12]

Sometimes, PTSD sufferers will shut out memories of painful periods in their lives and experience amnesia. Thus, a traumatized individual might not remember when his spouse died in a car accident. Another person who was abused might have gaps in her memory of childhood.

One person might obsess over worries or physical pain in order to avoid facing painful feelings. Another might use anger to avoid facing deeper feelings.

When memories are so painful, it makes sense that one would try to numb them. However, one cannot numb painful memories without also numbing joyful memories. One must suppress *all* feelings in order to numb painful feelings. So people with PTSD often avoid even pleasant activities, including those that were pleasurable before the trauma—such as travel, babies, hobbies, or relaxation. You might hear people say, "I don't know how to have fun or play anymore." Without feelings, these people naturally feel uninvolved with life.

Not surprisingly, people with PTSD commonly feel detached or estranged from others. People who have endured combat, rape, disaster work, and other forms of trauma often assume that they are now different and that no one could possibly relate to their experiences. They might feel that they can't tell others about what happened or what they did for fear of judgment, and the secrets and fear of being shunned lead to their feeling disconnected from others. Because they no longer feel comfortable in social situations, they might avoid gatherings—or they might go but find no pleasure in them. Of course, to connect with others, people need to be emotionally open. This is difficult when one is still struggling to contain memories of the past.

*Restricted range of affect* refers to the "psychic numbing" or "emotional anesthesia" that one does to try to escape from the painful memories. As we mentioned, anything that numbs pain acts as a general anesthesia. Thus, one with PTSD might have trouble laughing, crying, or loving. Feeling numb and closed down, he might wrongly assume he has lost his capacity to feel or be compassionate, intimate, tender, or sexual. Certain family or work environments such as the military or emergency service work might encourage the suppression of feelings. However, at some point, the healthy experience and expression of grief and pain must occur if one is to become a healthy, emotional person.

As trauma can lead one to feel disconnected from others, it can also lead one to feel disconnected from his or her future. This is called *a sense of foreshortened future*, which means that trauma victims can't envision or look forward to a normal, happy life. They might not expect to have a career, marriage, children, community connections, or a normal life span—so it is difficult to make plans for the future. Instead, their pessimistic expectations for the future might include disasters, repetition of the trauma, dying young, or simply finding no joy. This outlook has been called the "doomsday orientation"—no matter how good life seems, trouble is coming.[13] Said one person with PTSD, "I can't get past the past, so how can I think about the future?" If people are stuck in the past—preoccupied with unresolved pain, guilt, anger, grief, or fear and desperately trying to block these feelings out—they will often lack the energy or interest to plan for the future. If they worry that intrusive memories can spoil their moods at will, they will hardly make plans for a joyful future. Said another with PTSD, "I placed my memories behind prison doors and stand guard. I realized, however, that it is I who am the prisoner. I am so tired of standing guard that I no longer seem to care." It is a sad irony that when one tries to block out the past, one blocks out both the present and future as well.

## Duration

The symptom picture described in Table 1.2 under the categories "Reexperiencing of Event," "Avoidance," and "Arousal" must persist for at least one month for a diagnosis of PTSD. PTSD is specified as *acute* if the diagnosis resolves within three months, *chronic* if the diagnosis persists beyond three months, and *delayed* if the onset of PTSD occurs at least six months after exposure to the stressor. It has been observed that a large percentage of PTSD cases improve considerably within three months.

## Impaired Social and Occupational Functioning

The diagnosis of PTSD means that symptoms are significantly interfering with your relationships or work. Communication is disrupted by numbing, pulling inward, avoiding people and social situations, or by hostility and anger. Work suffers due to absenteeism, fatigue, or impaired concentration.

# CHAPTER 2

# *Making Sense of the Bewildering Symptoms*

## *Understanding Anxiety and Dissociation*

---

This chapter describes two of the major symptoms of PTSD, anxiety and dissociation, to include the role of memory networks and the triggering of trauma-related memories. PTSD will seem much less confusing when you understand these concepts.

### ANXIETY

PTSD is considered an anxiety disorder. Many of PTSD's arousal symptoms are common to anxiety. There is no mystery about this condition: anxiety is essentially worrisome thoughts plus excessive emotional and physical arousal.

Normally, when the brain perceives a threat, it sets off a chain of physical changes that prepares the body for fight or flight. Messages are sent via nerves and blood-borne hormones to the body's various organs. Muscles tense, the heart beats faster and stronger, and the rate of breathing increases. The brain becomes sharper and able to react more quickly. This is called the *stress response*, or just stress. Stress is very adaptive in the short term. It prepares the body for emergencies. The energy of the stress response is designed to be worked off physically; the body then returns to the resting state.

In anxiety, the mind stays vigilant, ever on alert. This, in turn, keeps emotions and the body aroused. Chronic or severe arousal changes the nervous system. We say that the nervous system becomes *sensitized* from overstimulation. The brain's alarm centers stay on alert and sound the alarm for smaller threats than usual, while the body takes longer to return to the resting state. A traumatic event, or even an overload of smaller stressors, can change the structure and function of nerve cells. The amounts of neurotransmitters (chemical messengers) in the brain can change, as can the number of receptor sites for these chemicals on the nerves. A vicious cycle is set off whereby worry maintains physical and emotional arousal and this arousal maintains worry. It feels like worry and arousal cannot be shut off. Anxiety seems to take on a life of its own and is not always proportional to what is going on in your life. Anxiety accounts for a bewildering array of symptoms:

- **Physical fatigue.** Tension, fatigue, trembling, tingling, nausea, digestive tract problems, hyperventilation (rapid breathing), pounding heart, suffocating feelings, panic attacks
- **Emotional fatigue.** Irritation, moodiness, fear, exaggerated emotions, loss of confidence
- **Mental fatigue.** Confusion; inability to concentrate, remember, or make decisions
- **Spiritual fatigue.** Discouragement, hopelessness, despair

The symptoms of anxiety are merely an exaggerated stress response. They lessen as we retrain our nervous system to be calmer. They increase as we tell ourselves that they are unbearable and must stop.

*Avoidance* is a hallmark of anxiety. We try to flee the things that trigger it. This avoidance brings temporary relief, but at quite a cost. First, we maintain the fear of the triggers. We don't allow ourselves to let the fear in and watch it subside as we relax. So we don't learn to master our fears. Each time avoidance is rewarded with short-term anxiety reduction, we will tend to use it again in the future. The distractions that we use to escape the fear, such as work, will become associated with the fear through conditioning. Soon the distractions become triggers by association. The antidote to avoidance is to face the things we fear and flow with the symptoms until the stress response runs its course and we retrain our nervous system to be less reactive. This is learned in a gradual fashion.

Although PTSD is considered an anxiety disorder, also viewing it as a dissociative disorder helps us to better understand the symptoms. In order to understand dissociation, let's first understand normal "associated" consciousness.

## NORMAL "ASSOCIATED" CONSCIOUSNESS

In normal consciousness or awareness, people are fully engaged in life's experiences. They are basically mindful of their surroundings, tuned in to people, and open to the full range of feelings. Despite feeling various emotions or being in different situations, they always feel like the same person. When normal memories are triggered or intentionally retrieved, they can examine them and then put them away at will. Distractions from present awareness are either pleasant or at least controllable. For example, if you are paying your bills and your mind drifts off to Bermuda, you can bring it back to the task at hand if you choose to. If adding numbers brings back an unpleasant memory of failing math, you might think about it for a moment and then bring your focus back quickly to the bills.[1] In other words, your mind functions in a smooth, integrated way. Memories are filed away in an organized way. They can be retrieved and smoothly put away again.

## DISSOCIATION

Have you ever observed an antelope clamped in a lion's jaws? It seems to stop struggling as its consciousness shifts. Where does its consciousness go?[2] There seems to be an innate mechanism—called *dissociation*—that allows mammals to temporarily escape distressing experiences. Thus, we can mentally escape a present distressing experience, as the antelope did, by mentally "going away." Or, we can temporarily escape a traumatic memory by separating and walling off the memory. Instead of being smoothly connected to all other memories, the highly charged traumatic memories become dissociated or isolated. While the memory may be walled off for a while, it is not filed in long-term memory. Instead of taking its place alongside other memories on file, the traumatic memory remains "on the desktop," where it repeatedly intrudes upon awareness and cannot, it seems, be put away for long. Dissociated traumatic memory material is said to be walled off, split off, fragmented, separated off, or compartmentalized such that the information does not become integrated with the rest of one's memory material, nor is it fully connected to present awareness.

Traumatic memories contain many aspects: thoughts, images, feelings, behaviors, and physical sensations. Wrapped up in the trauma material may be a unique sense of identity, or who you are, since people often feel very different during the trauma. So you might feel like a different person since the trauma or when traumatic memories intrude into your awareness.

**Figure 2.1**
AWARENESS AND MEMORY

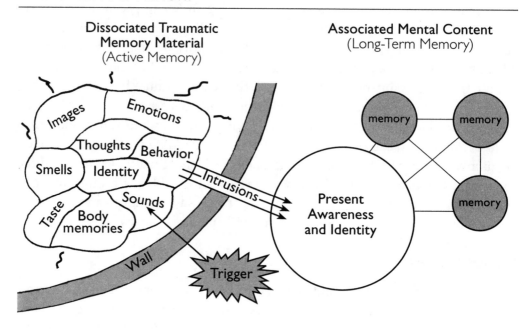

## MEMORY NETWORKS

A simplified picture (see Figure 2.1) helps to show how associated and dissociated memories are stored in the brain. Let's explore Figure 2.1 further.

### Associated Mental Content

On the right of the walled-off traumatic memory material depicted in Figure 2.1 is normal *associated* mental material. Normal memories are smoothly connected or integrated. Lessons learned and useful ideas from previous life experiences can be blended into present awareness and coping efforts. So a person who has had a very safe and secure childhood might approach a new challenge with the thought, "I'm safe; I'll probably be all right." Across all memories is the sense that you are the same person. Scientists have learned that under normal conditions various parts of the brain are activated to process memories in an organized way (see Appendix C). That is, the brain connects diverse aspects of a single memory to form an integrated whole. That memory is also filed alongside other memories in a way that a person can place it in time and space. Normal memories are processed logically and verbally. They are understood and make sense, and are then filed away. Although the memories contain appropriate emotions, they can be recalled without overwhelming emotion.

### Dissociated Traumatic Memory Material

On the left is *dissociated* trauma material. Notice several characteristics of this material.

*This "walled-off" material is highly unstable.* The parts of the brain that would normally file traumatic memories in long-term storage were overwhelmed during the trauma. So traumatic memories remain near the forefront of awareness, trapped in active memory, and easily triggered by reminders of the trauma—or even things associated with the *trigger*. For example, a woman who was raped on an elevator two years ago now reexperiences terror when she approaches any elevator. Since she got into the elevator after parking her car, parking garages have also become frightening. In fact, she feels frightened almost any time she parks her car, even when outside. A new association has been formed between the elevator and the act of parking. Now either can trigger intrusive memories. Sometimes traumatic memories can be triggered by stressful emotions that might seem unrelated to the trauma. For example, a firefighter "trapped" in traffic remembers being helpless to rescue a child in a burning building; a man who was abused as a child experiences intrusive memories when his boss criticizes him. These are called *state-dependent memories*, and the process called *mood-dependent retrieval*. A trigger may or may not be obvious as it passes through our awareness.

*The "wall" is highly permeable.* It is like a leaky dam. We expend much energy trying to maintain the wall, but memories keep seeping through, or intruding, into awareness.

*The dissociated material is highly emotional and relatively nonverbal.* Unlike normal memories, which are rather logically and verbally processed before storage, trauma material is walled off prior to complete processing. If verbal processing is done at all, it is usually quite incomplete, and thoughts related to the trauma will usually be automatic, unspoken, unchallenged, and disorganized. During a trauma, a person might have thought, "I am completely vulnerable." Now any stressful situation automatically triggers the same thought. The person may not even be aware of the unspoken thought. Instead, she just feels the intense emotions resulting from the thought. In this case, the very ideas that would help the person cope with traumatic memories are already stored in the associated memories. Normally, for example, she knows that all situations are not unsafe, especially when proper precautions are taken. However, the intrusive traumatic material, separated from this adaptive thinking, dominates her experience.

*Trauma material is not only walled off from associated adaptive material, but the traumatic memory itself might be fragmented into various aspects.* These aspects of memory include thoughts, images, emotions, behavior, identity, and physical sensations. Physical sensations include sounds, smells, tastes, and "body memories." These "body memories" can involve tactile, or touch, sensations, pain, and kinesthesia (the sensation of movement, tension, or position). Because of this fragmentation, a trigger does not usually set off all aspects of a memory. For instance, emotions from a traumatic memory might flood awareness without images or other memory aspects. Sheila was enjoying dinner with a group of friends. She became unaccountably anxious and sick to her stomach. She didn't realize that a man in the group was wearing the same cologne as the man who raped her. In this case, only fragments of the unprocessed memory (the emotions and physical sensations) were triggered by the fragrance.

Trauma material is like a screaming, emotional two-year-old trying to escape from a playpen in the middle of the living room while you try to watch a television program. You wish for a few moments of peace, but the more you ignore the child, the more the child demands attention, and the more effort it takes to concentrate on the show. Seeing a child on television reminds you of your own child. Eventually you give the child attention and the intrusions stop. This suggests how recovery will occur in PTSD.

## Triggers

Many triggers in the present environment can activate traumatic memory material and stimulate intrusions. *Triggers* are cues—often harmless—that have become associated with the original trauma. In some way, they remind us of the trauma or recall traumatic memories. The association may be obvious or subtle. They may trigger most of the memory or just certain fragments of it. Often, they trigger intrusions against our will. Recognizing triggers and realizing that their power to elicit intrusions is understandable are steps toward controlling PTSD symptoms. Table 2.1 lists a range of triggers and the traumatic memories they can stir up.

Some people find it helpful to understand triggers by conceptualizing them in the following twelve categories.

**Table 2.1**
## TRAUMATIC EVENTS AND TRIGGERS

| Trigger | Original Traumatic Event |
| --- | --- |
| Dark clouds, strong winds | Tornado |
| Entering subway tunnel | Trench warfare or tunnel rats in Vietnam |
| Lasagna or milk cartons | Firemen recovering bodies of children buried in school cafeteria by tornado |
| Firecrackers | Combat, gunshots |
| Popcorn popping | Helicopter in Vietnam, small arms fire |
| Campfire, cooking, barbecue grill | Burn victim or fireman who rescued burn victim |
| Rumbling truck | Earthquake |
| Aging, hospitalization | POW camp (loss of freedom, family, and purpose; helplessness) |
| Warm, damp day | Vietnam |
| Rain, clouds in sky | Flood |
| Bedroom, lying down, closing eyes | Rape |
| Asthmatic breathing | Hand held over mouth of rape victim |
| Nausea from illness or something eaten | Date rape (which led to nausea) |
| Neighbors | Child dies in neighborhood auto accident, neighbors at scene |
| The smell of fuel at gas station | Airplane crash for rescue worker |
| Perpetrator on television | Violent robbery |
| Pretzels | Eaten at frat party before being raped |
| Boss criticizes | Abuse by father |
| Depression, guilt, anniversary month, becoming a parent | Miscarriage |
| Throat swab during medical exam leads to nausea and shakiness[3] | Oral rape |
| Physical intimacy (emotional expressiveness elicits fear of losing control) | Sexually abusive, rageful father |

*(continued)*

**Table 2.1** *(continued)*
**TRAUMATIC EVENTS AND TRIGGERS**

| Trigger | Original Traumatic Event |
| --- | --- |
| Cold, snowy weather; uniformed security guards; hunger; watery soup; walking along roads in the winter; German vehicles; any unpleasant confrontation or rebuke by supervisors | POW in Germany |
| Firefighting, police, other paramilitary jobs | Soldiering |
| Elevator | Sexual assault |
| Scuba diving, beach | Rescue workers searching for bodies following airliner crash in ocean |
| Injections, vaginal exam | Torture |
| Seeing a crime on television | Policeman seriously wounded |
| Rushing, overload, stress | A disastrous decision made under pressure, without time to think |
| Egg white | Rape (semen) |
| Traffic, smell of diesel | Roadside bomb in Iraq |
| Lover's naked body | Bodies of civilians killed by terrorists |

1. **Sight** (visual). Seeing blood or roadkill reminds one of wounded bodies. Black garbage bags reminds a veteran of body bags. A secretary sees her boss standing over her and is reminded of her abusive father.
2. **Sound** (auditory). A backfiring car sounds like gunshot to a combat veteran; sounds during lovemaking with a spouse remind one of sexual abuse.
3. **Smell** (olfactory). The smell of semen or another's body during intercourse or the smell of aftershave reminds one of sexual assault.[4]
4. **Taste** (gustatory). Eating a hamburger reminds one of an automobile accident that occurred as one drove away from a fast-food restaurant.
5. **Body** (physical).
   - **Kinesthesia** means the sensation of movement, tension, or body position. Running when tense might be reminiscent of trying to flee a beating; trying to do progressive muscle relaxation (tensing muscles, lying on one's back with eyes closed) might trigger memories of sexual abuse.
   - **Tactile** or touch sensations can trigger intrusive memories. Pressure around wrists or waist, being gripped, held, or otherwise restrained

(perhaps even a hug), or feeling someone on top of you reminds you of torture or rape. A man accidentally kicked in bed by his wife while sleeping recalls torture; being touched during sexual relations with a spouse in the same place or in the same way as occurred during abuse might trigger traumatic memories.

- **Pain** or other internal sensations such as surgical pain, nausea, headaches, or back pain might trigger memories of torture or rape. Elevated heartbeat from exercising might remind one of a similar sensation during a bombing.

6. **Significant dates or seasons.**
   - Anniversary dates of the trauma
   - Seasons of the year with their accompanying stimuli (temperature, lighting, colors, sounds)
   - Other dates (a mother becomes distressed on the date when her murdered son would have graduated)

7. **Stressful events and arousal.** Sometimes changes in the brain due to trauma cause it to interpret any stress signals as recurrence of the original trauma.[5] At other times, seemingly unrelated events are actually triggers. The following scenarios are some common examples of this:
   - A woman visits her spouse in the hospital, which triggers a flashback of abuse. As a little girl, she was treated in the same hospital following the abuse.
   - An argument with a spouse triggers memories of parents arguing violently.
   - Criticism from a boss reminds a person of being abused by his father.
   - A frightening dream with no apparent related theme activates the fear of a traumatic memory. (Of course, a nightmare about the trauma would understandably elicit strong feelings of distress.)
   - Athletic competition reminds an athlete of being abused when she performed poorly.

8. **Strong emotions.** Feeling lonely reminds one of abandonment; feeling happy reminds a woman of a rape that occurred after having dinner with her best friends. Anything that makes one anxious, out of control, or generally stressed, such as premenstrual syndrome (PMS), can trigger intrusive memories. Some memories are state-dependent, meaning that the brain activates them only when the emotional state is the same as the original memory.[6] Thus, if one was drunk when raped, she may feel symptoms only

when drinking; if raped when sober, then drinking might provide an escape from the symptoms.[7]

9. **Thoughts.** Rejection by a lover leads to the thought, "I am worthless," which triggers the same thought that occurred when one was abused as a child.
10. **Behaviors.** Driving reminds a person of a serious accident.
11. **Out of the blue.** Sometimes intrusions occur when you are tired, relaxing, or your defenses are down. Often a thought or something you're not aware of will elicit symptoms; so might the habitual act of dissociating during stressful times.
12. **Combinations.** Often triggers contain several memory aspects at once. Here are some examples:
    - Walking to the parking lot on a dark summer's night (visual + kinesthetic + seasonal stimuli) triggers a memory of violent crime.
    - Fireworks (loud sounds + flarelike sight) trigger combat memories.
    - Intercourse (weight, touch, sounds, relaxing, the smell of aftershave or semen, the pressure of a hug or a squeezing sensation on the wrists) triggers memory of rape.

## WHY DOES DISSOCIATION OCCUR?

Dissociation is a defense against extremely distressful, painful experience. The mind walls off trauma material to try to contain it in much the same way as the body walls off infection. Dissociation is most likely to occur if the trauma was severe, repeated, or occurred at a very young age. We might regard dissociation as a very understandable coping mechanism.

As long as we wall off painful material, we gain some protection. However, the protection is temporary. Without exploration and processing, the material remains negatively and emotionally charged and will intrude in distressing ways. Intrusions are the mind's way of telling us that painful material needs processing. If we can view intrusions as such, then we will likely experience less distress when they occur.

## WHEN DOES DISSOCIATION OCCUR?

Dissociation might occur during traumatic events that seem too painful to cope with. For example, a teenager who was raped reported that she felt as if she were on the ceiling during the rape, looking down and feeling sorry for the person being raped. In this way, called *depersonalization*, she could "separate" herself from the trauma. Her usual self was watching the event from afar, while another part of her identity was walled off in the trauma memory. This defense is entirely understandable. It protects for a while. Yet notice what has happened. Walled-off material has been created. This material will eventually intrude in a distressing way until it has been processed enough to take its place among other memories on file. The sense of self has been split as well. Another way people who experience trauma dissociate during a traumatic event is *derealization*. In derealization, the person looks at the event as if it is not really happening, as if it is a dream, far away, or covered by fog. Dissociation at the time of the trauma will usually make healing more difficult.

Dissociation can also occur later in life as an escape from stress. We might simply be trying to escape an everyday stressful situation, or we may be reacting to intrusions or triggers. We are more likely to dissociate in the present if dissociation happened at the time of the trauma. Dissociation at the time of trauma is more likely when the victim is very young or if the offense was repeated or horrific. One seems to learn to use dissociation as a defense. We are also more prone to dissociate in the present if we are tired, drunk, sleepy, anxious, or depressed.[8]

## VARIETIES OF DISSOCIATION

People dissociate in many ways that do no harm. For example, immersing yourself in a book, movie, or play and "tuning out" your surroundings is generally a harmless escape. Daydreaming is another way to escape from reality. Usually, these are harmless because they are pleasant and under our control. We become concerned when dissociation occurs often, is not under our control, becomes distressing, or makes us feel detached from life. Let's take a look at the more distressing forms of dissociation. All signal that the person is elsewhere, not focused in the present, and is using energy to contain troubling material. All signal that the person is trying to distance himself from the unacceptable.

### Depersonalization
As discussed previously, in *depersonalization*, one feels as if he or she is an outside observer of self (e.g., on the ceiling looking down or across the room watching a movie of self).

### Amnesia
*Amnesia* means forgetting all or parts of the trauma. Some people forget the entire trauma. Others forget only the most stressful aspects of the trauma, such as the

moment when one was thrown from a car. Some experience gaps in their life story, for example, an entire year of school during which abuse occurred, or for all the years before it occurred. Others simply have a poor general memory, as if remembering anything might invite more intrusions. Amnesia is not explained by normal forgetfulness, but is more severe and distressing.

### Dissociative Flashbacks

After people try for so long to wall off traumatic memories, these memories eventually break through into awareness. *Dissociative flashbacks* pull us away from the present and into the memories. We suddenly and vividly experience the memories as if they are happening in the present. For instance, Bob was a combat veteran of the Vietnam War. While at a Fourth of July celebration, a teenager carelessly threw a firecracker near his young daughters. Bob immediately flashed back to the war, pounced on the teenager, and was choking him when bystanders pulled him off. He later had no recollection of the flashback.[9] As people explain to him what happened, he begins to think he is going crazy. He is not. It is simply the result of walled-off material that has never been processed. As with other intrusive memories, one might reexperience many aspects of a traumatic memory, or just certain aspects. One may or may not act as if he is back in the situation. Some still retain some awareness of present reality during flashbacks, as though they were watching a movie of the trauma. Some remember having the flashbacks.

### Fugue

*Fugue* is a form of amnesia in which a person suddenly travels to another town with no recollection of how he got there. Some may start a new life and forget their old identity.

### Dissociative Identity Disorder (DID)

*Dissociative identity disorder* is the most severe dissociative state. Here, people form at least two different personality states, or identities, in order to cope with unacceptable material. Ellen was a happy little girl until her father began to sexually abuse her. She could not figure out how a father who was often loving to her could also mistreat her. Her young mind could not make sense of this, nor was she old enough to seek help or talk about it. It seemed that part of her must be bad to deserve this. As she developed, Ellen formed two identities. Ellen was the good and outwardly happy girl that most people knew. At other times, particularly when trauma-related triggers occurred, she switched to an identity known as "Trixy"—a seductive, promiscuous woman who frequented bars to be picked up. Trixy is a way to contain the unacceptable trauma material. To Ellen, it seems that the trauma "didn't happen to me—it happened to someone else," in this case, Trixy. In DID, there may be many more personality states (sometimes called *alter egos* or *alters*). Each feels like a different person and may have a different self-image. This is why DID used to be called *multiple personality disorder*. However, there is only one person and one personality—but the aspects of the personality have not yet been integrated. There may be a host identity who knows the other identities and may be influenced by the alters' voices. The host is often compulsively good, logical, depressed, and overwhelmed. There may be an angry identity who blows up at people. Alternate identities might differ in age, may conflict with or deny knowing each other, or may hold different fragments of memories. The identities might have typical given names (like Barbara) or symbolic names (the Tramp, the Crazyman, etc.). Identities might sound or speak differently from one another. DID almost always results from a history of horrific childhood trauma. If, for example, a close relative repeatedly abuses a child before her personality integrates and parents are not there to help the child integrate the experience, then DID could occur. In treatment, the individual learns to challenge the distortions (e.g., "I must have deserved this") and to accept and integrate all aspects of the personality.

The above forms of dissociation are rather dramatic. However, dissociation is not always so. Some people who dissociate may just seem to "go away" or "space out" when triggers or intrusive thoughts occur or when present situations are stressful. If the skill was learned during the trauma as a protective defense, it makes sense that one would use the device in the present.

## HOW DO WE KNOW WHEN ONE IS DISSOCIATING?

While it may not always be apparent which form dissociation takes, a number of signs suggest that the dissociating person is trying to avoid the unacceptable. Table 2.2 provides a list of such signs, which are likely to continue until the trauma material is processed.

## IS DISSOCIATING BAD?

It depends. Dissociation is something most people do. At times it can be helpful. You might "escape" from work for a few moments to daydream about a romantic

## Table 2.2
## INDICATIONS OF DISSOCIATION

Body becomes still or stiff

Is slow to respond to others

Things seem to move in slow motion or fast-forward

Emotions become flat, numb, or nonexistent

Does not feel expected pain

Is out of touch with surroundings

Drifts off, goes away, spaces out, blanks out, loses track of what's happening

Stares off into space

Has downward or blank stare

Eyes dart anxiously from side to side or roll upward

Eyes blink rapidly or flutter

Gets a faraway or dazed look

Tunes out

Is not involved in present

Feels like an observer of the present situation, rather than a participant

Is careless, distracted

Suffers memory lapses

Fantasizes and daydreams excessively

Experiences overactivity or withdrawal

Is on autopilot (automatism behavior), feels like a robot

Falls asleep during the day

Is disoriented

Misses conversation

Experiences derealization (people or world don't seem real; familiar places seem strange; doesn't recognize oneself in the mirror; world seems like a dream, veiled, as if one is not really there)

Feels like one is watching things from outside his/her body

Experiences life split before and after ("I'm a different person since the trauma")

Twitches or grimaces

Alertness is clouded; foggy feeling (if you're suppressing traumas, you can't focus your thoughts; your mind goes blank)

Unusual, inexplicable behavior (hitting the ground when a car backfires; a dependable woman suddenly leaves the house for two days)

Attempts to remain grounded in the present (stroking side of chair; tapping, jiggling leg)

Self-soothes (rocking back and forth)

Things look or sound different: colors are faded or brighter; tunnel vision or "wide-angle view" develops; sounds are louder or more muffled than expected; things seem far away or unclear/fogged

---

evening. The famous concentration camp survivor Viktor Frankl mentally escaped the prison at times to consider a brighter future.

Dissociation provides some relief and some protection from overwhelming pain. In that sense, dissociation serves a useful purpose. On the other hand, continually blocking out memories requires enormous energy that can leave one fatigued and irritable. In numbing out the painful memories, we also lose pleasant memories and feelings. Inevitably, distressing intrusions will occur. Dissociation also delays or prevents healing because it keeps us from coming to terms with the walled-off material and prevents us from associating it with experiences of mastery and control. Dissociation might be likened, then, to a baby's bottle or security blanket. Both served a useful function at one time but are relinquished as one grows.

## WHAT CAN I EXPECT IF DISSOCIATION IS NOT MANAGED?

As a rule, unprocessed trauma material will continue to intrude until it makes sense—until you have processed it to the point where it can settle into long-term memory. We shall learn shortly how this is done.

# CHAPTER 3

# *Associated Features*

To complete our understanding of PTSD, we must understand a variety of symptoms that commonly occur following a traumatic event. In this chapter, we'll discuss thirteen associated features.[1]

## SELF-RECRIMINATION

Time and again we see traumatized people feel shame and guilt, whether they are responsible for the event or not. Although shame and guilt are similarly defined in the dictionary, guilt usually implies a feeling of responsibility, and shame has come to mean a feeling of badness, of worthlessness to the core. Soldiers who return from war often experience survivor's guilt. Upon examination, we often see questions of worth arise ("Why did I survive when John was a much finer human being?"). Victims of sexual abuse or rape often feel responsible ("I must have done something to cause it—if I had been more careful, it would not have happened."). Often, shame and guilt are experienced as a result of what the survivor sees as inappropriate behavior. For example, a child in the Oklahoma City bombing stepped on an electrical cord and assumed that she set off the explosion. A firefighter reflexively runs from an exploding building. Five seconds later he returns to try to find his buddy. Years later he reproaches himself for being a coward. The question often arises, "What kind of person would do that?" The answer, fair or not, is often, "One who is worthless, useless, unlovable, bad to the core." That is a difficult—and very erroneous—belief to live with.

Often people feel shame and guilt for what they did not do. Children who are victims of repeated sexual abuse self-recriminate, thinking, "Why didn't I do something to stop it?" Or the sibling thinks, "Why didn't I do something to rescue her, when I knew it was going on?" A police officer freezes for an instant as criminals open fire. His buddy is shot and he later thinks, "If I had returned fire immediately, he might still be alive."

Sometimes people with PTSD feel guilty for being unable to control their symptoms ("I must be a wimp to be depressed") or behaviors ("I can't believe I blew up at my wife like that—what's wrong with me?").

Guilt can be adaptive if it is realistic and if it leads to improvements in our behavior or character. Self-condemnation is never helpful. Unprocessed guilt and shame will make recovery very difficult. Fortunately, a number of very effective approaches can help to neutralize these emotions. We'll discuss them in Chapter 20.

## SHATTERED ASSUMPTIONS

Each of us holds basic assumptions that give order to our chaotic world and make stress bearable. A number of researchers have indicated that PTSD is due to the shattering of views of self, the world, and other people. In the now famous musical *Les Misérables*, Fantine is left with a newborn baby by the man she loves. In a stunned and socially isolated state, she is accused of being a whore at work and thrown out on the streets, where she later takes up prostitution to feed her child. In poignant song, she recalls a time when men were kind, when God was loving and forgiving, when the future was bright. Then all went wrong. Life killed her dreams, shredded her hope, and filled her with shame. Such are the changes often experienced by trauma victims. Table 3.1 lists several ways that people typically think before and after traumatic events. These assumptions summarize the work of Ronnie Janoff-Bulman, Seymour Epstein, and others.[2] The shattered, post-trauma assumptions are often imbedded in the walled-off material, so they are not well challenged or integrated.

## MOOD DISTURBANCES

These mood disturbances are common among those with PTSD:

- **Depression.** This follows logically from lowered self-esteem, hopelessness, shame, loss, feeling permanently damaged, and pessimism. Thus, victims of trauma might be at risk for suicide until such negative thoughts and feelings have been resolved.
- **Anxiety.** These symptoms can range from excessive worry to tension, a pounding heart, hyperventilation, feeling keyed up, and even panic attacks.

**Table 3.1**
SHATTERED ASSUMPTIONS

| Pre-Trauma Assumption | Post-Trauma Assumption |
|---|---|
| *View of Self* | |
| It can't happen to me; I'm not vulnerable; I'm safe and secure. I know what to expect. I can control things. | It will happen again; I'm vulnerable and helpless, fragile, threatened, endangered, insecure; I'm no longer safe. I can't succeed in relationships. I can't control my behavior, symptoms, or sanity. |
| I see myself in a positive light (decent, worthwhile, good, competent, guiltless). | I'm bad, unworthy, shameful ("tramp mentality"), incompetent, weak, different from others, permanently damaged. I question myself. I can't count on myself anymore. (Abused people conclude, "I'm an object existing for the needs of others—my needs are irrelevant.") Self-denigration and shattered identity—don't know who I am anymore; identity split into before and after trauma—are common. |
| I will have a happy future. | My lifelong goal of protecting others feels shattered. I am unworthy of a good life. I can't conceive of a happy future anymore or of finding love. I am not good enough. |
| *View of the World* | |
| The world is meaningful, fair, good, predictable, orderly, comprehensible, pleasurable, rewarding, kind, and safe. It makes sense and follows accepted social laws. | It just doesn't make sense. The world is confusing ("Why did this happen to me? What's the meaning of life?"). I can't believe in a God who permits this. God hates me. |
| People get what they deserve—if I'm cautious, I can prevent disaster. Bad things won't happen to me. | What I do just doesn't matter. I have no control. |
| *View of Others* | |
| People are good, trustworthy, comprehensible, worth relating to. | I can't trust people anymore—they're bad, exploitive, hurtful, etc. I can't relate to others; I feel alienated and isolated. Nobody understands. |

For example, a woman who compulsively washes herself might be trying to get rid of the feeling of being contaminated following rape or sexual abuse.

- **Hostility.** This is an attitude of dislike and distrust of others. It might show up as irritability, rage, or angry outbursts at

   Those who didn't go through the trauma and can't understand

   A perpetrator

   Those who did not protect the victim (such as parents)

   Secondary victimizers (those who are supposed to protect you but hurt you instead, such as police or insensitive doctors)

   Family members who happen to be nearby

- **Grief for losses.** This may not always be obvious, for reasons we'll discuss later.

## ADDICTIONS

Substances such as alcohol, cocaine, barbiturates, opiates, amphetamines, or other drugs are frequently abused in attempts to relieve the pain. Such self-medication provides only temporary relief from symptoms and interferes with healing.

## IMPULSIVE BEHAVIORS

In further attempts to escape the pain, people with PTSD might take impulsive trips, suddenly be absent from work, or make abrupt changes in lifestyle, such as compulsive shopping, eating, or sudden changes in sexual behavior.[3]

## SOMATIC (BODILY) COMPLAINTS

When trauma material cannot be processed and verbally expressed, the pain is often expressed physically, frequently around body areas that were physically traumatized. Often, the physical pain serves as a distraction from emotional pain. Physical complaints can include the following:[4]

- Chronic pain—headaches, heart pains, painful joints, back pain, pelvic pain
- Hypertension
- Allergies, asthma, rheumatoid arthritis, skin problems
- Heavy limbs, lump in throat, fainting, numb or tingling body parts, hypochondriasis

- Exhaustion—trying to contain the symptoms of PTSD is fatiguing, making one vulnerable to more physical (and psychological) symptoms[5]
- Gastrointestinal disturbances—ulcers, irritable bowel or spastic colon (the term "gut-wrenching" is apt to describe traumatic events[6])

It is often observed that physical complaints are more likely to occur in people who were traumatized in preverbal childhood. The physically painful part of the dissociated memory might then intrude as present pain. Other physical complaints are simply the common symptoms of anxiety and a sensitized nervous system.

## OVERCOMPENSATIONS

In an effort to regain lost control, some people with PTSD become driven for success, achievement, or fitness.[7] This can be a positive outcome of trauma, although it might also distract from healing.

## DEATH ANXIETY

A brush with death or serious injury will understandably lead to fear of recurrence until that fear or memory is processed and completed.

## REPETITION COMPULSION

Freud observed that people will often reenact traumas in attempts to master and complete them. (We hope this time to make things right.) This might take several forms:

- Many combat vets go into high-risk or rescue-oriented professions such as police, fire protection, emergency medical services, or crisis intervention work, perhaps in an attempt to transfer their experience in a meaningful way.
- High-risk behaviors might include skydiving, rock climbing, scuba diving, or reckless speeding. As with high-risk professions, living on the edge creates an adrenaline rush that might ward off depression and the feeling of helplessness experienced during trauma. At the same time, stress-triggered opiates in the brain act like a natural painkiller.
- A woman abused as a child marries an abuser and stays with him.
- A man who was abused as a child enlists in the military, seeking to do violence against the enemy.[8]

- Someone who was forced to go without food as a child might develop problems with eating, such as bingeing and purging.

Repeating the trauma gives an oddly comforting feeling of familiarity, predictability, and control. However, the original trauma is rarely resolved by such acts.[9] In fact, these acts might help one continue to avoid dealing with the original trauma.

## DELIBERATE SELF-INJURY

One of the ironies of PTSD is that victims might further harm themselves. As Aphrodite Matsakis observes, deliberate self-injury includes "burning, hitting, cutting, excessive scratching, using harsh abrasives on skin or scalp, poking sharp objects into flesh, head banging, pulling out hair or eyebrows for noncosmetic purposes, inserting objects into body orifices," excessive fasting, self-surgery, excessive tattooing, or refusing needed medication.[10] This seems like such a paradox. Why in the world would those who are already in intense pain further injure themselves? It seems to make no sense, yet it does. Most often, it follows a history of protracted childhood trauma (such as physical or sexual abuse), not a single exposure.[11] The person harms himself in response to overwhelming, dissociated pain. At least sixteen reasons account for this complex behavior. Deliberate self-injury:

1. **Expresses pain that can't be verbalized,** as when the abused child was told to keep the offense a secret or when the abuse happened before the child learned to talk. The nonverbal outcry says, "Something terrible has happened." Self-injury may be a plea for help.
2. **Attempts to convert emotional pain to physical pain.** Physical pain can be localized, displaced, and released, providing a temporary distraction from psychic pain.
3. **Paradoxically relieves pain.** Stress triggers natural painkillers in the brain, temporarily easing psychic and physical pain. This so-called "stress-induced analgesia" might also help explain why trauma victims become addicted to trauma-related stimuli.[12]
4. **Is a way to feel alive.** Numbing and dissociation make the PTSD sufferer feel dead—perhaps feeling pain is better than feeling nothing. Physical pain grounds one in reality and counters dissociation. It returns focus to the present, providing temporary relief from intrusions. Some people report that blood provides a soothing, warm sensation that relieves stress and

reminds them they are still alive. (Paradoxically, feeling pain can also cause dissociation as a way to escape emotional pain.)

5. **Provides an illusory sense of power, a sense of mastery and control of pain.** Reversing roles and assuming the role of the offender, a self-injurer might think, "This time when I am hurt, I am on the controlling end. I can determine when the pain begins and ends."[13] Another might think, "I'm stronger than others because I can tolerate pain."

6. **Attempts to complete the incompleted.** The idea of *repetition compulsion* states that we repeat what we've experienced until we've completed old business—processing it and learning a better way. Unfortunately, simply reenacting the abuse doesn't change the trauma material. Complete processing of the material does.

7. **Is a way to contain aggressive tendencies and pain.** The person thinks, "If I discharge my anger and hurt on myself, then I won't hurt anybody else." Maybe it is the only way to stop anger, at least for a time. Learning constructive ways to express emotions is the antidote for this approach.

8. **Vents powerful emotions that cannot be vented directly** (e.g., "I can't rage at the powerful perpetrator, so I vent on myself instead").

9. **Makes the body unattractive to spare further abuse.** This harmful defense makes sense to a child who was powerless to stop sexual abuse. Excessive thinness or weight might accomplish a similar purpose.

10. **Might become associated with pleasant moments.** Following abuse, some abusers become remorseful, attentive, and loving for a time. Thus, victims might be conditioned to think that pain signals the beginning of good times. Self-injury also calls forth self-care and nurturing and expresses a desire to heal.

11. **Imitates what the child has seen.** Children naturally imitate behavior that is modeled by adults. They learn to abuse if their parents are abusive, just as they learn kindness if the parents model that.

12. **Can be an attempt to attach to parents.** Children have a deep need to attach to parents, even if they are rejecting. In order to gain the abusive parent's approval, the child might internalize his punishing attitudes. The child's thinking might be, "I'll show I'm good and devoted to Mom by doing what she does to me." This makes more sense when we realize that abusers often isolate the victims, making them more dependent on them for approval. Need for approval causes the victim to identify with the aggres-

sor. A child might confuse abuse with emotional closeness, especially if abuse was the only form of attention the parent showed. The child might think, "If I keep hurting myself, eventually they will love me."

13. **Can mark a return to the familiar, understandable past.** The child thinks, "I don't understand loving, soothing behavior, but I do understand pain. It does not always feel good, but at least it is predictable."

14. **Is consistent with one's view of self.** People treat themselves consistent with their self-image. Abuse teaches the victim, "I'm worthless, bad, no-good, an object—so it makes sense to treat myself like an object." Self-punishment consistently follows from feeling blameworthy, bad, or inadequate.

15. **Is consistent with one's view of a maimed world and a nonexistent future.**[14] Recall that PTSD sufferers might view the world as unsafe and believe that they won't have a normal future.

16. **May ensure safety if it results in hospitalization.** Here self-nurturing might also take place.

The fact that you hurt yourself does not mean you are insane. You are simply repeating what you learned to cope with intolerable pain. As you learn productive ways to meet your needs, you'll no longer need to do this. The antidote is learning to honor yourself and soothe yourself in healthy ways.

## OTHER ADDICTIONS AND SELF-DESTRUCTIVE BEHAVIORS

Other self-destructive behaviors include eating disorders and accident proneness as well as compulsive exercise, gambling, sex, prostitution, and shopping. Of course, suicidal tendencies could be included here. Although these behaviors can be complex, understanding them in light of PTSD can help make them less confusing. Much of our discussion of self-injury sheds light on these as well.

Raymond Flannery estimates that 80 percent of prostitutes come from homes with abuse or alcoholism.[15] In alcoholic or abusive homes, children often learn that sex is separate from love and is useful for purposes other than love. Thus, a prostitute might use sex as the only means of survival she knows. Or she might use it to control men and relationships, a form of repetition compulsion. Prostitution is also consistent with one's core beliefs about self: "Sex is not only the only thing I'm good *at*, it's the only thing I'm good *for*." "What am I worth? Nothing, except for the morale of the troops."

Flannery adds that sex addiction is not really an attempt to appease the sex appetite but is an attempt to rework and master trauma. The victim hopes that this time sex will provide self-esteem, a sense of being lovable, and relief from the pain of rejection, abandonment, and loneliness. Of course, isolated from love, sex provides none of these. Nor does the addiction resolve the problems of dissociated material.

Much like self-injury, compulsive gambling can provide an adrenaline rush, a sense of control, and a distraction from the pain of dissociation. The vet who starts barroom brawls does so for similar reasons. The abused child who becomes an abusive spouse might wish to stop. Yet following the abuse, they feel a sense of control, a calmness attributable to the release of endorphins in the brain. Food becomes another way to soothe pain for overeaters.[16]

A final form of self-destruction that we'll discuss is *revictimization*. Repetition compulsion only partially explains why a woman would stay in an abusive relationship. Abuse tends to leave one feeling stunned, numbed, and unable to protect oneself.[17] The adult who was abused as a child will often seek a powerful authority figure to rescue her. Too often this is another abuser who can spot defenseless prey. Abusers typically isolate their victims, making them feel helpless, dependent upon them, and grateful for "any shred of affection." The victim increasingly views the abuser as powerful and respected. It becomes harder and harder to leave the relationship,[18] as the cycle of victimization continues.

## ALEXITHYMIA

*Alexithymia* is another name referring to the general shutting down of feelings. One becomes like a robot, capable of functioning but expressing little feeling. One might describe bodily symptoms to the doctor but be unable to connect them to emotional pain. Recall that traumatic memories are highly emotional. To permit any feelings will also invite negative emotions into awareness. So we dread and bottle up all feelings, even love, joy, and relaxation. People make us feel, so people might be avoided. Since empathy requires feelings, giving or receiving love will be challenging. People with alexithymia may appear overly intellectual or business-like. They will deny that anything is wrong: "Nothing bad happened." "I didn't do anything wrong." "It didn't bother me." "It bothered me then, but not now because I don't think about it." When resulting from trauma, alexithymia is a defense against painful dissociated material.[19] Some people hold the view that showing feelings is a sign of weakness rather than a normal aspect of being human and a necessary step in healing. This view tends to promote alexithymia.

## CHANGES IN PERSONALITY

Changes in personality may result from traumatic events. These changes may be substantial, especially if the events are severe, repeated, or happen early in life. As already suggested, an individual might become chronically distrustful, cynical, angry, irritable, aggressive, destructive, socially withdrawn, perfectionistic, dependent, anxious, moody, or depressed. Self-esteem often drops. Three personality disorders that can result from repeated trauma—antisocial, borderline, and narcissistic—and dissociative identity disorder are described in Appendix D.

## CHAPTER 4

# *Frequently Asked Questions*

We'll complete our overview of PTSD by answering some commonly asked questions.

## WHO GETS PTSD?

Anyone can get PTSD. A strong predictor is the stressful event. The closer you are to a severe event, the more likely you are to experience PTSD. The longer the duration of the event, or events, the greater the chances of PTSD, although a single exposure to an extreme event could also lead to PTSD.[1]

It is estimated that at least half of Americans have experienced at least one major trauma and that 7 to 12 percent of U.S. adults will experience PTSD at some point in their lives. These figures might increase with certain changes in society such as rising crime rates and the weakening of the family unit. Certain populations are more at risk, including children and people whose work exposes them to trauma. The latter group includes the armed forces, police, firefighters, rescue workers, emergency medical service workers, dispatchers, and disaster workers. However, anyone can be exposed to potentially traumatic events.

## ARE THERE FACTORS THAT MAKE US MORE VULNERABLE TO PTSD?

The primary cause of PTSD is the stressful event. The risk for PTSD increases if the events

- Are sudden and unpredictable[2]
- Last a long time
- Recur or are thought likely to recur—especially if there is insufficient time or resources to recover

- Involve real or threatened sexual abuse or physical injury (e.g., sexual abuse combined with violence is generally more traumatizing than sexual abuse alone)
- Involve multiple types of traumatic events (e.g., after an earthquake, a plane with relief supplies crashes into a village)
- Occur in the early years before the personality is fully integrated (abuse from family members is generally more destructive than abuse from strangers because a child's most significant relationships are involved)

Consensus is emerging, however, that a variety of secondary factors can increase the risk of developing PTSD following exposure to traumatic events. These factors become more influential as the severity of the traumatic event decreases.[3] They include pre- and post-trauma vulnerabilities and initial distress following the trauma.

### Pre-Trauma Vulnerabilities

These vulnerabilities are risk factors that exist prior to the development of PTSD. They can be innate or related to the environment and include the following aspects.

*Individual Differences.*  People are different; we meet traumatic events at varying degrees of preparedness. There is no shame in this. Some of the risk factors for developing PTSD include the following:

- **A history of prior traumatization.** For example, Vietnam veterans with PTSD were more likely to have experienced childhood abuse than those without PTSD. This is understandable since present traumas are likely to reactivate unresolved traumas from the past.
- **Underdeveloped protective skills, problem-solving skills, self-esteem, resilience, creativity, humor, discipline, ability to express emotion to others, and ability to tolerate distress.** All of these are learnable. PTSD can stimulate us to develop these skills.[4]
- **Personality and habitually negative thought patterns** (e.g., pessimism, depression, introversion).[5] These also are modifiable.
- **Biology.** Some people appear to have overreactive nervous systems. Heredity and a history of drug abuse appear to influence this factor.

- **Gender.** Females have a greater risk for developing PTSD. Interestingly, they also tend to respond better to treatment, perhaps because they are more likely to express emotions.

*Family Characteristics.* For optimal mental health, children need to bond to warm, loving adults in a secure, predictable setting. Here they can learn to trust others and themselves, and they learn to experience and express emotions appropriately and safely. Given reasonable demands, they discover that the world is predictable and that they can cope. They learn that in difficult times they can share their burden with others who will support them. Yet a variety of family environments can predispose the child to insecurity, shame, guilt, secrecy, distrust, alienation, or bottling of emotions—all of which increase vulnerability to PTSD. Consider a few of the possibilities:

- Watching parents divorce, children might conclude: the world is not safe; people don't stand by you, so don't trust.
- By watching parents cope with stress, a child might learn to blame others, take out anger on others, use illegal drugs to self-medicate, or avoid emotions.
- Parents with PTSD can indirectly transmit their wounds.[6] A combat vet may parent according to the following rules of war, thereby teaching his children the same rules: destroy your enemies lest they destroy you; don't show feelings such as grief or tenderness; do whatever it takes to protect yourself; it's safer to disguise your intentions. Fearing angry outbursts, the children of such vets learn to keep quiet. Since the outbursts are unpredictable, they learn to feel unsafe and out of control. They have no way of knowing the cause of their father's pain, but self-esteem will be disrupted if they do not realize that they are not causing the problem.

    A police officer protects his family but is emotionally disengaged. He takes the children to the park but is worried about danger instead of enjoying the experience with them. Another enmeshes the family: "We must always stick together for protection." "Avoid outsiders." "Don't leave home." "Never argue." In both situations, the children learn to be anxious and distrustful.
- An abusive, alcoholic father threatens to harm a child if she tells. The child learns to be secretive and ashamed. The child learns to "look normal" rather than heal.

*Recent Life Stressors.* These can weaken resistance. Accumulated stressors might include recent divorce, illness, financial pressures, natural death of a friend or relative, or losing a job.

Pre-trauma vulnerabilities might have limited you in the past and probably have limited your growth since the trauma. Sometimes the trauma highlights the opportunity to grow in these areas, which is why trauma can present certain positive aspects.

## Initial Distress at (or Shortly After) the Time of Trauma

PTSD is more likely to develop if one:

- Dissociates[7]
- Has the perception that she was responsible or acted inappropriately (how one thinks about the traumatic event is crucial, a point we shall repeatedly return to)
- Perceives that he is alone or isolated (e.g., a batterer threatens to kill his wife if she tells anyone; an abused child feels different from her friends and is too ashamed to talk with anyone)
- Experiences very strong emotions (such as extreme panic, anger, guilt, shame, sadness, grief, or disgust) or avoidance (disbelief, unwillingness to discuss, or social withdrawal)

## Post-Trauma Factors

These are risk factors that exist following the development of PTSD.

*Recovery Environment.* Lack of support from family, friends, and community can make the victim feel more alone, helpless, or worthless. Ideally, support systems will be believing, uncritical, and nurturing. They will encourage you to take care of yourself and express your feelings—they can feel and accept your pain, even if they don't understand it. Risk factors include the following:

- **Emotional unavailability.** Some adults feel threatened by pain. They don't know how to talk about it. Perhaps they too were victims and feel their unresolved memory material will be triggered by your trauma.
- **The victim's being disbelieved, stigmatized, shamed, or shunned.** Think of a rape victim who is blamed or rejected by her husband, or our troops

returning from Vietnam.[8] The rejection adds to the wound, while the victim is denied the healing balm of sharing one's burdens. In contrast, consider cultural homecoming or decompression rituals such as the Native American sweat lodge or homecoming parades for soldiers that help integrate individuals into society.

- **Secondary victimization.** This occurs when those who are supposed to help instead inflict further harm.
     - The police or lawyers treat a victim of rape as if she asked for it or could have prevented it had she been more careful.
     - A physician minimizes the symptoms, belittles one seeking assistance, or even refuses to render treatment ("There's nothing wrong with you, it's all in your head.").
- **Conspiracy of silence.** Perhaps the wife tells the child to keep silent about the father's incest for fear that he will be thrown in jail.

*Lack of Treatment.* This reinforces the victim's belief that she is alone and different from others. By contrast, some organizations provide group meetings and education to help prevent the development of PTSD and offer follow-up individual counseling.

*Ineffective Coping.* Some people keep the pain inside—unexpressed and unprocessed. They might then turn to drugs or alcohol to kill the pain, or to self-destructive behaviors. None of these solve the root problem—painful dissociated material. Effective copers take care of themselves and seek necessary help.

## WHAT COURSE WILL PTSD TAKE?

Mardi Horowitz has described the normal sequence of the traumatic stress reaction and recovery:[9]

1. **Outcry.** This stage involves strong, distressing emotions. One freezes or feels stunned, overwhelmed, or frightened. Perhaps one begins to feel strong emotions after having coped with an emergency, maybe when home relaxing. Strong anger might have helped them to cope.
2. **Avoidance and denial.** Some who experience traumatic stress may think, "Oh, no! It can't be true." They may feel numb or blunted. They withdraw, avoid potential supporters, constrict emotionally, and stare blankly into space. In a frantic attempt to keep life as usual, they compulsively return

to pre-trauma tasks that were important then (perhaps work, sports, sex, or cleaning). But the world looks gray. Feeling physically and emotionally numb, unable to talk about it, they might turn to drugs for relief.

3. **Intrusions.** Intense emotions and thoughts related to the stressful event begin to break into awareness, accompanied by signs of arousal. The strong waves of thoughts and emotions might wane for a time, giving one hope of coping. But they return. Arousal is signaled by startle reactions, hypervigilance (excessive alertness, looking around for threats), and compulsive repetition of actions that are linked to the event (constant searching for lost persons or situations, reenacting the event, and rehearsing ideal responses to regain control).

4. **Working through until completion.** Eventually, one faces the reality of the event, experiences all thoughts and feelings, talks it through with others, corrects erroneous thoughts, comes to terms with the experience, grieves, and restores equilibrium. New commitments are made to live, accept self, accept losses, find the silver lining in the trauma (e.g., resiliency, wisdom, or compassion), grow beyond the pre-trauma condition, and move on.

If one gets stuck at a step before completion, then the symptoms of PTSD will continue, including swinging between these stages. If stuck, Horowitz recommends early treatment so that maladaptive coping does not get rigidly fixed in place. Treatment involves going through the four stages just described to find out where one is stuck, and then progressing through to completion.

Most people will experience at least some symptoms of PTSD following a severely stressful event. As a general rule, about half of all adults diagnosed with PTSD will recover within three months.[10] Others will continue to experience PTSD for months to years if not treated. Without treatment, many people who do not meet the full criteria for PTSD will continue to experience symptoms for decades; people might indeed manage their symptoms for decades only to find them multiplying during retirement years. Perhaps one finally becomes exhausted from a lifetime of battling. Perhaps a hospital stay or failing health triggers old memories of helplessness and loss of control.[11]

The onset of PTSD usually occurs within three months of the trauma, although there might be a delay of months to years. However, so-called delayed PTSD is rare. Careful examination will usually detect PTSD early on, although the symptom profile and associated features might change over the course of the disorder.[12] Some people experience periods of remission followed by recurrence.

## WHY AM I STILL BOTHERED BY THE TRAUMA AFTER ALL THESE YEARS?

Persistence of your PTSD symptoms is not a sign of being "crazy" or "weak." PTSD symptoms are simply a sign that the trauma overwhelmed your coping abilities at the time and that you have not yet learned effective ways to cope or reduce the symptoms. As you learn new skills, you will likely feel much better.

## WHAT ARE THE COSTS AND CONSEQUENCES OF PTSD?

John Wilson summarizes that PTSD impacts one's psychology, self-concept, development, and attachment capacities (including the capacities for intimacy, love, bonding, and sexuality).[13] Untreated, PTSD is associated with greater rates of the following:

| | |
|---|---|
| Depression | Impaired relationships |
| Anxiety disorders (e.g., panic disorders, phobias) | Social isolation |
| | Sexual dysfunction or sexual acting out |
| Suicide | Unemployment |
| Low self-esteem | Drug addictions |
| Guilt | Eating disorders (e.g., anorexia, bulimia) |
| Personality disorders | Medical illness |
| Dissociative disorders | Homelessness |
| Cynicism | Loss of religious faith |
| Revictimization | Child and spousal abuse |
| Family disruption (e.g., conflict, divorce, secondary wounding) | Difficulty handling stress |
| | Violence |

A few notes on key items in this list follow.

### Suicide

Suicide may be viewed as an attempt to escape overwhelming pain. The suicide rate for incest victims is two to three times higher than rates for the depressed; the latter comprise the majority of suicides. Suicide attempts among rape victims occur ten times more frequently than the population average.[14] It is apparent that sexual abuse violates not only the body but the mind and soul as well. It sends the message that a victim is but an object. The lasting danger is that the victim accepts that message and fails to realize that things can get better. Battered women also attempt suicide at alarming rates, consistent with findings that women are on average more distressed by troubled relationships than are men.

## Revictimization

Incest victims are more likely to be sexually victimized in later years and to marry abusive spouses. Here is a complex irony. There is a great need to protect oneself. Yet experience might have taught the victim that self-protection is futile. One who dissociates is not in contact with lessons of the past. Vulnerable and in need of assurance, one becomes a "sitting duck" for an abuser.[15]

## Intergenerational Secondary Wounding

PTSD victims can infect their families. For example, children of Vietnam vets can feel neglected by emotionally absent fathers who transmit the expectation of silence. Children of Holocaust survivors might also bear scars of their parents' wounds. Through their parents, they might learn to fear separation, avoid intimacy, or overachieve. They might experience Holocaust-related nightmares, anxiety, difficulty concentrating, aggression, and psychosomatic disorders. Frequently children of victims wish to empathize with and understand their parents, but the parents remain emotionally closed. The children might then take on the symptoms themselves as a way to feel close. In short, any parental difficulties can be passed on to the family. The difficulties are compounded by the family's frustration at being unable to help the victim.[16]

## Sexual Dissatisfaction[17]

Many symptoms common to PTSD interfere with the enjoyment of wholesome sexual intimacy: difficulty trusting, guilt, depression, self-loathing, emotional numbness, preoccupation with emotional survival, disgust, drug abuse, and anger, to name several. The challenge is even greater when inappropriate sexuality was part of the traumatic experience. For example, home is no longer safe to incest survivors, who are most often females. Unhelped survivors are more likely to enter sexualized relationships to replace deeper intimacy and often become pregnant during teen years. They are more likely to experience sexual dysfunction and report that they do not like being a woman. They will often experience flashbacks during sexual closeness.[18] In relationships, they might experience great ambivalence about sex. They often find sex aversive and wish to avoid it. At other times, they need and seek closeness. So they might flip-flop between avoidance and excessive sexuality. Partners might interpret the flashbacks or the wish to avoid sex as rejection.[19]

## WILL TIME HEAL THE WOUNDS?

Perhaps. Some people seem to recover without treatment within a few months. For others, however, "work hard and forget" does not necessarily work.[20] Often, effects can be prolonged and may worsen without treatment. The good news is that research has taught us much about PTSD, including many strategies that help people to heal, recover, and grow.[21]

## WHAT ABOUT TRAUMATIC BRAIN INJURY?

Sometimes injuries to the brain can cause PTSD symptoms. Head injury can occur if someone is knocked out or whipped around or if someone experienced a coma or concussion. Such conditions might be a result of violence, explosions, a car accident, or other traumatic events. The victim might look the same but act differently.

Many of the symptoms of head injury are similar to PTSD, including concentration difficulties, aggression, depression, anxiety, irritability, mood swings (being demanding or verbally abusive), amnesia (usually loss of recent memory), fatigue, disrupted sleep, headache, decreased sexual interest (although 5 to 10 percent will exhibit increased interest), and shame.

However, additional signs might suggest brain injury. Look for these signs:

- Slowed processing (slowed memory storing or retrieval)
- Difficulty with abstract or complex thinking (e.g., a person can't explain what "people who live in glass houses shouldn't throw stones" means)
- Decreased muscle strength
- Headaches
- Seizures (sometimes looks like a fainting spell)
- Loss of coordination; dizziness
- Difficulty with vision, speech, hearing, smell, or taste
- Light or sound sensitivity

Brain injury is best evaluated by a neuropsychologist or other neurological expert, who is trained to detect abnormalities that might not be obvious on normal medical tests. The expectation that one will recover seems to promote recovery in many cases involving mild to moderate injuries. State-run head or brain injury foundations can assist in care of the victim and support of the family. If a brain injury is suspected, one should avoid caffeine, alcohol, or other substances, which can worsen symptoms.

## WHAT ABOUT FALSE MEMORIES?

The accuracy of trauma memories is one of the most controversial aspects of PTSD. Perhaps no one has summarized the research on this topic better than Dr. Jon G. Allen of the Menninger Clinic. He relates that a full range of recall is possible. Some people remember the gist of the trauma reasonably accurately and consistently. Some remember parts of the trauma consistently with varying degrees of precision. Some totally forget the trauma, and some of these later have varying degrees of recall. Sometimes the recall occurs spontaneously. Sometimes recall is prompted by a psychotherapist or hypnotist. Sometimes this recall can be relatively accurate, and sometimes totally false. Allen points to the need for caution in evaluating the accuracy of traumatic memories. We recall that traumatic memories are often stored in fragmented, dissociated bits, which are not filed in memory in proper perspective with respect to time. Trying to reconstruct them might lead to interpretation and the changing of details over time. Spontaneously recalled memories tend to be more reliable than those suggested by a therapist or gained through hypnotism because some people are somewhat prone to suggestion.[22] Thus it is generally considered unethical for a therapist to try to persuade a client that abuse has occurred, or to even suggest it.

# PART II

---

# About Healing,
# Recovery, and Growth

# CHAPTER 5

# *Principles of Healing, Recovery, and Growth*

**The story of PTSD is the tale of the indomitable and indefatigable human spirit to survive and adapt.**

**—*Dr. Donald Meichenbaum*[1]**

You might, like many other people, find it somewhat healing just to understand your PTSD symptoms and realize that they make sense. You are not crazy, although your symptoms might indicate the need for assistance. This book is to help you heal, recover, and grow. "Healing" and "recovery" are often used interchangeably, although we will use them to mean slightly different things. *Healing* means "to make whole." The word, in fact, derives from the same root as "health" and "whole." We'll use this word to refer to the process of becoming whole again. *Recovery* means a return to your former state of functioning. Although we are never the same following any new experience, we can again feel strong, whole, and functional—ready to move beyond the suffering and turn the negative experience of PTSD into growth.

When you recover, you will notice that your symptoms will be fewer, less severe, and less troubling when they occur. You'll notice these changes:[2]

1. You can recall or dismiss the traumatic event at will, instead of suffering from intrusive memories, frightening dreams, troubling flashbacks, and distressing associations (triggers).

2. You can remember the event with appropriately intense feeling—not false detachment.

3. Feelings about the traumatic event can be named and endured without overwhelming arousal, dissociation, or numbing.

4. Symptoms of anxiety, depression, and sexual dysfunction, if not absent, are at least reasonably tolerated and predictable.

5. You are not isolated from other people but have restored your capacity for trust, empathy, and attachment.

6. You have assigned meaning to the trauma and discarded a damaged sense of self, replacing it with a belief in your own strength. Losses have been named and mourned; self-blame has been replaced by self-acceptance and self-worth; obsessive rumination about the past has been replaced by realistic evaluation.

7. You are more comfortable with all your feelings—positive, negative, and neutral.

8. You are again committed to your future and take responsibility for your life, no matter how badly you were treated or defeated.

The road to recovery and growth is different for each person. In some cases, symptoms will resolve fairly quickly. In many cases, recovery will be a marathon, not a sprint. We might picture the process as shown in Figure 5.1.

PTSD puts one in the dark valley. This is a detour, a temporary derailment, not an endpoint. Steps to healing begin the upward climb, sometimes two steps forward and one step back. Often the course is not smooth, and you might feel like you are getting worse before you get better. Over time you will reach the recovery point and be ready to pick up where you left off.

## THE SEVEN PRINCIPLES OF HEALING

Understanding these important principles will greatly facilitate your healing process.

1. **Healing starts by applying skills to manage PTSD symptoms.** These include skills to reduce distressing arousal, manage anger, and manage intrusions. These skills are not curative, but they do help to reduce troubling symptoms to the point where life becomes more manageable. They enable us to begin the steps of healing.

**Figure 5.1**
HEALING, RECOVERY, AND GROWTH

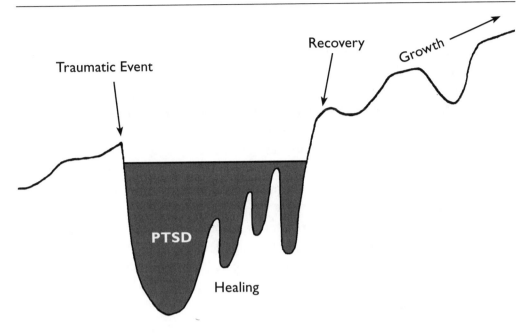

2. **Healing occurs when traumatic memory is processed or integrated.**
Recall that a dissociated traumatic memory is walled off, or separated, from adaptive memories that are associated and stored in long-term memory. Fragments of the memory are also separated from one another. Highly charged and stored in active memory, the traumatic memory intrudes into awareness as a call for processing and integration. In integration, memory fragments are recalled and explored so that they can be connected to each other—making the memory whole. The memory is connected to adaptive material, including adaptive thoughts and emotions. Inaccurate or unreasonable thoughts are identified. Adaptive thoughts blend into the memory in their place. In some cases, these thoughts come from stored memories. In other cases, they are introduced. Distressing emotions can literally be expressed, or released, and this time the memory is connected to calmer, more supportive emotions. The unspeakable memory is given words, since verbalizing helps to put the memory together and be viewed more logically.

Bringing the highly emotionally charged memories under the light of reason settles them down.

We come to see the memory in clearer perspective. The distressing energy of the memory is neutralized. We reevaluate the triggers and see them simply as reminders, not a repeat of the trauma. The traumatic event is viewed as part of the past, not the present. Now the memory can take its place in long-term memory, one memory alongside all other memories. The traumatic memory no longer seems to be the only one on file, but just one in an entire life history. As with other memories, it can be recalled, but without overwhelming emotion and arousal.

Integration means more than just thinking about memories. Intrusions are thought about, but that is not sufficient to heal. In fact, simply thinking about traumatic memory may simply reinforce the memory. Integration means that memories are transformed and reorganized in a meaningful way. We process the dissociated trauma memories until we come to terms with them, make sense of them, and can put them to rest. This healing process is referred to in many ways:

- Integrating
- Processing
- Assimilating
- Digesting or metabolizing (becoming aware of memory fragments and then neutralizing and assimilating each part)
- Coming to terms with the memory
- Making sense of the memory
- Reframing (changing the way we view the event)

3. **Healing occurs when confronting replaces avoidance.** Avoidance is a hallmark of the anxiety disorders. It seems natural to avoid pain and suffering. However, without awareness, integration does not occur. When we avoid, we do not master. We never learn that we can triumph over our fears. We never learn new coping skills, and we remain controlled by the past. So we shall confront in a safe and orderly way that which we find distressing.

4. **Healing occurs in a climate of safety and pacing.** When you were traumatized, you were not safe. This time, however, you will always remain safe and in control. You will progress steadily, but as slowly as you need to remain in control. Steady progress is more beneficial than going too fast. In fact, Richard Kluft has stated, "The slower you go, the faster you get there."[3]

You will only start when you are ready, and always move at a comfortable pace.

5. **Healing occurs when boundaries are intact.** The concept and maintenance of boundaries are so important that they merit a longer discussion later in this chapter.

6. **Kind awareness and acceptance of feelings aid the healing journey.** Acceptance of feelings begins with compassionate acceptance of self. In various ways, trauma therapist Beverly James communicates this to traumatized children early in treatment: "There are parts of you that are funny, heroic, strong, smart, warm, angry, gross, tender, weak, and tricky that make you wonderfully special. I like the whole, big, warm, smelly, alive package of you."[4] This is the view we strive for: "Even though I am imperfect, nevertheless, I am worthwhile; I matter."

7. **Balance in our lives is necessary to heal.** Healing is work. You can't work constantly on difficult material. You will need a break, a time-out from your healing work. You will need to nourish your mind and body. You'll need to permit time for recreation, laughter, play, and beauty.

## BOUNDARIES[5]

Think of yourself as a beautiful house, lovely outside and in. The house is a place of joy and comfort—a secure place from which you explore the world. Around the house is a sturdy fence with a gate. You also have strong doors and windows. You can open the doors and gates to invite in welcomed guests—neighbors, friends, and family. You keep them closed to keep out danger. Trauma blew open your doors and burst into your house. It may have convinced you that you are powerless to close the doors. Perhaps the door has remained open and danger has walked in too often. Or you may have locked the door so tightly that no one can get in anymore. Perhaps you no longer open the windows, so stale air remains trapped and no light and fresh air can enter. Maybe you have stopped beautifying the inside of your home, and your health is declining because you stay so confined.

Your boundaries are like doors, gates, and windows. Healing occurs as you learn to put into place very strong, secure boundaries. These boundaries allow you to feel safe. They open and close at your choosing. You are in control. You will learn to keep out dangerous people, and you will again invite in safe people to enjoy. You will choose when to open your windows to express feelings that need to be confided or shared and permit the light of friendship, love, and healing ideas to enter.

Building strong boundaries also means that you know what you are responsible for; you do not assume responsibility when you are not responsible. You can see clearly that you are responsible for your house and all that is in it (sometimes you need to call in the plumber for help). You will probably choose to assist your neighbors because that makes the neighborhood nicer, but you realize that they are responsible for their own houses. You can't personally fix all the houses in the neighborhood. The best you can do is bring your tools and offer to help.

You will beautify and take care of your own house, at a pace that is right for you. You will never berate yourself because your house is unique or because yours has not progressed as far as someone else's. In this way, you enjoy your house.

Boundaries give us a feeling of inner strength. Ultimately they enable us to enjoy ourselves and the world. They empower us to love and relate to others better.

## FEELINGS

Life is feeling. Not to feel is to be dead. To be at peace with all feelings is to heal. Nominated for the Nobel Peace Prize, the exiled Vietnamese monk Thich Nhat Hanh has put this in beautiful perspective in *Peace Is Every Step*. With permission, I wish to share his insights on feelings:[6]

> In us, there is a river of feelings, in which every drop of water is a different feeling, and each feeling relies on all the others for its existence. To observe it, we just sit on the bank of the river and identify each feeling as it surfaces, flows by, and disappears.
>
> There are three sorts of feelings—pleasant, unpleasant, and neutral. When we have an unpleasant feeling, we may want to chase it away. But it is more effective to return to our conscious breathing and just observe it, identifying it silently to ourselves: "Breathing in, I know there is an unpleasant feeling in me. Breathing out, I know there is an unpleasant feeling in me." Calling a feeling by its name, such as "anger," "sorrow," "joy," or "happiness," helps us identify it clearly and recognize it more deeply.
>
> We can use our breathing to be in contact with our feelings and accept them. If our breathing is light and calm—a natural result of conscious breathing—our mind and body will slowly become light, calm, and clear, and our feelings also. Mindful observation is based on the principle of "non-duality"; our feeling is not separate from us or caused merely by something outside us; our feeling *is* us, and for the moment we *are* that feeling. We are neither drowned in nor terrorized by

the feeling, nor do we reject it. Our attitude of not clinging to or rejecting our feelings is the attitude of letting go, an important part of meditation practice.

If we face our unpleasant feelings with care, affection, and nonviolence, we can transform them into the kind of energy that is healthy and has the capacity to nourish us. By the work of mindful observation, our unpleasant feelings can illuminate so much for us, offering us insight and understanding into ourselves and society.

[Like surgeons, some helpers] want to help us throw out what is unwanted and keep only what is wanted. But what is left may not be very much. If we try to throw away what we don't want, we may throw away most of ourselves.

Instead of acting as if we can dispose of parts of ourselves, we should learn the art of transformation. We can transform our anger, for example, into something more wholesome, like understanding. We do not need surgery to remove our anger. If we become angry at our anger, we will have two angers at the same time. We only have to observe it with love and attention. If we take care of our anger in this way, without trying to run away from it, it will transform itself. This is peacemaking. If we are peaceful in ourselves, we can make peace with our anger. We can deal with depression, anxiety, fear, or any unpleasant feeling in the same way.

**Transforming Feelings**
1. **The first step in dealing with feelings is to recognize each feeling as it arises.** The agent that does this is mindfulness. In the case of fear, for example, you bring out your mindfulness, look at your fear, and recognize it as fear. You know that fear springs from yourself and that mindfulness also springs from yourself. They are both in you, not fighting, but one taking care of the other.
2. **The second step is to become one with the feeling.** It is best not to say, "Go away, Fear. I don't like you. You are not me." It is much more effective to say, "Hello, Fear. How are you today?" Then you can invite the two aspects of yourself, mindfulness and fear, to shake hands as friends and become one. Doing this may seem frightening, but because you know that you are more than just your fear, you need not be afraid. As long as mindfulness is there, it can chaperone your fear.
3. **The third step is to calm the feeling.** As mindfulness is taking good care of your fear, you begin to calm it down. "Breathing in, I calm the activities of body and mind." You calm your feeling just by being with it, like a mother tenderly holding her crying baby. Feeling his mother's tenderness, the baby will calm down and stop crying. . . . So don't avoid your feeling. Don't say,

"You are not important. You are only a feeling." Come and be one with it. You can say, "Breathing out, I calm my fear."

4. **The fourth step is to release the feeling, to let it go.** Because of your calm, you feel at ease, even in the midst of fear, and you know that your fear will not grow into something that will overwhelm you. When you know that you are capable of taking care of your fear, it is already reduced to the minimum, becoming softer and not so unpleasant. Now you can smile at it and let it go, but please do not stop yet. Calming and releasing are just medicines for the symptoms. You now have the opportunity to go deeper and work on transforming the source of your fear.

5. **The fifth step is to look deeply.** You look deeply into your baby—your feeling of fear—to see what is wrong, even after the baby has already stopped crying, after the fear is gone. You cannot hold your baby all the time, and therefore you have to look into him to see the cause of what is wrong. By looking, you will see what will help you begin to transform the feeling. You will realize, for example, that his suffering has many causes, inside and outside of his body. If something is wrong around him, if you put that in order, bringing tenderness and care to the situation, he will feel better. Looking into your baby, you see the elements that are causing him to cry, and when you see them, you will know what to do and what not to do to transform the feeling and be free. . . . [In looking, you might] uncover causes of suffering that stem from the way [you look] at things, the beliefs [you] hold about [yourself], [your] culture, and the world. . . . After recognizing the feeling, becoming one with it, calming it down, and releasing it, we can look deeply into its causes, which are often based on inaccurate perceptions. As soon as we understand the causes and nature of our feelings, they begin to transform themselves.

The above beautifully expresses an important concept of healing. Feelings are not to be feared or avoided. As we calmly look into our negative feelings—without judging them, but accepting them with compassion—we discover the cause of our suffering and better see the pathways to healing, recovery, and growth. Healing is permitting feelings into awareness in a safe and paced way, while always retaining control.

# CHAPTER 6

# Treatment Approaches

## Professional, Medication, Group, and Self-Managed

**There is always an easy solution to every human problem—neat, plausible, and wrong.**
**—H. L. Mencken, A Mencken Chrestomathy**

In recent years, researchers have learned much about PTSD and its successful treatment. The prospects of overcoming or lessening your symptoms today are quite hopeful, especially with *skilled*, *appropriate* treatment.

Many ask whether or not they should treat PTSD, since some people seem to recover on their own. A point to remember, though, is that untreated PTSD can worsen and needlessly lead to problems like depression, anxiety, substance abuse, chronic pain, or personality disorders. Treatment can be very helpful and is suggested if

1. Symptoms are causing considerable suffering.
2. Symptoms are interfering with your capacity to work, enjoy life, and connect to others.
3. Symptoms are causing physical illness.
4. Symptoms do not lessen within one to three months. This is a rule of thumb. In many cases, immediate treatment might prevent worsening of symptoms and is recommended if symptoms are extremely disturbing. Treatment is a good idea even if symptoms have diminished but are still disturbing.

5. You are having suicidal thoughts, hallucinations (seeing or hearing things), or fear that you will hurt yourself or others.
6. You are taking any medication for your symptoms.

The saying "That which doesn't kill me makes me stronger" is not always accurate. Some traumatic wounding severely weakens people, and the symptoms can worsen with time. Treatment can help these persons heal and grow stronger.

Because PTSD sometimes runs its course, people might urge you to

- Just not think about it.
- Just get on with your life—be like you used to be.
- Get over it.
- Stop dwelling on the past.

Diane Everstine writes[1] that it is a myth that PTSD will go away and be forgotten if you don't talk about it, if you pretend it did not happen, or if you don't tell anyone. If willpower alone has not helped you dissipate dissociated traumatic material (it rarely does), then seeking treatment would be a wise choice—a way of caring for yourself.

We will explore many approaches that have been found to foster recovery. Research has not yet established one approach as vastly superior to any other. Rather, people are unique and respond differently to specific strategies. So the principles will be presented for each strategy. This will empower you to determine if the particular strategy is suited to you and decide when or if to apply it.

## CAUTION

Treatment is not easy. It generally does not provide a quick fix, although some gains might occur fairly rapidly. Homework is usually needed to heal. Be prepared to encounter feelings of depression and anxiety as you encounter difficult memories until they are resolved. You might initially experience the worsening of some symptoms and a desire for unhealthy comforts. However, the work of healing progresses with each appropriate effort and eventually becomes easier.

## PRINCIPLES OF TREATMENT

The following principles optimize treatment success:[2]

1. **Transcend your fears of treatment in order to facilitate treatment.** Understand that your fears of treatment are normal. There are good reasons for them, and they are shared by many others, at least initially. Fears might include these:[3]
   - **The fear of discovering the cause of the disturbance.** Although it may feel like you are the only one to have gone through an experience like yours, in fact many have. We learn that many people react in ways similar to the way we have. Feelings of disgust, humiliation, fear, and self-dislike are typical. They don't mean that you are inadequate. Understanding the root cause of the symptoms will help dissipate the symptoms.
   - **The fear of alienating the therapist.** An experienced therapist knows that PTSD reactions are normal and understandable. She is not shocked by the symptoms, and this response will help you realize that you are not crazy or abnormal.
   - **The fear of being overwhelmed or going crazy.** You will learn how to cope effectively with difficult thoughts and feelings so that you are less likely to feel overwhelmed.
   - **Fear of losing good memories.** In actuality, when negative memories are processed, the good ones come to awareness and can become stronger. Treatment just allows a negative memory to take its place properly in the past.
2. **Understand the treatment options and the reasons behind them.** Know what to expect, then formulate a plan in conjunction with your counselor. Be open to various treatment possibilities.
3. **You must be willing to give up harmful "retraumatizing behaviors" like drugs, violence, self-destruction, or dangerous thrill-seeking.** These all keep you in the survivor mode (vigilant, minimizing risk, detached from feelings) or the avoidance mode (isolated, numb).[4] Both are contrary to recovery. You will learn to understand the purposes of these behaviors and substitute constructive behaviors that better meet your needs.
4. **Stay in control as you gradually learn to trust the healing process.** Many strategies have demonstrated effectiveness. If you work with a helper, recognize that it may be difficult to trust. You might have learned from experience that other people are not trustworthy. Part of the role of trauma therapy is to teach the survivor how to relate in a relationship. Over time, if the therapist is constant and models good boundaries, the survivor will learn to trust. You may decide to give her a chance to earn your trust, grad-

ually letting her know of difficulties you are having so that she will know how best to help.

5. **Be willing to confront traumatic memories in a therapeutic, controlled way—if and only when you are ready.** Do not dig. Memories will come to the surface as a natural part of therapy.

6. **You must be willing to give up secondary gains.** *Secondary gains* are desirable payoffs for being sick. Thus, the person is unwilling to be well. Sometimes the payoff is not obvious. In order to heal, the person must be aware of any secondary gains and then be willing to release them. "Will you miss the problem when it's gone?" If you hesitate, you may have secondary gains.[5] We ask ourselves, "Would any bad things happen if we recover?" Then we formulate a plan to address these needs.

Here are a few secondary gains and their challenges to recovery:[6]

- For a vet, recovery must be more important than a disability check.
- An abused teenager will have to find a new place to live.
- A vet who has the identity of a wounded hero must expand his way of seeing himself.
- A member of a support group must find other ways to meet his social needs.
- A vet fears that an end to his pain will mean that he'll forget his dead comrades. He later learns to better honor the dead with a productive life. Releasing intense pain does not mean forgetting or being disloyal to comrades.
- A police officer who fears losing his edge must realize that constant vigilance degrades performance.
- A person with PTSD fears losing something that has been "a part of me for years." She must learn to see herself as more than her symptoms.
- A survivor of abuse fears giving up her justification for years of failure. She must learn to replace it with a gradual, achievable plan for success.
- A son of a Holocaust survivor with PTSD feels it would be disloyal to become different from his parents. He must learn that he can be happy *and* loyal.

The following questions can help to clarify secondary gains so that a plan to address the secondary gain can be formulated.

- What will I give up if I get better?
- What new challenges will I face if I recover?

- Who am I without this problem?
- Who will I disappoint if I recover?
- What would happen if I were happier or more successful?
- What would happen if I weren't experiencing these symptoms?

Try completing this cost/benefit analysis.

---

## PTSD COST/BENEFIT ANALYSIS

| The Benefits of Having PTSD Are | The Disadvantages of PTSD Are |
| --- | --- |
|  |  |

---

The ultimate questions are, "Is PTSD a problem in terms of its costs?" and "How can I meet my needs without PTSD?" This book will suggest various ways to meet your needs without PTSD.

## WHEN NOT TO TRY MEMORY WORK

An important part of treatment is the work of processing traumatic memories, or memory work. This requires that you be stabilized and functioning reasonably well. It should not be tried if any of the following conditions are not under control:

- Substance addiction
- Self-destructive behavior (self-injury, suicidal tendencies, eating disorder)
- Threats of violence or homicide
- Life chaos (the likelihood that the trauma will be repeated, abuse is ongoing, no home or income, etc.)
- Mental illness, especially schizophrenia, bipolar disorder (manic depression), or other illness needing medication
- The threat of mental health being overwhelmed

Flannery states, "Some victims appear so overwhelmed by the recall of such episodes that in some cases it is better to leave the event sealed in memory and to work on the other steps toward a more normal life. This would leave the victim subject to possible intrusive memories in the face of threat or loss, but given our current understanding of treating these events, this might be a better trade-off in some few victims." [7] A number of steps can help this person manage the stress in his life. At some point it may be appropriate to explore traumatic memories, perhaps in a controlled environment such as a hospital ward.

Matsakis[8] adds that memory work should not be undertaken if

- There is not a strong therapeutic alliance with a mental health professional.
- There is no support system.
- Severe rage, nightmares, flashbacks, and irritability are uncontrolled.
- The individual is not ready.

Remember, you are the one who is in control. You determine when to begin. You set a safe pace and say when to stop. Stop or ease up at any time you feel overwhelming or dangerous emotions, such as extreme or dangerous anger or panic. Likewise, ease up if you dissociate, experience psychotic episodes, or encounter strong physical upset—such as nausea, pain, dizziness, or panic attack.

## APPROACHES TO TREATMENT

There are many treatment approaches with demonstrated effectiveness.

### Professional Treatment

A skilled mental health professional can be an invaluable resource in helping you treat PTSD. If the PTSD is severe or long-lasting, a psychotherapist will probably be needed to guide you through the process of healing. Think of psychotherapy as crisis counseling for stress and anxiety, not counseling for mental illness. An important aspect of psychotherapy is that it provides a supportive relationship while you work through difficult material and learn new coping skills. A good therapeutic relationship will also help the individual learn to trust again.

Psychotherapists include psychologists, psychiatrists, clinical social workers, psychiatric nurses, clinical mental health counselors, certified pastoral counselors, and marriage and family therapists. Certified pastoral counselors consider both psychological and spiritual needs. All of these can be helpful if they are specifically trained to treat PTSD.

As Frank Ochberg observes: "There are not enough therapists in the world to treat the millions of men, women, and children who have been assaulted, abused, and violated as a result of war, tyranny, crime, disaster, and family violence. When people do seek help, suffering with posttraumatic symptoms, they may find therapists who are ill-equipped to provide assistance."[9] It is important, then, for a person with PTSD to be a good consumer. The resources listed at the back of this book will help you locate a psychotherapist who treats PTSD (see Additional Resources). However, not all clinicians are equally skilled. You must find one whose skills you respect and who you feel comfortable working with. You will want to select one whose values you are comfortable with, who is trustworthy and ethical. It is advisable to discuss the principles of therapy before you begin treatment. Before settling on a psychotherapist, ask questions such as the following (a therapist who is unwilling to discuss these important issues is not likely to be a good match for you):

- What is your training and experience in treating PTSD?
- What is your approach to treating it? (You will get a sense for the types of approaches you prefer by reading later sections of this book.)
- What are your views about dissociation and its treatment?
- Do you have experience treating those who have encountered traumatic events similar to mine?

- Are you experienced in treating the associated conditions that I experience (such as drug addictions, eating disorders, depression, generalized anxiety, or panic disorders)?
- What are your views about the use of medication in the treatment of PTSD? If needed, can you prescribe it, or do you have a working relationship with someone who does?
- Do you provide family counseling or have a working relationship with counselors who do?
- What are your policies about calling you during the week, should I need to?

The psychotherapist will ideally bring a number of attributes to counseling:

- **He will put you at ease and share control—you will hold primary control.** He will be comfortable in allowing you to set the pace and will work to ensure that you are as comfortable and safe as possible. He might remind you that "you don't have to tell anything you don't feel ready to or feel safe disclosing" or to feel free to control the timing or back away from uncomfortable material.[10]
- **She will explore your fears of treatment.** Everyone feels weak and helpless at times. After trauma, most people fear being overwhelmed. Emotions are temporary, not a permanent reflection of character. She will understand your fear of bringing up material that causes more pain and will work to help you replace that fear with trust and understanding.
- **He will be skilled in forging a strong therapeutic alliance.**

Early in the course of treatment, the therapist will make a thorough assessment of your trauma and your life history. This will be useful to both of you. This process helps you to see that you will not go crazy talking about the trauma. The process begins to name the pain. The assessment also helps the therapist to plan the course of treatment. If, for example, you have a history of distrust in your family where it was not OK to express feelings or needs or take care of yourself, treatment might start by addressing these issues before addressing the trauma. The assessment will also identify factors that could impede treatment. For example, a treatment plan would have to include provisions for treating a drug addiction, should that exist (if you are addicted to any substance, be sure to find a therapist experienced with treating addictions or who collaborates with those who do).[11]

Expect the counselor to be respectful and supportive but not infallible. She will not always be available nor able to fill all your needs. Some days will be less productive than others. Don't worry about expressing your secrets. Keeping secrets is part of the problem of PTSD. Experienced counselors will not be uncomfortable with such material. Keep going to therapy even after you feel better, since return of symptoms is likely at some point.

It can prove helpful to involve family members of the survivor in counseling since they can be troubled by the victim's symptoms. The therapist will help them understand PTSD and realize the real cause of the symptoms. Family members will learn what is helpful and what is beyond their capacity to fix. They might learn new ways to take care of themselves. If they are unwilling or unable to provide support to the survivor, then other social supports would be recruited. Of course, if the family member is the perpetrator, he would be excluded as a social support.

Remember that you will form a working team with your therapist but you are the one in control. You will learn to be more tolerant of distressing feelings that may arise. You will learn to watch them come and go. Pay attention to how you are feeling. If you experience any of the following, stop and talk to your therapist:[12]

- Feeling that you are losing touch with reality, such as experiencing flashbacks, hallucinations, or derealization
- Feeling disoriented, spaced-out, or loss of control
- Hyperventilation (rapid, irregular breathing), uncontrollable shaking, pounding or irregular heartbeat, panic attack, gasping for air
- Extreme nausea, diarrhea, bleeding, new or intense pain, exacerbation of existing medical conditions (e.g., diabetes)
- Desire to hurt yourself (e.g., cutting or suicide)
- Desire to perform self-defeating behaviors (vomit, use drugs, overspend, engage in inappropriate sexual activity)
- Thoughts of hurting others
- Emotions so overwhelming that you fear you are going to die, go crazy, or lose control

## Medication

Medications do not cure PTSD. However, they may be useful under certain situations to lessen symptoms so that other forms of treatment can work. For example, medications might help reduce symptoms of depression or anxiety when these symptoms are severe and blocking treatment success. Psychiatrists and other medical doctors prescribe medications. Seek a psychiatrist who is skilled in working with people with PTSD. General practice physicians will be unlikely to have such experience. Psychiatrists do not usually provide psychotherapy, although some do. All medications have side effects, and a wise consumer will discuss these considerations with the prescribing physician. Appendix H discusses other medication considerations.

### Survivor Groups

The use of groups to treat PTSD was pioneered with Vietnam War veterans. Survivor groups typically include five to ten people meeting weekly to provide support and encouragement as they process their experiences and learn coping skills. Some groups are run by or advised by mental health professionals. Others are self-help groups organized and directed by nonprofessionals. Groups can prove a useful adjunct to individual counseling and individual efforts, once symptoms are stabilized. Experience has taught that groups accomplish a number of critical steps in healing:[13]

- **Alienation and estrangement are countered.** The group member comes to realize that others can understand what he has gone through because they have had similar experiences themselves. Survivors realize that they are not the only ones to react as they did or do. They see that others are struggling, too, and that others can understand. They feel less abnormal, less weird, less different. It can also be helpful to see that those in the group with different experiences can still understand you.
- **Groups provide a sense of community, a feeling of security that is akin to family.** This is important since safety and security are needed for recovery. This breaks down further the feeling of isolation and helps people transition back into society.
- **Groups destigmatize the experience.** Members can assure the victim that they are not abnormal for what they experienced. Seeing the worth of those who have experienced a similar trauma helps counter feelings of worthlessness.
- **Groups facilitate the disclosing of secrets, thus unburdening the secret-keeper and countering the idea that "my story is too horrible to tell."** The saying that we are as sick as our secrets suggests that there are appropriate ways to express our secrets so that we can move beyond them.

- **Group members will challenge each other to take a more realistic view.** This might be helpful, for example, when one carries unreasonable guilt.
- **Groups help survivors to talk about and process their traumatic memories in a supportive climate.** Sometimes aspects of memories missed in individual counseling will surface in a group setting.
- **Groups permit the sharing of coping ideas.** Members see coping attempts modeled and can try out new ideas and behaviors.
- **Groups are especially empowering when they are not run by therapists.** However, a disadvantage is that needed clinical skills may be absent.
- **Groups combine the strengths of many individuals, not just one or two.** Thus, members might brainstorm ways of coping, ways to assign meaning, and ways to grow.
- **Families can be involved to increase social support.** The important benefits of involving family members in treatment are further discussed in Chapter 35.
- **Groups create an environment where members can learn to trust others and repair their ability to relate to others.** The group format allows members to create relationships that simulate the world but are in some ways safer. In that controlled environment, then, group members can practice necessary skills while learning how to relate to people in healthy ways.

Certain cautions apply. The frank discussions of some groups might trigger troubling dissociated material. An individual should not, therefore, enter a group until he is in fairly good control of his symptoms. He might, for example, seek individual psychotherapy until he is comfortable confronting traumatic memories. Or he might seek a group that focuses on coping but not memory processing, or combines individual with group work. Group work is generally not advisable for one who has never talked about his traumatic memories or for one whose life is chaotic. Groups are usually not appropriate for people who are suicidal, homicidal, violent, abusing drugs, injuring oneself, or who have borderline personality disorder, at least until these are controlled. Groups for dissociative identity disorder can be a useful adjunct when secondary to one-on-one psychotherapy (see Appendix D).[14]

## Self-Managed Treatment Approaches
There are many steps that people with PTSD can take to help themselves, especially with regard to managing symptoms and restoring balance, stability, and health to

one's life. Should people with PTSD try to treat themselves? As a general rule, professional help is suggested since, by definition, PTSD means that one's present coping abilities have been overwhelmed. While a minority of survivors seem to fully recover on their own, most will continue to experience troubling symptoms for a long time afterward without treatment. Properly trained specialists can help the survivor along the road to recovery faster, much like a skilled coach can help an athlete improve performance. Mental health professionals can help survivors develop new coping skills and process material that is "stuck." Acknowledging the need for help and seeking it is a sign of self-esteem.

### Be Aware of Your Choices

Unfortunately, many of those who need help will not find it. Sometimes skilled professionals are not readily available. Sometimes individuals cannot afford treatment or feel embarrassed to seek it. Sometimes people with PTSD do not know where to look for help or don't realize how useful it can be.

This book will guide you to finding and facilitating the correct treatment. As much as possible, specific instructions for treatment strategies are provided, since an informed client will progress better in treatment. Use this book as a resource. Discuss it with your mental health professional. Together, you might decide to practice certain treatment strategies at home as part of your comprehensive treatment plan. Some people who do not have a formal diagnosis of PTSD but are nevertheless troubled by symptoms might find some of the strategies herein useful. In some cases, the originators of certain techniques indicate that they can be used without supervision. However, these should be used with caution. The main principle to remember is that dissociated material can be more troubling than needed if it is not managed in a controlled and safe way. If in doubt, consult with a mental health professional skilled in treating PTSD before using any of the treatment strategies in this book. Take responsibility for your recovery. Seek to be as self-reliant as possible but also know when to ask for help.

### FINDING THE BEST HELP

Various organizations listed in the Additional Resources section in the back of this book will help you find the right mental health professional and/or group. Remember to be a good consumer. Check out credentials and experience. Make sure that you are comfortable with a therapist before committing to therapy.

# PART III

# Preparing for the Recovery Process

# CHAPTER 7

# *Stabilization and Balance*

Before beginning treatment, restore as much equilibrium in your life—balance, order, and health—as you can. You can't concentrate on recovering if you don't feel reasonably safe and strong. Treatment is more like a marathon than a sprint. Recovery may take months or longer, depending on the amount of upheaval in your life. So you'll need to have your life in good balance. This section will help you regain control of your life and prepare for the work of healing. Many of the steps are themselves healing. They send a soothing signal that you are willing to rebuild damaged boundaries and take care of yourself. Don't feel like a failure, though, if you feel a need for professional help in getting started.

## PHYSICAL SAFETY

You have the right to be safe and protected from harm. Building physical safety includes protecting against harm:

### From Others

Take all necessary precautions to insure your safety. Consider doing the following:

- **Removing yourself from an abusive partner or causing the partner to be removed.** Shelters or crisis centers will advise you of your rights and assist in obtaining protective or restraining orders (which are not always well enforced) or other legal protections. Know how to summon the police to quickly report battery (being attacked or beaten up).
- **Making an emergency escape plan.** Plan in advance how you will find shelter or safe relatives or friends. Pack a bag or make a 72-hour emergency

preparedness kit (see Appendix E). This can provide a tremendous sense of security should you need to flee criminals, abusive partners, civil unrest, terrorism, or natural disaster. If you live with an abuser, keep emergency supplies elsewhere such as at a trusted friend's home.

- **Checking the security of the house.** It is quite normal for people who have suffered a traumatic event to make frequent checks of locks and windows or to look under beds and in closets. If your house has been violated, you might put up protective bars, install dead bolts on doors, or change locks or telephone numbers. Join a neighborhood watch group or form one with help from the police.
- **Learning self-defense.** This may prove lifesaving in an emergency.
- **Being fully mindful of the environment.** Trauma victims might temporarily lose their protective instinct, becoming stunned and feeling helpless. Take control of your safety again. Carefully scan for signs of danger. Look around parked cars, for example, or inside your car before entering it. Do this with a sense of confident anticipation. That is, if you detect potential danger, you will have a sensible action plan (e.g., run away, blow a whistle, loudly call for help).
- **Avoiding risky places and/or arranging for companionship** (e.g., a college student calls for a security escort before walking to a dark parking lot).

### From Self

Commit not to harm yourself in any way. Drugs, self-injury, and other self-destructive acts are ways you might have learned to deal with painful dissociated material. They undermine treatment. Seek professional help if you need assistance in controlling these practices. It is an act of self-caring to arrange for hospitalization if you anticipate the need for protection.

### To Others

Violence must be halted, and anger must be controlled (see Chapter 13). Family crisis centers often provide anger counseling for individuals and couples. Hospitalization might be necessary if you suspect that you might harm others. Some family members might be harmed simply by your withdrawal or mistrust. You might explain, "I went through a rather difficult experience some time ago. I have my ups and downs. If I seem distracted or unreasonably upset sometimes, it's not because of you. I will recover, but it will take some time." You may or may not choose to disclose the details of the traumatic event. People can be known emotionally without their disclosing private facts. The important point is that feelings can be openly communicated so that family members can make sense of their world.

## EMOTIONAL SAFETY

A strong therapeutic alliance with a mental health professional that you respect and feel comfortable with can be a crucial component of healing. Social support can also be provided from family and friends (if they are available and willing) and support groups. Fight the tendency to isolate yourself following exposure to a traumatic event. Do choose your social supports wisely. Be sure that you disclose information only to people whom you discern to be safe and trustworthy. That is, you will be reasonably confident that they will keep confidences and will not negatively judge you or harm you. Again, recognize the limits of family members. They may not understand the nature of PTSD. Perhaps they won't understand why you just can't bounce back to normal. You might let them read this book. They themselves may be overwhelmed or unavailable for other reasons. In such cases it will be wise to cultivate additional social supports.

## LIVING CONCERNS

These include food, shelter, employment, medical and legal care, bills, and time management (see Appendix I). Most counties have organizations to help people find employment and low-cost or free shelter. Medical care may be needed to help heal physical wounds, check for sexually transmitted diseases or pregnancy, or clear you for physical exercise. A thorough medical exam can also detect physical conditions that can increase symptoms of arousal and anxiety. For example, thyroid disorders can create a wealth of anxiety and depression symptoms. An inexpensive test called the TSH test can frequently detect subtle abnormalities that normal blood tests will miss.[1] You might have to specifically request this test from your doctor. A biopsychiatrist specializing in PTSD might be more likely than a primary care physician to look for such conditions. Sleep apnea can also lead to fatigue, depression, nightmares, and loss of sexual interest. Sleep apnea (see Chapter 8) is signaled by loud snoring followed by silence and gasping for air. It is very treatable but frequently goes undiagnosed.

Learn how not to be harmed by the legal system. The National Organization for Victims Assistance (NOVA) helps victims of crime, for instance, navigate the criminal justice system, including the risks of police investigations (giving details might be traumatizing), precourt appearances, trials, and sentencing hearings (see Additional Resources). Be prepared for messages from insensitive lawyers or police who might suggest that you caused the crime or asked for it, or did not respond "correctly." Personal details of your life history will also become a matter of public record should you choose to prosecute an offender.

See Additional Resources in the back of this book for a list of resources that can help you get back on your feet following a traumatic event. Some services will not apply if you let too much time elapse after the trauma, so act as promptly as you can.

## PROBLEM SOLVING

Serious problems of immediate living will need to be solved, or at least reasonably controlled, for recovery to progress. During times of extreme stress, we often get tunnel vision, so focused on fear and so desirous of a quick solution that we fail to consider all of our options. Problem-solving skills enable us to explore our options and enact a plan. Problem-solving skills have been taught even to children, resulting in less anxiety and stress. Solving problems is more satisfying than escaping them with drugs. When a problem arises, tell yourself, "This is an opportunity for growth, not a stumbling block." Here is the procedure:

1. Clearly identify the problem. Some people find that writing the problem down on paper helps to focus their thinking.
2. Determine what the desired outcome is. (What do you wish to see happen?)
3. Brainstorm a list of possible solutions. When we brainstorm, we think of as many ideas as we can, as quickly as we can. We don't judge, at this point, whether possible solutions are good or bad, possible or not possible. We simply list. Being critical of ideas stifles the creative process.
4. Appraise the list of solutions. What are the strengths and weaknesses of each? Can any solutions be combined? Are there any solutions that have not been thought of? Do you need more information?
5. Pick what seems like a sensible solution.
6. Make a thorough plan.
7. Try it out.
8. Reevaluate and make adjustments.

You need not attempt problem solving alone. The list in Additional Resources suggests many sources of help. Trusted acquaintances can be especially helpful in brainstorming. However, studies have suggested that the best creative problem solving occurs when people alternate between working in groups and working alone. Thus, it might be wise to solicit ideas and information from sensible people, but rely on yourself to think through all aspects of your plan. It is unlikely that you will find a perfect solution; it is likely you'll find one or more reasonably good solutions.

You can use this problem-solving process for the immediate problems of living. Later, you can use it when stressful situations arise or when you wish to manage troubling PTSD symptoms.

## HEALTHY PLEASURES

Your physical and mental well-being depend on a healthy balance between work and play. Plan to incorporate a variety of healthy pleasures into your lifestyle to sustain your mood and recreate (literally, *re*-create). Perhaps you'll want to try things that used to be pleasurable. Perhaps you'll wish to try new things that might prove enjoyable. Remember activities such as warm baths, gardening, getting together with friends and family, pleasant reading, or other forms of recreation that you found enjoyable in the past. At this point, you might not feel capable or worthy of pleasure. These ideas will wane over the course of treatment. For now, set some simple, modest goals to regularly engage in pleasant activities and then experiment. Try some events alone and some with others. On a one-to-ten scale, predict how pleasurable you expect an event to be. Afterward, rate how pleasant it actually was. The actual rating might be higher than you predicted. Don't get down on yourself if events don't seem as pleasant as they used to. This is a normal symptom of PTSD. This will change. Avoid violence in the media—movies, videos, television—that will trigger arousal.

# CHAPTER 8

# *Taking Care of Your Health*

The mind and body are connected. The condition of your body will profoundly affect your moods, energy level, performance, and symptoms, including sleep quality. Developing a healthier body will help you through the course of treatment.

**EXERCISE**

*Note:* If you hyperventilate, do not begin an exercise program until you are skilled in automatic, slow, regular, and rhythmic abdominal breathing. Complete Chapter 11 on retraining your breathing before proceeding with this one. If physical activity is a trigger, see Chapter 15 for managing intrusions before beginning an exercise program.

Virtually everyone who engages in a *regular, moderate* exercise program knows how remarkably effective it is in reducing stress. Exercise has been shown to measurably reduce muscle tension and other stress symptoms without the side effects of medication, improve self-esteem and mental health generally, reduce blood pressure, increase energy levels and stamina, reduce resting heart and breathing rates, strengthen the heart, improve the quality of sleep, promote weight loss, strengthen the immune system, and reduce PMS symptoms.

The stress response is designed to culminate in physical movement. Exercise allows the body to expend the energy of the stress response and return to a more restful state. It also gives the mind a break, time to distract and spin free, so that we return to work mentally and physically refreshed. This is why the exercised person can accomplish more in less time. Some think they are too busy to exercise. It helps to think of exercise as an important investment. It enables people to be more productive, accomplishing more in less time. It also enables people to remain more relaxed and in a better frame of mind while they cope with problems.

## What Kind of Exercise Is Best?

Any kind of exercise is better than none. There are three kinds of exercise:

1. **Aerobic exercise.** This is rhythmic, continuous exercise, such as walking, swimming, low-impact aerobics, jogging, biking, stair-climbing, and some racket games.
2. **Strength training** (lifting weights, calisthenics, or similar activities).
3. **Flexibility exercises** such as yoga or stretching.

If you are limited for time, aerobic exercise is generally recommended, at a gentle pace, on most days for at least twenty minutes. Daily, longer, gentle exercise (e.g., walking for forty minutes daily rather than running for twenty minutes three times a week) is best for stress reduction and weight loss. However, these are just goals to strive for. Even a ten-minute energy walk can bring ninety minutes of energy, elevated mood, and stress reduction. Try a quick energy walk to get away from your desk for a few minutes every hour or two. And don't overlook the other two types of exercise. Yogic postures can slow the effects of aging and stiffening, and the improved muscle tone from weight training facilitates weight loss and greatly reduces anxiety.

Start your exercise program gently and build up gradually. You are not in a race. Exercise should leave you refreshed and energized. It should not hurt or exhaust you beyond a pleasant fatigue. If you eventually work up to a total exercise time of thirty to ninety minutes on most days, great. If not, do what you can to start. Do make a plan for regular, moderate exercise. If you have trouble falling asleep, try exercising before dinner, or earlier. Allow five to ten minutes before and after exercising for warm-up and cooldown. If you are older (age forty for men; fifty for women) or have any health risk factors (such as being overweight, symptoms or family history of high blood pressure, heart disease, or diabetes), have a physical examination first and discuss your exercise plans with your doctor.

## SLEEP HYGIENE

Poor sleep can be both a cause and effect of anxiety, and attempts to improve sleep typically lessen PTSD symptoms. Two considerations for improving sleep quality are crucial: amount and regularity. Most sleep researchers believe that almost all adults function and feel at their best with at least eight hours of sleep. Many do better on considerably more. Sleep shortage has been associated with shrinkage of the hippocampus, a region of the brain that helps store traumatic memories properly. Regular sleep and wake-up times are needed to keep the body's sleep cycle consistent. Retiring at irregular hours (e.g., getting to bed much later on Friday and Saturday nights than on weekdays) can lead to insomnia. In this century, a number of developments have interfered with sleep: the lightbulb permits people to stay up later and do shift work; worldwide communication allows people to work or be entertained around the clock; twenty-four-hour shopping promotes irregular sleep patterns. It is no wonder that today's American is sleep-deprived but does not realize it.

The idea is to get a little more sleep than you think you need and to keep sleep and wake-up times as consistent throughout the week as possible, varying no more than an hour from night to night. This will probably take considerable discipline, given all the temptations of modern society. The payoffs will surprise you.

Beyond the major issues of amount and regularity, the following tips can also improve sleep:

- **Use the bedroom only for sleeping.** Sex is an exception when it is enjoyable and relaxing. Remove phones, computers, and television. Don't pay bills, work, or read arousing material in bed. All can condition you to be aroused in bed.
- **Reduce light and noise, which can disturb sleep.** If your clock emits light, cover it or turn it away from you. Be sure that early morning light does not enter through the window.
- **Don't eat a big meal within four hours of retiring.** A light carbohydrate and/or low-fat dairy snack before bed can help you fall asleep quicker (e.g., warm milk, crackers and cheese, sweetened yogurt, bread).
- **Avoid stimulants, like caffeine, for at least seven to ten hours before bedtime.** It can take hours for stimulants to clear the body.
- **If you are having difficulty sleeping, either eliminate naps altogether, or try them regularly each day for fifteen to ninety minutes around 1:00–2:00 P.M.** Most people find regular naps beneficial; others find that eliminating naps consolidates nighttime sleep.
- **Once in bed, try slow breathing and/or progressive muscle relaxation to unwind.** Later chapters will explain how these are done.
- **If you wake up and cannot fall back to sleep within fifteen to twenty minutes, get out of bed and do something quiet.** Do not reward your-

self for not sleeping with television or something else enjoyable. Rather, try something like paying bills. Some people prefer to meditate to calm down.

- **If you are afraid to go to sleep because of nightmares, read Chapters 10 and 25.** Useful skills can help neutralize troubling nightmares.
- **If the bedroom itself is a trigger (e.g., for a rape victim), try the arousal reduction techniques in Part IV.** Typically, processing traumatic memories (see Part V) also reduces sleep problems.

## SLEEP APNEA

A treatment for sleep apnea, continuous positive airway pressure (CPAP), is associated with reduced nightmares, insomnia, and PTSD symptoms in several studies. Apnea occurs when the airway closes while one is sleeping, typically caused by excess tissue in the throat. The brain registers the lack of air and wakes the sleeping person up just enough to resume breathing. The cycle of falling asleep and waking up can occur hundreds of times during the night, without conscious awareness. A partner might notice a pattern of loud snoring interrupted by a sudden stoppage of breathing. During the day, the person is likely to feel exhausted, sleepy, depressed, and disinterested in sex, in addition to the PTSD-related problems already mentioned. If apnea is suspected, ask your physician to arrange a sleep study in a sleep clinic to diagnose and correct this condition, which is highly treatable.[1] Sleep apnea is also a risk factor for strokes, heart attacks, and high blood pressure. Losing weight through exercise and proper nutrition can also help to reduce sleep apnea and snoring in general.

## EATING HABITS AND NUTRITION

Sensible eating habits are essential in managing stress. Simply stated, good nutrition raises resistance to stress and anxiety, while poor nutrition is a stressor. (See Figures 8.1–8.3 and Table 8.1 at the end of this chapter.) If you visualize a plate where less than one-fourth of the plate comprises meat products and plant foods fill the rest of the plate, then you have a pretty good idea of eating goals, which include the following:

- **Get most of your calories from complex carbohydrates, which come from plant foods** (e.g., vegetables, fruits, and whole-grain breads, rice, pasta, and cereals). Foods that are fresh, frozen, or minimally processed are usually better choices because they tend to have less added sugar, salt, and fat, but more fiber.

- **Reduce meats, which contain saturated fats and cholesterol, to about 6 ounces daily.** Use mainly poultry without skin, fish, lean meats, or meat alternates such as dry beans and peas, nuts, or seeds.
- **Reduce fats, sugar, salt, caffeine, prwocessed foods, and alcohol.** If sleep is troubled, avoid caffeine altogether or for at least seven to ten hours before bedtime. (Nicotine and recreational drugs can also increase anxiety, so gradually reduce or eliminate these too, over a period of several weeks.)
- **Take adequate calcium.** Adults need at least 1,000 mg of calcium each day. A glass of skim milk provides 300 mg. Even if one drinks three glasses of skim milk each day (or eats yogurt or cheese equivalents), then additional calcium would still be needed from sources like spinach, broccoli, or tofu.[2] Do not exceed 2,500 mg daily.

Here are some additional guidelines that can improve health generally, help control weight, and help stabilize the mood:

- **Keep blood sugar steady throughout the day.** This can be done by eating breakfast, not skipping meals, and eating smaller, more frequent meals. There is evidence that five or six smaller meals will reduce fatigue and irritability while also facilitating weight loss. "Meals" can include midmorning and midafternoon snacks such as wa half-sandwich, yogurt, soup, or fruit. Avoid concentrated sweets, which cause blood sugar fluctuations.
- **Shift food so that some of the calories that would normally be eaten at a big dinner are eaten at breakfast, lunch, or as snacks.** This also keeps blood sugar steadier throughout the day and may help regulate appetite and mood.
- **Choose foods often that are less than 30 percent fat.** To quickly estimate fat content, multiply the grams of fat by ten and divide by the total calories. The result should be less than 33 percent. A candy bar contains 250 calories, and 14 grams of fat. Thus:

$$\frac{14 \text{ grams fat} \times 10}{250 \text{ calories}} = 56\%$$

This choice is quite high in fat. The sugar would also tend to give a momentary energy lift but would make one more tired and tense an hour later (a brisk walk would give a similar energy lift that would be sustained). Similar calculations for bread, potatoes, or almost all other plant products (before adding butter or oil) would show these to be healthy choices. Although meat can exceed the 30 percent fat goal, meats can be mixed with vegetables to reduce overall fat (e.g., meat stir-fried in a little oil).

- **Stay well hydrated.** Too little fluid in the body can lead to fatigue and hunger. A urine stream that is clear or pale yellow indicates adequate fluid intake. Water is an excellent beverage because it contains no calories, so stop by the water fountain when you pass it.

**Figure 8.1**
## MY PLAN TO TAKE CARE OF MY BODY

There is power in making a written plan and committing to stick to it. Please make a realistic plan that you can follow for life. It is alright to give yourself several days to "work up" to the goals in your plan.

1. **Exercise.** Exercise most days of the week for a total of thirty to ninety minutes; make sure to get at least twenty minutes of aerobic exercise. Describe your plan below:

2. **Sleep.** _____ hours a night (a little more than you think you need—most adults require about 8¼ hours of sleep or more per night to feel and function at their best) from _____ (time you'll retire) to _____ (time you'll wake up)

3. **Nutrition.** Eat at least three times a day using healthy choices. Make a written one-week menu using the worksheet on the next page and check it against the eating goals and guidelines, including the dietary guidelines on pages 86–87.

**Figure 8.2**
SAMPLE MENU:  A WEEK OF MEALS

(Write down what you plan to eat each day, with corresponding amounts.)

|  | Mon. | Tues. | Wed. | Thurs. | Fri. | Sat. | Sun. |
|---|---|---|---|---|---|---|---|
| Breakfast | | | | | | | |
| Snack | | | | | | | |
| Lunch | | | | | | | |
| Snack | | | | | | | |
| Dinner | | | | | | | |
| Snack | | | | | | | |

**Table 8.1**
DIETARY GUIDELINES

Check to see if your sample menu meets the following guidelines for healthy eating.

1. Does your plan provide the needed servings from each food group as indicated below? (Someone trying to lose weight might reduce the number of servings from each group by one, except for the milk group, which should remain at three servings.)

| Food Group | Servings Needed Each Day (with a daily total intake of 2,000 calories)* | One Serving Is . . . | Comments/Benefits |
|---|---|---|---|
| Fruits | 4 (or a total of 2 cups) | ½ cup. This is equivalent to ½ cup fresh, frozen, or canned fruit; 1 medium fruit; ¼ cup dried fruit; ½ cup fruit juice. | Fruits and vegetables provide fiber, energy, many vitamins, minerals, and phytochemicals that reduce risk of various diseases (e.g., potassium lowers risk of high blood pressure). |
| Vegetables | 5 (or a total of 2½ cups) | ½ cup. This is equivalent to ½ cup cut-up raw or cooked vegetable; 1 cup raw leafy vegetable; or ½ cup beans (black, garbanzo, soy/tofu, lentils, etc.). Count beans here or in meat group, but not both. | Seek a rainbow of colorful fruits and vegetables—green, red, orange, and yellow. |
| Grains | 6 ounce-equivalents | 1 ounce-equivalent. This is equivalent to 1 slice bread; ½–1¼ cups dry cereal (check label); ½ cup cooked rice, pasta, or cereal; or 3 cups popcorn. | At least half of servings should be whole grains, which reduce risk of heart and other diseases. Whole grains contain fiber, B vitamins, antioxidants, minerals, and various plant chemicals. Whole grains include oatmeal, whole wheat, bulgur, hulled barley, popcorn, quinoa, and brown rice. |

| Lean Meat and Beans | 5 ½ ounce-equivalents | 1 ounce-equivalent. This is equivalent to 1 ounce cooked fish, poultry, or other lean meats; 1 egg; ¼ cup cooked dry beans or soy/tofu; 1 tablespoon peanut butter; or ½ ounce nuts or seeds. | Most or all days should include nuts, seeds, and/or legumes. Legumes include all cooked dry beans, peas, and soybean products (pinto beans, kidney beans, lentils, tofu, etc.). ½ ounce nuts = 4½ walnuts = 6½ cashews. |
|---|---|---|---|
| Milk | 3 | 1 cup. This is equivalent to 1 cup low-fat or fat-free milk or yogurt; 1½ ounces low-fat or fat-free natural cheese; or 2 ounces low-fat or fat-free processed cheese. | Major source of calcium, potassium, protein, B vitamins, and other vitamins and minerals. |
| Oils | 6 teaspoon-equivalents | 1 teaspoon. This is equivalent to 1 teaspoon vegetable oil; 1 teaspoon soft margarine; 1 tablespoon low-fat mayo; or 2 tablespoons light salad dressing | Provide needed unsaturated fatty acids and vitamin E. Olive and canola oils are particularly beneficial. Avoid trans and hydrogenated fats found in commercially made snacks, baked goods/mixes, stick margarine, and fried fast foods. |

2. Does your plan provide variety in order to get all needed nutrients? That is, do you vary your choices within each food group? For example, instead of an apple each day, try bananas or strawberries as alternatives.

3. Does your plan follow the other guidelines discussed in this chapter?

* Most people's caloric requirements will not vary significantly from this figure.

Source: USDA Dietary Guidelines for Americans, 2005. See www.mypyramid.gov for interactive information. Adapted with permission from Schiraldi, G. R. The Self-Esteem Workbook. Oakland, CA: New Harbinger, 2001.

**Figure 8.3**
DAILY PROGRESS RECORD

Keep a record to see how well you stick to your plan for two weeks. Throughout this period, make whatever adjustments are necessary, and then continue the plan.

| Day | Date | Excercised (Minutes) | Number of Meals Eaten | hours | Sleep time to bed | time out of bed |
|---|---|---|---|---|---|---|
| 1 | | | | | | |
| 2 | | | | | | |
| 3 | | | | | | |
| 4 | | | | | | |
| 5 | | | | | | |
| 6 | | | | | | |
| 7 | | | | | | |
| 8 | | | | | | |
| 9 | | | | | | |
| 10 | | | | | | |
| 11 | | | | | | |
| 12 | | | | | | |
| 13 | | | | | | |
| 14 | | | | | | |

# PART IV

---

# Managing Symptoms

# CHAPTER 9

# Affect Management

---

**The most damaging feelings are those
that are never discussed.**
—*Dr. Don R. Catherall*[1]

Throughout the course of your recovery, you will likely encounter times of high emotional and physical arousal, especially when you experience intrusive recollections. This part of the book will describe approaches that help to manage these symptoms so that they become less troubling.

Remember the caution about trying to do too much, too fast, or too much by yourself. You'll likely find better success if you read and apply the skills in this part under the guidance of a skilled therapist, who can act as a coach and help ensure that you do not become overwhelmed. A therapist's guidance is especially important for the skills in Chapters 14 and 15 (and for any skills involving imagery or hypnosis or that might trigger dissociation). And discuss with your therapist the best order for reading the chapters in this part. You might find that the present order makes the most sense. However, if intrusions are so troubling that they interfere with symptom management, you might wish—again under your therapist's guidance—to start with Chapters 14 and 15 in order to permit you to succeed with the other chapters. Again, if you have any questions, discuss them first with your therapist before proceeding.

Before we discuss learning to control your physiology, let's begin by discussing emotional or feelings skills. Often, people who have experienced very painful emotions have learned to control their pain by shutting down their emotions. It is as if they think, "Feelings are too painful—I refuse to feel." They might also have picked up messages along the way that reinforce this decision not to feel.

- **Family messages.** Perhaps family members were mocked if they cried or expressed tenderness or anger (big boys don't cry; ladies don't get angry). Perhaps they grew up in a family in which feelings simply were not expressed. In some families, people were too preoccupied with survival to feel.
- **Occupational messages.** Perhaps there is an occupational mind-set that does not permit feelings. Spoken or unspoken messges might erroneously assert that soldiers, policemen, firefighters, doctors, or nurses shouldn't cry—they'll be sissies, unable to perform.
- **Fear messages,** such as "I won't be respected if I show my feelings" or "If I feel at all, I will lose control and not be able to regain it."

## IMPORTANCE OF EMOTIONS

Certainly some people lose control of their emotions in unwholesome ways. This is the case with violence and uncontrolled anger. It is the case with those who say things in the heat of emotion that they later regret. It might be the case with those who repeatedly give in to their fears. We'll advance here the proposition that the wholesome experience and expression of feelings is necessary for mental health, peak performance, and relationships that go deeper than mere superficiality. We are referring here to being aware of our feelings, distinguishing between appropriate and inappropriate behaviors, and knowing how to constructively channel and express our feelings. Feelings make us human. Wisely schooled, they elevate us to a higher level of humanity. I think, for example, of combat veterans shedding tears at their fallen comrade's funeral. The tears signaled their love for their friend and validated their sadness. It showed that it was OK to feel sadness at the loss. The commander's tears revealed a heart. Respect for him increased. It is easier, perhaps, to follow such a leader than one who has little regard for human life or for the feelings of his people.

The wholesome release of emotions returns our system to equilibrium, better prepared to react to the next emergency. Those who remain on constant alert are often the ones who blow up or burn out. In PTSD, while people seem to feel little, there are often many intense emotions that have been numbed. They remain under the surface, though, ready to explode. Often, anger is the closest to the surface. However, anger usually covers up more primary emotions such as fear and hurt. As long as only the anger is experienced and expressed, the other emotions will never heal. So our goal is to be fully aware of the range of feelings, and their gradations, so that we can channel them constructively. A person who can view her feelings without judgment is in the strongest position to control them.

All feelings serve a protective purpose. Without fear, we don't take wise precautions. Without anger, some protective acts would not be initiated. If we pay attention to it, grief tells us where healing is needed. Uncomfortable feelings tell us that something is wrong so that we can take appropriate action. Even numb feelings protect us from overwhelming emotions at first and signal a need for healing later. It is said that the difference between a coward and a brave person is that one acts despite fear. Feelings make life interesting. Without fully feeling, we do not fully respond to life. To shut down some feelings is to shut down others.

Our goal, then, is to learn to experience and express feelings as normal, constructive, and wholesome. If we don't, we are more likely to experience intrusions, rage, bodily complaints, fatigue, and self-destruction.

## RECOGNIZING EMOTIONS

Relax and ask yourself, "What am I feeling right now?" It is normal for victims to have a tough time identifying their feelings.

Realize that all feelings are valid and a normal part of life. Don't judge them. Feelings change. Tears do not last. They are expressed, and then we return to normal. The idea is to first recognize feelings so that we can control what we do with them. It is a beautiful thing to see a child with joyful feelings so openly expressed. Likewise, it is comforting to see an adult who feels—joy, love, tenderness, and even negative emotions if they are directed constructively and lovingly. Again, we can't shut down the negatives without shutting down positive emotions. Perhaps you weren't permitted to grow emotionally. That was then. Now the goal is to feel comfortable with all emotions, identify them, and channel them constructively.

### Emotions/Feelings Skills

1. **Learn to name your feelings and recognize gradations.** For example, there are differences between rage, anger, irritation, and frustration. Naming emotions gives us a sense of control over them; it helps us to express emotions verbally rather than needing to act them out inappropriately. You might consult the following list for the varieties of emotions (see page 94).
2. **When you notice yourself feeling, just observe the process without judging.** Do not think, "This is awful to feel such things. I shouldn't feel

# WORDS OF EMOTION

| | | | |
|---|---|---|---|
| accepted | ecstatic | interested | safe |
| affectionate | edgy | irritable | satisfied |
| afraid | elated | isolated | scared |
| aggressive | embarrassed | jealous | secure |
| aggrieved | enthusiastic | joyful | sensitive |
| agitated | envious | lonely | serene |
| alienated | excited | loved | shocked |
| alive | exhausted | love-struck | shy |
| ambivalent | fearful | manipulated | silly |
| amused | friendly | mischievous | sorry |
| angry | frightened | miserable | stubborn |
| annoyed | frustrated | misunderstood | stupid |
| anxious | furious | moody | supportive |
| apathetic | generous | negative | sure |
| appreciated | glad | nervous | surprised |
| ashamed | gloomy | old | suspicious |
| awkward | graceful | optimistic | tender |
| bashful | grateful | outraged | tense |
| beautiful | grouchy | overjoyed | terrified |
| bored | grumpy | pained | threatened |
| brave | guilty | panicky | torn up |
| calm | happy | paranoid | touchy |
| cautious | hateful | passionate | unappreciated |
| confident | helpless | peaceful | uncertain |
| confused | hopeful | persecuted | uncomfortable |
| courageous | hopeless | pessimistic | undecided |
| curious | horrified | playful | understanding |
| cynical | hostile | pleased | uneasy |
| daring | humiliated | possessive | uptight |
| defeated | humorous | preoccupied | used |
| dejected | hurt | pressured | useless |
| delighted | hysterical | protective | victimized |
| depressed | impatient | proud | violated |
| desperate | inadequate | puzzled | violent |
| determined | incompetent | quiet | vulnerable |
| devastated | indecisive | rejected | warm |
| disappointed | inferior | regretful | weary |
| disconsolate | inhibited | relieved | withdrawn |
| discontented | innocent | remorseful | worthwhile |
| discouraged | insecure | resentful | |
| disgusted | insulted | sad | |

like this. How dare she make me feel like this." Just notice the feelings arise and notice them subside.

3. **Feelings always make sense.** Like a scientist who observes with detachment, see if you can identify the cause of the feelings. Something happens. You think about it. Then you feel. You might with curiosity try to identify the thoughts that led to your feelings. If you can't determine what brought on the feeling, try to discover if there was a trigger related to the trauma. Distinguish between feelings and actions. You don't have to do anything with feelings if you choose not to. On the other hand, you might constructively express your feelings in a journal or drawing, or you might talk it over with a trusted friend or relative.

If becoming aware of your emotions in any way becomes overwhelming or causes you to fear harming yourself or others, do not try these skills for now. The skills will become easier as the dissociated material is digested.

# CHAPTER 10

# *Reducing General Arousal*

Many PTSD symptoms are caused by your sensitized nervous system. Trauma overwhelmed the brain's arousal center and sent it into a condition of high alert. The alarm center has since remained on alert, overreacting to stressful situations and keeping your body aroused. In turn, bodily arousal feeds back to the brain, keeping it sensitized. A vicious cycle now exists between anxiety and physical arousal. Reducing general arousal in the body is an important step in desensitizing the nervous system. Although it may take from several weeks to months to desensitize the nervous system, this section can help you notice relief from many of the symptoms of arousal fairly rapidly. When arousal symptoms do occur, they will often be less severe, and you'll learn how to relax *into* them to prevent additional arousal as a result of becoming alarmed at the symptoms.

## RELAXING INTO THE SYMPTOMS

Let's consider panic attack as a worst-case scenario of arousal. In a panic attack, the brain's alarm center goes off full blast. Every pathway of the stress response is triggered to a maximum degree. The pounding, racing heart, dizziness, air hunger, and other physical reactions are bad enough for the person affected. But in his terrified state, the panic attack sufferer also feels that he might do something drastic (like run or hit someone) or lose control. This is a normal response to a threat and would make sense provided there was a real threat and provided there was a physical outlet for the energy of the stress response. We might consider the recurring panic attack, then, as a normal, physical stress response when there is little or no threat. It is simply an alarm response caused by sensitized nerves. The body is designed such that the maximum stress response can only be maintained for five to ten minutes. After peaking, the symptoms begin to subside of their own accord, often quite rapidly—especially if we relax so as not to induce further arousal.

Even in panic sufferers, reducing general arousal can settle the chronically agitated nervous system and reduce the number of attacks. However, a goal more important than *avoiding* symptoms of arousal is learning how to *master the fear* of arousal. As we master the fear of symptoms, anticipatory fear and general arousal also decrease.

Dr. Claire Weekes is sometimes referred to as the "grandmother of anxiety" because she has helped so many people learn to deal with the symptoms of nervous arousal due to sensitized nerves. She has given four principles of recovery from sensitized nerves. Although these principles are designed for panic, they also apply to any anxiety symptoms.

1. **Face the symptoms.** Confront them until they no longer matter. A little girl is invigorated by facing into the wind and learning that she can stand up to it without being defeated. Even panic will not defeat you. The body is designed to adapt to the stress response. The mind becomes sharper under stress. Arousal does not cause people to act crazy. Indeed, a certain amount of arousal sharpens reactions. It is dissociation, not moderate arousal, that impairs performance.

2. **Willingly accept the symptoms.** Relax, let go, and invite in the body's "rattling." Let the body go loose as much as possible, then go toward, instead of withdrawing from, the feared symptoms and experiences. Go with the symptoms, "bending like the willow before the wind—rolling with the punches."[1] Realize that with time, the arousal and the intensity of the symptoms will diminish because the secretion of chemical messengers of stress decrease. As Weekes says, "so many people allow an electric flash to spoil their lives by withdrawing from it in fear."[2] Go into it; never withdraw. At their worst, symptoms will pass.

3. **Float.** With a deeply relaxed body (the paralysis in panic is simply from overtensing the body), breathe gently and peacefully and see yourself floating forward as in a cloud or on the water. There is no struggle, grim determination, or clenching of muscles—these increase arousal. Likewise, trying to erase or forget memories also creates tension. Accept them as ordinary. Act and do anyway what you want to do. As you read more in

this section, you will learn how to more deeply relax your breathing and your body.

4. **Let time pass.** A sensitized nervous system will not be cured overnight. So allow time for chemical readjustment and to learn new ways to react to stressors.

It is important to learn that anxiety symptoms will not defeat you. Under professional supervision in clinical settings, panic attack sufferers are often helped to induce their own panic attack (by intentionally hyperventilating, spinning around, or exercising too intensely) and then float through the symptoms. This helps them in two ways: They realize that there is a reason for the attacks. There is not something drastically wrong with their bodies; they are not having a heart attack, and it is not a brain tumor causing the symptoms. They also learn as they relax and stifle the urge to run away that the symptoms subside on their own. It's not as bad as they had feared. They don't die. They can tolerate the symptoms of anxiety. This is a major step in reducing their fear.[3]

## REDUCE CAFFEINE, NICOTINE, AND OTHER ANXIETY-PRODUCING DRUGS

The caffeine in just two cups of coffee can be enough to trigger intense anxiety symptoms. You might, therefore, consider reducing or eliminating caffeine gradually over the course of several weeks to reduce withdrawal symptoms. If you are having difficulty sleeping, avoid caffeine for at least seven to ten hours before bedtime. Caffeine is also found in tea, chocolate, certain soft drinks, and various nonprescription medications and weight-control aids. Check the label. You might consider switching to decaffeinated coffee, herbal teas, or soft drinks without caffeine.

A variety of other substances can cause arousal and anxiety symptoms. Recreational drugs (nicotine, alcohol, marijuana, PCP, LSD, cocaine, etc.) and a variety of prescription and nonprescription drugs can also trigger anxiety. Discuss this with your doctor. You might consider their discontinuation, reduction, or replacement.

## EXERCISE, SLEEP, AND NUTRITION

Exercise, sleep, and nutrition are all extremely important foundations in your plan to reduce anxiety. Exercise directly reduces arousal by expending the energy of stress. It also strengthens the body and builds resistance to stress-related disease. Sufficient sleep and sound nutrition also help us to be more stress-resistant. Diets high in white sugar (found in processed foods) and white flour (which is handled by the body like sugar) have been linked to anxiety and arousal. Eating more fresh, frozen, or minimally processed foods in accordance with the food pyramid discussed in Chapter 8 can help reduce anxiety symptoms. A complete discussion of important general health guidelines can be found in Chapter 8.

# CHAPTER 11

# *Breathing Retraining*

## BREATHING AND HYPERVENTILATION

Many people are surprised that very subtle shifts in breathing can cause anxiety symptoms ranging from muscle tension to migraines, panic attacks, and high blood pressure. The highly respected researcher and physician Chandra Patel sums it up:

> Behind the simple act [of breathing] lies a process that affects us profoundly. It affects the way we think and feel, the quality of what we create, and how we function in our daily life. Breathing affects our psychological and physiological states, while our psychological states affect the pattern of our breathing. . . . Hyperventilation causes not only anxiety but also such a variety of symptoms that patients can go from one specialty department to another until a wise clinician spots the abnormal breathing pattern and the patient is successfully trained to shift from maladaptive to normal breathing behavior.
>
> It has long been known that slow, rhythmic, diaphragmatic breathing can soothe our inner storms and make us feel calm and composed. It is difficult to apportion the benefit contributed by breathing exercise, but I now believe it is likely to be larger than I had originally imagined.[1]

Hyperventilation, or overbreathing, means that you expel carbon dioxide ($CO_2$) faster than your body is producing it.[2] This usually occurs with rapid, shal-

The author wishes to express appreciation to Dr. Ronald Ley, University of Albany, for reviewing this section, which has drawn much from his work: B. H. Timmons and R. Ley, eds. 1994. *Behavioral and Psychological Approaches to Breathing Disorders.* New York: Plenum.

low "chest" breathing, but can also occur with deep breathing. Hyperventilation is seen in many, and perhaps most, people with anxiety disorders. It accounts for many visits to primary care physicians and most of the calls for ambulances.[3]

When blood $CO_2$ drops, at least two major changes occur in the body. First, certain blood vessels constrict, causing less oxygen to reach the brain, heart, and extremities. Second, the blood acidity changes, causing less oxygen to reach the tissues[4] and certain ions to flood body tissues.[5] These changes account for a wide array of symptoms that are virtually identical to the symptoms of anxiety (see page 102). The change in blood acidity is thought to play a role in sensitizing the nerves.

## WHAT CAUSES HYPERVENTILATION?

When stressed or worried, we tend to tense the muscles of the neck, throat, chest, and abdomen. Especially when we tighten the abdominal muscles, we begin to breathe with rapid, shallow breaths primarily in the upper chest region. As the drop in $CO_2$ causes distressing symptoms, we become afraid of the symptoms. Arousal remains high, and a vicious cycle of worry and arousal occurs.

Hyperventilation is more likely when one becomes stressed and remains immobile such as when driving, watching an upsetting television show, or freezing during trauma. If worrisome thoughts trigger hyperventilation, one might learn to manage such thoughts. Learning to relax while one faces these thoughts will reduce the arousal.

In addition to stress, hyperventilation can be caused by several other factors:

- **Lung or airway disorders,** such as asthma, bronchitis, and interstitial lung diseases.
- **Impaired breathing caused by problems of the nose, throat, or ear.** Some of these problems only appear during sleep. If nothing else accounts for your symptoms, an ear, nose, and throat doctor experienced in rhinomanometry (the measurement of nasal airway resistance) and nasopulmonary testing might be able to detect disturbed or impaired breathing.[6]
- **Certain postures.** Under stress, some people seem to assume an "attack posture" (hunched shoulders, head and neck thrust forward, clenched teeth). Others puff up their hard, firm chests on inhalation and under-deflate during exhalation.[7] Relaxing the body and roughly equalizing the inhalation and exhalation phases of breathing helps.

# SIGNS AND SYMPTOMS OF HYPERVENTILATION
## (Breathlessness and Chest Pain Are Most Common)

**Cardiovascular:** palpitations, missed beats, tachycardia, sharp or dull atypical chest pain, "angina," vasomotor instability, cold extremities, Raynaud's phenomenon, blotchy flushing of blush area, capillary vasoconstriction (face, arms, hands)

**Neurological:** dizziness, unsteadiness, or instability; faint feelings (rarely actual fainting); visual disturbance (occasional blackouts or tunnel vision); headache (often migraines); paresthesia (numbness; deadness; uselessness; heaviness; pins and needles; burning; limbs feeling out of proportion or that they "don't belong," commonly of hands, feet, or face, sometimes of scalp or whole body); intolerance of light or noise; large pupils (wearing dark glasses on a dull day)

**Respiratory:** shortness of breath (typically *after* exertion), irritable cough, tightness or oppression of chest, "asthma," air hunger, inability to take a satisfying breath, excessive sighing, yawning, sniffing

**Gastrointestinal:** difficulty in swallowing, lump in the throat, dry mouth and throat, acid regurgitation, heartburn, "hiatus hernia," flatulence, belching, air swallowing, abdominal discomfort, bloating

**Muscular:** cramps, muscle pains (particularly in the back of the head, neck, shoulders, between shoulder blades; less commonly, the lower back and limbs); tremors, twitching, weakness, stiffness, tetany (seizing up)

**Psychological:** tension, anxiety, "unreal feelings," depersonalization, feeling "out of the body," hallucinations, fear of insanity, panic, phobias, agoraphobia, catastrophizing

**General:** weakness; exhaustion; impaired concentration, memory, and performance; disturbed sleep, including nightmares; emotional sweating (armpits, palms, whole body); woolly head

**Allergies**

---

*Source: From personal communication from Lum, Dr. L. C. (1991) in B. H. Timmons and R. Ley, eds.* Behavioral and Psychological Approaches to Breathing Disorders. *New York: Plenum, 1994. Copyright © 1994 Plenum Press. Used by permission.*

- **Other causes of irregular breathing patterns that are not associated with diseases.** These include excessive, fast, breathless talking and taking large breaths of air; tight clothing; heat, humidity, or a steep fall in barometric pressure; strong perfume or smells; excessive caffeine, nicotine, and other stimulants.
- **Blood sugar in the low-normal range in combination with hyperventilation can aggravate symptoms.** The antidote is having multiple meals spread out over the course of the day and avoiding simple carbohydrates, found in foods such as sugar and white flour.
- **Progesterone causes $CO_2$ to drop.** Hyperventilation can contribute to PMS or pregnancy symptoms such as fatigue or headache.
- **Uncontrolled diabetes, kidney or liver failure, or heart disease.** All of these can alter breathing patterns.
- **After hyperventilating for about ten days, the body makes certain accommodations to adjust to low $CO_2$ and restore the blood's acid-base balance.** Breathing may slow down, but when it increases (as when one is under stress), the symptoms of anxiety will be even more pronounced. Even a deep breath or sigh can then trigger symptoms.[8] Some people may be symptomatic most of the time. Some are symptomatic only during stress.

## HOW DO I KNOW IF I HYPERVENTILATE?

There is great relief that comes from knowing that hyperventilation is contributing to your distressing symptoms and that it is treatable. First, rule out medical causes.

### Observe Breathing Rate and Other Signs

Simply paying attention to your breathing can help you breathe correctly. Notice if any of these indications of hyperventilation exist:

- A breathing rate in excess of fourteen breaths per minute usually indicates hyperventilation.
- Breathing is mostly chest, or *thoracic*, breathing. Little use is made of the diaphragm, the muscle below the lungs that normally moves down when inhaling while pushing the abdomen out. So the chest breather will show little abdominal movement. Instead, the breastbone, or *sternum*, moves up and out, with little lateral expansion.[9] Sometimes, you'll also see the neck, shoulders, and clavicles (collarbones) move up and down.

- Once established, low blood $CO_2$ can be maintained by normal breathing plus occasional deep breaths or sighs. So look for other signs: occasional deep breath or sigh, repeated sighs, air hunger, inability to take a satisfying breath, coughing, frequent yawning, clearing the throat, sniffing, or nasal drip.
- Other possible indications: moistening lips (excessive breathing dries out the airways), occasional spasmodic twitching of facial muscles, tenderness of chest wall,[10] and irregular inhale/exhale ratio.

### Provocation Test

An expensive but sometimes useful test performed in a lung function laboratory or other specialty clinic, the provocation test involves intentionally breathing fast (thirty to sixty times per minute) and deeply or thoracically for two to three minutes. The appearance of symptoms or the inability to complete the test indicates that hyperventilation is the cause. Determination of low blood $CO_2$[11] and decreased acidity of the blood confirms the diagnosis. By demonstrating to the person that symptoms are only the result of breathing and that they are safe and reversible, this test can be very reassuring.[12] In some cases, as few as twelve rapid breaths while standing will produce symptoms.

### Think Test

This test is often used along with the provocation test. Sometimes just thinking about and recalling a stressful time when great physical distress was experienced will bring on hyperventilation and anxiety symptoms. After the provocation test, patients close their eyes and re-create the situation at the time of a panic attack. That is, they think about circumstances, such as disturbing topics they were thinking about at the time of the attack, feelings, sensations, and symptoms. The combination of the two tests is more likely to create hyperventilation symptoms, thus confirming the diagnosis.[13]

### HOW DO I TREAT IT?

The effects of stress-induced hyperventilation can be reversed by altering the breathing so that $CO_2$ is conserved or by increasing through exercise the amount of $CO_2$ produced by the body. The first approach is called *breathing retraining*, a most important skill that we'll discuss next.

## Breathing Retraining[14]

Normal breathing is slow, effortless, regular, fluid, and quiet with virtually no movement above the diaphragm. Some master breathing retraining quite rapidly, while others may require months of practice. The goals are to change from erratic breathing to slow, regular, rhythmic abdominal breathing and to make this kind of breathing automatic. This shift in breathing results in long-term changes in the nervous system and anxiety symptoms. Here are the steps:

1. **Loosen your clothing** (belts, ties, collars, clothing around waist and abdomen). Remove contact lenses or glasses if you wish.
2. **Lie on your back or in the half-lying position.** Place pillows under your back and knees to relax the abdominal muscles.
3. **Relax your entire body.** Especially warm and relax the abdomen. Also release tension in the chest, shoulders, neck, face, and jaw. Using the upper body's muscles to breathe wastes energy.
4. **Place a telephone book over the abdomen** (the area below the diaphragm down to the pelvis; practically, this means putting the book below the ribs and over the navel). The book provides resistance to strengthen the diaphragm and encourages abdominal movement.
5. **Bring your lips together.** Breathe comfortably and rhythmically, not deeply, through your nose. As you breathe in, let your stomach rise slowly, gradually, quietly. Think of your stomach as a balloon easily filling gently with air. Move smoothly into the exhalation without pause. Expiration is quiet, passive, and relaxed. The in-breath and out-breath are approximately equivalent in duration, the out-breath perhaps a little longer. Transition smoothly between the out-breath and in-breath, with little pause between phases.[15] Keep all of your body above your diaphragm relaxed and still, moving only your abdomen. You'll see the book gently rise as you breathe in and fall as you breathe out, while the upper body remains still.
6. **Practice.** It might take a few weeks until abdominal breathing becomes automatic. Here are the suggested guidelines:
   - Practice twice a day or more, for five to ten minutes each time.
   - For the first few days, just breathe at your regular rate. If at any point you feel dizzy or faint or if your diaphragm cramps, stop immediately. You might need to build up gradually to five to ten minutes over the course of days or weeks, beginning with only a few seconds of practice. Generally,

dizziness and faintness result from improper breathing. These symptoms will disappear if you get up and walk (e.g., up stairs) to increase the body's $CO_2$ production. When you resume practice, *be sure that you are not breathing fast or deeply, only slowly and regularly.*

- After about a week, begin to gradually slow your breathing rate. Perhaps you'll eventually reach a rate of six to ten breaths per minute (i.e., about six to ten seconds for each complete breath cycle). *However, don't worry about the rate. Focus on achieving a rate that feels comfortable.*
- After the second week, progress to the seated position, then to standing and leaning against a wall, standing unsupported, slow walking, and fast walking. Remember, first relax your entire body, warm and relax your abdomen, then breathe slowly, regularly, abdominally.
- Try rebreathing (i.e., relaxed, abdominal breathing) in a variety of situations (in bed as you wake up or before sleeping, walking down the hall, jogging, watching TV, on the train).
- As you gain confidence, try consciously rebreathing in slightly stressful situations before anxiety symptoms appear (e.g., in a traffic slowdown). Then try it in situations where anxiety symptoms have already begun to appear. Just notice the symptoms. Think to yourself, "My breathing is causing this. I'm not going mad or having a heart attack. These symptoms are harmless and reversible. I know how to breathe." Then relax your body, warm your abdomen, and breathe slowly and regularly. Watch your symptoms come and watch them subside, like a scientist watching an experiment.
- Do not attempt breathing retraining without first discussing this with your doctor if you have diabetes, kidney disease, or other disorders that might cause metabolic acidosis. In such cases, breathing may have become rapid to normalize the metabolic acidosis, and slowing down your breathing could be dangerous.

### Tips for Breathing Retraining
- If you can, breathe through your nose, which increases resistance and helps to slow breathing. If you can't, breathe through pursed lips.
- Don't be too concerned with technique. Just be aware of your breathing and attempt to breathe in a manner that is restful for you. Simple awareness of

how you're breathing is often all that is needed to slow down and encourage abdominal breathing.

- Visualizing air being drawn through the toes into the abdomen and pelvis helps to slow down breathing. As you practice, think, "Low and slow."
- Some find it helpful to visualize being on the beach, breathing in refreshing air and likening the breath to the easy rhythm of the waves.
- When first practicing, use a mirror to check for tension or movement in the face, jaw, shoulders, or chest. Insure that the abdomen, or belly, is moving up and down rhythmically.
- Wear looser clothes around the neck, chest, and abdomen.
- When you feel confident, move on to progressive muscle relaxation, explained in the next chapter, to learn how to further relax.
- Don't sigh or yawn, which will expel more $CO_2$; suppress coughs and sniffles. Instead of sighs or yawns, swallow. Or hold the normal breath for a count of five, then breathe out slowly, hold to five, then resume easy abdominal breathing.
- Learn ways to express feelings constructively. You might have learned to smother your feelings. This can be unlearned. We can school our feelings, thus giving them constructive outlets. More about this later.
- When speaking, relax your muscles. Go more slowly and smoothly. Use short sentences with gentle breathing through your nose—no gasping or gulping air. Seek natural pausing places to breathe gently.

## Troubleshooting

- If you can't relax your abdominal muscles while seated, Jonathan Weiss advises putting your fists on the back of your hips and trying to bring your elbows together behind you. Someone behind you can assist. Getting on all fours with the abdomen relaxed is another way to learn to relax and move only the abdomen.[16]
- If rebreathing frightens or frustrates you and you find that anxiety increases or you tune into the physical symptoms, try the following:
    Relax into the symptoms. Let them happen. Keep practicing until the nervous system is desensitized. Remind yourself that the symptoms are harmless. Or consider enlisting the help of a mental health professional specializing in anxiety and breathing retraining (call the Anxi-

ety Disorders Association of America, listed in Additional Resources, for referrals).

In an emergency, should all else fail, hold a paper bag over your nose and mouth with thumbs and forefingers of both hands. Take six to twelve easy natural breaths, then breathe abdominally. Breathing into and from a bag recaptures $CO_2$. The bag should have a capacity of about one liter.

## Physical Activity

Recall that the *fight-or-flight response* is designed for activity. When the muscles move, more $CO_2$ is produced. The breathing increases just enough to expel the appropriate amount of $CO_2$. So hyperventilation does not usually occur with exercise. Regular, moderate exercise is recommended to decrease arousal; it also decreases resting heart and breathing rates. However, those with a pattern of hyperventilation need to learn first to breathe abdominally before engaging in exercise. *Warning:* Slow down *gradually* after exercise. Suddenly stopping can produce acute hyperventilation. Cool down for several minutes by walking, perhaps followed by stretching.

Yoga is a form of exercise that improves the physical condition of people of all ages and promotes breathing control. However, deep breathing that fills the entire lungs, holds the air, and then emphasizes long exhalations should be avoided by overbreathers.

# CHAPTER 12

# *Relaxation*

---

In stress, both the mind and body are aroused. Muscle tension in the chronically anxious body keeps the nervous system sensitized. Relaxation is the opposite of stress. Relaxation means that the mind and body are calm. As the mind and body remain in a calm state of reduced arousal, they become restored. In particular, the nervous system is allowed to desensitize.

As Harvard's Herbert Benson notes,[1] four to six weeks of relaxation training typically result in reductions in anxiety symptoms, stress, headaches, insomnia, and blood pressure; prevention of hyperventilation; control of panic attacks; greater inner peace; and enhanced creativity.

He notes that relaxation training is particularly useful for those who feel their worries are justified and reasonable. Among the many other advantages of relaxation training are greater feeling of control, better mood, enhanced immune system functioning, ability to think more rationally, better judgment, improved work efficiency, and fewer errors.

Because the mind and body are connected, relaxation can be achieved in two ways: First, the body can be relaxed, and the mind follows. Second, the mind can be relaxed, and the body follows. We'll explore both approaches. Regardless of the form of relaxation, the following general guidelines apply:

1. **Regular practice.** Relaxation is a skill that improves with practice. Most methods recommend practicing once or twice each day, for ten to twenty minutes each time. If possible, find a quiet place free from distractions. Soon this place—through association—will become a cue to relax.
2. **Concentration.** Relaxation techniques usually ask that you focus on one thing rather than scattering your attention. A singular focus allows the mind

to calm down. You might wish to develop a way to "store" your worries during relaxation sessions. Some people put their worries in an imaginary box outside of the room or house. Some write down their worries first. Some simply say, "I'll deal with you later, but right now I wish to relax."

3. **Relaxation training works well after exercise or yoga, when the body is calming down and the mind is clear.** However, digestion seems to interfere with relaxation, so don't practice right after a meal.

4. **Relaxation techniques work very well for people wanting to fall asleep at night.** You will probably want to use these techniques for this purpose at times. However, as a rule, try to keep your mind alert and focused when you practice to gain the most benefit.

5. **Trust that the technique will bring benefits.** Develop a confident attitude. Also, develop a passive attitude that simply allows whatever is to happen with each practice session to happen. Don't force or hurry relaxation. Just accept and enjoy whatever happens. It is the process, not the immediate outcome, that matters.

6. **Some people need less medication when practicing relaxation, so speak with your doctor about the need to monitor dosages.** Requirements may lessen for insulin or medications for high blood pressure, epilepsy, depression, or anxiety.

7. **Rise slowly after relaxation training.** Allow ample time for your blood pressure to return to normal.

8. **For each form of relaxation, you will find a script that you can read.** Alternatively, have someone read the instructions to you, or put them on an audio recording.

9. **Some people feel as if they are floating or losing track of time as they relax.** Most people feel this is pleasant. If it is not, simply stop.

## WHAT IF I FEEL MORE ANXIOUS AS I TRY TO RELAX?

Occasionally, you might be surprised to find that your anxiety actually seems to increase as you try to relax. This is understandable. First, as we relax, our awareness increases, so we are usually more aware of our physical symptoms, such as tension. Some feel like they are vulnerable and out of control when relaxing. For example, if one had been abused while prone, lying down might understandably feel frightening. If we are carrying around suppressed fears or worries, relaxing will let down our guard, allowing them to come into awareness. This is similar to the person who suppresses worries all day by keeping busy but then becomes preoccupied with them at night when he wants to sleep. Others might worry that they should be accomplishing something tangible.

There are a number of ways to deal with these concerns:

1. **Remind yourself that you are safe now.** Look around. Make sure you are safe. Is the door locked? Remind yourself that a frightening event from the past was then; this is now. If you wish, sit up and/or practice with your eyes open.
2. **Remind yourself that anxiety symptoms are just a result of sensitized nerves.** Stay with the practice and notice how they subside. Allow time for this to happen.
3. **Write out your worrisome thoughts in a journal before you try to relax.** For about twenty-five minutes, write down facts and feelings about what worries you.
4. **Persist, and counter the belief that bad things will happen if you relinquish control.** This is a step toward confronting fears and learning to master them.
5. **Remind yourself that people who take a relaxation break usually accomplish more.** As is the case with exercise, nutrition, and sleep, relaxation practice helps us work longer and more efficiently.

Remember this important point: any relaxation practice is helpful. It does not matter whether perfect relaxation is attained. Each attempt is an effort toward desensitizing your nervous system.

If you still are not having a good experience practicing relaxation, don't despair. You might wish to try some of the other strategies in this book to increase your sense of control and then return to the practice of relaxation.

## PROGRESSIVE MUSCLE RELAXATION

This relaxation technique is generally tried first because it is so effective for almost everyone who tries it. Developed in the 1920s by Dr. Edmund Jacobson, progressive muscle relaxation (PMR) is so named because it calls for one to tense and then relax the muscles in the body from toe to head, relaxing increasingly deeper as you go. The point of focus in this technique is the tension and then relaxation in your muscles.

Jacobson showed that you cannot relax your muscles and still worry at the same time. He demonstrated that just thinking about throwing a ball increased tension in the throwing arm. Conversely, relaxing that arm quieted worries in the mind. There is a paradox in muscle tension in that simply willing oneself to relax leaves residual tension in the muscles. So even bed rest is not necessarily relaxing. The brain becomes used to chronic muscle tension. It takes an *increase* in muscle tension to jolt the brain's arousal center into relaxing unnecessary tension. In this technique, we purposefully tense our muscles, then relax deeply. As we concentrate on the contrast between tension and relaxation, we retrain our brain to recognize tension when it starts. This can aid us greatly in warding off tension headaches and backaches.

The instructions for this relaxation technique follow. You may read the script to yourself as you practice, use the summary at the end, or place these instructions on an audio recording. They are easily adapted to the sitting position, if you prefer that position.

*Note:* The tensing in PMR might be a trigger for some people. If so, you might view practicing it as a way to challenge your fears, using calming self-statements, such as "Tension is just a reminder of an old memory. I am safe now. It's OK to relax now." Try keeping your eyes open as you practice, and start initially with briefer periods of practice.

**Progressive Muscle Relaxation Script**

We are about to progressively tense and relax the major muscle groups in the body. This is a very effective way to reduce general arousal and muscle tension. I'll explain first the exercise for each area and then ask you to tense by saying, "Ready? Tense." Tense relatively hard but always stop short of discomfort or cramps. Tense until you are aware of tension in the area. Fully pay attention to it, and then study its contrast, relaxation. You'll tense for about five to ten seconds and then relax for about twice as long. For areas that are injured or sore, simply avoid tensing those areas or else tense very gently and slowly.

To prepare, please loosen tight clothing. Remove glasses, contact lenses, or shoes if you wish. Lie down comfortably on a firm mattress or on the floor with a small pillow under the head and another under the knees. Rest your arms at your sides and let your legs lie straight with your feet relaxed.

1. **To begin, please let your eyes close, if this is comfortable.** As you shut out visual stimuli, it is easier to notice the pleasant rhythms of your breathing. Just pay attention to your breathing. Breathe gently and peacefully, noticing a slight coolness on the air entering your nostrils on the in-breath and

a slight warmth on the out-breath. Throughout this exercise, just breathe normally—slowly, rhythmically, abdominally.

2. **When I say "tense," I'd like you to point both of your feet and toes at the same time, leaving the legs relaxed.** Notice the pulling sensation, or tension, in the calves and the bottoms of the feet. Form a clear mental picture of this tension. Now relax all at once. Feel the relaxation in those same areas. When muscles relax, they elongate, and blood flow through them increases. So you might feel warmth or tingling in areas of your body that you relax. Just let your feet sink into the floor, feeling completely relaxed.

3. **Next, pull your toes back toward your head.** Ready? Tense. Observe the tension in the muscles below the knee, along the outside of the shins. Now relax all at once and see and feel the difference as those muscles fully relax and warm up.

4. **Next, you'll tense the quadriceps muscles on the front part of the leg above the knee by straightening your leg and locking your knees.** Leave your feet relaxed. Ready? Tense. Concentrate on pulling in these muscles. Visualize it clearly in your mind. And relax. Scan your quadriceps as you relax. Sense them loosening and warming, as though they are melting.

5. **Imagine now that you are lying on a beach blanket. Keeping your feet relaxed, imagine pressing the back of the heels into the sand.** Ready? Tense. Feel and visualize the tension along the backs of the entire legs. Now relax as those muscles loosen and relax.

6. **A slightly different set of muscles, those between the upper legs, are tensed when you squeeze your knees together.** Ready? Tense. Observe the tension. Then relax and observe the relaxation as you deeply relax, and keep relaxed, all the muscles in the legs as we progress upward. Just let the floor support your relaxed legs.

7. **Next you'll squeeze the buttocks, or seat muscles, together while contracting your pelvis muscles.** Leave your stomach relaxed as you do this. Ready? Tense. Visualize the tension in these muscles. Then relax and observe what relaxation in those muscles feels like—perhaps a pleasant warm and heavy feeling.

8. **Next you'll tense your stomach muscles by imagining your stomach is a ball and you want to squeeze it into a tiny ball.** Ready? Tense. Shrink your stomach and pull it back toward the spine. Notice the tension there and how tensing these muscles interferes with breathing. Now relax. Let the

abdomen warm up and loosen up, freeing your body to breathe in the least possible fatiguing way. Continue to breathe abdominally as you progress.

9. **Now leave your shoulders and buttocks down on the floor as you gently and slowly arch your back.** As you do, pull your chest up and toward your chin. You'll observe the tension in the back muscles along both sides of the spine. Now gently and slowly relax as your back sinks into the floor, feeling very warm and relaxed. Study that feeling. Notice where relaxation is experienced.

10. **Tense the lower back muscles by pressing the lower back against the floor.** Ready? Tense. Observe the tension there, then relax and observe the relaxation in that area.

11. **Prepare to press your shoulders downward, toward your feet, while you press your arms against the sides of your body.** Ready? Tense. Feel the tension in the chest, along the sides of the trunk, and along the backs of the arms. You may not have been aware of how much tension can be carried in the chest or what it feels like. Relax and feel those muscles loosen and warm. Realize that you can control and release the tension in your upper body once you become aware of it.

12. **Now, shrug your shoulders.** Ready? Tense. Pull them up toward your ears and feel the tension above the collarbones and between the shoulder blades. This is where many headaches originate. Now relax and study the contrast in those muscles.

13. **Place your palms down on the floor.** Pull your relaxed hands back at the wrists so that the knuckles move back toward your head. Observe the tension on the tops of the forearms. Relax and study the contrast.

14. **Next, make tight fists and draw them back toward the shoulders as if pulling in the reins on a team of wild horses.** See the tension in the fists, forearms, and biceps. Relax and notice the feelings as those muscles go limp and loose. Just let your arms fall back beside your body, palms up, heavy and limp and warm. Pause here to scan your body and notice how good it feels to give your muscles a break. Allow your entire body to remain relaxed as you move on.

15. **Let's learn how to relax the neck muscles, which typically carry much tension.** Right now, gradually, slowly turn your head to the right as if looking over your right shoulder. Take ten seconds or longer to rotate the neck. Feel the tension on the right side of the neck pulling your head around. The sensation on the left side is stretching, not tension. Hold the tension for just long

enough to observe it. Then turn around slowly back to the front and notice the difference as the muscles on the right side of your neck relax. Pause. Turn just as slowly to the left and watch the left side of your neck contract. Rotating back to face forward, see the left side relax.

16. **Now press the back of your head gently against the floor while raising your chin toward the ceiling.** Do you notice the tension at the base of the skull, where the skull meets the neck? Much headache pain originates here, too. Study the tension. And relax. Allow those muscles to warm up and elongate. Relax the neck completely and let it remain relaxed.

17. **Lift your eyebrows up and furrow your brow.** Feel the tension along the forehead. Relax. Imagine a rubber band loosening.

18. **Wrinkle up your nose while you squeeze your eyes shut and your eyebrows together.** Observe the tension along the sides of the nose and around and between the eyes. Now deeply relax those areas. Imagine pleasantly cool water washing over the eyes, relaxing them. Your eyelids are as light as a feather.

19. **Frown, pulling the corners of the mouth down as far as they'll go.** Feel the tension on the sides of the chin and neck. Relax. Feel the warm, deeply relaxing contrast.

20. **The jaw muscles are extremely powerful and can carry much tension. When I say "tense," clench your jaw.** Ready?

---

## SUMMARY: TENSE, OBSERVE; RELAX, OBSERVE

1. Close eyes (if comfortable)
2. Point feet and toes
3. Pull toes and feet back toward head
4. Straighten legs; lock knees
5. Press back of heels down
6. Squeeze knees together
7. Squeeze buttocks together; tighten pelvis
8. Squeeze stomach
9. Arch back
10. Flatten small of back down against floor
11. Press shoulders down, arms against body
12. Shrug shoulders
13. Bend hands back at wrists
14. Make fists; pull back to shoulders
15. Rotate neck
16. Press head back against floor while raising chin
17. Lift eyebrows up
18. Wrinkle nose; squeeze eyes shut; squeeze eyebrows together
19. Frown
20. Clench teeth
21. Smile

Tense. Grit your teeth and study the tension from the angle of the jaw all the way up to the temples. Observe the tension. Now relax and enjoy the contrast, realizing that you can control tension here, too. Relax the tongue and let the teeth part slightly.

21. **Make a wide smile.** Open the mouth wide. Ready? Tense. Grin ear to ear and feel the muscles around the cheekbone contract. This really requires little effort. Now relax and let all the muscles of the face become smooth and completely relaxed.

Allow a pleasant sense of relaxation to surround your body. Imagine that you are well supported and floating on a favorite couch, bed, or raft—all your muscles pleasantly relaxed. When you are ready to end this session, count slowly to five, send energy to your limbs, stretch, sit up slowly, and move your limbs before standing slowly.

Practice this twice a day for two weeks or more. At first you might be more aware of aches or tension in your muscles. This tends to disappear with practice as those tense muscles get a break and your nerves desensitize. With practice, you'll notice that you can relax your muscles passively just by reminding yourself to relax them. Some people use a reminder, like a dot on their watch or a picture on the wall, as a cue to relax their muscles throughout the day.

When you feel that you are aware of the first signs of tension and can cause those muscles to relax, then you might progress to other relaxation exercises. Or if you wish to stay with this one, keep practicing daily as you move on to Chapter 13.

## RELAXATION RECORD

Keeping track of your practice and progress can be very motivating and revealing. Keep a record for several weeks on the form in Figure 12.1. You can also use this form to track your progress with other relaxation methods.

## AUTOGENIC TRAINING

Originally developed and researched in Europe, autogenic training is another very effective relaxation method. In this method, people simply give themselves the suggestions of warmth and heaviness in order to induce deep relaxation. Start by sitting or lying comfortably, with eyes closed if that is comfortable, breathing abdominally. Imagine that you have just returned from a refreshing walk and you

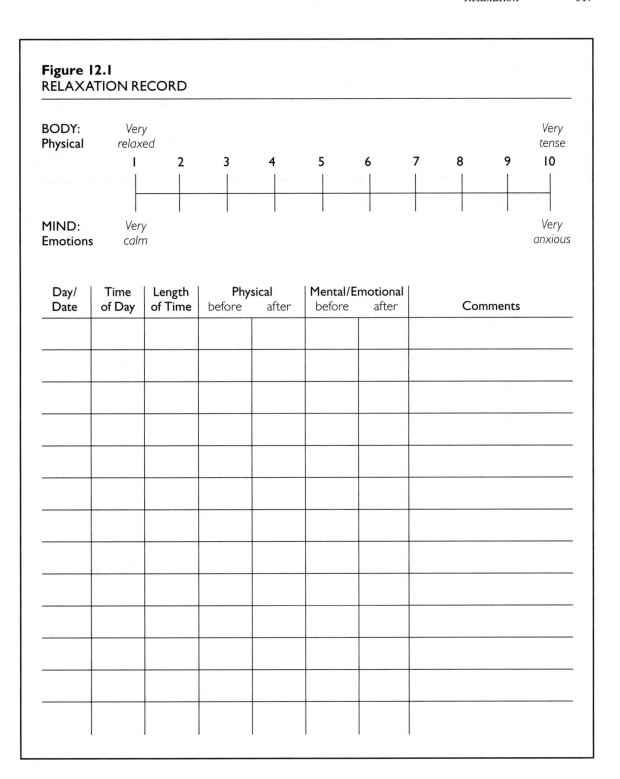

**Figure 12.1**
RELAXATION RECORD

**BODY:** *Very relaxed* ................................................ *Very tense*
**Physical**

1   2   3   4   5   6   7   8   9   10

**MIND:** *Very calm* ..................................................... *Very anxious*
**Emotions**

| Day/ Date | Time of Day | Length of Time | Physical | | Mental/Emotional | | Comments |
|---|---|---|---|---|---|---|---|
| | | | before | after | before | after | |
| | | | | | | | |
| | | | | | | | |
| | | | | | | | |
| | | | | | | | |
| | | | | | | | |
| | | | | | | | |
| | | | | | | | |
| | | | | | | | |
| | | | | | | | |
| | | | | | | | |
| | | | | | | | |

are sinking into an overstuffed chair by the fireplace. Let the abdomen and chest be warm and soft. You slowly repeat to yourself each of these suggestions three times: "My right arm is heavy." "My right hand is heavy." "My fingers are heavy." Suggestions for heaviness are repeated for the left arm and hand, the right leg and foot, and then the left leg and foot. The same sequence is followed, repeating suggestions of warmth ("My right arm is warm," etc.). Upon completion of this sequence, you then repeat, "My right arm is heavy and warm," and so on, for each part of the body. End by imagining that you are relaxing in a warm tub of water, with a relaxed smile on your face.

## MEDITATION

Meditation may be thought of as awareness of our true, happy nature. In meditating, we go beneath the wounds and batterings, beneath our worries and racing thoughts, and rest in the center of our being, which is still calm, peaceful, dignified, wise, and joyful. A study with Vietnam veterans found that meditation greatly reduced PTSD symptoms.[2] You might find a meditation teacher in your area, or try the meditation script at Appendix F. Chapter 16 also describes mindfulness meditation, which shows promise in the treatment of PTSD.

# CHAPTER 13

# Managing Anger

**He who gives way to violent gestures will increase his rage.**

*—Charles Darwin*

Intense anger is common in PTSD for reasons that all make sense. Normal day-to-day living rarely demands intense, extreme emotions. But during traumatic events, raw emotions are often unleashed. For example, a soldier in combat for the first time encounters a destructive rage at the enemy who killed his comrades. A victim of rape for the first time encounters intense bitterness and desire for vengeance. It is said that PTSD is "lots of fire temporarily numbed." Such highly charged emotions are likely to erupt repeatedly until they are resolved—often the anger will be misdirected at loved ones or colleagues. People with PTSD live with pain and frustration. Anger is usually the least painful emotion to acknowledge because the focus of anger is outside of yourself. You can focus outwardly in anger without acknowledging inward feelings of sadness, shame, fear, or self-dislike. In fact, anger tends to distract from such feelings. Angry aggression overrides fear. That is, for a little while, we no longer feel as helpless and out of control.

People with PTSD might be angry at any or all of the following:

- A perpetrator of a crime or accident—especially if the offense was senseless, intentional, or preventable (e.g., a drunk driving accident is not really an accident, because the person chose to drink and then chose to drive)
- God or life for letting the traumatic event happen
- Everyone (e.g., a man who was struck by an oncoming car now views all drivers as enemies)

- "Normal people" who are still happy and act like nothing has happened
- Self—for being unable to function better or "get over it" for hurting one's family
- The imperfections of people (e.g., a victim who was hurt by the weaknesses of another is now impatient with all imperfections in others)
- People who don't understand or know how to help
- Family members for annoying or disappointing them
- Firefighters, police, parents, or others who failed to protect them
- The criminal justice system for failing to find or punish the offender
- Secondary wounders—people who are hired to help them but end up offending them further
- Everyday stressors

Intense, uncontrollable anger from the past will likely be reduced as traumatic material is fully processed and the concerns underlying the anger are addressed. In the meantime, this chapter will furnish you with the skills needed to control present anger so that your health and relationships are not damaged.

## WHAT IS ANGER?

Anger is a negative, uncomfortable feeling that follows from specific thoughts about something that we view as threatening or frustrating. Along with this feeling, anger leads to physical arousal (increased heart rate, breathing rate, muscle tension, blood pressure, stress hormones in the blood, flushed face) and certain chosen behavior responses. For example, when angry, you might choose to clench your fist, raise your voice, become quiet, or leave the room. Some people become physically violent. Others become critical or sarcastic. Such behaviors are learned habits that become reinforced through repetition. Just as ineffective ways for coping with anger might have been learned during or after trauma, so can effective coping styles be learned or relearned.

Table 13.1 lists the varieties of angry feelings, metaphors, and behaviors that we sometimes use to describe the experience of anger.

## UNDERSTANDING ANGER

Anger is something we experience as we try to control our world and avoid pain. Some people are troubled by their difficulty in managing anger better. Others feel completely justified in their anger and see no reason to change it. Anger provides some distinct payoffs. If it did not, we would probably experience it far less often. Before deciding, then, if anger management is something you'd like to work on, let's sharpen our understanding of anger and its impact on our lives. Please list below all the advantages and disadvantages of anger that you can think of:

---

### ANGER COST/BENEFIT ANALYSIS

**BENEFITS: The Good Things About Anger Are**

**COSTS: The Bad Things About Anger Are**

---

**Table 13.1**
VARIETIES OF ANGER

| I feel . . . | Metaphor | Behavior |
|---|---|---|
| Aggravated | Angry enough to kill/shoot someone, | Argue |
| Agitated | cut someone off, cry, strangle | Attack posture, body tightens |
| Angry | someone, explode | Avoids eye contact |
| Annoyed | Blew a fuse/gasket | Backbite |
| Churning | Blind with rage | Becomes quiet |
| Defensive | Blood boiling | Blaming |
| Disappointed | Boiling mad | Clench fist |
| Embittered | Breathing fire | Clench teeth |
| Enraged | Burning mad | Criticism, put-downs, sniping |
| Exasperated | Couldn't see straight | Cry |
| Frustrated | Fighting mad | Destroy property |
| Fuming | Flew off the handle | Drink, use drugs |
| Furious | Flipped his wig | Glare |
| Hostile, hate | Hit the ceiling | Harassment |
| Hot | Hopping mad | Insults |
| Hurt | Hot potato | Interrupt others |
| Incensed | Hot under the collar, hot as | Makes demands |
| Indignant | a firecracker | Physically attack or harm |
| Infuriated | Icy cold | Pout |
| Irate | Loaded and ready to fire | Raise voice |
| Irked | Mad as a bat out of hell | Sarcastic comments |

These are some benefits that people have identified over the years:

- Anger honestly communicates my feelings about other people's faults.
- Others might quickly comply with my demands.
- It shows that I care.
- It gives the feeling that I am in control and viewed with respect.
- Anger clears the air—it vents my frustration so that I don't explode.
- Anger protects me from injustice and/or danger.
- Anger lets me at least feel something—I feel more alive; I have a sense of self.
- Anger is a cue that something is wrong and in need of fixing.
- Anger energizes me.

| I feel . . . | Metaphor | Behavior |
|---|---|---|
| Irritated | Madder than a mad hatter | Silent treatment |
| Livid | Madder than a wet hen | Sneer |
| Mad | Madder than a wet hornet | Sulk |
| Malicious | Madder than hell | Threats |
| Offended | Popped his cork | Throws things |
| Out of control | Raging bull/maniac | Vulgar language |
| Outraged | Ready to explode | Walk away, storm out, |
| Peeved | Seeing red; red hot | withdraw |
| Perturbed | Sizzling | Yell |
| Pissed off | Slow burn | |
| Royally pissed off | Smoke coming out of ears | |
| Riled up | So angry I could explode/bust | |
| Seething | So angry I could spit | |
| Slamming | So angry I couldn't speak | |
| Spiteful | Spitting nails | |
| Steamed, steaming | Steaming mad | |
| Teed off | Went through the roof | |
| Ticked, ticked off | | |
| Upset, uptight | | |
| Vengeful | | |
| Vexed | | |
| Violent | | |

On the costs side, people have identified these:

- Communication suffers.
    People hear only my anger, not the issue.
    They're afraid to have a dialogue with me, so all useful ideas don't
        surface.
- Anger sours relationships—people distrust me and may see me as mean.
- I feel out of control—humiliated because I can't control my own emotions.
- When I am not cool, my job performance suffers. I don't think clearly.
- I get fired when I blow up at work.
- Conflict increases. Some people don't cooperate with me; some argue
    more.

- My kids are learning violence from watching me.
- I feel guilty for blowing up at my family.
- Some of the people I've offended have sabotaged me.
- As long as I'm angry, I don't heal underlying hurts.
- I avoid learning better coping skills.
- My health suffers (heart disease, ulcers, high blood pressure, higher death rates from all causes).
- I don't give people the chance to show me that some people are trustworthy and good.
- Anger is unpleasant; I've lost my sense of joy and peace.
- Anger escalates. The more I lose patience, the angrier I get.

As we consider the pros and cons, it is apparent that anger sometimes makes sense. Anger has a number of apparent payoffs, at least in the short term. People who get angry are not bad people. They are behaving in a way that makes sense to them. Perhaps they have not learned other ways to meet their needs. On the other hand, anger has many disadvantages, especially in the long run.

Perhaps anger is a long-term habit that has worked for you in many ways. Before considering changes you might consider answering these questions:

- "Is anger a problem for you in terms of its costs?"
- "Are you getting what you really want when you are angry?"
- "Could you get your needs and wants met with less anger?"
- "What are the positive consequences of being less angry?" People have suggested these answers to this last question:

    I'll be cooler, more in control, more powerful.

    I'll have relationships based on more trust, better friendships, better relationships with my wife and kids.

    I might see that some people will respond to me because they want to, not because they fear me.

    I'll see myself as more patient, tolerant, kinder, cooler, more in control of my emotions.

    Others would probably view me as calmer and more in control.

    I'd be more respected.

    I'd give people a chance to do good things because they choose to.

    Communication with others will improve. People will be more open and creative.

I'll be able to funnel my energy more effectively and work more logically. I'll be more relaxed, healthier.

## ANGER MANAGEMENT SKILLS

Everyone has a limbic system (the seat of emotion in the brain) and so will experience anger at times in his or her life. The question is how you experience it and how often. Do you hold anger in at work and then explode at home? Does anger build until you let it out at work and then get reprimanded or fired? Many people debate whether it is better to hold in anger or let it out. At times, both approaches can be useful choices, but there is a third option: the choice to be angry. We'll explore a number of ways to be less angry and to be in greater control of the anger we do experience.

### Take Responsibility for Your Own Anger

The first principle taught in military spouse abuse programs is that no one *makes* us angry. We choose who we let under our skin and how we will express the anger that results. We can choose to talk calmly rather than scream or become violent. We can choose to walk away from a fight rather than give in to conflict. Giving others control of our lives—by choosing to let them annoy us—places us in the victim role and reinforces the feeling of powerlessness. Violence to self or others is not an option. It only temporarily relieves tension, while destroying inner peace and relationships.

### Put Your Anger into Words

Refer to the feelings list in Table 13.1. Select the four that represent your most intense anger levels (or come up with your own). Also select the four that describe your lowest anger levels, and the four that represent your midrange anger. Within each category, rank in order these feelings from most to least intense. This helps to reinforce the idea that there are gradations of anger. That is, there are many ways to experience anger between having none and being out of control. It will help you to later be able to calmly describe your feelings in words rather than to act them out physically. If you prefer to draw, place the variety of angry feelings on a thermometer from cool to hot.

Try writing about your anger in a journal. Describe the event that triggered your anger. Then describe the emotions and body sensations. Next, identify why you felt the anger. Remember this important point: anger is a secondary emotion. Under the anger is the primary emotion: hurt or fear of being hurt. Try to calmly identify what the underlying hurt is and put it into words. Perhaps you felt that you were not respected or treated fairly. Perhaps people were not as loyal as you would have liked. It's OK to identify and feel that hurt. You realize that you can identify it, and just watch it. You will learn ways to soothe the hurt rather than retaliate. If you can think of another way to view the hurt, write that down too.

## Soothe the Hurt

Anger in the present is often just a button that is pushed, where the button symbolizes an unhealed hurt from the past. This imagery technique developed by Ron Klein provides practice to soothe yourself.[1] It is described from the perspective of the therapist, who acts as a guide.[2]

- Hear the complaint. Help the client identify the present unwanted and/or inappropriate behavior and the associated feelings of anger that occur in these situations.
- The therapist will require that the client is desirous and motivated to change.
- Have the client recall a time when he was supportive and comforting to someone else, and/or engaged in an activity where he was competent. Assist the client to experience fully the feelings and the details of being resourceful in that situation. Ask the client to describe these feelings in a word or phrase, which becomes Anchor A (e.g., "secure, affectionate, here, and competent").
- Instruct the client to imagine sitting in a movie theater or in front of a TV with a blank screen waiting for the movie to start. Tell the client that she can move the screen as far away as desired, the picture can be brightened or darkened, and the volume of the sound can be adjusted from her seat. When the client feels a sense that the picture is at a safe distance, a word describing this distancing becomes Anchor B (e.g., "safe; screen over there").
- Ask the client to access a recent example of experiencing the unwanted behavior but to watch the scene unfold as if it were on the imaginary screen. While the client watches this situation play out as a motion picture, the therapist helps the client to remain comfortable by utilizing Anchor A and Anchor B.
- When the scene has reached some sort of completion, ask the client to evaluate what resource(s) the younger self needed in that situation—resources

that would have allowed the client to have responded favorably, such as self-acceptance, humor, or curiosity. Next, direct the client to remember and to access an example of being resourceful in this fashion. Instruct the client to [fully experience this] resourceful experience and to describe the related resourceful feelings with a word that becomes Anchor C [e.g., "reassuring"].

- The therapist repeats Anchors A, B, and C as needed, while requesting that the client access earlier and earlier representations of the unwanted behavior on the screen until she comes to the one that appears to be the earliest experience. Remind the client that she is a full-grown adult, that she has many resources that the younger self needed, and that the younger self is having the experiences *over there* on the screen.

- As the therapist continues to utilize Anchors A, B, and C, the client watches the younger self go through the above earliest scene until it reaches completion. Ask the client to then imagine going over to the younger self as an older, and more resourceful, adult. The client is, in effect, a "visitor from the future" who can comfort and encourage the younger self to express and relieve the emotions (such as loneliness, fear, sadness, shame) present in that old scene, for example, by telling the younger self that it's "OK to feel what you feel."

- The client is directed to suggest to the younger self that he did his best at that time and that he survived that unhappy event and went on to have many positive experiences in his future. Tell the client to send, by mental projection and/or imaginary touch, the appropriate resources, insights, and understandings that were needed (therapist again utilizes Anchors A, B, and C).

- The client now is asked to start the scene from the beginning and to watch as the younger self goes through the decisive experience again, *but this time* with protection, the new resources and understandings that have been conveyed from the older self. Tell the client to observe the changes the younger self makes at the conclusion of the scene. Suggest that the client congratulate and embrace the younger self—that she bring the younger self into her body and experience the integration as positive energy and vitality. Give the client permission to take a few moments to feel the body making adjustments as these new ways of being are assimilated.

- Ask the client to imagine going through three or four situations from the past *but to realize* that he is behaving and feeling differently in each of them. The therapist uses all three anchors as needed.

- Future mental rehearsal. The client mentally constructs a situation in the future like the ones that used to generate the unwanted behavior and/or feelings. Have her imagine going through the experience to test that she can now do so resourcefully.
- Personal impact considerations. Invite the client to think through the consequences of the changes that have taken place and to make any adjustments if needed.

## Communicate

Tell your loved ones that the anger comes from hurts you are trying to heal—that they are not the reason for the anger's intensity. Tell them you love them at every opportunity and whenever you experience even the smallest positive feelings. Focus more on complimenting what they are doing well rather than criticizing what is wrong.

- **Communicate preventively.** Rather than waiting for problems to develop, set aside an hour a week with your partner. Sit down with your calendars and "wish lists." Identify what is going well. Then anticipate problems and plan to solve them. For example, an Army officer got very angry when his wife would bombard him with problems as he came home from work. He and his wife found that a weekly meeting enabled them to calmly anticipate most problems and plan solutions. If something came up in the meantime, they would wait until he had had a few minutes to relax and then discuss it.
- **If someone verbally attacks you, you might feel the urge to fight back.** Instead, try this:
  Put your ego on the shelf and just listen. Don't defend yourself; just notice that you can absorb the speaker's information without undue arousal. Quietly think, "This is not an emergency situation. It's just useful feedback. I'll calmly listen and evaluate it. I'm still worthwhile even though he is angry now." Try to see things from the speaker's point of view.
  Gently ask questions to show the person that he is being listened to and respected. ("Are there other ways I have offended you? When did I do that? Would you help me better understand how that upset you?")
  Paraphrase to check for understanding. You might say, "Let's see, it sounds like I offended you by doing such and such. Do I have that right?"

If possible, find a point of agreement. "I understand what you're saying and I agree. I wasn't as sensitive as I'd have wished to be." If he has called you dumb, you might agree, "I certainly feel dumb sometimes." Or you might try, "I see your point and I'll correct X, Y, or Z."

Only then try to solve the problem. You might ask, "What would help?" You might want to negotiate a solution. Remember to compromise ("How about a compromise. If I do X, would you do Y?"). This technique works nicely with someone who is fairly reasonable, but not with someone who is abusive. For such a person, you might say, "I'll discuss this with you, but not until you calm down."

- **Constructively express your feelings and preferences.** Remember this three-step formula: (1) Make a positive statement; (2) Describe your feelings related to another's behaviors; then (3) State your preferences. Bob was a combat vet who got angry and frustrated that his teenagers would not clean the truck after using it. He learned to firmly but without anger assert, "I really love you guys and I don't want to be nagging you. But I get upset when you return the truck without cleaning it. I'd like you to pick up the trash inside and hose it down after you take it out. Will you do that?" They responded, "Sure, Dad. We didn't realize that mattered to you." Had they responded differently, Bob could have stated the consequences. "If you don't clean the truck, I won't permit you to use it for a month." Then he would have to follow through on these consequences.
- **Take time-outs.** In athletic events, teams take time-outs when things start to get out of control. Should anger start to build, take a time-out from the discussion. Explain to your partner that you are trying to manage your anger better. So whenever anger is building, either partner can say, "I need a time-out to collect myself. Let's take a break for _____ (specify the time, usually less than an hour) and then meet to continue." This is not a sign of rejection, just a strategy to keep anger from getting out of hand. During the time-out, take a walk, write in your journal, take a bath, or do any of the other things that help you reduce anger (don't drink alcohol, drive, or take drugs).

## Channel Vengeance Fantasies

It is common that women who have been raped will have a strong and constant desire for vengeance that will not dissipate over time. This can be very upsetting to women who have not previously been violent or who feel that violence violates their values. So they try to bottle up these feelings and pretend not to feel them. Like dissociated material, however, such intense feelings might intrude in unhealthy ways. It might manifest as physical illness or erupt as anger misdirected at loved ones. One possibility, stated with caution, is the option of verbalizing vengeance fantasies in a support group or with your therapist. The caution is that verbalizing does not authorize or encourage violent retaliation. In one group, women laughed with relief to realize that others had the same feelings. It almost became a humorous "Well-I-can-top-that-one." The process enabled the safe venting of anger in a setting that formed new associations with the anger. Shame for the feelings was replaced with understanding, acceptance, and humor. Simple venting (e.g., screaming at a loved one) does not put a person in touch with the real cause of the anger. Talking about the underlying hurt in a safe setting can.

### Remember the Opposites

Creative problem solvers can conceive many opposites to the problem. Thus, they have many options. What are the opposites of anger? Consider friendliness (stand up to a bully in a friendly way and he might become your friend), patience, understanding, happiness, compassion, acceptance, trust, enjoyment, conciliation, indifference (I don't have to hook into every problem), optimism, happiness, flexibility, or inner security.

### View the Offender Differently

Compassion is a beautiful word. It means sorrow for the suffering of others and a desire to help. When people disappoint you or hurt you, try to view them with compassion. Longfellow wrote, "If we could read the secret histories of our enemies we should find sorrow and suffering enough to disarm all hostility." When people disappoint you, try to ask yourself, "Why would someone do that to another? What need is he trying to fill? How is he trying to protect himself?" You will usually find insecurities and fears. Since overrunning Tibet, China has killed hundreds of thousands of its citizens and destroyed countless beautiful temples. Yet the Tibetan religious leaders have refused to be embittered or loaded down with hate. One of the Tibetan teachers has written that no one in his right mind would knowingly harm another human being. One who behaves unkindly is never completely in his right mind. So instead of becoming embittered, we might cultivate compassion and remember that hostile people are hurting people. Instead of condemning the person or taking offense, we might ask ourselves, "I wonder if I could wish him well." If this is too difficult to do just now, remember the idea and return to it when you have healed.

## Humor

If someone seems unbearable, just think, "That poor fellow must have a brain tumor." Or see him as a baby dressed in diapers screaming for his bottle. If you think, "He is such a butthead," you might ask yourself what a butthead would look like and try to draw it. We realize, of course, that he is not a total butthead, nor has he got a brain tumor. Rather, he is just a flawed, suffering fellow traveler who is behaving badly. In this way, humor can give problems perspective and provide a certain sense of mastery.

## Practice Relaxing Others

In interchanges with others, try to model calmness. Encourage others to talk, as you listen calmly. Show that you are trying to understand. Practice reassuring others. Help them save face. In many arguments, the real issue doesn't surface because the communication degenerates to attacks and trying to save face. Rather than criticizing the other person for coming home late ("You irresponsible idiot!"), you might get to the heart of the issue by saying, "I'm disappointed because I didn't get to spend time with you last night."

## Distinguish the Two Forms of Anger

*Disturbed anger* is out of control and disproportionate to the offense (rage, fury, etc.). *Nondisturbed anger* is functional (e.g., annoyance that stimulates us to rational communication, reasonable action to prevent disrespectful treatment, or problem solving).[3] The question really is not should we give up all anger but can we choose when and how to experience it.

## Choose Cool Thoughts

Angry feelings follow from our thoughts. During traumatic events, we develop thought patterns that seem appropriate for survival. Getting fighting mad, for instance, might have saved us from harm or spurred us to seek justice afterward. We might call these thought patterns the "emergency mode." Once learned, the emergency mode can be automatically triggered by everyday stressors, like traffic jams or disrespectful people. Explosive anger follows from our thoughts, even though the emergency mode is no longer needed. The emergency mode is learned. We can also learn another thinking mode that is more suitable for nonemergency

**Table 13.2**
HOT VS. COOL THOUGHTS

| Emergency Mode (Hot Thoughts) | Nonemergency Mode (Cool Thoughts) |
|---|---|
| *Catastrophizing* | |
| "This is awful. I can't stand it. I hate this! I can't let myself be helpless again. I've got to do something. I must stay in control." | "This is certainly inconvenient and frustrating. But this isn't combat, rape, or any other present emergency. In fact, compared to the trauma, this isn't nearly as bad. No one is now shooting at me or assaulting me. It's OK if I'm not in total control. No one ever has that. But I'm never powerless. I can at least always control my thoughts and actions. This is a problem to be solved, not the end of the world." |
| *Dehumanizing* | |
| In war it was easier to shoot a faceless enemy. If you were abused as a child, you know what it is like to be treated as a worthless object. In either case, you might now find it automatic to think of someone who disappoints or hurts you, "That worthless loser deserves my outrage." | "As disappointing as his behavior is, no one is worthless. I don't like it when I'm treated that way. This person is fallible, but he is nevertheless worthwhile." |
| *Angry Demands* | |
| In battle, incompetence lost lives. Now Fred, an ex-Marine, finds himself demanding perfection of his kids ("I must keep them in line at all times"), himself, and most other people. | "No one ever had perfect kids, no matter how demanding the parents were. If I kindly and gently support, lead by example, and allow them to be fallible, they'll probably turn out to be decent human beings." |
| *Thinking in Extremes* | |
| "He's an enemy—out to get me." | "Maybe he's indifferent. He probably has reasons why he's doing this that makes sense to him. If he really is out to get me, he's just one bad apple among many good ones. Everyone isn't like that, so why should I let him get under my skin?" |
| "I have to win or I'll lose." | "It's OK to compromise or even yield on many matters. I can bend." |
| "I won't be respected if I'm not angry and in control." | "Anger might win me victory by intimidation and fear. Respect, however, is earned by respectful treatment." |

situations. The nonemergency mode lets us respond to stressors more calmly. We think more clearly and thus function better. Table 13.2 shows some of the most common hot thoughts and how they can be challenged and replaced.

## Other Strategies

Exercise or do physical work. Exercise is a wonderful outlet for pent-up anger. So is gardening or other physical labor. Such physical outlets reduce general arousal. Also avoid watching media violence, which reinforces the tendency to react aggressively.

# CHAPTER 14

# *Eye Movement*

At this point, we will introduce a very useful skill called the *eye-movement technique*, described by trauma specialist Dr. Larry D. Smyth.[1] Used as a quick distraction and a way to gain temporary relief from distressing thoughts, this technique helps about two-thirds of those who try it. Remember that this and the techniques in Chapter 15 especially are best taught and learned in the context of a therapeutic relationship. It is not recommended they be first tried alone. Please note that this skill is not to be confused with the comprehensive treatment strategy of eye movement desensitization and reprocessing (EMDR) described in Chapter 21.

1. **Identify something that upsets you.** It might be a stressful present situation that triggers intense emotions. Perhaps it is seeing one of your triggers and trying to fight off the intrusive thoughts. It may be thinking about the trauma. In a moment, you will think about it to the point that you feel 5 to 6 subjective units of distress (SUDs). SUDs are simply a rating of how distressed you are feeling. A SUD number of 0 means you feel pleasantly relaxed with no distress. A reading of 10 means extreme distress, as uncomfortable as you have ever felt or could imagine yourself feeling. When you have identified the upsetting event you wish to work with, continue to Step 2.

2. **Imagine the upsetting event.** Now add worry, the "What-ifs . . . Oh nos . . . I can't stand it . . . here we go again." Stew about the event until you get your SUDs to the 5–6 range, but not higher, because we don't want this to become overwhelming. A SUDs score of 5–6 suggests moderate distress that is unpleasant but tolerable. Although you might notice fear, anxiety, or other uncomfortable physical and emotional states, you are still able to think clearly. (For reference, a SUDs rating of 3 is the amount of arousal needed to concentrate—it is not unpleasant. A SUDs rating of 4 suggests

mild distress that is easily tolerated; a SUDs rating of 8 is high distress that can't be tolerated for very long and impairs thinking.)

3. **With your eyes open and your head still, watch as I (the mental health professional) move my hands.** Notice if this helps reduce your discomfort. (The therapist moves his hand back and forth at a distance of about fourteen inches from your eyes. The hands move a horizontal distance of about two feet. About twenty-five back-and-forth cycles are completed.)

4. **Where are your SUDs now?** A typical drop might be to 4–4½ SUDs. What happened to your images and thoughts? (Often people will say they are blocked, suppressed, blurred, they shrink or fade.)

5. **If your SUDs dropped a little, if your thoughts and images altered somewhat, then this technique seems like a useful skill to practice.** If so, let's put this skill under your control and learn to self-direct it.
   a. Pick two spots in the room to focus on, maybe on the wall or your hands on your knees.
   b. Think about something that upsets you, that could take you to the 5–6 SUDs range.
   c. Get a clear image of it.
   d. Add the worry.
   e. Bring yourself to the 5–6 SUDs range.
   f. Complete about twenty-five cycles of eye movements.
   g. Check for any alterations in your SUDs, images, and thoughts.
   h. How easy is it when you self-direct? (Often people find it to be a little easier when the therapist directs, but most people can do it alone.)

6. **You might be in situations when you cannot conveniently move your eyes back and forth.** In such situations, you can do the eye-movement technique with your eyes closed. You might even wish to do it with your hand over your eyes, as though you are deep in thought. Are you willing to try it with your eyes closed?
   a. If so, let your eyes close.
   b. Get an image of the stressful event.
   c. Now add the thoughts until you reach the 5–6 SUDs range. Let me know when you reach that level.
   d. Now try moving your eyes back and forth about twenty-five times.
   e. Check your SUDs and notice what happened to the images and thoughts.

If you observe a drop in your discomfort, then the eye-movement technique seems like a good skill to practice. Try practicing it several times a day over a one- or two-week period to gain mastery of the skill. You can use this as an effective distraction from upsetting intrusions and as a rapid stress reducer. It might be used later in the course of treatment to calm intense emotions that might arise during processing work.

*Note:* Thought field therapy can also rapidly reduce distressing symptoms of PTSD (see Chapter 22). It can be especially useful before one feels ready to talk about traumatic events.

# CHAPTER 15

# *Intrusion Management*[1]

Over the course of your recovery, there will probably be times when you'll want a break from intrusive thoughts, images, feelings, or sensations, including flash-backs and other forms of dissociation. Fortunately, a number of intrusion manage-ment tools can provide relief until traumatic memories are neutralized or should trauma processing become too distressing. Try to use these tools, rather than drugs or self-injurious behaviors, when intrusions become too distressing.

## EYE MOVEMENTS

If intrusions occur when your eyes are closed, open them and perform about twenty-five cycles of the eye-movement technique that we learned in Chapter 14. If opening your eyes is not practical, do it with them closed. Although some peo-ple find that simply closing their eyes tightly distracts from the intrusive thoughts, most people find they cannot get oriented to the present and away from reliving the past without seeing where they are.

## GROUND YOURSELF

This means do things to bring your awareness solidly back to the present, cen-tered in the here and now. Knowing how to do this helps you feel less controlled by intrusions from the past or worries about the future. There are several ways to do this:

- **Ground in your body.** Simply notice without judging what your body feels like, such as clenched muscles or tight stomach. Breathe low and slow, and focus on your breathing (this is especially useful for hyperventilation). Rub fabric or the arms of the chair and pay attention to what that feels like. Push your feet down or stomp them. Rub your elbow or wiggle your toes. You might also try tapping various parts of your body, as explained in Chapter 22, or tensing and releasing muscle groups, as explained in Chapter 12.

- **Ground in your surroundings.** Describe five objects that you see in the room in great detail (name them, describe colors, etc.). Then describe five sounds that you hear. Now handle and describe five objects. Notice if the intrusions become less troublesome. Now try this again, describing four objects and four sounds, and handling four more objects. Repeat this sequence three times, then twice, then a final time.[2]
- **Ground in symbols of the present.** Handle and look at a recent photograph, birthday card, driver's license, newspaper, or gift that reminds you that you are in the present, not back in the trauma.
- **Ground verbally.** Repeatedly tell yourself the following:[3]

    This is just a memory from the past talking—old stuff. It will pass.
    My feelings are understandable. They come and go.
    I am safe now.
    That was then. This is now.
    I'm here now. Today is _____ (think of today's date). The time is _____ .

- **Count something** like beads or your pulse. As you count, you might use verbal grounding statements.
- **Name or describe your favorite television shows, people, cars, or songs** (hear/see them in your head).
- **Slowly bring your age to the present.** Notice your age regarding the intrusive memories. Slowly count back to the present ("I'm twenty-two now . . . now I'm twenty-three . . . etc.")
- **Ground in your posture.**[4] Notice how intrusions cause your posture and facial expression to shift. You might slouch, tighten, or even assume a fetal position. Notice how that feels. You might feel vulnerable, afraid, or even angry. Exaggerate that posture and expression. Stand and take a strong, adultlike posture and confident expression. Feel in control. Now really exaggerate that strong posture and the feelings of control. Alternate between the two postures several times, describing the feelings, thoughts, and images associated with each posture. Notice that you are in control, able to describe and shift the different feelings associated with each posture.

You might also want to exercise, splash water on your face, take a shower, or play with pets.

## SAFE PLACE IMAGERY[5]

The object is to create a safe place in your imagination, a haven or place of rest. This skill is very effective anytime that you feel overwhelmed during or between sessions. It is also a pleasant way to start the day and is frequently used for restoring calmness at the end of a therapy session.

1. **Select an image that evokes calm and safety** (not the safe place yet—just some image that makes you feel safe and calm).
2. **Focus on the image. Feel the emotions.** Identify the location of the pleasant sensations in your body. Just allow yourself to experience and enjoy them. (The therapist allows time and asks you to signal when you feel the soothing emotions and sensations. She asks you to identify where in your body you feel the sensations.)
3. **Now bring up the image of your safe place, the place that feels safe and calm to be in.** Your safe place can be real or imagined, outdoors or indoors. Maybe you have really been there, or maybe you've made it up. You may go there alone, or some person that makes you feel safe can be there. You are the boss. If you can't think of a safe place, then imagine the safest place you can think of.[6]
4. **Notice all your physical senses in that safe place.** Notice where you feel the pleasant sensations in your body and allow yourself to enjoy them. Now concentrate on those sensations. *Optional:* If the eye-movement technique has been helpful, the therapist will ask you to follow her fingers with your eyes as she does a set of about twenty-five hand movements. She will ask how you feel and try four to six additional sets of hand movements. If positive emotions don't increase, she'll try alternate directions, such as up and down or at an angle. Some experts feel that this reinforces the image and also builds a pleasant association with the hand movements for future memory work.
5. **What single word fits that picture** (you might pick a word such as "relax," "beach," "mountain," "trees," etc.)? Think of that word and scene, allowing yourself to again experience the pleasant sensations and a sense of emotional security. *Optional:* Therapist does four to six more sets of eye movements.

6. **Self-cueing.** Repeat the procedure on your own, bringing up the image and the word, and experience the positive emotions and physical sensations without the eye movements.

7. **Self-cueing with disturbance.** You can use this technique to relax during stressful times. To emphasize this point, bring up a minor annoyance and notice the accompanying negative feelings. Now use your cueing word and bring up the emotions and physical sensations of peace and safety.

8. **Bring up a disturbing thought once again.** This time access your safe place on your own.

9. **Practice at least once daily.** Call up the positive feelings (and word and image of the safe place) while you use the relaxation techniques that you like best.[7]

You might wish to get creative. You might envision the safe place very nearby, with a door you can open and step through into the scene. Take a nice, relaxing breath before entering. You might find there a couch, next to which is a feelings dial, which allows you to turn down the intensity of the negative emotions. You might rush there to tell your concerns to the safe person, or just go to be safely alone.

## SAFETY OBJECTS

Rub a ring, another piece of jewelry, or even a smooth stone that you associate with someone safe or a safe time in your life. Keep a picture of a safe place or a safe person where you can look at it often.

## SAFETY AND SUPPORT CLUB

Dr. Ana Baranowsky and colleagues[8] suggest this strategy to counter the distressing feelings of intrusions:

- Taking a comfortable position, either seated or lying down, relax, close your eyes, and focus inwardly. Imagine a safe object and let it bring you back to your safe place. Recall details and the feelings of safety that these bring to memory.
- Begin to call in toward you all the people in your life who you feel would be good members of your "safety and support club." These could include those who are involved in your life now or those who have been helpful in the

past. They could be real or imagined, alive or dead. They are people who wouldn't judge you but who make you feel very safe and supported. Call them in one by one, becoming very aware of who they are, what they look like, their names, and how they feel to be with.

- Remember these are figures you can call on when you need support in everyday life—for wisdom, play, or emotional support. You can ask anyone in the club to leave, politely and firmly, if you don't feel comfortable at any time.
- Once the club is formed, imagine a club member moving toward you and sharing words of support and genuine care. Imagine that internal dialogue for a minute or two.
- Slowly bring attention back to the place you are in. Open your eyes and write out all the names of club members. Describe the effect of this exercise on you.

## FEELINGS DIAL

You can use this imagery to gain better control over the intensity of your feelings. With practice, you can learn to "turn down" overwhelming feelings. This technique is not a way to avoid or get rid of feelings—these must eventually be processed for healing to occur. Imagine a volume dial, as on a radio. This is like a "feelings dial." It has numbers from 1 to 10, from low to most intense. Notice what the dial is made of. Notice if it is smooth. Think of an unpleasant feeling you sometimes feel. Notice whether you are feeling it right now. What number on the dial reflects how weak or strong the feeling is now? What number is the dial on now? What is it like to be on that number? What would it be like to be at 1? 8? How about somewhere in the middle? If you'd like to try turning down the feelings dial, which number would you turn it to? Turn the dial down lower and lower until it goes down a number. And keep turning it lower and lower and lower. Would you like to keep going? Keep going nice and slowly until you go to the desired intensity. Please repeat several times so that you can master this skill. Do easy deep breathing. Time your breathing so that each time you exhale, you turn the dial a little lower.

Anytime that your negative feelings are too high, imagine the dial. Turn it down. It can be a revelation to some that feelings can be controlled in this way. This is a good technique if you feel angry, demoralized, anxious, out of control, or depressed. It can be useful for feelings associated with flashbacks or for ending a therapy session.

## CONTAINMENT SKILLS[9]

These are additional steps to help you firmly control intrusive thoughts on a temporary basis, until you are ready to process them. Containment helps you function each day without being overwhelmed. It provides a way to tolerate intense feelings and choose when you wish to work on them. Containment also helps you keep the past separated from the present.

### Split Screen

This skill is like watching a television screen where two sports events appear at once. You divide a mental TV screen, putting the past on one side and the present on the other. You have remote controls that allow you to mute, slow down, shrink, fast-forward, turn to black and white, or turn off the past. You download the difficult memories to a video recording as the therapist counts from one to three. You turn the TV off, take the recording out, and store or file it in a safe place (wherever you want, maybe a safe with a special key). Place it there until you are ready to take it out.

### Freezing

Imagine that the intrusive thoughts, images, feelings, or recollections are ice cubes, which you'll store at your therapist's office. Visualize a big scoop that scoops up the ice cubes and drops them into Tupperware containers. Tight-fitting lids on the containers seal in the ice cubes. See the containers safely stored in a freezer outside your therapist's office. You and your therapist can retrieve the ice cubes, one container at a time, and use them in an appropriate way to help your therapy progress.

### Dirty Laundry

Imagine the intrusive thoughts, images, feelings, or recollections as soiled clothing that needs to go to the laundry. See yourself stuffing the soiled clothing in a laundry bag and calling the laundry collection service. Imagine that the laundry truck arrives. The laundry bag is placed in the laundry truck, the truck doors are closed, and you watch through a window as the laundry truck drives away. Watch the truck turn the corner and disappear. The cleaner's is next to your therapist's office. You and your therapist can pick up your laundry together, sort it out, and use it in an appropriate way to help your therapy progress.

## Shrinking Techniques

Imagine that you are looking at distressing material through a reverse telescope, so that it becomes very small and far away. Or imagine that you are in a plane flying over the material and looking down. You are in control, the boss. You say how high and far away you wish to go.

## Other Containment Techniques

There is no one best way to do this. The best technique is the one that works for you. Create a strategy that you like to get better control of your symptoms. You might, for example, imagine the distressing material written on a chalkboard, then erased, written on a letter and mailed to a safe place, or packed in a suitcase and stored in a locker.

# CHAPTER 16

# *Before Starting Memory Work*

## *Helpful Strategies*

In addition to psychological suffering, PTSD is linked to greater risk for a variety of medical illnesses and death from all causes.[1] Thus, prompt, effective treatment is essential. However, everyone is not ready or willing to engage in the work of processing traumatic memories. This chapter explores new options that help survivors prepare to do memory work.

These approaches consider that a central feature of PTSD, avoidance, prevents victims from successfully resolving traumatic memories. In trying to turn from the pain, victims might use a variety of maladaptive strategies that ultimately increase suffering, including addictions to substances, gambling, sex, anger, food, and work.

### DUAL DIAGNOSIS: PTSD AND SUBSTANCE USE DISORDER

Often, people with PTSD also have a substance use disorder (SUD). SUD refers to the abuse[2] of alcohol, hard drugs (such as cocaine and opiates), prescription pain medications, marijuana, sedatives, or other drugs.

PTSD usually occurs first, with people later turning to drugs for symptom relief. This is called self-medicating.[3] However, drug use can also put one at risk for PTSD. For example, after drinking, one might be more vulnerable to rape, traffic accidents, or domestic violence.

It was previously thought that one should be drug-free prior to treatment, since drug misuse can impede memory processing. However, abstinence often removes the victim's only way to numb the overwhelming emotions of PTSD. Lacking coping skills, the person soon returns to using drugs. Today, most experts feel that it is best to treat PTSD and SUD at the same time. This approach is preferred by most people with PTSD.

## The Seeking Safety Program[4]

The Seeking Safety program has been applied to a wide variety of groups with dual diagnoses (men, women, adolescents, combat vets, emergency service workers, prisoners, homeless persons, victims of domestic violence[5]) with encouraging results. It has reduced both substance use and PTSD symptoms in a number of studies, and it appears to help with other addictions.

Over a period of at least three months, Seeking Safety typically covers twenty-five topics before trauma memory processing starts.[6] Each topic teaches safe coping skills common to both disorders. These skills are then practiced at home. The topics are independent of each other and can be covered in the order best suited to the individual or group:

1. Introduction
2. Safety
3. Taking back your power over PTSD
4. Grounding
5. Substances and PTSD (understanding the role substances play in PTSD, counting the costs, options for reducing substance use)
6. Asking for help
7. Self-care
8. Compassion
9. Red and green flags (catching signs of danger before we spiral out of control)
10. Honesty
11. Recovery thinking
12. Integrating the split self
13. Commitment (to a better life, ideals, and relationships to self and others)
14. Creating meaning (thoughts relative to PTSD and substance abuse disorder)
15. Community resources
16. Setting boundaries in relationships
17. Discovery
18. Getting others to support your recovery
19. Coping with triggers

20. Respecting your time
21. Healthy relationships
22. Self-nurturing
23. Healing from anger
24. Review
25. Termination

Notice that Seeking Safety does not seek to process traumatic memories, but only helps to provide a secure foundation and the coping skills needed for treatment to start.

### What If I Don't Want to Start?[7]

What if you are not ready (or don't want) to start treatment or give up substances? What if, for example, you consider it smart to remain angry and hypervigilant in a dangerous world? If you've used substances for a long time, this might seem like a natural way to cope with pain. Perhaps you have mixed feelings about giving up drugs because of the benefits that they give you. Part of you might want to give drugs up, and another part of you might not want to.

Some PTSD treatment programs begin with a motivational enhancement group. In a supportive group setting, individuals do the following:

1. **Discuss the rationale for acknowledging PTSD problems**, lest they be "blindsided by the enemy." Consider, for example, the use of alcohol, as it affects social isolation. Although PTSD treatment might be successful, the excessive use of alcohol might cause one to slip back into bad habits, such as social withdrawal, anger, or depression. These habits could disconnect one from needed social support.

2. **Generate a list of PTSD problems that survivors *might* have.** These are defined as problems that you *might* have wondered if you had or that other people told you that you had but you disagreed. In addition to anger (the most frequently cited problem among vets), other frequently reported problems include substance use, isolation, depression, lack of trust, conflicts, difficulty with intimacy, and restricted emotions. You will make a three-column list with these headings: "I'm Sure I Have This Problem"; "I'm Sure I Don't Have This Problem"; and "I Might Have This Problem."

3. **Compare how problematic the behavior might be, compared to the average person who doesn't have PTSD.** Through discussion, problems

are rated as average, moderate, or extreme, considering frequency, severity of consequences, and purpose.

4. **List pros and cons of the "might have" behaviors.** This helps one see more clearly if a behavior is a problem in terms of its costs. The pros also reveal real needs that the behavior is filling—needs that can be met in other ways.

5. **Discuss roadblocks to change**, such as fear of being overwhelmed if you acknowledge the problem, fear of being rejected if the problem is acknowledged, fear of admitting failure, or other feelings or beliefs, such as "Only homeless bums have a drinking problem."

6. **Determine at the end of discussions if behaviors are reclassified.** There is no judging of whether such shifts are good or bad. The goal is simply to see clearly and accurately one's present situation.

This process can indeed be motivating. People see that everyone struggles with something. Seeing others acknowledge problems and contemplating the issues for oneself makes it easier for one to recognize one's own problems and thus be more prepared to change.

## MINDFULNESS-BASED STRATEGIES

In recent years, mindfulness-based strategies have been applied to reduce many types of mental and physical suffering, including stress, depression, anxiety, chronic pain, sleep disorders, eating disorders, and many other conditions. More recently, mindfulness has been used to help those suffering with PTSD.[8]

Mindfulness means awareness of our present inner and outer experience, including painful memories and their associated thoughts, feelings, and body sensations. However, it is a special kind of awareness. It is completely accepting, letting things be just as they are for the moment without protest, complaint, or struggling to change them. We see ourselves as separate from and deeper than memories, thoughts, feelings, and sensations.

Five assumptions underlie mindfulness-based strategies:

1. **PTSD is an avoidance disorder.** It is not memories and associated thoughts, feelings, and sensations that are the problem, but the attempts to erase or escape these. We increase our suffering with disbelief, anger, fear, and wanting things to be different. That is, the more we tense and fight our symptoms, the more we become aroused.

2. **We can't change our history.** The more we try to, the more we become attached to the painful memories. Forty years after serving in Vietnam as a Marine, Rob said, "I wish I could just laser these memories out of my head." Feeling contaminated to the core, he wished to kill off and push away the memories. Of course, we can't erase the past, and the more we fight the memories, the more we think of them. So we ask, How long have you been fighting your traumatic memories? Has it worked? What has been the cost of the battles? Would you be willing to try a different approach?

3. **Although we can't change our history, we can change our response to our experience.** Turning gently toward the memories actually decreases their intensity and enables us to more fully live in the present. Intrusions lessen. We become less emotionally reactive. We learn to tolerate, not fear, unpleasant experience.

4. **Suffering is an opportunity to learn kindheartedness and a different way of being.** We learn to embrace and soothe pain. We again learn to be in touch with our true selves, our feelings, and our bodies. PTSD often separates people from such awareness. We gain freedom and flexibility by giving up the obsession with controlling our pain.

5. **Mindfulness is the opposite of dissociation.** It helps us to stop running away, resisting, and trying to change memories.

In the mindfulness view, all people are of two minds. Visualize a circle, which represents the *wisdom mind*, or one's true, happy nature. The wisdom mind is wise, dignified, compassionate, and good-humored. It is also peaceful and humble. Like a cloud, however, the *ordinary mind* surrounds and obscures the wisdom mind, causing much suffering. The ordinary mind fixates on painful emotions and thoughts: "I can't stand this!" "I'll never recover." "I'm damaged goods." "I feel so badly." The ordinary mind worries, obsesses over symptoms, and judges: "What's wrong with me!" "I hate this." "I should be better by now." When one feels beside himself with worry or anger, it means that he is caught up in the ordinary mind. Much of the drama of PTSD results from being stuck in the ordinary mind. Mindfulness teaches one to go beneath the ordinary mind, to recognize thoughts and feelings as simply thoughts and feelings—temporary, not who one is at the core. One learns to rest in the wisdom mind, experiencing its deeper inner peace. The "idea of being broken" exists only in the ordinary mind. The deeper self and hope are not actually shattered. It is as though the wisdom mind is asleep and covered and in need of awakening.

Mindfulness, then, focuses less on thinking and more on the way we are. At the heart of mindfulness practice are certain key attitudes:

1. *Compassion* means sorrow for people's suffering, plus the desire to help. However, mindfulness teaches that compassion also means compassion for oneself. Compassion is often equated to loving kindness, or gentle friendliness. Holding our experience in gentle, friendly awareness reduces the intensity of disturbing negative emotions.

2. **Vastness.** Rather than trying to run from or get rid of painful symptoms, we create a place to hold them in compassionate awareness. The wisdom mind is vast—like the ocean, wide and deep enough to hold any disturbing emotion. It is as though we watch from the calm depths of the ocean. PTSD symptoms are like waves arising on the surface and then being absorbed by the ocean. The waves don't alter the essential nature of the ocean.

3. *Acceptance* means that we willingly allow into awareness whatever we experience, without trying to change, fix, or escape it. Paradoxically, when we simply observe our experience as a scientist would, without judging, we stop reacting with as much arousal. With acceptance, we adopt the stance "Whatever I am feeling is OK, let me feel it." Ironically, as we accept what is, without bracing, tensing, and fighting our experience, things begin to change. More correctly, *what changes is our response* to what is.

4. **Beginner's mind.** The beginner is open to learning and change. The expert assumes she already knows, and thus changes little. In mindfulness, we commit to practice with an open mind, willing to experiment with a new approach to symptoms. The expectation is that things *might* change with practice. The expert's mind assumes that the way one feels is a permanent reality. The beginner's mind realizes that circumstances change and that one is able to again experience one's true happy nature.

5. **Good humor.** PTSD makes people overly serious. In mindfulness, we remain open to our wisdom mind and to again experiencing a somewhat playful attitude.

Let's briefly discuss some of the mindfulness-based strategies.

## Mindfulness-Based Stress Reduction (MBSR)

This eight-week, group-format program started at the University of Massachusetts Medical School and is now being taught at various clinics and schools around the world. The program teaches a new way to be with whatever arises, eventually helping people to be grounded in the present and more comfortable even with unpleasant emotions—such as anger, disgust, or guilt.

Below is a sampling of some of the MBSR strategies. MBSR is not simply a collection of techniques. Rather, each skill builds on the one before it. So regular practice is emphasized. As a reminder, do not continue if practicing any of the following causes you to destabilize, including experiencing any types of dissociation or extremely uncomfortable emotions. Discuss this with your counselor. You might also decide to try more physically oriented mindfulness practices, such as walking meditations or yoga, which help one to stay grounded in one's body.

*Mindful Breathing.* Practice this very effective strategy for about ten minutes each day until it feels comfortable.

1. **Sit comfortably with feet flat on the floor and hands resting in the lap.** The back is comfortably straight but not rigid. The chin is neither up nor down, neither back nor forward. You might think of yourself as a mountain, which is always steadfast and dignified, even if covered by darkness or storm. Allow your eyes to close gently (or if that is uncomfortable, keep them half open, resting on a spot on the floor in front of you).
2. **Release tension in the shoulders, jaw, mouth, and abdomen.** As you permit your body to relax and settle, allow yourself to also settle in your wisdom mind, which is kind, peaceful, and good-humored.
3. **As you breathe abdominally, low and slow, place awareness on your breathing.** Pay attention to the rising and falling of the abdomen with each breath. Notice what your body is doing and what it feels like. Perhaps you notice the air flowing through your nostrils and down your throat and in and out of your lungs. Notice what the body feels like when you simply pay attention to something you do every moment of every day.
4. **As you are doing this, you will notice that thoughts enter your mind—** perhaps worries, plans, questions, judgments, and so forth. This is what the ordinary mind does. Simply notice the mind doing this without comment or judgment. Simply say to yourself, "There's a thought." Congratulate yourself for noticing that thought. Then simply bring your attention back to your breathing. When the next thought comes into awareness, gently bring your attention back again. Do this again and again and again, without getting upset. Remember, the goal is not to avoid thoughts, but to simply notice thoughts and bring your attention back to your breath.

People often find this strategy extremely relaxing, as they give themselves a break from constant, racing thoughts. However, the goal of this strategy is not to relax, nor is it to avoid thinking. The goal is simply to recognize thoughts as they occur without reacting emotionally and to realize that you can gently return your focus to the breath. The breath is always with you, just as the wisdom mind is.

***Compassion Meditations.*** As important as compassion is to the healing process, many people find it a new and challenging experience to cultivate compassion. So you might practice some of the following strategies until compassion feels familiar. Sit comfortably as you did in Steps 1 and 2 of the mindful breathing exercise above, grounding yourself in your breath as you try these:

- Imagine a very compassionate being standing in front of you. The being is gentle and kind and makes you feel safe, accepted. Perhaps the being is one you have known, a loving relative or friend, for instance. Or, it might be someone that you imagine. For a few moments, notice what it feels like to be in that being's presence. As you exhale, see that being absorbing your suffering. As you inhale, you absorb that being's compassion and loving kindness, much as the body receives warm sunshine. Notice what that is like for a few minutes.
- Remember a time when you witnessed loving kindness shown by one to another.
- Remember a time when you experienced or imagined loving kindness from another.
- Remember a time when you felt or showed loving kindness to another.
- Remember a time when you were kind to and accepting of yourself. (If this is difficult, try imagining yourself being that way to yourself.[9]) Follow this by saying this to yourself with intention:
     May I be kind.
     May I care about my pain.
     May I see myself as whole.
     May I be happy.
     May I find peace.
     May I be free of suffering.
- Write a cue word, words, or phrase, such as "compassion," "gentle friendliness," or "be kind to myself," on a card. Sit with this cue for five minutes. When thoughts arise (e.g., "This feels phony"), rest in your breath and gently return your attention to the cue word, words, or phrases each time.

*The Body Scan.* We feel the full range of sensations and emotions—pleasant and unpleasant—in the body. Yet people with PTSD are usually out of touch with their bodies. They try to manage pain in their heads. In thinking, "Not again. I can't deal with this. I've got to get rid of this," they actually become more tense, which causes discomfort to increase. This powerful strategy teaches a different way to calmly welcome in each bodily sensation, noting that it often changes as we pay attention to it. Then we learn to release the sensation as we shift attention elsewhere in the body. This prepares us eventually to respond to painful emotions in a similar way. So this important strategy develops body awareness, which people often discover is pleasant. Being grounded in the body, beneath thoughts, is also a good way to be present in the true self.

The body scan typically takes forty-five minutes or more. However, you can get a feel for this very important strategy by practicing the following for five to ten minutes initially each day for several days.

1. **Sit comfortably** as you did in Steps 1 and 2 of the mindful breathing exercise, and allow your mind to settle in your breath. Alternatively, you can lie down, if that feels comfortable.
2. **Bring awareness to the toes of your left foot.** You might wiggle them if that helps. Imagine that your mind is actually resting in your toes.
3. **Now imagine that you are actually breathing in and out of your toes.** Follow the air as your breathe in down through your nose, lungs, abdomen, and legs into your toes. As you exhale, imagine the air flowing out through the legs, abdomen, lungs, and nose.
4. **As you continue to breathe this way, notice any and all sensations in the toes.** Notice what they are touching and what that feels like, such as a sock, shoe, or each other. Notice whether they feel warm or cold, comfortable or not, tense or relaxed. Do you feel the blood pulsing through them? Notice any changes in these sensations as you breathe. Whatever you notice, do so without comment or judging.
5. **As thoughts arise (such as "I wonder what time it is," "I have things to do," "What's for lunch?"), simply notice each one.** Each time gently return your attention to your toes, resting your mind and your breath there.
6. **After a while, when you have experienced whatever sensations you notice there and you feel ready to, take a deeper, more intentional breath into the toes.** As you release that breath, also let awareness of your toes dissolve, as you begin to focus on the sole of the left foot.

7. **As you did with the toes, rest your mind in the sole of the left foot, breathe into it and out from it, and patiently notice any and all sensations and what happens to those sensations as you breathe.** Escort your mind back to that area each time it wanders. When you are ready, take a deeper, more intentional breath and release awareness of the sole as you bring attention now to the left ankle.

This process continues until you have scanned the entire body, bringing gentle, nonjudgmental awareness to each part of the body.[10]

*Happiness Meditation.* This strategy starts as the others, sitting comfortably, settling your mind in your breath. Begin by thinking about what it would be like to smile, perhaps to feel the warm, playful, good-humored aspects of your true self. You might think of something that made you smile in the past. Notice what this feels like. Perhaps you notice that just the thought of a smile makes you feel content and relaxed, softening the face. Allow your face to form a genuine half-smile, allowing your eyes to soften. Then allow your mind to rest in your belly, settling peacefully there. As you breathe into the belly, allow yourself to feel happiness there. Perhaps that evokes a feeling of contentment or light in that area of the body. After enjoying that pleasant feeling for a few moments, allow the warm and light feeling of happiness to spread to and settle in the heart.

Continue in this way, allowing happiness to settle into the lungs, throat, and other regions of the body in turn.

*Flexible Awareness.* The greatest control, paradoxically, comes from flexibility and releasing attempts to control everything rigidly. Flexible awareness asks people to simply notice whatever comes into awareness with equanimity—the same gentle calmness whether what surfaces is pleasant or unpleasant. Practice this for five minutes at first:

1. **Begin in the usual way.** Follow Steps 1 and 2 in the mindful breathing exercise, allowing your mind to settle in your breathing.
2. **Notice where the mind wanders with nonjudgmental, softhearted acceptance.** If a thought arises, simply say, "There's a thought that I can't do this right," or "There is a memory of a past event." If a bodily sensation arises, simply say, "There's the sensation of tightness in the gut," or "There is a pain in the back." For an emotion, you might say, "There is a feeling

of sadness." For an urge, "There is the urge to use alcohol for comfort." Hold each thought in cordial awareness, breathing. Let awareness of each thought dissolve as a new thought enters awareness.

A number of benefits result from this exercise.

1. We realize that we can acknowledge pain and urges without being controlled by them (for example, by drinking alcohol, ignoring needs, tensing up and fighting them). Even if we'd prefer not to have unpleasant experiences, we can welcome them into awareness without reacting emotionally. This exercise reinforces that a thought is just a thought, not who we are.[11] Likewise, bodily sensations, emotions, urges, and memories happen. They come into awareness and go; they are not who we are.[12]
2. Describing emotions and putting them into words has been found to regulate regions of the brain associated with fear and anxiety.[13]

Again, if memories surface and become too troubling, don't force yourself to try this or any other mindfulness exercise. Perhaps you can return to mindful practice at a later time.

*Other Mindfulness Practices.* Try doing an everyday activity mindfully. For example, try eating a meal, and only eat. Eat slowly, savoring each bite. Notice aromas, textures, and flavors. Notice what your body feels like after you swallow. You can also try mindfully showering, driving, talking to someone. Notice how often we miss pleasures of the moment when we are not fully in the present.

Some people prefer more active forms of mindfulness, such as walking mindfully and paying attention to each sensation as you slowly place a heel down, roll your foot forward, feel tension in the various muscles of the legs, and so forth.

## Dialectical Behavior Therapy (DBT)

Dialectical behavior therapy was developed for the treatment of people with borderline personality disorder (see Appendix D). Those with this disorder frequently have a history of childhood abuse (physical, sexual, and/or emotional), adult trauma, and habitual invalidation.[14] Understandably, these people often have difficulty regulating strong emotions and might struggle with deliberate self-injury (including suicide), depression, bipolar disorder, anxiety, eating disorders, substance abuse disorder, and PTSD.

Today, DBT is also used to help PTSD survivors who are not ready to process traumatic memories or who don't yet have the skills to handle the strong emotions associated with PTSD. It has been adapted to help those with PTSD and substance abuse disorder and can help those who destabilize when practicing mindfulness-based stress reduction. The goal is to strengthen people to the point that they can practice other skills described thus far and eventually be able to process traumatic memories.

DBT is offered in certain clinics and hospitals (see Additional Resources). Typically lasting around a year, it combines group skills-training with individual therapy and individual coaching. A unique component of DBT is that it affords a great amount of acceptance and validation before change is encouraged.[15] The groups meet weekly, covering four basic modules, for which homework practice is assigned.

1. **Basic mindfulness** (does not focus on memories).
2. **Basic relationship skills** (asking for what you want, accepting "no" for an answer, resolving conflict, saying no).
3. **Emotional regulation** (identifying and labeling current emotions and why they arise; understanding related sensations, behaviors, and aftereffects on functioning; understanding that emotions make sense; being willing to have and not judge emotions; increasing positive emotions; understanding that you are not your emotions; behaving in opposition to the feelings, such as facing what is feared).
4. **Distress tolerance.** This includes accepting oneself and the situation and surviving a crisis that can't be changed (by doing something to distract, helping another, realizing it could be worse, leaving the situation, self-soothing through pleasant tastes or sounds, prayer, relaxation, taking a vacation, mindful breathing, examining the pros and cons of tolerating distress rather than hurting oneself, living a good life despite pain).

## Acceptance and Commitment Therapy (ACT)[16]

ACT (pronounced as a word, not initials) combines many of the principles that have been discussed in this chapter in a very effective and creative way. Used with groups or individuals, ACT has been found to help depression, anxiety, substance abuse, and chronic pain—all associated with PTSD. It is also being used for PTSD with and without substance use disorder, sometimes as a follow-up to DBT.

For example, the originator of ACT, Dr. Steven Hayes, explains that we all have battles raging in our minds as we try to fight against painful memories of the past. We go on the attack, thinking, "I shouldn't have done that," "Why didn't I do more?" and so forth. The more we fight against the unchangeable past, the more *fused* we become with it. However, it is possible to notice that the battle is raging but then step back away from the battlefield so that we might be freer to live again. Hayes introduced the process of *defusion*, which helps one to accomplish this.[17] One defusion strategy directs people to completely accept the reality of past events, letting the pain in with a kind and welcoming attitude, and noticing the associated thoughts, feelings, memories, images, and bodily sensations. One might think, "These are just memories." Now one selects a single word to represent oneself in regard to the past memory, such as "loser," "bad," "damaged," or "shamed." The word and other aspects of the memory are welcomed into awareness with complete and kind acceptance. Then the word is repeated out loud as quickly as possible for a period of about forty-five seconds, as one notices if the distress associated with that word decreases. Another defusion strategy is to draw a picture of your head with all the negative thoughts and feelings inside it regarding the past that you carry around with you. Put this picture in your pocket and realize that you can carry on despite the inner struggles.

Other metaphors help one commit to live a valued life. For example, your life's journey is like a bus that you are driving. In the back are passengers, who scream things like "stop!" "don't go that way!" "turn here." The passengers are just thoughts, just what the mind does. They are on for the whole ride, but the driver realizes that she can choose to drive the bus anywhere she wants. She still has that capability. If one has a craving to drink alcohol as a temporary escape from pain, one can break down the urge into thoughts ("I'm having the thought that I need a drink"), sensations ("There's the sensation of tightness in the chest"), feelings (anxiety), and urges (to drink). These become "passengers on the bus" as we drive on despite their noise. Another "passenger" might try to keep you from sleeping. The "driver" thinks, "I'm just having the thought that I'm going to have a nightmare if I fall asleep," or "I'm having the thought that I'll be in danger if I fall asleep," and goes to bed anyway.

# PART V

---

# Treatment

# CHAPTER 17

# *Principles of Memory Work*

---

**I don't want to remember but I can't seem to forget.**
*—PTSD sufferer*

A major goal of treatment for PTSD is to integrate dissociated traumatic memory material with your associated memories. Think of a young boy in your neighborhood whom you have watched grow up with great enjoyment. Imagine that he is called to war and returns quite shaken. At the airport, you notice that much of the sparkle has left his eyes. The town holds a parade and welcome-home party to celebrate his return. The neighborhood goes out of its way to integrate him back into normal life. He is embraced again and again. Eventually the life begins to return to his eyes. If the young man is to resume his life again, he hopefully will not be shunned or shamed but will be made to feel a part of the community again. Now think of a personal traumatic experience. If you are to heal and pick up again, you will need to embrace your traumatic memories and integrate them with the rest of your life experience. You will not try to destroy them or cast them out. To do so would be to disown the part of you that experienced them.

## TURN TOWARD THE MEMORIES

It is normal to wish to flee from painful memories. Yet these memories continue to pursue us, much like a little barking dog chases a person until that person stops, turns, and faces the dog. As Mary Beth Williams notes, "Only a remembered trauma can be worked through and then let go."[1] It is easier to live with a memory when all aspects are remembered and processed.[2] How is this done?

In memory work, you will give yourself the opportunity to call up memories in sufficient detail so that you can accurately see what happened and understand their impact. You will learn to view trauma like a scrapbook of an event that you can store on a shelf and take down as needed. The trauma gives you a unique experience, but you don't have to look at it everywhere you go, and you don't equate the owner of the album with the album.[3] You are more than the traumatic event. Eventually you will see your traumatic experience in the context of your broader life experience, neither exaggerating nor underemphasizing your role or its impact. As you confront rather than avoid traumatic memories, you find that the memories no longer are as frightening.

In the process of healing, you will answer questions like the following:

- What does the trauma mean? Why did it happen?
- How do I make sense of my world again?
- Who or what was responsible, and how do I make peace with my actual role(s)?
- Why haven't I adapted better, and what coping skills will help me cope better?
- What does it mean to process memories so that I can let them go? How is it done?

In telling your story and recalling memories, you will have the opportunity to break the secrecy that maintains dissociation and correct misinterpretations and unrealistic expectations.

## YOU'RE IN CHARGE

A word of caution is important to reemphasize. During treatment, intrusions (memories, nightmares, flashbacks, reactions to triggers) are likely to increase. This simply signals the need to process traumatic material. Information in the intrusions can be very useful as long as you are not overwhelmed by the intrusions. Remember that you need to be the boss, to dictate the pace of memory work. Remember to work in partnership with your therapist. Communicate if you are beginning to feel overwhelmed. Allow yourself time to prepare for memory work and time at the end of sessions to restore a feeling of safety and balance. Safety and balance can be restored by grounding, eye movements, safe place imagery, relaxation, and/or containment exercises, as we learned in Part IV. Continue to practice the skills you have acquired thus far. You might hear your therapist use the word *titrate* to refer to the process of gradually bringing up enough memory detail to allow processing but not so much that you feel overwhelmed. As a rule, the more aspects of a memory that can be processed, the more effective the integration will be. Eventually as you "tell your story" repeatedly, you will be able to tolerate more and more detail without being overwhelmed. Do not rush the process, however. Like building a house, slow and steady progress is better than rushed, sloppy work.

Note that some people choose not to or cannot face traumas. Discuss with your therapist when to do this work, if at all. For example, some people feel the need to be in therapy for a year or two before talking about trauma because they need to learn the techniques and/or feel safe enough to process memories. Poor health may prevent others from having the strength to do memory work.

## YOU HAVE MANY TREATMENT OPTIONS

Your therapist will explain various ways to do memory work. Some proceed more slowly, while others are somewhat accelerated. Some are primarily intellectual, while other approaches involve more emotions and/or behavior. PTSD can be responsive to all of the approaches summarized in this part of the book when they are applied appropriately. Become familiar with the treatment options described herein so that you can create a treatment plan with your therapist that makes sense for you. For many cases of PTSD, treatment could logically follow the general sequence as outlined in this book. However, the treatment plan is usually affected by the skills, resources, and preferences of both the survivor and the clinician, as well as the particulars of the case.

When children face distressing setbacks, they bounce back when embraced with love, faith, hope, humor, and a sense of purpose. You, too, will recover as you embrace your experience in similar ways.

# CHAPTER 18

# Cognitive Restructuring

---

**When circumstances don't fit our ideas,**
**they become our difficulties.**

*—Benjamin Franklin*

We remember that a major PTSD treatment goal is to integrate dissociated trauma material with associated memories so that the fabric of our memory becomes like one continuous memory. The problem is that traumatic memory doesn't mesh with the way we want to look at the world. The dissociated memories often contain misinterpretations and inaccurate conclusions that were formed under great duress, while strong emotions and arousal continue to interfere with processing.

Integration is facilitated by restructuring unproductive ideas that maintain emotional arousal and interfere with processing. Unproductive ideas can relate to the present (our normal assumptions about life, people, and ourselves; thoughts about triggers, symptoms, or everyday stressors), the past (e.g., misinterpretations about the traumatic event), or the future. Each can keep arousal dysfunctionally high. Reworking these ideas is the goal of cognitive therapy, a mainstay in the treatment of PTSD. Cognitive therapy asserts that thoughts significantly influence our reactions to events. Let's see how this works.

---

This chapter summarizes the ideas and therapeutic strategies of several cognitive theorists. Albert Ellis originated the ABC model and the concepts of *catastrophizing* and *shoulds*. Aaron Beck originated the concept of *automatic thoughts*, the term *distortions*, most of the distortions presently used in cognitive therapy, the idea of basic (core) beliefs, and the idea of recording thoughts, distortions, and moods. David Burns wrote *Feeling Good*, a very useful application of Beck's theories. The book is recommended for further reading.

Paramedics Harold and Anne received an urgent call one dark, rainy night. A popular teenager who lived in an unfamiliar section of the county was having difficulty breathing after he returned from playing in a basketball game. Reacting quickly, they drove toward the house but found that the bridge en route had washed away. Quickly looking at the map, Anne directed Harold to an alternate route. In their haste, however, they sped past the turn and lost several precious minutes. When they arrived at the house, the teenager had stopped breathing and could not be resuscitated. Harold thought angrily, "Why did such a fine young man have to die? Life is so unfair!" Then sadly, "If only I had heeded my instincts and turned sooner. I could kick myself for being so dumb." Later he worries, "What if something like that happens to my kids?" Harold begins to have trouble sleeping and can't get the thought of the young teenager out of his mind. He starts worrying about his own children and becomes overprotective of them. He starts to notice his heart pounding and worries that maybe he'll have a heart attack. He can't seem to unwind and eventually takes a leave of absence. Anne processed the event differently, however. She thought, "It is so sad that that fine young man died. He had such a bright future. I'll always wonder if we might have saved him had we arrived sooner. But we were in unfamiliar territory with such poor visibility. We did the best we could." Anne grieved at the loss but returned to her job with a renewed commitment to serving others. Both Harold and Anne are capable, bright, and dedicated professionals. Their responses to the traumatic event, however, were largely determined by their thoughts.

Cognitive therapy enables us to stop, identify unproductive thoughts, and replace them with more functional thoughts. We stop running from arousing thoughts—or only partially confronting them—and begin to persistently confront and challenge them. In so doing, we shift from the helpless victim mode to the action mode, gaining mastery over the one thing we can consistently control—our thoughts. This process usually lessens arousal. Should emotional and physical arousal occur, knowing how to replace unproductive thoughts helps keep it within bounds and allows it to subside more quickly. The model is fairly simple:

$$A \longrightarrow B \longrightarrow C$$

**A** stands for the Activating (or upsetting) event. **B** is the **B**elief (or *automatic thoughts*) that we tell ourselves about **A**. **C** is the emotional and physical **C**onsequences (or arousal). Most people think that **A** causes **C**. In reality, it is **B**, our self-talk, that has greater influence. Productive self-talk would likely lead to appropriate emotional upset that allows us to focus and concentrate on functioning. On the other hand, unproductive thoughts lead to emotional *disturbance* that prevents cool thinking and functioning.

## AUTOMATIC THOUGHTS AND DISTORTIONS

When an upsetting event occurs, automatic thoughts (ATs) run through our minds. Although we're all capable of thinking reasonably about upsetting events, sometimes our automatic thoughts are *distorted*—or unreasonably negative. Distorted automatic thoughts occur so rapidly that we hardly notice them, let alone stop to question them. Yet these automatic thoughts profoundly affect our moods, our body's arousal, and our ability to process clearly.

Distortions are learned. Sometimes we learn them in childhood. Sometimes they are taught from others; sometimes they are learned from previous traumatic experiences. Distortions are not a reflection of intelligence or strength. They are simply learned habits. When we submit them to new evidence and logic, we can learn new, more productive thought patterns. In this section, you'll improve your skill in catching troublesome distortions, challenging their logic, and replacing them with thoughts that are less arousing.

The distortions that increase PTSD symptoms fall into only thirteen categories, as described in the following sections. Learn them well. You will use them repeatedly throughout treatment. Beyond PTSD, cognitive therapy teaches skills that facilitate coping and growth in all people. In addition to being able to quickly spot distortions, the goals are to rebut and replace them as well. Rebuttals generally take the form of three questions: What's the evidence? What's another way to look at the situation? So what if it happens?[1]

### Flaw Fixation

Here we tend to zoom right in on what is wrong or what went wrong. This is also called "fear focus" because the mental camera focuses on the fearful. It is like seeing only one aspect of a picture. Here are some examples:

- A firefighter saves twenty people from a fire but dwells on the five that he could not rescue. He ignores the good things that he did before and during the fire and fixates only on the bad outcomes.
- On vacation, a paramedic sees a cross on the side of the road, reminding him of a life that he could not save. He stops noticing the beauty of the countryside.

- A rape victim surveys a crowd of people and only notices the face of a man who reminds her of the perpetrator.
- A soldier thinks of his shortcomings in a battle when he recalls his three years of military service. He ignores the fact that he persisted in his duty and showed great skill in surviving many difficult situations.
- A father concentrates on his child's C and doesn't praise the As and Bs on the report card.

The problem with this "worm's-eye view"[2] is that it ignores the very aspects that make life satisfying and enjoyable. And through conditioning, related negatives snowball so that many places and events now remind us to feel guilt, anger, fear, sadness, or insecurity.

The antidote is to expand our focus—use a wider lens to see the whole picture. Ask, "What else could I notice? What isn't wrong? What's gone well? What is right? What percentage of the time did I perform well? What's here to enjoy?" Notice that the suggestion is not to ignore the negative aspects but to see more aspects.

## Dismissing the Positive

Whereas flaw fixation ignores the good, dismissing the positive actually discounts it, as if it didn't matter. You don't give yourself deserved credit, so you feel badly. When armed terrorists seized her school, a teacher coolly led her class out a basement passage. When complimented on her cool functioning, she replied, "It's not worth thinking about. I was just lucky to survive; there was no skill to it." The teacher might have thanked the giver of the compliment and privately thought, "I am glad that I had the presence of mind to function so well." Good always counts.

## Assuming

There are three kinds of assumptions. Each kind results in distress without testing the evidence.

1. **Mind reading.** Here we assume that we know what others are thinking. Examples:
   - "My colleagues think I'm a wimp for being so stressed about this."
   - "They hate me for letting them down."
   - "God doesn't love me and couldn't possibly forgive this kind of mistake."

These distortions are challenged by asking, "What's the evidence? Is there another possibility?" Some people will have empathy and understanding for your suffering. Others might be indifferent or curious—not mocking. People may or may not be disappointed in your behavior. On the other hand, some, most, or all of them may find it understandable under the circumstances.

2. **Jumping to conclusions.** You hear a noise and assume that a burglar is in the house. You literally jump at this conclusion, which is called the *startle response*. This is tested by asking, "What is the evidence? Is it possible that this is not a repeat of my trauma?"

3. **Fortune-telling.** Here we pessimistically predict a negative outcome without testing the evidence. Table 18.1 shows some examples and replacement thoughts. Fortune-telling often starts with a fear focus ("It *might* happen. After all, it's happened before. Or it could happen for the first time.") and subtly shifts to "It will *undoubtedly* happen," which arouses one further. To challenge this distortion, we think somewhat tentatively and openly like a scientist. "Certainly bad things might happen, but what's the probability or odds of this happening?" Other antidotes include asking, "Why might this negative *not* happen? Why might something *good* happen?"

## Catastrophizing

This means making things much worse than they actually are. We assume that something is so horrible, dreadful, disastrous, or awful that we can't stand it. In exaggerating the badness of the situation, we also magnify our arousal and create a feeling of helplessness. Table 18.2 shows some examples.

What-ifs commonly signify catastrophizing ("What if this awful thing happens! What if I screw up again! What if I can't recover!"). What-ifs keep the focus on the worst possible fear, so we remain aroused, while distracting us from what we can resolutely do to maximize the possibility of a good outcome.

There are many rebuttals to this pervasive distortion:

- Ask, "How likely is this to do me in? Will the world really end?"
- Think, "It's not so bad. This is inconvenient, not a catastrophe."
- Think, "OK, let's assume the worst is really happening or will happen. What will I *do* then?" There is something calming about fully facing the worst, accepting that it could happen or is happening, and then determining what you would do to improve upon the worst. Turn a "*What if* . . . " to

**Table 18.1**
FORTUNE-TELLING

| Distortion | Replacement Thought |
|---|---|
| If I let myself feel, I'll lose control and never stop crying. I'll go crazy. | It's highly unlikely that feelings make people crazy. Tears eventually stop. Bottling feelings is more dangerous than processing them. I'll learn ways to process feelings gradually in a safe and controlled setting. |
| Talking about it will make me feel worse. | The research shows that talking about it helps most people feel better eventually. |
| If I express my anger, I'll explode. I'll become violent and beat my kids, just like Dad did to me. | I can verbalize feelings. That's different from acting on them. In fact, only a minority of adults who were abused as children abuse their own children.[3] |
| I'll never recover. I'll always be thinking of this bad stuff. | These thoughts are just the effects of trauma. They are understandable when someone has felt helpless and out of control. They are also depressing, frustrating, and unreasonable. The only evidence that I won't recover is that my present methods have not been effective to date. As I learn new skills, I'll likely start to climb the staircase to recovery. |
| If I leave the house, the trauma will occur again. | Perhaps, but maybe the trauma was a glitch, an exception to the rule. Rather than constantly worrying and expecting the worst, I'll do all I can to be prepared. |
| I'll never feel safe again. | Life is never 100 percent safe. If I take reasonable precautions, I might feel reasonably safe. |
| I'll never fit in. No one will understand me. I'll never be attractive to others. No one will love me. They'll shun me if they know what I've been through. | Some might shun me. Some might be unable or unwilling to understand. On the other hand, some might appreciate me, knowing what I have battled to overcome. |
| If I go to the party, I'll have a rotten time. | I might have a mediocre or somewhat enjoyable time. Maybe some aspects will be pleasant. I won't really know until I experiment. |

**Table 18.2**
CATASTROPHIZING

| Distortion | Replacement Thought |
| --- | --- |
| These intrusions are unbearable. | It's OK. It's just a symptom of dissociation and a cue to process when I am ready to. |
| It's awful to feel these bad feelings. | It's a sign that I can still feel. Good feelings will likely return as I heal. |
| I hate that reminder of my trauma. | Yes, this is difficult, but it is just a trigger, not a repeat of the traumatic event. |
| I can't stand it when things don't go the way I want. | I can stand it even if I don't like it. |
| This is hell all over again. | Five years from now, maybe this won't seem like such a big deal. It's OK to not get my way all the time. |

an "*If . . . then . . .* " (If such and such happens, then I'll do such and such to make the best of the situation and salvage what I can.) For example, "If I were unable to fully recover and were to lose my job, I'd grieve for a while that I couldn't do some things anymore, but not forever. I'd retool for a job I can handle and find new ways to enjoy life." Remind yourself that the negative may never happen, but if it does, you'll make the most of it. Instead of "What if this negative happens?" ask, "What if it doesn't?"

- Look calmly and fully at your symptoms. Think, "This is common to PTSD. With treatment, they'll most likely improve. I can handle it. Though frightening, arousal is just my normal stress response that hasn't turned off. This is a real opportunity to relax, process my disturbing material, and improve my health."

- Remember to focus on the here and now to redirect your focus from catastrophic, arousing thoughts. For instance, instead of focusing on a racing heart and intrusive thoughts, count backward, focus on abdominal breathing, concentrate on what people are saying or wearing, look around the room, and notice colors, sounds, smells, and other aspects of your surroundings.

- To realize that there are many coping options, ask what others have done in similar situations.

• Try humor. "Oh, no! I'm losing it. I'm going to blow up like an atomic bomb." Or, "Bad things happen in life. Tough!" Or, "Maybe I can find a certificate guaranteeing me perpetual tranquility."

## All-or-None Thinking

Here we think in extremes that create arousal and often lower self-esteem. Think of a pole-vaulter who sets the bar very high and considers himself a loser for not making it over. There is no middle ground and no partial credit in this distortion. Examples:

• Either I handled the trauma perfectly or horribly.
• I'm a hero or a heel, a success or a failure.
• If I make a mistake, I am a complete failure.
• I'm brave or I'm a coward.
• I'm completely competent or I am incompetent.
• I'm not fitting in very well since the trauma. I'm a social retard.
• I'm either a good guy or a bad guy. I performed badly during the trauma. Therefore I am bad, irresponsible, and inadequate.
• Either I am symptom-free or I am out of control—strong or an emotional wimp.

In reality, most humans operate in the middle much of the time. (Half of all brain surgeries are below average.) No one excels in all things at all times. Falling short of perfection makes you fallible, not worthless. In some situations, just surviving or performing reasonably well is quite a feat. All you can do is your best. If you are already committed to your best, then worrying or condemning yourself adds nothing to your performance. Rating your performance on a one-to-ten scale helps correct this distortion. For example, "I performed at about 80 percent today." (Notice, we rate *behavior*, not people, who are too complex to rate.) Also, redefine success as trying your best and progressing, not reaching perfection.

Extreme thinking can also be applied to others. "I must trust you 100 percent or I can't trust you at all," might lead one to trust a person who really is not worthy of trust. Or it might cause one to reject a kind and sensitive person who occasionally acts irresponsibly but is willing to improve. Trust is earned gradually. There can be many shades of gray between complete trust and complete absence of trust. Some people are somewhat trustworthy, honest in certain situations and dishonest in others—sometimes dependable and sometimes not. People are not all good or all bad, but are a combination of bad and good attributes at varying degrees of development. It takes time to build trust, and it can be earned and given in varying degrees. If we are willing to patiently walk the middle ground, we might make better judgments about people and be disappointed less often.

In addition, extreme thinking might apply to the way we view the world (life was ideal before the trauma, completely good—now it stinks). There is a tendency to forget that some aspects of life before the trauma were good and some bad. That's life . . . and this is generally true, even after a trauma. To remember this lessens upset at the parts that are not yet going well.

Another example of extreme thinking is to think that if we are not completely relaxed and calm, then we are out of control and back in emergency mode. There are many gradations in the middle, and it is OK to be there.

Finally, extreme thinking includes the view that I am either strong or I am emotional. The middle ground might be "I can be strong and have feelings. Having genuine feelings makes me human, not weak. Shedding a tear does not mean that I will become a complete basket case. The constructive expression of feelings will let me bend without breaking."

## Shoulds (Musts/Oughts)

These are rigid demands that we make of ourselves or the world. These demands insist that the world be somehow different than it is. The unspoken assumption is that the consequences are dire if the demand is not met. It is clear how this distortion keeps arousal high. Examples:

- "I should have handled the traumatic event differently. I should have acted better."
- "It's not fair. It should not have happened to me. Only good things should happen."
- "I shouldn't be feeling so distressed. John Wayne never felt this way."
- "I must be strong."
- "I must have control over my life. Now. I must no longer make mistakes since mistakes caused me pain in the past."
- "I should be over this by now."
- "People should understand what I'm going through." "I shouldn't be afraid, tired, imperfect, etc." "I must be absolutely sure that nothing can go wrong before I risk it. Life ought to be predictable."
- "I must not allow my kids to mess up—ever."

A powerful antidote for a should is a *would* or *could*. Woulds and coulds preserve ideals but in a gentler, more flexible way that accepts the world as it is. For example:

- "It would be nice to be less distressed during a crisis and perform more coolly. I wonder how I could do this."
- "It would be nice to be recovered by now, but everyone's timetable is different, and forcing things will just make me more stressed. In the meantime, I wonder what I could be trying."
- "It would be nice if things were better. But I accept that

   People will always be fallible, never perfect.

   Life will always be unfair, and things will happen that we don't always deserve.

   No one can ever achieve total control of events. I won't make myself crazy by insisting that things be perfect. I'll just aim to do a very good job and expect I'll probably improve with experience."

Also, ask, "Why should I? Where is this *should* written?" For example, is it written somewhere that humans should not be frightened when confronted with an overwhelming event for the first time? Or the hundredth time?

A final antidote is to see what happens when you don't do the thing you think you must and realize that the world does not end (e.g., "If I allow myself to be vulnerable, I might learn that people like me better." "If I allow my children to make some mistakes, they might learn some valuable lessons. This is not a combat zone, after all.").

## Making Feelings Facts

This is thinking that your feelings represent reality. For example:

- "I feel so anxious all the time—I must be in danger; I must not be as capable as others; something bad must be about to happen."
- "Because I feel so anxious, there must be a real and present danger. If not, I'm going crazy."

Remember that feelings result from thoughts. During traumatic events, it is easy to formulate inaccurate ideas that don't get challenged. So question your feel-

**Table 18.3**
MAKING FEELINGS FACTS

| Distortion | Replacement Thought |
|---|---|
| "I feel so diminished by the trauma, so unworthy, so bad. I must be bad." | Separate the trauma from the resulting feelings of worth. It's the trauma that's bad. Not you. If someone did something offensive to you, you might think, "Something bad happened to me." If your behavior fell short of your ideal, you might think, "I made a mistake. That makes me fallible and human, not worthless." |
| "I feel so dirty." | When people are abused, it is natural to feel that way. Again, separate the event from your worth. |
| "I feel hopeless." | Are you hopeless, or just in a situation that feels hopeless? |
| "I feel crazy. I must be crazy." | "This feeling is the result of defending against unpleasant feelings. This doesn't make me crazy. As I learn to gradually process those feelings, I'll start to feel better." |
| "I feel so totally out of control and powerless." | "I was out of control and powerless then. That was then. This is now." |
| "I feel so numb—like I'm incapable of feeling." | "I feel numb now. But feelings will grow gradually as the wounds begin to heal." |

ings now. Ask, "Is this reality, or just a feeling?" Some common distortions and their antidotes appear in Table 18.3.

## Overgeneralizing

To overgeneralize is to decide that your negative experience applies to all situations. For example:

- "People always let you down."
- "All men want only one thing."
- "Everything in life is so unfair."
- "All new or strange situations are dangerous, especially those that are like situations that frightened me in the past."

- "All authority figures are fearful."
- "I can't do anything right. I never do things right. I always let people down."
- "Nobody has confidence in me."
- "My whole life stinks."
- "Since I was helpless and out of control then, I am that way in all situations."
- "Things always go wrong. It never fails."

Words like *always, never, everyone, nobody, all,* or *none* indicate overgeneralizations. The opposite to these words is *some* ("*Sometimes* I do pretty well; *Some* authority figures are safe; *Some* new situations can be exciting and fun.") Ask yourself if a negative event could be an exception to the rule. Maybe the world isn't always like this.[4]

Some people overgeneralize in the positive direction ("All the world is good and safe." "Good people always make good decisions."). When a traumatic event occurs, they cannot reconcile the traumatic memory with this thought. Again, the word *some* helps. For example, Joan was raised in a very close family with a very loving father. She assumed that all men are trustworthy. She could not get over it when her boyfriend raped her. She learned to view reality on a continuum. Between the extremes of *men are totally trustworthy* and *men are untrustworthy,* she viewed a new middle ground: *some men are mostly trustworthy and some are mostly untrustworthy.* She learned to accept responsibility to evaluate each individual separately.

## Abusive Labeling

Here you give yourself a label, or name, as though a single word could describe a complex person completely. For example, to say, "I am a loser," means that I am *always* and *in every way* a loser. Obviously, this isn't fair or true. Children often internalize spoken or unspoken messages. For example, a child who is repeatedly molested comes to think of herself as just a sex object, a whore—even in adulthood. The antidote is to rate behavior or experience—but not people. Thus, think, "That was a really difficult experience for me," not, "I'm bad."

Table 18.4 shows some other examples of thought distortions and rebuttals related to trauma.

Notice that labels can be levied at other people as well, which is common in anger reactions. To reduce another human being to an "always and in every

**Table 18.4**
ABUSIVE LABELING

| Distortion | Antidote |
| --- | --- |
| I'm damaged goods—worthless. | I was raped. I am more than my wound. |
| I'm a coward. | I was frightened and unsure of what to do. I made some bad choices. |
| I'm a slut for climaxing when my stepfather molested me. | Orgasm is an automatic physiologic response to direct stimulation. It means that I am a normally functioning woman. |

way" label is just as inaccurate and unfair as doing it to yourself, even if it feels justified.

## Personalizing

This is seeing yourself as more responsible or involved with a given situation than you really are. See Table 18.5 for examples.

The antidote to this distortion is to see things accurately. Separate influences from causes. Figure out how much responsibility truly is yours, and keep what is beyond your control outside of your boundaries.

## Blaming

Blaming is the opposite of personalizing. Whereas personalizing puts all the responsibility on yourself for your difficulties, blaming puts it all on something outside of yourself. For example:

- "He treated me so miserably. He has ruined my life and my self-esteem."
- "I'm stressed-out today because of _____ (my crummy childhood, Iraq, the doctor's incompetence, etc.)."
- "Dogs make me so afraid."

The problem with blaming, much like catastrophizing, is that it tends to make us think of ourselves as helpless victims who are too feeble to cope. Blaming keeps us stuck in the past problem; we are powerless because the past is unchangeable. The antidote to blaming is to acknowledge outside influences but to take responsibility for your own welfare. "OK, I see how these things have influenced my development and challenge me. Now, I commit to get back on track and move on."

**Table 18.5**
PERSONALIZING

| Distortion | Antidote |
|---|---|
| It's all my fault that I was raped. I must have asked for it because of the way I dressed. I deserved it. | This is a faulty way to try to make sense of a crime. Rape is a crime. No one deserves a crime. Dressing attractively is not the same as asking for a crime. The cause was the perpetrator, not me. I'm not responsible for a crime, only my recovery. |
| There must be something about me that invited the battering, or caused my husband to do it. | Battering is a crime. Perhaps I could learn some social skills, but lack of skills does not justify being bullied or brutalized. Crimes happen for reasons outside of my influence. |
| A firefighter is asked about a fire caused by an arsonist and he replies, "We lost twenty people." | I didn't lose twenty people. They were murdered by an arsonist. |
| Why did this happen to me? Why was I singled out? | The world is not for or against us. Both bad and good things happen to people. |
| That driver is out for me. | That driver doesn't even know me. I am not the central figure in his bad day or life. Maybe he hates the world, not me. Maybe he is neutral to me or completely oblivious to me. |
| In an argument, a husband tells his wife, "You are either for me or against me." | People will inevitably disagree about issues. That doesn't mean she is against me, just my idea. |
| If I worry enough, I can keep bad things from happening. | This is trying to be responsible for too much. I accept that I cannot have total control. All I can have is responsibility for what I can control. Instead of worrying and staying aroused, I will make a good action plan, do my best, then release worry. |

For present stressors, we might think, "Nothing makes me do anything—I now choose how I respond."

## Unfavorable Comparisons

Here you magnify another's strengths and your weaknesses while minimizing the other's faults and your strengths. So by comparison, you feel inadequate or inferior. For example, you think, "Brian is a bright surgeon. He makes so much money. He was even on the news the other night for treating the governor. Me, I'm just a nurse. I could never get up in front of a camera and talk like he does. Sure, I have wonderful friends, and I'm active at the homeless shelter. And it's true that Brian's got a drinking problem and his kids are really struggling. And yeah, he told me he really depends on me in the operating room. But look at what he does!" On a rescue team, Marty is constantly comparing himself to the sharpest, bravest individual. Sometimes he compares himself to movie stars, like Chuck Norris, who never seem to show fear or make mistakes in their scripted settings. A way to challenge this distortion is to ask, "Why must I compare? Why can't I just appreciate that each person has unique strengths and weaknesses? Another's contributions are not necessarily better, just different." Someone humorously noted that doctors have more status than garbage collectors, but one wonders who does more for public health. We generally function better and with less stress when we focus on doing our personal best, not drawing comparisons.

## Regrets

In looking back, we think, "If only I hadn't . . . (performed so poorly, been so anxious, said what I did)." Beyond a period of introspection where mistakes are acknowledged and courses are corrected, regrets are unproductive because we can't go back and change the past. Regrets are another way to reject our imperfections. We might beat ourselves up, thinking, "I deserve to be punished for that." What we actually deserve is the opportunity to try again, improve, and learn from the mistakes. We can think, "I've learned from mistakes in the past and I can do so again. That was then and this is now."

George Everly and Jeffrey Mitchell[5] advise the following for dealing with regret regarding difficult experiences from the past:

- A mistake isn't usually a deliberate act. Ask, "What did I want/intend to happen?"
- If it was an honest mistake, think, "This could have happened to many people."

- Ask, "What did I learn that could prevent this from happening again?" Focus on remedial action.
- How much was I actually responsible for? Were there factors beyond my control?
- What good things are a result of this outcome? What is the possible silver lining?
- Will there be more chances to learn better approaches, new skills, ways to grow?

*Note:* Turn questions to statements when you analyze your self-talk. For example, asking, "Why can't I get over this?" keeps us aroused and provides no resolution. Changed to the statement "I can't get over this," the fortune-telling error becomes obvious. We can then change this to "I'll probably learn how to come to terms with this."

"Why" questions are intellectual. The intellectual response is straightforward: "I am suffering because I haven't learned how not to yet." However, the real issue is the emotional frustration. It is better to state directly, "I am feeling so frustrated with this pain." Then take steps to soothe yourself as you learn additional skills.

## THE DAILY THOUGHT RECORD

Now that you know about distortions, the next step is to use them to help you. When stressed or anxious, thoughts and feelings can swirl in our minds and seem overwhelming. Putting them down on paper helps us to sort it all out and see things more clearly. The daily thought record in Figure 18.1 takes about fifteen minutes each day. It is good to do it right after you notice yourself feeling upset. Or it can be done an hour or two before you go to bed. Here's how it works.

### Step 1: The Facts
At the top of the daily thought record, briefly describe an upsetting event from the past, present, or future and the resulting feelings (such as sad, anxious, guilty, or frustrated). Rate the intensity of these feelings (10 means extremely unpleasant). Remember, getting in touch with disturbing feelings is a way to stop them from controlling us.

### Step 2: Analysis of Your Thoughts
In the first column of the "Analysis of Your Thoughts" section, list your automatic thoughts. Then rate how much you believe each. Ten means it's completely

**Figure 18.1**
DAILY THOUGHT RECORD

DATE: _____

## THE FACTS

| Event | Impact of Event | Intensity |
|---|---|---|
| (Describe the event that "made you" feel bad/unpleasant.) | (Describe the emotions you felt.) | (Rate the intensity of these emotions from 1 to 10.) |
| | | |

## ANALYSIS OF YOUR THOUGHTS

| Initial Responses | | Thought Fallacies | Reasonable Responses | |
|---|---|---|---|---|
| (Describe the automatic thoughts or self-talk. Then rate how believable each is from 1 to 10.) | | (Find and label the distortions.) | (Talk back! Change the distortions to more reasonable thoughts. Rate how much you believe each from 1 to 10.) | |
| | Ratings | | | Ratings |
| | | | | |

## RESULTS

Based upon your thought analysis, rate again how much you believe your initial responses. Then rate the intensity of your emotions again.

believable. In the second column, identify the distortions (remember that some automatic thoughts might be reasonable). In the third column, try to respond, or talk back, to each distorted automatic thought. Realize that your first automatic thought is only one of several possible choices. Try to imagine what you would say to a friend who said what you did, or try to imagine yourself on a good day saying something more reasonable. Ask yourself, "What is the evidence for the reasonable response?" Then rate how much you believe each response.

## Step 3: Results
After all this, go back to the "Initial Responses" column and rate your automatic thoughts again. Then at the top, in the "Facts" section, rate the intensity of your emotions about the event again. Even a slight drop in your upset feelings is significant. With this process, upsetting events will still probably be upsetting, though not as disturbing.

Remember, work out your thoughts on paper. It is too complex to do it in your head. Be patient with yourself as you learn how to do this. It usually takes a few weeks to become good at this skill.

So each day for two weeks, select an upsetting event and do a daily thought record. (Figure 18.1 may be photocopied for this purpose.) You might consider working on symptoms, triggers, feared situations, or past events. Then proceed to the next section in this chapter, entitled "Getting to the Most Distressing Ideas."

Figure 18.2 is an example of a simplified daily thought record. Mark asked his sixteen-year-old son as he was leaving if he had mowed the grass yet. The son responded, "Sometimes I feel like a slave around here—I'll do it tomorrow," as he slammed the door. Mark smashed the banister. When asked why, he could not really explain his reaction. His therapist helped him to slow down the action and put his thoughts on paper. By way of background, Mark grew up in a family with a violent, alcoholic father. The father was sometimes kind when he was sober. Once he stood up to his father in an attempt to protect his mother. He was brutally beaten. A teacher noticed Mark's bruises and reported the situation. Eventually, the children were placed in a foster home. Mark later joined the Army and tried conscientiously to raise a good family. Here is what the daily thought record looked like.

**Figure 18.2**
EXAMPLE OF DAILY THOUGHT RECORD

DATE: _____June 10_____

| Event | Impact of Event | Intensity |
|---|---|---|
| My son was disrespectful as he left the house. | Angry<br>Powerless | 9 ⟶ 6<br>8 ⟶ 5 |

### ANALYSIS

| Automatic Thought | Distortion | Reasonable Response |
|---|---|---|
| He shouldn't be rude.<br>7 ⟶ 5 | Should | It would be good if he were more civil, but we're both still learning. It's not the end of the world. We'll probably figure out a way to reach an agreement.     9 |
| He should know better than to leave before doing his chores.<br>9 ⟶ 6 | Should | It is silly to expect him to always follow my example. His response makes sense to him. Most teenagers prefer being with their friends to doing chores. If he really thought that doing chores makes one wildly happy and successful, he'd do his chores willingly.     8 |
| This disobedience is awful.  9 ⟶ 4 | Catastrophizing | This is inconvenient, but pretty normal for teenagers. This is not combat. Lives won't be lost. There's time to calmly figure out a solution.     6 |
| He'll get fired from his job.  8 ⟶ 6 | Fortune-Telling | Maybe he won't.     8 |
| People will think I'm a poor dad.  10 ⟶ 5 | Mind Reading | Maybe I won't be named Father of the Year. But maybe people will just consider him an average teenager.     7 |

## GETTING TO THE MOST DISTRESSING IDEAS: THE QUESTION-AND-ANSWER TECHNIQUE[6]

So far you have learned to use the daily thought record to identify and replace distorted automatic thoughts. While replacing distorted automatic thoughts can reduce distressing symptoms, uprooting *core beliefs* provides an even greater benefit. Core beliefs are deeply held beliefs that lead to many present distortions.

Because they are usually learned early in life, they are rarely challenged. We discover core beliefs by starting with an automatic thought and using the question-and-answer technique. In this approach, you take an automatic thought and keep asking the following questions until you reach the core belief:

> Assuming the automatic thought is true:  What does that mean to me (or say about me)?
> Why is that so bad?

For example, on his daily thought record, Mark expressed feelings of anger and loss of control because of his son's disrespect. He decided to apply the question-and-answer technique to the automatic thought "He shouldn't be rude." It went like this:

He shouldn't be rude.

**Question:** What does that mean to me?
**Answer:** He'll get fired!

**Question:** And what else?
**Answer:** He'll repeat my mistakes and be like me.

**Question:** What does that mean?
**Answer:** If I hadn't provoked my father, my family would still be together.

**Question:** Assuming that's true, why is that so bad? What does that mean?
**Answer:** I did something pretty shameful.

**Question:** And what does that mean?
**Answer:** I was a bad son.

**Question:** And what does that say about me?
**Answer:** I'm a bad person.
        ( = CORE BELIEF!)

In reaching this core belief, we did not pause to challenge the ideas. Now let's go back and look for distortions along the way, responding reasonably at each step. Table 18.6 shows what the whole process looks like, using the three columns

**Table 18.6**
**THE QUESTION-AND-ANSWER TECHNIQUE**

| Initial Response (Automatic Thought) | Distortion | Reasonable Response |
|---|---|---|
| He'll get fired. | Fortune-Telling | Most of the time he's quite responsible. |
| Q | | |
| He'll repeat my mistakes and be just like me. | Fortune-Telling Catastrophizing | Maybe he won't. If he does, that will be too bad, not a catastrophe. |
| Q | | |
| If I hadn't provoked my father, my family would still be together. | Fortune-Telling Personalizing | I don't know that. My dad had a history that went well beyond one incident. |
| Q | | |
| I feel so ashamed for what I did. | Making Feelings Fact | What I did was to try to protect my mother. This is not a shameful act. |
| Q | | |
| I was a bad son. | Label | I was trying my best. |
| Q | | |
| I'm a bad person. (Core Belief) | Label | I am a fallible, yet worthwhile person. |

of the daily thought record. The Qs represent questions, which need not be written down.

## SOME COMMON CORE BELIEFS

Table 18.7 shows a number of core beliefs common to PTSD and their more reasonable alternatives. As a drill, cover up the alternatives and see how you would talk back to each of the core beliefs. There are no perfect or "right" answers. What matters is that the response works for you.

For a week, use the question-and-answer technique once a day to find your core beliefs. Use previously completed daily thought records or a newly completed thought record.

**Table 18.7**
COMMON POST-TRAUMA CORE BELIEFS

| Core Belief | Possible Alternative |
| --- | --- |
| I am weak. | I am a combination of weaknesses and strengths. I am strengthening the weaker areas. |
| My weaknesses/flaws will be exposed— how horrible! | Everyone is fallible; each person has flaws. To have them exposed makes me human. That's not awful, just life. Actually, some flaws are endearing. |
| My worth equals my behavior during a traumatic event. | My worth as a unique individual is far too complex to reduce to isolated performances. Mistakes reflect our skill level or development at the time. A mistake does not totally and irrevocably define a person. |
| I am no good since the trauma. | My life does not equal my trauma. |
| If I am not respected by others, I have no value; I cease to exist. | Nobody's opinion determines my worth. |
| To lose control is awful. | Loss of control is inevitable. Many things in life are beyond my control. Sometimes all I can control is the way I look at the loss of control. Paradoxically, to accept loss of control helps me control my stress. I *can* endure loss of control. |
| I shouldn't need to work at recovery. I shouldn't need help. I should be able to cope like normal people. | I really should be just as I am, given my present skill level and sensitized nerves. No one is entirely self-sufficient. It's OK to seek skilled help. |
| If I don't worry, it will more than likely happen. | Since most bad things don't happen, I'm just reinforcing this belief. Instead of worrying, I'll make a good plan, take reasonable precautions, and remain cautious but relaxed. |
| If I obtain perfection, nothing fearful will happen. | Perfection is not possible. Trying to attain it will just keep me frustrated and aroused. I can commit to doing a very good, steady job. |
| Bad things won't happen if I am good enough and careful enough. | Rain falls on the good, the bad, and the in-between. Some things happen randomly and are not indicative of divine disfavor. The best we can do is to be prepared. |
| I must always prepare for the worst. | Certain precautionary measures might lessen the likelihood of some negative outcomes. Constant worry doesn't. I'd rather take reasonable, intelligent, thorough precautions, and then release the worries. |

*(continued)*

**Table 18.7** *(continued)*
COMMON POST-TRAUMA CORE BELIEFS

| Core Belief | Possible Alternative |
| --- | --- |
| I can only function if I have a strong individual to depend on. I must lean on a strong individual because I am so helpless. | Nonsense. While everyone needs to rely on others at times, I can learn to be self-sufficient, or at least as self-sufficient as most others. |
| I should judge and punish myself for my shortcomings and failings. | I can greet myself cordially and with encouragement—this is a better way to grow and develop. I'll leave the judgment to others. |
| My past failures mean I'm incapable and out of control. | Mistakes mean I am human and fallible—just like everyone else. I have every right to try again, to grow from the level where I am. |

# CHAPTER 19

# *Confiding Concealed Wounds*

**Give sorrow words: The grief that does not speak**
**whispers the o'erfraught heart, and bids it break.**
**—*Shakespeare*, Macbeth[1]**

Traumatic wounds are complex. For some, the damage is quite obvious. Sometimes it is not apparent on the surface. Sometimes we anticipate the trauma's recurrence or worry about the consequences of the event. Sometimes it is just the memory that keeps us aroused after the actual threat has passed. All these aspects need to be processed so that traumatic material can be filed away like other memories.

Those who bounce back quickly, "rolling with the punches," seem to figure out a way to process the experience, bringing it to closure so that it no longer matters. Many, however, remain troubled by past events. Concern for this latter group led a psychologist at the University of Texas at Austin, Dr. James W. Pennebaker, toward an extraordinary line of research.

Pennebaker initially asked students to write their deepest thoughts *and feelings* about events from the past that they would not even share with their close friends. They wrote fifteen minutes a day for four days while a control group of students wrote about neutral subjects such as what their living rooms looked like where they grew up. The results were surprising.

---

This chapter summarizes the work of Pennebaker, Dr. James W. 1997. *Opening Up: The Healing Power of Expressing Emotion.* New York: Guilford Press. Copyright © 1997 James W. Pennebaker. Instructions for confiding in writing, cautions, and summary of supporting research are adapted with permission.

First, Pennebaker was surprised about the range of traumas that had been experienced by a seemingly normal group of college students. These are some of the traumas that they related:

- A ten-year-old girl failed to clean up her room when asked in preparation for her grandmother's visit. The grandmother slipped on a toy, broke her hip, and died.
- A boy taught his sister how to sail. The sister drowned on her first solo outing.
- A father announced to a nine-year-old boy that he was leaving his mother and that the problems in the marriage were caused by the birth of the children.
- A drunken father beat the mother, then the child.
- Rape, molestation, and sexual abuse by relatives were not uncommon. Suicide attempts were also reported.

Among those who confided their feelings in writing, as expected, there was a short slip in mood during the days of the study. Some cried as they wrote or dreamed about the past events. However, after the study, those who confided were significantly happier and less anxious than the controls, who did not confide. They often reported that they understood their experience better after writing; it no longer hurt to think about it. The writers also showed stronger immune system functioning immediately after the experiments and became ill less often over the ensuing months than the controls. The greatest improvements were observed in those who had wanted to confide, but never had before the study.

Surveying working adults, it was found that traumas from childhood are the least likely to be confided. Those who had experienced childhood traumas were more likely to be ill as adults, especially if they had not confided the experiences. Among survivors of the death of a spouse, those who had talked about the death felt better afterward and ruminated less than those who had not. The more they spoke, the better they felt.

Pennebaker repeated his research with subjects among various populations. He found, for example, that persons fired from their jobs were more likely to be rehired if they wrote about their feelings surrounding their job loss. Apparently, expressing the feelings of frustration, humiliation, and shame helped people to rebound quicker compared to those who just "pressed on." Similar findings were observed among Holocaust survivors: low disclosers were found to be the least healthy.

Pennebaker concluded that confiding is healthy. It can help people to confront, understand, and organize traumas.[2] If you have lost a loved one, broken up, moved, or had some past trauma, find a quiet place and write continually for four to five days about the trauma. Confronting the trauma often quells its devastating effects. If not, seek professional help. A therapist can help you pace and maintain safety as you process trauma-related memories.

## TRAUMA AND AVOIDANCE

It appears that suppressing powerful emotions requires such effort that it takes a devastating toll on health. Following a trauma, such as sexual trauma or the suicide of a spouse, people might find ways to avoid the topic by

- Staying occupied with trivial distractions such as work, cleaning, or exercise.
- Avoiding people who might broach the subject.
- Being with people but saying, "I'm not upset by that." Or, "I was upset, but I'm not anymore."
- Not crying as a way to block out the pain.
- Ruminating, worrying, or mentally rehearsing the event. This is done, however, without feelings or tears. Thus, it is a way to avoid the emotional pain of the trauma.

Pennebaker identified what he called "low disclosers," people who inhibited their emotions. These people wrote about superficial topics or were less emotional and self-reflective, showing less emotional awareness. Some in this group were rigid, chronic, high-level worriers. These people used the *mental* process of worry as a way to avoid contact with their *feelings*. Consistent with other research on repression, the low disclosers were the least healthy.

We might ask why, then, one would choose to inhibit emotions? There are several possibilities.

1. **Concern with image.** One may believe that he'll be perceived as weak or incapable if he is troubled by events (e.g., a policeman or soldier after witnessing a shooting death). Or, he might be ashamed or embarrassed by the trauma (e.g., a transgression or abuse).

2. **One might be too involved with coping with present demands to allow feelings to arise.** This may become a habit.

3. **One might have been punished for or discouraged from expressing feelings in the past.** Perhaps a child was beaten for crying or told, "Be strong for the younger children."

4. **One might have learned that feelings are futile.** For example, a child finds that feelings are ignored by her distant, distracted parents.

5. **Society might not encourage grief related to certain traumas.** Many modern cultures do not acknowledge grief for miscarriage or provide a way to mourn. People may be reluctant to talk to those whose family member has committed suicide or been imprisoned.

6. **One might fear being overwhelmed by feelings.** Paradoxically, allowing oneself to be "overwhelmed" by feelings and realizing that the world doesn't end is usually an extraordinarily effective way to liberate oneself from this fear.

7. **One might simply have never learned to express feelings.** Perhaps a person's parents were both emotionally numb from their own traumas.

Pennebaker observed that intrusive thoughts commonly surface after a trauma or when reminded of traumas. The more people ruminated on them or tried to suppress them, the larger and more threatening they became. The intrusive thoughts included thoughts about sex or sexual trauma, aggression (e.g., hurting a baby), illness, death, failure, relationship problems, dirt and contamination, and food.

## RESILIENT COPING

Those who cope well with trauma seem to have at least two factors in common:

1. An outlet for their feelings.
2. A way of viewing the trauma that brings it to closure, so that they can view the event and think, "It no longer matters." Notice the striking parallel here with Dr. Weekes's counsel to face and accept anxious symptoms until they no longer matter.

Psychologist Mardi Horowitz has described three stages for the resolution of trauma-related grief: (1) denial; (2) working through; and (3) completion. Typically, people good at coping with trauma feel they can communicate about the trauma in some form. They can confide to a spouse, friend, or diary. Some use prayer or religious confession. This overcomes denial and facilitates completion of the second and third stages described by Horowitz.

Disclosing with emotional awareness and expression leads to the many benefits already mentioned. Pennebaker cites several theoretical reasons why communicating feelings, especially in writing, is so useful.

1. **Language unifies and completes our conscious experience.** Kurt Lewin and Bluma Zeigarnik[3] explained that we remember interrupted tasks until they are completed. Once resolved, we cease thinking about them. That is, understanding, seeing clearly, sorting out, or organizing our thoughts settles issues. It appears that different aspects of a memory are stored in different parts of the brain. Language appears to unify the diverse elements of experience. Writing increases our focus and understanding. As teachers often discover, they know that they understand something once they can teach it. Putting a complex issue into words helps us organize it, understand it, and then remember it with less stress. For example, once we organize complex material, the mind remembers it with less work. It relaxes and stops rehearsing the material. This is the principle behind a "to do" list. Once we have done the work of sorting out what needs to be done and put it on paper in a clear, meaningful way, the mind relaxes without swirling confusion. So writing helps bring order, detachment, and meaning.

2. **Because writing is slower than talking, it promotes more detailed thought.** A pattern emerges. The goal is flexible engagement. That is, we willingly face the pain as needful. We face the worst and see it clearly, without fear. Sometimes we see a way to improve upon the worst. Sometimes we see a new way to interpret the event. Sometimes we simply accept life with more peace and understanding.[4] We look until it no longer matters. *Then* we can turn our attention from the trauma and focus on other aspects of life.

## SHOULD I TRY CONFIDING IN WRITING?

If you are still anxious or depressed by a past event, writing could help. If you still think about it or spend significant energy trying to avoid thinking about it, you will likely find this strategy helpful. It may be difficult and stressful at first until you get used to disclosing. Once the gates finally open, it usually becomes easier. The instructions for this strategy follow.

### Confiding in Writing Exercise

1. **Find a place where you won't be interrupted for fifteen to thirty minutes.** A neutral place (a table placed in the corner of the room) works well.

2. **Write continuously for fifteen to thirty minutes on four or five consecutive days.** Pennebaker's original instructions to the study subjects follow:

> I want you to write continuously about the most upsetting or traumatic experience of your entire life. Don't worry about grammar, spelling, or sentence structure. In your writing, I want you to discuss your deepest thoughts *and feelings* [italics added] about the experience. You can write about anything you want. But whatever you choose, it should be something that has affected you very deeply. Ideally, it should be about something you have not talked about with others in detail. It is critical, however, that you let yourself go and touch those deepest emotions and thoughts that you have. In other words, write about what happened and how you felt about it, and how you feel about it now.[5] Finally, you can write on different traumas during each session or the same one over the entire [period]. Your choice of trauma for each session is entirely up to you. [Remember to write continuously. If you run out of words, repeat yourself.]

3. **It isn't necessary to write about the most traumatic event of your life.** Remember to pace your healing. If a topic makes you overly distraught, ease up. Approach it gradually or try a different topic.

4. **Especially write about topics that you dwell on and/or you would like to talk about but are embarrassed.** Write mostly about your feelings. Avoid wishful thinking (e.g., I wish he weren't dead; I'd like to get even), which is a way to avoid the underlying feelings. Instead, focus on your feelings and what they mean.

5. **Write just for yourself.** If you worry about someone reading it, you may not write what you honestly feel.

6. **Expect sadness immediately afterward.** This usually dissipates within an hour or, rarely, within a day or two. Most people then feel relief/contentment for up to six months afterward.

7. **Balance writing with action.** Don't let writing be a method of avoidance.

8. **Use any comfortable medium.** Talking into a recorder, writing, and speaking to a therapist are similarly effective.[6] (Talking to a therapist was found to elevate the mood somewhat quicker over the four-day period and is recommended for difficult problems. Other media can be used for home assign-

ments.) Art can be a useful medium if verbal expression is used to interpret the art and the feelings it conveys.

9. **You can try this before bed if insomnia is associated with intrusive memories at bedtime.** This is a useful way to accept the worries, rather than fight them, and then clean out the mind. (Some with severe PTSD must stop writing several hours before bed or they'll feel worse. You might also find it useful to set a timer to help pace yourself. Monitor your feelings and stop writing if you become too uncomfortable.)

### Cautions

1. This is not a substitute for therapy for intractable problems.
2. This is not a substitute for remedial action. For example, you'll probably still need to tell others if they hurt your feelings and you want them to stop. Don't merely complain, which is a way to keep things the same and avoid action.
3. Confiding to friends might change the relationship if they are threatened by the content; they become burned out themselves by listening; the listener feels a need to confide what you have told him or her to unburden; your motive is to hurt the listener. If any of these are a concern, try writing or talking to a counselor.
4. Look ahead after discharging and analyzing your traumas. Don't stay in a wallowing stage.

### ISN'T IT BETTER TO LEAVE THE PAST ALONE?

Perhaps. If the past no longer troubles you and feels completed, then revisiting the past might not help. However, if the past is truly settled, revisiting it does not usually hurt and may often lead to even greater insights and resolution.[7] Most people feel that confronting traumatic material is the hardest but most helpful part of treatment. As a rule, if you can express and reframe it, you'll replay it less.

If you feel that your life is now extremely chaotic, you might wish to regain some control first. See Chapter 7 for information on how to stabilize your life and find some balance before confronting traumatic memories.

### HELP FOR CONFIDING IN WRITING

Some people find it difficult to express feelings because they have not learned words for feelings. What people typically find is that as they express negative feelings, they become more comfortable with their emotions in general. It then becomes easier to experience and express positive feelings as well. If you feel the need for help in identifying feelings, you might again refer to the list of emotions on page 94. When writing, you might use direct statements, such as "I feel sad about . . .", "I'm so frightened"; "I'm feeling so . . ."; and "I was so scared that . . ." You might also use metaphors, such as "I feel like the weight of the world is on my shoulders"; "I feel like the roof is caving in on me, and that makes me feel . . ."; "I felt like a used shoe"; "I felt torn up inside"; and "I feel like my life is out of control, like a runaway train."

Bruno Bettelheim wrote, "What cannot be talked about can also not be put to rest; and if it is not, the wounds continue to fester from generation to generation."[8] Thus, we might view confiding as an opportunity to stop transgenerational wounding.

Beverly James likens unresolved trauma material to carrying around a bag of smelly garbage throughout life. Instead of carrying it around, she suggests briefly identifying traumatic events on separate pieces of paper and placing these papers in a plastic trash bag, which is left at the therapist's office. At each session, a piece of paper is taken out for processing. In this way, trauma material is contained and processed in small, manageable steps.[9]

Aphrodite Matsakis[10] advises recording as many details as possible before, during, and after the event, including what others were thinking or what you thought they were thinking, regarding your experience. To make material less threatening, she advises imagining that you are watching the event through a one-way mirror or imagining that the trauma is happening to someone else, not you. Prompts, such as photos of yourself before, during, or after might help recall, as might a visit to the scene of the event (if that is not too upsetting).

Memory work with your therapist should not be done until you have developed a trusted therapeutic alliance. Your therapist will be like a traveling companion as you view old sights, someone who will help you surround the memories this time with respect and calmness. Use enough emotion to evoke the memories,[11] but not so much that you overwhelm feelings of mastery and control.

Cognitive processing therapy (CPT) is used successfully in group and individual settings to treat survivors of rape, combat, and other traumas. It combines writing about the trauma with cognitive restructuring. CPT might be helpful for those who wish to have more structure and support in applying the skills in Chapter 18 and this chapter.[12]

## FINAL THOUGHTS ON CONFIDING

Timmon Cermak and Stephanie Brown have observed that "No pain is so devastating as the pain a person refuses to face and no suffering is so lasting as suffering left unacknowledged."[13] In support, Bessel van der Kolk and Jose Saporta have stated that "numerous studies for the past one hundred years have established a causal relation between the inhibition of expression of traumatic experience and psychophysiological impairment. These studies have demonstrated a marked increase in symptoms of the respiratory, digestive, cardiovascular, and endocrine systems in people with PTSD."[14] It appears, then, that confiding past wounds is an important skill to cultivate. Remember, however, not to rush. Slower is faster.

# CHAPTER 20

# Resolving Guilt

---

**It is a human prerogative to become guilty and it
is a human responsibility to overcome guilt.**

—V. Frankl, *concentration camp survivor*

Your progress in treatment will be blocked by unresolved guilt. So it is fitting that
we turn our attention now to its resolution.

Guilt is an unpleasant feeling. As with other feelings, it arises from our
thoughts. In guilt, we feel responsible for what happened. Our conclusion is that
our role in the event resulted in the negative outcome. Guilt is not, as some assert,
a useless emotion. Guilt affirms morality. We would be concerned, for example,
about a drunk driver who felt no remorse for injuring someone. We would hesitate
to form a relationship or enter into business with someone who has no conscience.
Guilt is a motivator for change. If we hurt someone we care about, guilt helps us
to improve our behavior. Guilt is an ally when it leads directly to a satisfactory
resolution. We see clearly what did happen so that we can identify needed adjustments, make those adjustments, and then put the guilt to rest. Unresolved guilt,
however, keeps memories emotionally charged and in active memory.

To integrate memories, we must recall the memory fragments in sufficient
detail to put them back together again, and then emotionally defuse the whole
memory so that it can be stored in long-term memory. To begin this process, let's
consider how we might be experiencing guilt.

## WHAT DO WE FEEL GUILTY ABOUT?

What we do, think, or feel. Examples are:

- Drinking too much
- Feeling afraid
- Going along with the demands of the perpetrator (rapist, terrorist, batterer, abusive parent, robber)
- Feeling relief for surviving when others did not
- Causing the offender to commit the crime (e.g., by making oneself attractive, wanting attention)
- Saving myself but not others, abandoning others
- Killing (as in combat), which violates cherished values
- Resistance fighting that leads to the enemy's retaliatory killing of civilians
- Errors in judgment (e.g., permitting a teenager to travel with an irresponsible driver)
- Identifying with the victimizer (seeing good points, trying to win favor or privileges, becoming a participant in the offense)
- Wanting to die and be released from pain
- Living a life that we think is so imperfect as to warrant traumatic events
- Feeling ambivalent about those who died
- Carelessness, thoughtlessness
- An innocent mistake or accident
- Hating the perpetrator, wanting to harm him
- Enjoying aspects of sexual abuse
- Acting unkindly to someone who was later injured or killed
- Trusting someone's judgment or decisions, which later resulted in harm to people

What we fail to do, think, or feel. Examples include:

- Failing to save or protect others (parent doesn't stop kidnapping, firefighter does not save burn victims)
- Failing to take suitable precautions
- Freezing and doing nothing, didn't fight harder
- Failing to leave a relationship with a batterer who severely injures a child
- Failing to stop chronic abuse

- Wishing that you could have done more
- Failing to live up to your ideal or normal expectations
- Failing to control symptoms or recover
- Failing to say "I love you" or tell the deceased how much you valued them
- Not having a proper way to say good-bye to someone who has died
- Not pressing charges or reporting a crime to the police
- Not feeling sympathetic to others' suffering

Unreasonable accusations that we internalize ("I feel guilty, so I must be."):

- Police don't believe your story and imply you are making it up or asked for it
- The lawyer defending the perpetrator attacks your character
- People think that the crime against you was your fault

## STAGES OF RESOLUTION

The successful resolution of guilt follows a course similar to other intense feelings common to PTSD:

1. **Denial.** Because guilt is so uncomfortable, we may deny responsibility at first. We may be shocked and numb.
2. **Processing.** In time, we accurately assess the harm done and legitimately assess our responsibility. We learn our lessons and neutralize emotions by clarifying faulty thinking.
3. **Resolution.** Here we express appropriate sorrow for the hurt we have caused and make amends as appropriate. Guilt and self-punishment are released. The focus transitions to constructive change and growth. We again look ahead, concentrating on elevating humanity—self and others.

Integration is blocked if we get stuck prior to the completion of any stage. We can't process what is not adequately retrieved from memory. If we avoid thinking about the event, then memory fragments will intrude, but not sufficiently for processing. Thus, unresolved guilt continues to be replayed like a broken record. In attempts to kill the pain, we numb our conscience and sensitivity to the pain of others while becoming unable to emotionally connect with them.

Many inaccuracies can enter our memories during the stress of a traumatic event. During the event, it is typical to develop tunnel vision: being so narrowly focused on survival, we do not see the whole picture. We may assume an exaggerated sense of responsibility and underappreciate mitigating circumstances. These views are never effectively challenged, as one tries to "just forget the past and move on."

Without complete processing, many other unkind ideas remain unchallenged. Shame often rides in on guilt's coattails. Shame goes one step further than guilt, saying, "Not only did I *do* something bad, but I *am* bad to the core." Shame is frequently a pattern learned in childhood. Perhaps the survivor felt worthless when she was abandoned or was constantly given messages of badness. The child does not think to question these messages and so remains vulnerable when a traumatic event later occurs. A variety of other unkind ideas can be learned and connected to the trauma. Again, if they remain unchallenged, they retain their ability to disturb the survivor. The list below is a sampling of distortions and core beliefs that are often associated with guilt.

- I am either all responsible or not at all. I cannot be partly at fault.
- I feel so badly that I must be completely responsible.
- I don't deserve to live or to live happily because of my behavior.
- I should have done better.
- The more I punish myself, the more I show I care.
- The more I suffer and punish myself, the more I will ease another's suffering.
- The more I suffer, the less likely I will be to repeat the mistake.
- If I give up guilt, I will be disloyal to my values, God, or those who have suffered.
- If I suffer enough, I will somehow restore fairness and justice.
- I should be able to fix all problems, right all wrongs, save all who are in trouble, vanquish all evil.
- I shouldn't have been afraid.
- I am somehow responsible—even totally responsible—for a crime committed against me.
- There is absolutely nothing I can do to improve upon the past.
- My character is flawed and unchangeable. (In truth, everyone's character is flawed, but not unchangeable.)
- I should have acted in a way that only came to me later (hindsight bias).

These ideas create further pain and foster increased attempts to wall off the memories. Instead of relief, more intrusions occur.

## HOW IS GUILT RESOLVED?

PTSD authority Dr. Charles Figley[1] has proposed five questions that need to be answered in a kind, sensitive, and healing way in order to come to terms with traumatic events. These apply particularly well to the processing of guilt. In order to begin the processing of the guilt aspects of your traumatic memory, please respond to the following questions. This is now just a fact gathering exercise. You might think of yourself as a reporter researching a story. I suggest writing the answers because writing tends to make the processing slower and more deliberate. However, you might prefer to speak your responses to your therapist.

1. **What happened?** (Describe the event. List all the facts. What did I do that was good and bad? What did I fail to do that was good and bad?)
2. **Why did the event happen?** (Why did it happen to me? Was it a random act of nature or of God? Was it something about me?)
3. **Why did I act the way I did during the event?**
4. **Why have I acted the way I have since that time?** (How and why have I changed as a result of the event for good and bad?)
5. **If something like this were to happen again, what would I do differently to cope and survive?** (What strengths and knowledge would lead to a more optimistic outcome?)

## DETERMINING PERCENTAGES OF RESPONSIBILITY[2]

Dr. Raymond M. Scurfield developed this impressive technique to help Vietnam combat veterans accurately assess their responsibility. It is useful both for those who overestimate their responsibility, as well as for those who inappropriately disavow any responsibility. It has clear applicability to adult trauma other than war and can be used in both individual counseling or group treatment settings.

The following case study will reveal how the technique is applied. This veteran is forty-three years old and served a tour in Vietnam primarily as a truck driver delivering and unloading supplies to various military units.

> I had finished unloading a truck full of supplies to this unit; I was really tired, and was just sitting in the cab, resting . . . I happened to glance over and saw a guy in the distance by a tree; I assumed he was on perimeter (guard) duty. I also saw a second guy who was a little ways apart from the first guy and was moving in his direction. I assumed they were both Americans. All of a sudden, I heard

this loud sound, a rifle shot. One guy looked like he was laying down next to a tree; the other guy was running away. I found out that the second guy must have been a VC [Viet Cong], and he had killed the American . . . and I had just *sat* there in my truck and had *assumed* he was an *American*! My God, I could have checked closer, or I could have yelled out, or done *something*!

Application of the steps of assigning percentages of responsibility is as follows.

## Step 1: Narrative and Self-Assessment

This step facilitates a clear explication of the event and the survivor's perception and rationale for the degree of self-responsibility assumed. The veteran is helped to verbalize the *details* of the event, preferably in the first person as if the event were occurring now. Hazy or unclear descriptions *must* be clarified *or* it must be determined that a remembrance actually *is* hazy or unclear. Then the veteran must verbalize exactly *how much* of the responsibility he has assumed, in this case for the death of the American who was shot by the VC.

**Therapist:** Let me clarify something right away; are you feeling *totally* responsible for this guy's death?

**Veteran:** Yes . . . well, almost totally.

**Therapist:** Let's give a percentage to it. If we can assume that there is a total of 100 percent responsibility for this guy's death, what percentage have you blamed yourself for? You don't have to be *exact*, just give an approximation.

**Veteran:** About 95 percent.

**Therapist:** Are you sure that your responsibility is about 95 percent? Is it maybe *more* than that, or *less* than that?

[The purpose of] this therapeutic interaction is to stimulate new thinking by the veteran regarding the percentage of responsibility that he has assumed responsibility for. The veteran is then challenged to *convince* the clinician (group) how it is that he *deserves* to be 95 percent responsible. The clinician [group] does *not* rescue at this point, in order to force the veteran to *fully acknowledge "publicly"* that which he has already decided and has been persecuting himself about all these years. It is critical for the veteran to indicate *how* and *what* he has been remembering and saying to himself to remain convinced of his (exaggerated) sense of responsibility.

### Step 2: Examination of Others' Direct Roles

[The purpose of this step is to challenge] the survivor's exclusion or minimization of the role of others who were at the immediate scene of the trauma. Here is the continuation of the dialogue:

**Veteran:** I would give the other 5 percent of the responsibility for the death to the vet himself; I guess if he had been a little more careful, maybe the VC wouldn't have gotten that close to him.

**Therapist:** Wait a minute. Let's look closer at this guy's responsibility. *Were you responsible for sentry duty that night?*

**Veteran:** No, actually I think the guy killed was one of the guys pulling sentry duty.

**Therapist:** And so, he is only *5 percent* responsible for allowing that VC to get that close to him that night, and he was on sentry duty, and somehow you are 95 percent responsible for his death? Does that make sense to you?

**Veteran:** Well, no, now that you put it that way, maybe he was 15 percent or 20 percent responsible.

**Therapist:** Really? Are you sure that is a fair percentage to assign to him? Should he get more or less than 15 to 20 percent?

Once the veteran arrives at what appears to be a more realistic percentage of responsibility that might be assigned to the most obvious other person who bears some responsibility, the veteran is further challenged to consider how responsible he is for that other person *even being there* that night.

**Therapist:** By the way, did you have any responsibility for that veteran being in Vietnam? [And being in that unit, being there that night, being on guard duty, that he obeyed somebody's order to stand guard, for him being in-country or for being in the Army . . . ]

If the veteran claims that indeed he *did* have some influence over the other person's being in the actual situation that occurred, he then is challenged to convince the clinician (group) how that person himself had *absolutely no responsibility for being there* and how the veteran had *totally "forced"* or caused the other person to be there.

The above strategy is also systematically applied to *all other persons who were present* at the actual scene of the trauma:

- The other veterans who were on sentry duty that night
- Whoever *assigned* that deceased American to be on sentry duty
- Whoever was responsible for the selection of the site where the unit was located (would this event have occurred if the unit had been elsewhere?)
- Any other Americans who were in the area, and do *any* of them have *any* responsibility for what happened that night?
- The Viet Cong who actually shot the American

**Therapist:** Let's talk for a moment about the "enemy." *Were the VC any good at what they did? You* tell *us* how good the VC were at infiltrating behind perimeter lines.

**Veteran:** Well, of course, they were good, they were *damned* good.

**Therapist:** And if the men in that unit all were doing their jobs to the best of their abilities that night, does that mean that the VC would never have been able to kill anyone? Let's get real: DOES NOT THAT VC DESERVE SOME OF THE RESPONSIBILITY FOR THE DEATH OF THAT AMERICAN?!

**Veteran:** Well, yes: maybe about 30 or 40 percent.

**Therapist:** Wait a moment; isn't that *too much* to give someone whom you hadn't given *any* responsibility to all these years? Make sure that you are now giving what *you* consider to be a fair and realistic percentage to the enemy, no more and no less.

Thus, the veteran *comes to his own conclusion* that, indeed, his perception and remembrance of the event and delegation of blame have been extremely constricted. It may now be timely to bring to the veteran's attention that *the percentages of responsibility that the veteran has assigned to various people—including his own—now total well over 100 percent!*

**Therapist:** By the way, you have now assigned well over 100 percent responsibility for the American who was killed. That is impossible; that total can only equal 100 percent. Do you think that you need to recalculate some or all of the percentages you have assigned? Is yours still 95 percent, which means that all of these other people split up the remaining 5 percent?

The veteran is not specifically directed to precisely recalculate the percentages at this time. (Usually the clinician or a volunteer from the group will write down what percentages have been assigned to whom by the veteran during the group session to give to the veteran after the session is over.)

## Step 3: Examination of Others' Indirect Roles

[This step] challenges the survivor's exclusion or minimization of the indirect responsibility of others who were not at the immediate scene of the trauma. To not expand the circle of responsibility beyond individuals actually at the trauma site promotes continuation of an exaggerated responsibility for individual acts or non-acts that occur in the war zone. This is "society victim-bashing" of our war veterans, that is, blaming our veterans for licensing them to be agents of death and maiming. We allow them to carry their own *and everybody else's share* of the consequences of our nation's war policy.

Thus, the veteran is now asked to consider *if senior military officials* in the war zone deserve any share of responsibility for the various traumas that occur. In other words, did the military strategies facilitate the most likely positive (military) outcome, was the minimization of loss of U.S. casualties a primary concern, and did their strategies and policies contribute to "unnecessary" loss of life and destruction among the veteran and civilian populations in the war zone? Ultimately, does not the military command structure at its higher levels in the theater of operations deserve to receive a piece of the responsibility?

Next, the veteran considers *the war itself.* The therapist may ask, "Would any of you even have been in-country that night if the United States were not fighting in Vietnam?" What percentage of responsibility for the Vietnam War should be assigned to our political leaders, and to all the civilians who sat around and watched the latest Vietnam casualty reports on television and then proceeded with their lives, irrespective of what was happening in Vietnam? (This author contends that *when a nation goes to war, every adult in that nation bears a piece of the responsibility for every single traumatic result that occurs.*)

## Step 4: Reorienting Responsibility/Blame

[This next step] rechallenges the veteran's sense of his own percentage of responsibility for behaviors and consequences in the war zone.

**Therapist:** Now, let us return to *you* and what *you* did and did not do and how much responsibility you had for being in the military, for being in the war zone, for being there that night, and for what you did and did not do that night. Because you *were* there that night, you *did* sit in that truck, you *did not* say anything, and an American *was* blown away. We are not here to try and help you to explain away *any* of whatever percentage of responsibility you truly believe and feel that *you* deserve for what happened that night—once you have fully considered *all* the others who deserve some responsibility, too. And so, considering all other factors, what piece of the responsibility for that American's death do you now believe is yours?

[Once the veteran has been reoriented on this issue, the clinician moves to the next step.]

## Step 5: Assessing Self-Punishment
[The veteran is now challenged] to consider if he has been "punished" enough for his personal share of the responsibility for what happened.

**Therapist:** Now, tell us how much you have suffered and punished yourself all these years over the *95 percent* or so of the responsibility that you had blamed on yourself for this American's death. In other words, take into account *all* the times you have suffered pain from remembering and agonizing over what happened, criticizing yourself, feeling guilty, etc. How much?

**Veteran:** A lot; I mean a whole lot: not a week goes by these twenty-three years that I haven't relived that event.

The clinician (group) and veteran then discuss the degree of responsibility that the veteran has now assigned internally and how this percentage compares with the self-punishment suffered (which has been based on a much higher assumption of responsibility). The veteran must make a clear statement to the clinician (all the group members) and decide if he has engaged in (self-punishment) "enough," "not enough," or "more than enough" in comparison to his *newly assigned* percentage of responsibility. (It is often helpful for the veteran to repeat this statement to *several* individual veterans in the group.)

The above procedures are also utilized to address responsibility issues of veterans who seem to significantly deny that they had any responsibility whatsoever for particular experiences that occurred.

## Step 6: A Plan for Realistic, Proactive Amends
[Next is the explication of] a non-self-destructive plan to provide additional "payback" for one's share of the responsibility. If the veteran concludes that he still has

not suffered enough for this, his conclusion can, of course, be confronted by both the clinician and the group. However, if the veteran can live with this reframed, less rigid percentage of responsibility, the therapist and group may now facilitate the implementation of a non-self-destructive plan. This plan provides additional payback through its positive, life-sustaining, proactive stance, rather than through a self-destructive, reactive stance. The significant reframing process will require considerable readjusting of cognitions, feelings, and memories.

### Step 7: Reflection and Reframing

Next is a homework assignment, which permits the veteran some time to reflect and reframe; to refine and recalculate the set of percentages of responsibility that add up to 100 percent and truly take into account the full circle of persons and circumstances involved; and to develop an initial longer-range plan to provide additional payback, if any, that the survivor feels and believes he still must provide. The veteran provides at least a brief account to the clinician/group of the results of this homework assignment to allow for group sanction or lack of sanction. Establishing specific steps to undertake the positive, life-promoting payback plan is important, as are follow-up activities to ensure that movement has occurred.

### Summary of Steps

Let's briefly summarize the steps in the percentage of responsibilities exercise.

1. Verbalize the details of the event in the first person.
2. Ask/answer, "What percent are you responsible for? Are you sure? Is it possible that the percentage is *more* than that; or less?"
3. Convince the listener(s) that you deserve to be _____ percent responsible. Indicate how and what you've been remembering.
4. Challenge. Who else shared responsibility? What is their fair share of the percentage?
   - Was there a perpetrator who shares responsibility?
   - Who else was involved? Other individuals at the scene? People distant from the scene? Societal influences? Can you reasonably support the argument that you, but nobody else, is responsible for what happened?
5. Recalculate responsibility so that the total is 100 percent, and accurately focus on what you did and did not do.
6. Describe how much you have suffered for the responsibility you have assigned yourself.

7. Indicate if your suffering is enough, not enough, or more than enough in comparison to your actual percentage of responsibility.
8. Establish specific, life-promoting steps to facilitate payback, if appropriate, and commit to productive living rather than being stuck in the punishment mode.

## ADDITIONAL APPROACHES TO RESOLVING GUILT

Once appropriate responsibility has been assessed, the following steps continue the process of grief resolution.

### Concern vs. Guilt

Feel your feelings, but distinguish between concern and guilt. You feel very deep sadness and compassion for someone who was injured and whose car was damaged in a car accident that you are in. Upon reflection, however, you realize that you were not responsible for the accident. So you realize that your feelings reflect appropriate concern, not immobilizing guilt.

### Attack Any Remaining Distortions

You might isolate distortions that still trouble you. Write each down on a separate sheet of paper and list the advantages and disadvantages of believing it. List the positive consequences of disbelieving it, and then list as many alternatives as you can.

### Accept Your Limits

Say out loud, repeatedly, "I am imperfect. I was imperfect then; I am imperfect now. I accept my fair share of responsibility and commit to improve." Why do humans make mistakes? Because we are imperfect. It has always been this way.

### Provide Acceptance and Understanding

For a year, a teenager kept the fact that she was raped secret from her parents for fear they would reject her. After she could hold it in no longer, she told her father, who embraced her and said, "I wish you had told me sooner. This must have been so hard for you to bear alone." An emaciated soldier returned to the United States after a year in Vietnam. The customs agent looked kindly upon the young man and said, "Do you have any contraband?" The soldier replied that he had none. The agent then said, "Welcome home, son."[3] How much more healing is kindness than condemnation. Yet we see that victims are often more self-critical than self-supporting. It is easier to be kinder to ourselves when we clearly understand what has happened and why we reacted the way we did. Let's consider how accurate reflection leads to understanding.

- A college student was raped by her boyfriend. Shocked, she went to see him the next night, when he raped her again. She felt guilty for letting it happen not once, but twice. With counseling she learned that her behavior was very understandable. In acquaintance rape, women are not prepared to use force to stop someone they trust. They are usually so stunned that they simply hope that their stronger offender will come to his senses and stop. Stunned, confused, hurt, the student had returned hoping for an apology. She had so many confused feelings and was very vulnerable. Now, after recovery, she describes the event with justifiable anger for the crime it was and has released the guilt. She says, "I was vulnerable then. I am stronger now." (See Appendix G for myths regarding rape.)
- A woman stayed in a relationship with a batterer and thought, "I must be sick to tolerate this. I should have stopped it." A relationship with a batterer is very complex. It starts with a relationship between two people who deeply need each other. The insecure batterer begins to isolate his partner. He brainwashes her into thinking that she is helpless and dependent on him. Since he can easily hurt her, she starts to feel she owes her life to him and becomes thankful for his protection, affection, and financial support. If she married young, she will likely feel insecure about her job skills. She will likely fear retaliation against herself and/or the children if she leaves. He may also have threatened suicide.[4,5] In addition, male batterers report that once battering starts, there is nothing the victim can do to stop it—so self-blame by the victim is misplaced.[6] In a similar fashion, a child is totally dependent upon adults for basic needs. The child may learn to comply with an abuser for protection and to be seductive for acceptance.[7]

### Understand Decision Making Under Extreme Stress

By definition, a traumatic event is overwhelming. That is, it overwhelms our present abilities to cope. We are not prepared for it by virtue of insufficient experience, practice, training, knowledge, or resources. Decisions are made under duress. This means that extreme emotion exists that interferes with logical processing. There is too little time to figure out the best way to cope and examine the consequences of your options.

In traumatic events, there are usually no apparent "right" decisions nor truly good solutions. All options place us in "double binds"[8] where you are "damned if you do and damned if you don't." Thus, a woman ordered into a car by an armed man is not completely sure if complying, screaming, trying to talk the offender out of the crime, attacking him, or trying to run is the best course of action. All approaches pose grave dangers. No matter what she does, each option risks safety, life, health, values, and/or property. Thus, indecision is to be expected.

The stress response leads a person to fight, flee, or freeze, all of which are normal, instinctual ways to survive. Especially in extreme stress, fleeing or freezing is to be expected. Do not feel guilty for that inborn desire. During traumatic stress, most people instinctively think of survival first and not initially about protecting others. Caring for others typically returns later—sometimes later in the event, sometimes later in life. Perhaps if a similar crisis occurs later in your life, you might learn better ways to respond to the needs of others; but go easy on yourself about your survival instinct.

As Michael Simpson[9] observes, to expect one's best in times of crisis is often unreasonable (e.g., think of a person being tortured). Hostile environments create fear and poor choices. Might this help to explain why athletic teams usually have better records at home? We don't perform at our best when overwhelmed, terrified, out of control, and unable to see the big picture. At the time of the trauma, you were in life training. You hadn't learned all of life's lessons. You hadn't learned yet to channel such strong emotions, and trauma creates a horrible learning environment. Lessons learned from trauma usually become apparent only later in life.

The following sequence of questions can greatly help to place your reactions in perspective:

1. Were you thinking coolly at the time?
2. Were you aware of *all* your options?
3. What were your choices?
4. Were any of them good ones?
5. Had you ever been in that situation before?
6. Was there any way of knowing for certain what was the best option?
7. Were you clearly aware of all the outcomes of the options?
8. What would have been the outcome for each choice?
9. Were any of the choices *clearly* the right one? Best one? Were any choices without a cost? Were you aware of all of this at the time?
10. Were any of your options taken away?

11. Did you lack certain information that would have helped you make a wiser choice? (You're not responsible for solutions or information that only came to light after the traumatic event.)
12. Did you have time to fully weigh your choices, to see all the angles?
13. Were there mitigating factors (fatigue, hunger, drugs, chaos and confusion, no support from family or friends, no one to ask for advice)?
14. Was the outcome what you intended? Did you deliberately try to harm someone? Was it an honest mistake?
15. What was a reasonable expectation given the situation?[10] Rather than asking, "Did I make the *right* decision," ask, "Did I make a *reasonable* one under the circumstances?"[11]
16. Did you accomplish your initial objectives? Will there be other opportunities to do better?
17. How could you have coped worse? (Are you maybe stronger than you thought?)
18. Did your imperfect actions avert a worse disaster? In what ways?
19. How might you have responded better to create more of a sense of mastery and control? Did you know how to do that then? Was it reasonable to expect that then? Can you imagine yourself doing that now? (Try imagining your ideal response.)
20. If this were your daughter, son, or best friend who reacted as you did, how would you feel? What would you tell them? Could you understand their actions? Would you forgive them? How would you comfort them?

### Separate Guilt from Shame

Both feel unpleasant and are easily confused. Remember, guilt is feeling bad for what you *did* (or didn't do), while shame is feeling bad for who you *are*. Guilt focuses on behavior, which is readily changeable. Shame focuses on character, which is slower to change. With shame, character feels polluted by the behavior. We ask, what kind of person would act that way? The answer is "A bad one." This unfruitful thought keeps you bound to the past, while modifying behavior allows you to move ahead to the future. If you were truly as bad as you think, you would not be suffering as you are now. So rate behavior, not your core worth. Think, "I don't like what I did and would hope to do better now. But I am worthwhile, even though I reacted imperfectly."[12]

If you were victimized, it is natural to feel shame, but not necessary. What *happened* to you was wrong, bad—*you* are not. Alternatively, you might think,

"Something is fundamentally wrong with *all* people." It is called fallibility, a universal aspect of the human condition. *Fallible* does not equal bad or worthless, though. You might think, "I am not bad. I was afraid, having my problems, pressured, trying to get out of a crummy situation. Maybe I had a bad choice then, but I can choose a good life now."

## Gestalt Chair Technique

This process involves an interchange between yourself and an imaginary understanding friend. You play both roles, one at a time, switching chairs as is appropriate. The technique allows feelings, thoughts, and sensations to be expressed and processed at an experiential level, rather than just at an intellectual level.

- Set up two chairs facing each other, one for you and one for an understanding friend.
- Sit in the friend's chair and assume the friend's role. Ask the survivor in the other chair to describe the traumatic experience, including the survivor's role, responsibility, and feelings.
- Change seats and respond to the questions, this time assuming the role of the survivor. When you are finished, sit quietly and allow yourself to feel the feelings. Notice what your body is sensing. Then switch seats.
- As the understanding friend, try to feel what the survivor is feeling. Offer support, encouragement, advice. Ask if anything else is needed.
- Switch seats and respond. Keep switching until the situation feels settled.

A variation is to let the intellectual self speak to the feeling self (that finds it hard to express emotions). In a similar exercise,[13] imagine that you are two distinct people. The first person is kind, forgiving, comforting—a friend who you can count on to listen to you with understanding and empathy. The second person is the part of you in pain—the part that feels hurt, guilty, or misunderstood. Inhale slowly and deeply. As you do so, imagine that the first person lovingly takes in the damaging, hurtful feelings of the second. As you exhale, the second person, in response to the love and acceptance of the first, releases the pain, guilt, or frustration that has been causing pain. Inhaling, imagine the second person receiving strong feelings of love, joy, and acceptance from the first. As you exhale, the distinction between the two persons dissolves, leaving you whole, complete, and healed.

## Consider Transition

For the present, just *consider*, but do not act upon these yet: What did I learn from this experience that could prevent the traumatic event from recurring or better prepare me should it happen again? That could make me a better person? That could lead me to make the world a little better place?

Where could I go from here—what's the next step? Will I accept that I am not perfect?

## Utilize Spiritual Resources

Most religions teach ways to heal from legitimate guilt and reconcile with deity. A sensitive clergyperson or pastoral counselor might be of help. The peaceful Tibetan Buddhists teach this exercise for feeling forgiveness. It can be adapted to one's religious orientation.[14]

- Visualize in the sky before you a figure who, for you, embodies truth, wisdom, forgiveness, and compassion—this can be God or perhaps a figure you revere.
- Focus on the figure in front of you. Ask that figure to cleanse you of all your negative, destructive, harmful feelings and emotions. Ask to feel yourself forgiven.
- Visualize the figure smiling on you and your request with warm and personal affection. From the figure, visualize a stream of light flowing out and into your heart, and from your heart into your entire body, bringing you a feeling of great peace, forgiveness, and joy.
- Visualize the light filling you until you feel yourself made up entirely of that light. You soar up into the sky and are united with the figure. Relax and enjoy the bliss of that oneness for as long as possible.[15]

# CHAPTER 21

# Eye Movement Desensitization and Reprocessing (EMDR)[1]

A growing number of studies have indicated that eye movement desensitization and reprocessing (EMDR) can be very effective in the treatment of PTSD.[2] Dr. Bessel van der Kolk, a Boston University and Harvard psychiatrist and leading PTSD authority, has observed that encouraging studies indicate that EMDR "seems to be capable of producing powerful therapeutic effects in some patients with PTSD."[3] Many respected organizations worldwide recommend its use.

EMDR was originated by Dr. Francine Shapiro in 1987 and was initially employed for survivors of rape, molestation, and war. Since then, it has been applied to survivors of diverse traumatic experiences across a wide range of ages. Therapists consistently report that EMDR lessens negative images, thoughts, and feelings, while increasing positive images, thoughts, and feelings.

## WHAT IS EMDR?

EMDR is a comprehensive treatment plan involving eight phases. A unique and central component of EMDR is that the client holds upsetting memory material in mind while following a rhythmic set of eye movements (or other rhythmical stimuli), which are thought to accelerate the processing of that material.[4] Dr. Shapiro stresses that EMDR should only be done by a licensed, EMDR-trained mental health professional; laypeople should not try it on their own except as instructed by such a clinician. Here is a general overview of the eight phases of EMDR.

1. **Client history and treatment planning.** A thorough history identifies people for whom EMDR might not be appropriate. For example, people with

cardiac or respiratory problems or who are pregnant should consult doctors because EMDR may at times bring up intense arousal (this is usually brief and occurs in about 10 to 15 percent of people). The history also helps to make a treatment plan that targets obvious traumatic events from the past that need to be reprocessed, as well as other disturbing events from the past that might be related to the trauma (e.g., times of feeling out of control). Clients are often asked to identify the ten most disturbing experiences from their life. Symptoms (nightmares, flashbacks) or triggers might also be targeted for processing. Coping skills that need to be learned also become part of the treatment plan.

2. **Preparation.** A relationship with the therapist marked by trust and ease must be developed so that clients can be free to report disturbance and progress accurately—information that is essential to the clinician. EMDR theory, procedures, and expectations are explained. Clients are taught ways to relax, comfort, and calm themselves as methods to cope with distressing arousal. Then they're taught to maintain awareness during eye movements of disturbing material, knowing that they are now safe (e.g., they're taught to imagine themselves in a safe train that is speeding by upsetting scenery).

3. **Assessment.** The client and clinician identify aspects of the target to process that best represent the traumatic memory. The client then identifies a negative belief about herself that is associated with the event. For example, negative beliefs that are locked in the traumatic memory might include "I'm no good"; "I'm bad"; "I'm incompetent"; or "I'm unlovable." Then the client chooses a positive, preferred statement (e.g., "I'm in control, I'm safe now, I can succeed, I did the best I could, or I now have choices."). The clients also identify negative emotions and physical sensations, such as a tight chest, constriction in the throat, or a heavy feeling in the stomach. The client rates the strength of the negative and positive cognitions, as well as the degree of disturbance of the negative emotion and physical sensations. These ratings will help the clinician know how the treatment is progressing.

4. **Desensitization.** Clients are instructed to think of the targeted material (an image might be part of this, although the image is not necessary), the negative belief, and disturbing feelings and sensations. While holding all this in mind, the client is asked to do a set of eye movements by following two fingers on the therapist's hand, held about twelve inches away and moved rhythmically back and forth across the field of vision. The head is held still as the eye movements are performed. Processing begins, and new mental

material typically emerges with each set. After each set of eye movements, the client is instructed to blank it out (clear his mind) and take a deep breath. The therapist asks what the client "gets now." The client often feels the image or feelings change somewhat, or helpful insights might emerge. An associated memory or chain of memories that need to be processed also might emerge. The client is asked to "stay with that" as she follows additional sets of eye movements. Eventually all disturbing aspects linked to a disturbing memory are "cleaned out," or processed.[5]

5. **Installing and strengthening the positive cognition.** When distress has been sufficiently reduced, the preferred, or positive, cognition is repeated. The therapist might say, "As you think about the original incident, how do the words 'I did my best' (or other previously identified positive cognition) feel now?" That positive cognition is reinforced with additional sets of eye movements until it feels sufficiently valid to the client. Anything that blocks the positive cognition from feeling sufficiently valid to the client is processed.

6. **Body scan.** To further ensure that all aspects of a traumatic memory have been processed, the client is then asked to notice if any disturbing physical sensations remain as she brings up the target. If so, that sensation is targeted for reprocessing with additional eye movements.

7. **Closure.** The therapist helps the client leave the session feeling safe and comforted, even if processing is not complete. Self-calming strategies are done, and the client is advised that processing will likely continue between sessions. (Even new disturbing material that comes up suggests the need for processing and is thus a positive sign.) The client is instructed to use a journal to record that processing and calming techniques to contain arousal.

8. **Reevaluation.** At the beginning of the next session, the clinician ascertains if positive results have been maintained from the last session. New targets are identified, or old targets that still need processing are identified—and processed.

When processing seems stuck, the cognitive interweave can be tried to prime the processing pump. The therapist poses a question to stimulate the connection of an appropriate positive cognition to the target network. For example, the therapist might ask, "Can a little child cause a rape?" The client thinks of that as a set of eye movements is done. Perhaps guilt changes to anger as the survivor realizes she wasn't to blame. The EMDR-trained clinician can also make a number of other adjustments to facilitate processing that is stuck.

## STRENGTHS OF EMDR

As the above discussion suggests, EMDR possesses quite a number of unique advantages:

- **EMDR often leads to rapid improvements.** Up to 90 percent of survivors with single-incident traumatic events show significant relief in only three sessions. EMDR can also accelerate the treatment of multiple incidents, although such treatment often takes longer.
- **EMDR processes various aspects of traumatic memories together: cognitions (thoughts/images), feelings, physical sensations, and behaviors related to the troubling memories.** Thus, integration of the different aspects of memory is facilitated.
- **Control remains with the client.** Aspects that need to be processed arise naturally in the course of treatment. The therapist does not tell the client what to think. Clients can also stop processing at any time. For example, if processing becomes too uncomfortable, the client can signal the therapist to stop eye movements by raising a hand or turning away.
- **EMDR defuses and clears out all aspects of memory networks that might be related to a traumatic memory.** Thus, processing a recent traumatic memory with EMDR might lead a client to process a childhood memory of feeling similarly out of control.
- **The benefits of processing one type of memory may generalize to other similar memories.** For multiple or repeated trauma, similar traumas may be grouped together. Processing a representative incident from each group is often sufficient to neutralize the other incidents in that group. Thus, all traumatic events may not need to be processed.
- **Traumatic memories need not be discussed in detail.** Some clients might not wish or feel ready to do so.[6]
- **Homework is not required.**[7] Treatment can be quite efficient, making EMDR useful for individuals and for disasters affecting many people.

## WHY EMDR WORKS

Although the mechanisms are uncertain, Shapiro offers what she thinks might explain EMDR's effectiveness. Just as a bone will heal naturally once it has been set, dissociated memories will heal naturally once processing is stimulated. EMDR helps people to confront—not avoid—disturbing memories, in small doses, in a controlled and safe way. This helps pair the memories to less fearful emotions.

It is possible that moving the eyes rapidly stimulates electrical connections between parts of the brain that process memories. Theorists have noted that rapid eye movements during dreams appear to help the brain process, while high levels of negative emotions seem to freeze eye movements and stop processing. Similarly, people with PTSD sometimes have frozen eye movements (e.g., the "thousand-yard stare" of shell-shocked soldiers). Thus, moving the eyes (or performing similar rhythmic movements) might accelerate the integration of traumatic memory with adaptive cognitions that are stored elsewhere in the brain. It is possible that the gentle processing biochemically alters the brain so that it becomes desensitized.

Clients are asked to notice memory material, by visualizing that they are a passenger on a train safely speeding by the disturbing memory. This teaches them that they can step outside the memory and observe it with safety and detachment—similar to the way meditation teaches one to view experience with detachment. Thus, disturbing memories are paired with neutral or comforting emotions, not fear. They then are told to dismiss the memory, teaching them another way to gain a sense of control and mastery over the material. Concentrating on the eye movements provides somewhat of a distraction from the pain of distressing memories while processing occurs.

Paying attention to physical responses and relating them to emotions allows the client to break down the various aspects of a traumatic memory and see it as less overwhelming. Finally, the structure of EMDR helps to prevent overanalysis and endless ruminating, and reminds clients that they are bigger than the trauma.

### What EMDR Can Treat
- PTSD
- Grief reactions that were avoided during the trauma
- Disturbing memories that are not always identified as traumatic (death of a loved one or excessive grief from other causes, abandonment, rejection, feeling powerless)
- Mental disorders that can be traced to earlier troubling events in life (e.g., trauma-related depression, certain anxiety disorders, low self-esteem, or addictions that are connected to childhood abandonment)[8]

- Self-defeating, ingrained beliefs whose origins are unknown (e.g., "I'm not worthwhile" or " I can't control my life" might come from an upsetting but not traumatic event)
- Future events that are anticipated to be stressful (desirable coping strategies can also be reinforced with EMDR)
- Fear of deciding upon a distressing medical experience (e.g., cancer treatment might be overwhelming for a person who previously had an unresolved negative experience with chemotherapy)

**EMDR Can Target**
- A single trauma from adulthood
- A single trauma from childhood
- Multiple traumas—targeting a representative incident for each group of related traumas is usually sufficient
- Triggers
- Symptoms such as dreams, nightmares, or startle response (Processing a nightmare can lead to identification of an earlier disturbing real-life experience that can then be processed.)
- Negative thoughts (e.g., the present thought "I'm powerless" often is connected to a disturbing memory)
- Symptoms of walled-off memories, such as memory lapses, dissociations, or the ability to access only negative material; such symptoms might exist without a memory of a traumatic event
- A recent experience that is not traumatic yet is inexplicably distressing (e.g., an authority figure might be unconsciously triggering memories of an adult molester; a failed business reminds you of abandonment). Processing often uncovers a root memory. If not, coping skills can be taught.
- Memories of people who contributed to low self-esteem
- Secondary gains
- Individual issues that interfere with couples and family therapy[9]

# CHAPTER 22

# *Thought Field Therapy*

Noted PTSD researcher Professor Charles R. Figley, Ph.D., Director of the Traumatology Institute, Florida State University, has systematically investigated four treatment approaches that appear to hold therapeutic promise: thought field therapy (TFT), traumatic incident reduction (TIR), visual-kinesthetic dissociation,[1] and eye movement desensitization and reprocessing (EMDR). All four of these techniques share many characteristics. Each attempts to recover traumatic material, hasten processing, and neutralize strong negative emotions. They can all be very effective when used as part of a comprehensive treatment plan, and they are particularly useful for those individuals who are significantly and regularly distressed by other treatment approaches. He notes the following:

> All four of the approaches we investigated generated impressive results. But TFT stood out from all other approaches of which I am aware because of [these] reasons:
>
> 1. It is extraordinarily powerful, in that clients receive nearly immediate relief from their suffering and the treatment appears to be permanent.
> 2. It can be taught to nearly anyone so that clients cannot only treat themselves, but treat others affected.
> 3. It appears to do no harm.

---

This chapter is adapted slightly with permission from correspondence from Dr. Charles R. Figley to colleagues in traumatic stress 27 June 1995. Also referenced is Callahan, R. J. and J. Callahan. 1997. "Thought Field Therapy: Aiding the Bereavement Process" in C. R. Figley, B. E. Bride, and N. Mazza, eds. *Death & Trauma: The Traumatology of Grieving*. Washington, D.C.: Taylor & Francis, 249–67. This excellent chapter provides rich background and additional algorithms for anger and guilt.

4. It does not require the client to talk about his or her troubles, something that often causes more emotional pain and discourages many from seeking treatment.

5. It is extremely efficient (fast and long-lasting).

Although Dr. Figley cautions that much research is still needed, he presents the steps in order to permit individuals and therapists to try thought field therapy as follows:

1. **Think about the problem.** Think of the causes of your anxiety (we all have them from time to time), including the traumatic experience, and work up as much discomfort as you can. However, do not spend more than a few moments on this phase.

2. **Rate discomfort.** At a point where you feel your anxiety is at its peak, choose a number between 1 and 10 that best represents the intensity of your discomfort, with 10 being the highest and 1 being the lowest. Thus, circle a number below:
   1 . . . 2 . . . 3 . . . 4 . . . 5 . . . 6 . . . 7 . . . 8 . . . 9 . . . 10

3. **Tap the beginning of the eyebrow.** After you have circled a number, using two fingertips, tap solidly five times while thinking about the anxiety (but not hard enough to cause bruising or pain) just above the bridge of your nose, approximately where either eyebrow begins.

4. **Tap under the eye.** Then tap five times approximately one inch below the bottom of either eye (again, not too hard).

5. **Tap the body.** Next, tap five times on the side of your body, approximately four inches below the pit of the arm.

6. **Tap under the collarbone.** Then tap five times on your chest just below the collarbone, approximately one inch on either side from the center of your chest.

7. **Rate discomfort.** Now take a deep breath and measure your anxiety again: Choose a number between 1 and 10 that best represents the intensity of your anxiety right now. Then, circle a number below:
   1 . . . 2 . . . 3 . . . 4 . . . 5 . . . 6 . . . 7 . . . 8 . . . 9 . . . 10

8. **Decide.** If the intensity of your anxiety is now at least two numbers lower than it was initially, go to Step 9. However, if it is not, follow this procedure: Tap the little-finger side of either hand (on the fleshy part midway between the wrist and base of the little finger, where you would do a karate chop) while saying the following: "I accept myself, even though I still have this

kind of anxiety." Repeat this statement three times while thinking about the problem and continuing to tap. Then, repeat Steps 3 through 7.

9. **Tap the back of your hand.** Next is a sequence of nine activities that are done while tapping at a spot on the back of either hand. The spot is just below and between the knuckle of the little finger and the knuckle of the next finger. (Find this spot by making a fist. Place the index finger of the tapping hand in the gap between the knuckles of the little finger and the ring finger. Slide the index finger an inch back toward the wrist.) With the hand flat, tap this spot continually while doing the following activities (about five taps for each of the nine activities):

   - Eyes open
   - Eyes closed
   - Eyes open, look down and to the left (head still)
   - Eyes look down and to the right
   - Roll eyes in a circle
   - Roll eyes in a circle in the opposite direction
   - Hum a few bars of some tune with more than one note
   - Count to five
   - Hum some tune again

10. **Follow Steps 3 through 6.**

11. **Rate.** As you did before, take a deep breath and measure your anxiety again. Choose a number between 1 and 10 that best represents the intensity of your anxiety right now. Then, circle a number below:

    1 . . . 2 . . . 3 . . . 4 . . . 5 . . . 6 . . . 7 . . . 8 . . . 9 . . . 10

12. **Repeat.** Follow the above procedure at least four times to give the procedure a fair test. If your anxiety rating has fallen at least two units, TFT might be a helpful skill for you to practice. You might also try it at a time when your anxiety is higher and the cause is very clear to you. You may come up with all kinds of explanations for why your anxiety level came down. Experiment with your explanations.

If your anxiety rating has fallen to a 2 or 1, do the following to solidify these gains. Hold your head level. Begin tapping the same spot on the back of the hand that you tapped in Step 9. As you tap, look down at the floor, then steadily raise your eyes all the way up toward the ceiling, taking six to seven seconds to do so.

# CHAPTER 23

# *Other Brief Processing Techniques*

This chapter explores three brief, integrative techniques that are sometimes tried to process specific traumatic memories of finite duration: the rewind technique, traumatic incident reduction, and the counting method. Each approach encourages processing in a safe and controlled way. The rewind technique uses visual processing alone; traumatic incident reduction and the counting method add verbalization of the memory to facilitate processing.

## THE REWIND TECHNIQUE*

The rewind technique[1] has been reported to be very effective for specific traumas of finite duration in adults, usually within three to four treatment sessions.[2] According to its originator, Dr. David Muss, the rewind technique will allow people with PTSD to get rid of[3]

> the various involuntary, unwanted memories of the event, such as the nightmares, the flashbacks and the dreams. As a result of this you will no longer succumb to the emotional distress which these bring about. The technique does not cancel your voluntary recall of the event. You will always be able to remember the event if you choose to. However, when you choose to recall the event, you know you will be mostly in control of your emotions and not overpowered by

---

*This section is adapted with permission from Muss, D. 1991. *The Trauma Trap*. London: Doubleday. Copyright © 1991, David Muss. Dr. Muss is director of the PTSD Unit, Birmingham Nuffield Hospital, Birmingham, U.K.

them as you are now when the event is unexpectedly recalled by a chance remark from a friend or a sudden news flash on the TV or radio. You will no longer be imprisoned in the trauma trap—you will be released from it.

The instructions for practicing the rewind technique follow. It is recommended that you first try this in a safe setting, with your therapist, after you are stabilized and a therapeutic alliance has been formed.

1. **Time.** Choose a time when you will be undisturbed.
2. **Place.** Find somewhere comfortable to sit for about fifteen minutes. You may feel more comfortable with your feet up and your hands unclasped.
3. **Relaxation.** Close your eyes and start to relax each muscle group of your body from your feet all the way up to your head by first tensing and then relaxing. You will find that a feeling of calmness will come over you as you slowly and systematically relax all these muscle groups. Indulge in this pleasant feeling of calmness for a while (you might also wish to use imagery of your safe place or a pleasant scene to increase pleasant, relaxed feelings). When you are feeling truly calm, continue.
4. **Background.** The rewind technique consists of watching a film of your traumatic event, in the exact way that it haunts you, first forward and then backward. However, it is not quite as simple as that, and it is very important that you follow precisely all the steps that follow. Some of the things I am going to ask you to do may seem a little odd, so let's pretend that I am introducing you to a new game. As with all new games, you need to understand the rules and the setting before you play. So before you start the treatment, learn the rules with me.
5. **Floating.** First, learn to float out of yourself. Another way of saying this is, learn how to *watch yourself*. Have you been on a boat or car journey and felt terribly sick? Or have you been on a roller-coaster and felt frightened? Stop and think about this for a moment. Have you remembered what it felt like? You probably didn't enjoy that memory, did you? This is because you didn't detach yourself.

    Try now to look at the same event in a detached way. Float out of the boat, leaving your body in it, and watch yourself from the shore. Do you feel as bad as you did when you saw yourself before? I hope the answer is no. This is because you are watching yourself and not reliving the event as it [actually] happened.

6. **The setting.** You will be watching two films in a cinema. Let's assume that you have a completely empty cinema hired just for you. Imagine that you are sitting in the center with the big screen in front and the projection room behind you. Now I would like you to float out of your body and go to the projection room to watch yourself watching the film from there. From the projection room, you will be able to see the whole cinema, the empty chairs with just your head, and perhaps shoulders, sitting in the center seat, and the screen in front of you, as in Figure 23.1. (Do not proceed until you can clearly see yourself in the projection room watching yourself watching the film.) Now let's consider the two films.

7. **The first film.** The first film is a replay of the traumatic event as you experienced it or as you remember it in your nightmares, dreams, or flashbacks. In this film, you will see yourself on the screen—just as if someone had unexpectedly taken a video on the day and is now showing it to you.

Run the film forward at its normal pace and stop when your memory begins to fade (or at a time when you realized you would survive). You will find it very helpful if you can start the film a little before the point where your memory of the traumatic event begins. In other words, if you were involved in a car accident with a truck, begin the film by seeing yourself driving along happily, as in Figure 23.2. You will see the truck appear (see Figure 23.3), and finally the accident (see Figure 23.4). I call Figure 23.2

**Figure 23.1    THE REWIND TECHNIQUE**

**Figure 23.2**   THE "NEW STARTING POINT"

**Figure 23.3**   MOVING TOWARD COLLISION

**Figure 23.4**   THE ACCIDENT

the "new starting point." It is the peaceful point you return to when you rewind the film.

So, for the forward film: remember first where you are sitting and where you are watching the film from. Then begin from the "new starting point." Next, see yourself on the screen. Finally, let the film run along until your memory fades.

8. **The rewind.** The second film is called the *rewind*. You do not exactly watch the rewind. You are actually in it, *experiencing* it *in* the screen, seeing everything as if it were happening to you now and experiencing the sounds, smells, feels, taste, and touch sensations. The really odd thing is that you see and feel everything happening *backward*. Thus, in the case of the car accident, first you are in the car after the impact (see Figure 23.5). Then you feel the car pulling away from the truck. You see the front of your car returning to its normal shape, as does the truck (see Figure 23.6). The vehicles pull farther and farther apart until the truck disappears and you finally end up with the "new starting point," as in Figure 23.7—you *see yourself* driving along in your car as you did at the beginning of the forward film.

Remember, in the rewind, you are actually in the film, reexperiencing the event—which is now, however, all happening in reverse. The rewind must be done rapidly. You may find this difficult at first. If so, practice it slowly at the start. Once you've got it right, run it through straight after the forward film.

To give you an idea of the speed of the rewind, if the forward film takes one minute, the rewind should take ten to fifteen seconds at most. You should end the rewind at your "new starting point," which represents a good image.

## Summary of Rewind Technique

To sum up, with the forward film, you are sitting in the center of the cinema, leaving your body there and floating in the projection room, from where you will watch the forward film. See yourself on the screen. Begin with your new starting point. Run the first film until it fades. At this point, get into the film. You are no longer watching the film, but reexperiencing the traumatic event in reverse. Rewind the event rapidly. End with your new starting point.

**Figure 23.5**   IN THE CAR AFTER THE IMPACT

**Figure 23.6**   COLLISION IN REVERSE

**Figure 23.7**   BACK TO THE "NEW STARTING POINT"

## Caution

I must warn you that going through the first film can be painful and may cause you to become pale, sweaty, or even tearful. Please don't be upset or put off. Remember that this should be the last time you remember the event in this way. After this treatment, you will find that whenever the memory is sparked off, the rewind will rapidly come into play and will, on its way back, scramble the sequence, leading you very quickly to the new starting point. The new starting point is a good image, and that is the memory you will be left with. This process will happen faster and faster as every day goes by. As a result of this treatment, you will find that you are now able to resume all the activities you haven't been able to do for a long time.

## Troubleshooting

Some people find rewinding difficult and slow at first. Don't be discouraged; practice the rewind on its own until you get it right. Then go through the complete sequence without hesitating or stopping.

If you gloss over the really frightening or ugly part and do not look at the film in its full detail, you will find that your PTSD symptoms will not disappear completely. You will therefore have to go back and deal with that particular section again.

You may be deeply shocked to find that once you have got rid of a major haunting memory, another one appears. This shouldn't surprise you. Quite often we suppress several disturbing images, and, once the major one has been removed, the next most disturbing one rises to take its place. If a deeper, concealed memory surfaces, just deal with it in the same way—rewind it.

## TRAUMATIC INCIDENT REDUCTION (TIR)*

In this technique, the client treats a traumatic incident like a videotape that is rewound to the beginning and played through to the end without talking. After viewing the "videotape," the therapist asks the client to describe what happened in the viewing. The therapist then asks the client to "rewind the videotape" to the beginning, again viewing the incident and then describing it. The client views and describes only what he or she is relatively comfortable with. However, with each repetition, the client typically contacts more and more details and emotions

---

*This section is adapted with permission from Traumatic Incident Reduction Association (TIRA) webpage (www.tir.org), "Traumatic Incident Reduction (TIR) FAQ." TIR's originator is Frank A. Gerbode, M.D.

until an emotional peak is reached. On successive run-throughs, the amount of negative emotions usually diminishes more and more as the memory is faced and mastered. Helpful insights might surface, and the client often feels calmer and more positive. Should the process become too upsetting, the client simply stops the procedure. TIR is not recommended for clients who are psychotic or nearly so, currently using drugs or alcohol, not ready or wanting to do it, or immersed in overwhelming life situations. When the client suffers from unaccountable distress but there are no obvious traumatic memories in evidence to address, a type of TIR called "thematic TIR" can be used to trace these "themes" back to their source. For more information on TIR, see Additional Resources.

## THE COUNTING METHOD*

In this approach, a client silently recalls a troubling memory while the therapist counts to one hundred within a two-minute interval. The client is instructed to allow the worst feelings to crest toward the middle of the counting and then gradually come out of the past and into the present toward the end of the counting. Afterward, the client is asked to describe what was remembered. Processing of memory material that emerged may be done, if tolerable. In most cases, clients report reduction in the frequency and intensity of troubling intrusive recollections, without negative consequences. This approach provides a sense of control with the realization that one can deliberately recall the event and give it a beginning, middle, and end. The memory becomes linked to the calm and safety of the therapist's voice.

---

*Adapted from Ochberg, F. M. 1996. "The Counting Method for Ameliorating Traumatic Memories." *Journal of Traumatic Stress* 9 (4): 873–80. This article provides much useful detail.

# CHAPTER 24

# *Prolonged Exposure*

As we have discussed, trying to avoid or forget traumatic memories does nothing to neutralize them. In fact, the more we fear and flee them, the more negative energy we give them, enabling them to remain so negatively charged. The opposite of avoidance is exposure, or fully confronting troublesome memories. Prolonged exposure (PE) is a method of inviting traumatic memories in a controlled way fully into our awareness in a safe environment. Extensive research validates its effectiveness.

In PE, we bring *all* aspects of traumatic memories into awareness. When we stay with the memories we fear, we soon realize that they can't really hurt us; they are distressing but not dangerous. Confidence replaces fear and begins to neutralize the memories. When we connect those distressing memories to feelings of deep relaxation rather than more fear, the memories are neutralized further. Connecting traumatic memories to soothing emotions is called *deconditioning*. That is, the nervous system breaks the conditioned response of reacting to recalled memories with arousal. We are actually training our nervous system to be less sensitive to these memories, hence the process is sometimes called *desensitization*. Exposure to all aspects of traumatic memories permits the memory material to be fully processed and integrated. Recall that intrusive memories usually do not contain all aspects of traumatic memories. If we were to permit full recall in a safe environment, the mind would have a chance to integrate these memories and place them in long-term memory. However, traumatic memories are typically avoided before integration occurs because they are so unpleasant.

When we voluntarily let fears come fully into awareness, some people will feel some relief right away. Some will feel troubled initially, much as Pennebaker found in those who began writing about their traumas. However, because processing is occurring, benefits might begin to become apparent fairly quickly, often within two to three weeks.[1]

### How Prolonged Exposure Is Done[2]

1. **PE is done with a psychotherapist, usually in less than fifteen exposure sessions.** Each session typically lasts one to two hours. Usually sessions are held once or twice a week.

2. **Start by making a hierarchy of distressing events.** Think of a ladder. At the top of the ladder is the most traumatic event that you experienced. At the bottom is the least traumatic event. Between these two endpoints are other traumatic events arranged in order of intensity. Or you might choose to break one traumatic event into parts, with the most distressing aspects at the top of the hierarchy. Assign a SUD rating (as explained in Chapter 14) to each rung (e.g., 0 = not at all distressing; 10 = most distressing).[3]

3. **Relax deeply.** Usually this is done with two easy, deep breaths followed by progressive muscle relaxation. To deepen feelings of safety, you might use safe place and/or pleasant memory imagery.

4. **Choose a starting point on the hierarchy.** Some wish to start at the highest rung, hoping that positive results will generalize. However, the potential for retraumatizing exists if memories flood and overwhelm awareness. Most approaches start at a rung associated with moderate levels of distress. This permits one to be challenged but not overwhelmed, while confidence is gained.

5. **Recount the selected event.** Tell what was happening before, during, and after. Use the first person and the present tense, as though it were happening now ("I'm walking to my car . . ."). Describe what you see, hear, smell, touch, and taste. Describe your body's reactions, your surroundings, weather, clothes, and what you are thinking, feeling, and doing. Recall what the perpetrator or others are doing. Verbalizing seems to help integrate the material.

   - The therapist will help you set up the scene by giving some details, such as the date, and ask you to begin retelling. In the approach developed by Dr. Edna Foa, the client simply retells whatever details can be tolerated for the first few recountings. Usually more details surface with repeated tellings.
   - With successive tellings, the therapist will prompt you to include more and more details. It is especially important to process the most distress-

ing aspects of a memory, the so-called hot spots. Thus you will take more time with hot spots, slowing down and recalling more detail. Your therapist might prompt you to recall other aspects, such as feared consequences.

- If you finish retelling the story before time is up, go back and repeat it in even more detail. As additional details come to light, more processing occurs. Although this might be more distressing, eventually your nervous system will react less to the memories, a process known as *habituation*.
- Monitor SUDs every five to ten minutes. Your therapist will ask you to rate your discomfort quickly, without your leaving the scene. You will continue to retell the story until SUDs drop by half or to a mild to moderate distress level.

6. **End the exposure with relaxation.** Use low, slow breathing and any of the relaxation techniques described in Chapter 12.

7. **Cognitive restructuring is done before and after exposure to eliminate distortions that increase arousal** (e.g., "This shouldn't be so hard" and "The world is totally unsafe") and to connect the memories with more adaptive thoughts and new insights (e.g., "It's okay that I need to work at this" and "The world is *sometimes* unsafe"). Evidence for unproductive thoughts is tested, and core beliefs are uncovered. The amount of time spent in cognitive restructuring increases as the amount of detail retold increases.

8. **Your therapist will give you an audio recording of your recounting, and you'll listen to it at least once per day.** As you listen, new details might arise for processing, and you'll likely tend to get less aroused with repetition. Perform a relaxation strategy such as progressive muscle relaxation before you begin and after you listen to the recording. You might also wish to end with pleasant memory imagery. Do not listen to the recording before bed because of its potential to trigger nightmares. Find a unique place to listen to the recording. You would not wish to associate negative emotions with places such as your bed, favorite sofa, or kitchen table. Instead, find a neutral place, such as a chair in the corner of a room. Monitor your SUDs and notice decreases.

9. **Sometimes variations might be introduced to the exposure portion of therapy sessions.** Your therapist might ask you to project yourself into the future, imagine the worst case happening, and stay with it until even that can be tolerated (e.g., imagine that loved ones discover your secret and reject you). Exposure to feared situations can later be supplemented with

role-playing, where you practice coping in situations you'll likely confront to gain confidence.

10. **As soon as possible, you'll also confront in real life fearful situations that you've avoided.** You'll make a hierarchy and gradually encounter these situations, staying in them long enough to notice a drop in SUDs by at least half or for thirty to forty-five minutes to gain confidence. For example, rungs of this hierarchy might include wearing clothes worn when one was traumatized and walking near the scene of the traumatic event if that is now safe to do. Before doing this real-life, or "in vivo," exposure work, review your coping skills. You might wish to carry flash cards with coping skills and adaptive thoughts. At first, your therapist or a skilled and trusted friend might accompany you.

11. **Remember the other strategies that you have learned thus far to feel safe, reduce arousal, and lift your mood.** Use these regularly during or between sessions as needed.

### Cautions and Considerations

1. **Prolonged exposure can increase distress, especially if done too soon or too fast.** Again, the distress is usually tolerable and temporary, and typically abates by treatment's end. Some experts feel that PE can yield greater, more lasting improvements than some of the other PTSD treatments. Yet many clinicians prematurely stop exposure for fear of destabilizing the person with PTSD. The general rule is to stay with exposure as long as you can but to stop should it become overwhelming. Prior to starting, be sure to have good calming and grounding skills and a strong therapeutic alliance. Learning mindfulness skills (see Chapter 16) can also help one to tolerate discomfort.

2. **PE is generally contraindicated in certain cases.** These cases include people who are experiencing current substance abuse, risk for suicide or self-injury, ongoing life crises, difficulty using imagery, inability to tolerate intense arousal, and uncontrolled mental illnesses (such as active psychosis or extreme anxiety).

3. **PE is indicated for people who are motivated, who become aroused when exposed to specific memories, and who can describe concisely the traumatic event.** Before using PE, insure that your symptoms are stabilized, that you have good self-esteem (see Chapter 33), and that you have developed a range of coping skills.

4. **Don't allow your SUDs to get so high that processing is blocked.** If retelling becomes too stressful
   - Slow down the retelling or shift to past tense.
   - Recall helpful reminders, which can be written on flash cards, such as "This is difficult, not dangerous—I can handle it; This is just a memory—the event is past; I know how to calm myself down."[4]
   - Remind yourself of the positive aspects of the traumatic event as well as the negatives. For example, you might recall what you did to survive or help others. You might recall that blood is also a sign of life and creation, not just death and hurt.[5]
   - Try to calm yourself without avoiding the memories.
   - If you have to take a break from the process, calm down and compliment yourself for doing as much as you did.
   - Discuss with your therapist the possible use of EMDR to process hot spots, or the worst parts of the memory.
5. **PE might not be effective with unresolved guilt, anger, or sadness.** If not, other cognitively oriented treatments described in this book might be tried before or after. (These can also be tried if PE is too distressing.)
6. **Don't expect to not have distress after prolonged exposure.** However, the levels of distress are likely to become more reasonable.

## VIRTUAL REALITY EXPOSURE

Often people are not very good at using their imagination to fully recall traumatic memories. Or perhaps the trauma scenes are too far away or too dangerous to revisit in order to practice real-life exposure. For such people, a new form of prolonged exposure called *virtual reality exposure* (VRE) can be helpful. In this treatment, the client dons a headset and begins to explore, at his own pace, a 3-D computer-generated scene that is similar to a trauma scene. The client recounts details of the trauma scene. Using this information, the clinician gradually introduces (in later sessions) sights, sounds, vibrations, smells, and even temperature adjustments to approximate the trauma scene more closely. After each exposure, the experience is processed through discussion with the therapist. Homework might include the client's listening to a recording of the session. As the memory is repeatedly faced and processed in a safe environment, it typically becomes more integrated, and the strong emotions associated with it tend to shift.

There are certain advantages to using this treatment. First, the treatment introduces greater realism than the imagery of typical prolonged exposure might. The more vividly the senses are engaged, the more the emotions are engaged as well. For example, a combat scene might involve the sounds of rockets, helicopters, yelling, civilians crying, and radio chatter. Scents might include burning rubber, diesel fuel, ethnic spices and cooking, and body odor. Vibrations can approximate explosions or the rumbling of a Humvee. Hot air can further help to approximate a war zone climate. Second, the clinician has greater involvement in the process, as she is able to add such cues as the client describes in the scene. Third, computer monitoring of the client's physical arousal can also help the clinician titrate the cues appropriately. And fourth, VRE is especially useful for younger people who are used to computer gaming technology.

A disadvantage is that the use of VRE is limited by what is currently programmed. Programs are or have been developed for car accidents, the September 11 tragedy, and the Iraq War.

## INTEROCEPTIVE EXPOSURE

In this final type of exposure therapy, clients are exposed to bodily sensations related to anxiety or dissociation. In confronting these sensations, clients realize that these feared sensations are actually harmless, that they are not going insane or losing control.

For example, one might create feelings of anxiety by breathing through a straw, breathing fast, spinning in a chair, or tensing muscles. Derealization might be created by staring at a fluorescent ceiling light for a minute and then trying to read or by staring continuously at oneself in a mirror for two minutes. In facing these self-created sensations, the fear and discomfort gradually decrease.[6]

# CHAPTER 25

# Dream Management
# and Processing

**All things one has forgotten scream for help in dreams.**

*—Elias Canetti*

This chapter begins an exploration of other commonly used approaches to healing (presented in Chapters 25 through 36). You'll be wise to remain aware of the opportunities these approaches present.

Post-traumatic nightmares so frequently become a terrifying aspect of PTSD. They can jolt people awake in a cold sweat and feel so petrifying that sleep is avoided for fear of having another. Because sleep is troubled, the victim becomes fatigued, which makes him more prone to intrusions during the day.

Nightmares can be demystified by viewing them as simply the normal intrusion of dissociated material. They are just the brain's attempts to process walled-off memory material. The obvious difference is that these intrusions appear during sleep, often in more creative ways than the intrusions in waking life. Think of nightmares as an ally to recovery. Accessing them, rather than avoiding them, facilitates the recovery process.

Dreams are a fairly accurate barometer of recovery. Dr. Deirdre Barrett, a Harvard psychologist and president of the International Association for the Study of Dreams, has written:[1]

> Several studies have delineated a pattern of post-traumatic nightmares in which the initial dreams are fairly close to a literal reenactment of the trauma (i.e., an almost exact replay), sometimes with the twist that an additional horror, averted

in real life, is added to the dream reenactment. Then, as time passes, and especially for those whose PTSD is gradually improving, the dream content begins to make the trauma more symbolic and to interweave it with concerns from the dreamer's daily life.

The more severe the trauma, the more likely nightmares are to occur, although dreams might not occur or be remembered until after the processing of some aspects of the trauma. Barrett and her colleagues have identified several common themes and symbols in PTSD nightmares:[2]

- Monsters
- Danger
- Being chased
- Rescues
- Dying
- Revenge
- Being threatened again by an assailant or other traumatic event
- Being punished or isolated
- Being trapped, powerlessness
- Sexual abuse (dreams might include shadowy figures, snakes going in holes, worms, blood, good and bad sex, injury, being trapped, paralysis, shame, guilt, anger, violence, or death)
- Filth, excrement, and garbage (can symbolize evil, lack of purpose or dignity, disgust, or shame)
- Physical injury (losing teeth is fairly common, which might symbolize losing control, being powerless or unattractive, or being wounded emotionally)
- Being visited by the deceased

Just as dissociated material can get stuck in waking life, so too can nightmares get stuck, so that we replay and rehash the same nightmares with little change. Nightmares typically remit as memory material is processed in waking life. Now we'll discuss different ways that dream material can be directly processed.

## CONFIDE YOUR DREAMS

Sometimes all that is needed to diminish the intensity of nightmares is to share your dreams verbally with a supportive person or by writing in a journal. Verbalizing in a supportive environment helps to neutralize the intense emotions and integrate the memory fragments.

- Relax and describe your dream in detail. Break it down into the following specifics:

  What is the setting?

  Who are the characters?

  What is happening?

  What are you doing? Feeling? Thinking? What physical sensations are you experiencing?

  What are the symbols?

  What are the symbols saying?

- Create a system to recall your dreams. You might keep a dream journal for such details. You might keep a pad of paper and a pen, or a tape recorder, beside your bed.

## "THIS IS JUST A DREAM"

Imagine that you see yourself at a specific, intense point in the dream carrying out a simple task, such as looking at your hands, and saying in the dream, "This is just a dream." Practice this before you go to sleep to serve as a cue to remind yourself that this is just a dream, should the dream, in fact, recur.[3]

## TURN TOWARD THE NIGHTMARE

Confront the nightmare and find appropriate ways to modify it. Here are some ideas:

- Confront the monster chasing you and ask in a direct and friendly way, "What is it you want—what are you trying to tell me?" One person confronted the monster and discovered that it represented himself and his guilt. He assessed his guilt and made some growth-promoting changes. See if you can make the monster laugh, smile, or get it to dance.
- Create a new ending. For example, see the assailant being caught. See yourself coping. A veteran from the Gulf War sees his buddy, "now with God." You might simply visualize yourself saying, "I am safe now, I survived," or any other positive cognition.

- Write out or talk out what you did above. (Others can sometimes suggest helpful changes you didn't think about.)
- Use art to draw the nightmare and then the more positive ending. Consider all the positive choices you have now.[4]
- Imagine the new dream for about ten to fifteen minutes before going to sleep, followed by a relaxation exercise.

Remember, dreams—like walled-off memories—change as we learn to cope and better process dissociated material. You might dream about positive outcomes. Dreams of the deceased might include assurances that they are now well-off or opportunities to say good-bye. As your recovery proceeds, pay attention to the quality of your dreams. Johanna King and Jacqueline Sheehan have written:[5]

Dreams of growth and understanding excite both the survivor and the therapist. In them, the dreamer behaves or feels differently, sees things from a different point of view, attends to some element of the situation that she has ignored in the past, sees new possibilities emerging. The affective tone of the dreams becomes more positive. The dreamer may come to realize for the first time that she did the best she could at the time of the [traumatic event] or that she had no viable options. She may see more clearly the role of significant others, then and now.

# CHAPTER 26

# Healing Imagery

Health is the movement towards wholeness. Imagery
is the movement towards wholeness made visible.

—*Rachel Naomi Remen, M.D.*

Embedded in traumatic memories are images that powerfully affect our moods, behavior, and health. Mental images even affect our immune systems. While changing our verbal thoughts can neutralize strong negative emotions, changing our mental pictures can sometimes bring about even more positive changes.[1]

Using imagery, we can create mental pictures that are profoundly soothing. You have already used imagery to create a safe place and visualize comforting people. In this chapter, we will explore ways to directly promote healing of the inner emotional wounds. Unlike the chaotic and overwhelming experience of your traumatic event, healing imagery will be conducted in a safe, accepting setting. You will have the chance to infuse your memories with dignity, respect, and control. In this chapter, you'll find a number of imagery exercises to try with your therapist.

## REPLACING PAIN WITH ACCEPTANCE

This imagery exercise is simple yet profound. The minimal use of words helps to discourage overanalysis, while the powerful image elicits strong healing emotions. If your therapist is guiding this exercise with gentle, soothing instructions, you can signal with a raised finger when each step is accomplished.

1. **Sit or lie down in a comfortable and safe place.** Deeply relax your body from head to toe.
2. **Take two easy, deep breaths.** Say to yourself a calming word or phrase such as "relax" as you breathe in and as you breathe out.
3. **Just think of your traumatic event.** Notice what it causes you to feel.
4. **Locate those feelings in your body.** Give them a boundary and a color.
5. **Push the feelings away in front of you.** As you do, give those feelings a shape, a color, and boundaries. Think of your feelings forming a barrier.
6. **See yourself walk around the barrier.** And as you get around it, you are welcomed by a most loving figure with open arms (perhaps a loving family member, deity, or an imagined figure). You hesitate for a moment, but the peaceful loving expression beckons you and invites you forward. You move forward and embrace and are embraced by this loving figure. And you just feel that loving acceptance.
7. **Perhaps no words need to be said.** Perhaps you hear that loving figure say words like, "You are safe and secure now. You have suffered enough. Let my love surround and heal you."

When you have fully experienced the feelings of this imagery, gently return to the present and open your eyes. Tears might appear, but they are usually warm tears, tears of relief and healing.

## TIME TRIPPING[2]

1. **Find a quiet place where you can be undisturbed for about thirty minutes.** Again, get very relaxed and take two easy deep breaths, using your calming word or phrase.
2. **Identify an event in your life that is still painful.** You might wish to start with a memory that is not highly distressing.
3. **Call the person who experienced this difficult time your "younger self."** Call your present self—who possesses greater experience, wisdom, and love—your "wiser self."
4. **Imagine that you, the wiser self, travel back in time to the difficult event and you approach your younger self.** Your younger self looks up and sees you. Your eyes meet, and there is an affinity and trust; your younger self is willing to listen to you.

5. **You enter into a dialogue with your younger self.** You ask the younger self, "What is troubling you?" The younger self expresses the facts *and* feelings of the event. You listen with great empathy and understanding.

6. **You ask, "What would help?"** You listen intently with your ears and heart for what is expressed verbally and silently. You perceive and provide for needs such as the following:

   • Understanding
   • Instruction; perhaps you can teach coping skills that you have recently learned or help the younger self to correct distortions
   • Support and encouragement (e.g., "Considering your experience and training, you're doing well!" "It *will* get better!" "You'll make it through this. I know that you will.")
   • Physical help or protection
   • Advice. Think together. Use the experiences and wisdom of both to brainstorm solutions like these:

     > Perhaps you could coach the child who was abused to say, "That's no way to treat a child. I am trying so hard." The wiser self stands alongside the child for protection and support.

     > The adult might help the child say to a critical parent, "I see your point. I'd like you to help me. I think I'll develop faster if you point out the positives, too."

     > If the younger self made a bad decision, the older might say, "I see why that made sense then. Here's a better way." Imagine helping the younger self improve.

   • Above all, communicate love in any or all of the forms that are needed:

     A loving, gentle, accepting look where eyes meet eyes
     Loving words (e.g., "I love you")
     A hug/embrace
     A soothing touch
     A token to remind the younger self of the wiser self's love

7. **The wiser self now returns to the present or future.** See the wiser and younger selves fused, strong, solid, and whole.

## THE EXPERIENCE OF MATTERING

Ideally, parents will provide children with a safe, secure environment where the children feel loved, accepted, worthwhile, and safe to explore. The children from such homes tend to feel resilient. If people lacked this kind of environment as children, they will likely feel insecure, vulnerable, and defective to the core. They may need to learn how to be loving and protective to themselves. This imagery exercise provides that feeling of security and acceptance. It is especially useful for people who cannot remember pleasant times prior to their traumatic event(s). These instructions for a corrective experience are adapted from the works of John Bradshaw and Pam Levin:[3]

1. **Write down the names of your most cherished friends, family, and loved ones—people you felt good to be with, people who made you feel warm, safe, accepted, loved.** First identify couples, then individuals (including friends, colleagues, teachers).
2. **Find a place to sit quietly and comfortably.** Make this a place where you won't be disturbed for about fifteen minutes.
3. **Relax your entire body.** Take two very deep breaths, saying to yourself the word "relax" as you breathe in and as you breathe out.
4. **Imagine yourself an infant surrounded by loving people.** These can be a circle of the loving people you identified or two warm, loving grown-ups— one a male and one a female—parents as you would like to imagine parents ideally, perhaps composite figures of people you have known and loved, who made you feel like a somebody.
5. **As an infant, you needed to hear these words.** Imagine yourself hearing these alternately from a male voice and a female voice:

   > We're so glad you're here . . . Welcome to the world . . . Welcome to our family and home . . . I'm so glad you're a boy or a girl . . . You're beautiful . . . All our children are beautiful . . . We want to be near you, to hold you and love you . . . Sometimes you'll feel joy and laughter . . . Sometimes sadness and pain and anger and worry . . . These feelings are all OK with us. We'll be there for you . . . We'll give you all the time you need to get your needs met . . . It's okay to wander and separate and explore and experiment . . . We won't leave you . . .

   Imagine them cradling you, loving you, gently gazing upon you with eyes of love—and you respond to these feelings.

## HEALING LOVED ONES

Imagine a loved one has been killed in an auto accident and you didn't have the chance to say good-bye. Talking about the event and your feelings has helped, but you still are having very distressing intrusions about the accident. Dr. Mary S. Cerney of the Menninger Clinic has taught this technique.[4] The client was a teenage girl who lost her sister in an accident. Her belief is that her sister is safe in heaven, yet she cannot get over the gruesome image of her sister's injury, which in this case, was an amputated arm.

1. Get very relaxed from head to toe. Again, use your calming word or phrase as you breathe in and as you breathe out.
2. Can you imagine seeing your loved one now, after the accident? And what do you notice? (Perhaps she is smiling and well, but the injury persists.)
3. Can you now reach out and heal your loved one? Anything is possible in imagery. (Perhaps you reach out and restore the lost body part or otherwise heal the injury.)
4. And what does that feel like? And is there anything else that you want to do? (Perhaps you want to tell your loved one that you love her and then say good-bye.)

## COPING IMAGERY

See yourself in the present confronting a trigger. See the memory of the original trauma intruding while you become very distressed. Now see yourself becoming very calm and peaceful. You feel in control. See yourself telling yourself the following:

- I'm safe and in control now.
- That's just past stuff—just old memories. I'm safely in the present now.
- I've survived. I'm not defeated.

# CHAPTER 27

# *Healing Rituals*

Following the Gulf War, American troops marched proudly as their country welcomed them home. Many a Vietnam veteran shed a tear and found the ceremonies vicariously healing.[1] A family holds a memorial service for a man whose body was never recovered from a flood. His little granddaughter launches a balloon heavenward with a love note saying good-bye.

Rituals are structured activities that help us heal. They help us focus our thoughts and feelings, experience them, and process them. They help us consider the meaning of what has happened, grieve losses, receive support, and develop helpful new ways to view ourselves and move ahead. Some rituals are formally structured; others can be quite simple. This chapter will explore the nature of rituals and give suggestions for developing healing rituals.

PTSD authority Dr. Don Catherall has suggested that most rituals generally contain seven parts.[2] Think of a funeral, and you can easily identify them:

1. **A location** might be a gravesite, a sacred religious structure, a place where someone experienced a traumatic event, or a beloved spot in nature.
2. **A symbol.** A gravestone, for example, helps us to experience our feelings. The Vietnam Veterans Memorial is a powerful symbol. The visitor descends into what feels like a dark valley of death, pauses to pay sacred respect to the fallen individuals, then walks upward toward life and light again. A family at the grave symbolizes a new family—not diminished but unified.
3. **Props.** These include flowers, candles, photos, or written speeches.
4. **Personal support.** People verbalize love and support and communicate it nonverbally through hugs, touch, or caring expressions. Grief is shared as people communicate their sorrow. People help survivors prepare food or

perform other helpful tasks. Comments such as "I'll see you again" remind survivors that they are part of the community.

5. **Healing words.** Remembrances help to put traumatic events and individuals' lives in perspective. For example, a eulogy by someone who knows the family can recall both the strengths and quirks of the deceased and reminisce in a loving, and even at times, humorous way. A woman nursed her husband for three years before he died from a fall. She was feeling ashamed for the times that she had gotten frustrated and impatient with him. A minister in the eulogy correctly reminded her of her extraordinary saintly patience at a time when she was open to hearing that. Informal reminiscing recalls cherished memories that may be otherwise lost.

   Meaningful poems, songs, or music and invoking divine comfort can also promote healing. Expressions of hope for the future and enduring commitment to relationships help survivors see beyond the traumatic event.

6. **A knowledgeable, trusted guide or director.** This might be a recognized leader, a funeral director, clergyperson, or one who has gone through similar difficult times and rituals before. Sometimes it is simply a family member or friend who is perceived as trusted and caring. Sometimes you might choose to lead your own ritual.

7. **Farewells.** Tossing a rose into the grave communicates acceptance of a person's passing, the wish to preserve loving memories, and the reality of moving into the future. One community drew pictures of feelings they wished to release, tore them up, and placed them in an inexpensive rocket, which together they watched fly into the night.

Catherall continues that the preparation of a ritual contributes to the meaning of it. Individuals can plan how to dress appropriately, create poems, pick flowers, walk down the aisle, and make other plans. It is good to invite all people who are involved to participate—even children. A good time to hold a ritual might be at the anniversary of the trauma. The season will tend to trigger strong emotions anyway, and a ritual could provide great support to the survivors. Other significant dates might also be meaningful. For example, at class reunions, the service academies hold chapel services where a roll call of deceased classmates honors their memory and gives survivors further opportunity to reminisce and grieve. The citizens of Oklahoma City gather annually on the anniversary date at the site of the tragic 1995 bombing.

Designing your own ritual will usually make it most meaningful. Consider how your family has conducted rituals over the years. This might suggest what would be most meaningful. Catherall suggests the following:

1. Specify the trauma(s).
2. Identify who has been affected and how.
3. Develop symbols for life before the trauma, the trauma itself, and transition and transformation. The loss of illusions of security might be symbolized by an unlocked door, a picture of a child confidently leaping into a parent's arms, or a photo of an infant sleeping peacefully. A rape survivor wears one closed rose to symbolize the rape and one open rose to symbolize becoming open again to life. Religious symbols of hope and resurrection can comfort.

Again, rituals can be quite formal or relatively simple. A pilgrimage to a place that you remember with fondness and safety can symbolize a sense of security that was lost. Catherall relates another creative ritual. A young four-and-a-half-year-old girl was molested at school but was not considered a credible witness at the trial. Although the older children testified, young Catherine did not and had difficulty moving beyond the trauma. So her mother set up a pretend trial, with the policeman who had been talking to Catherine serving as the judge and the social worker and therapist also participating. Catherine prepared by learning about how trials work, discussing the roles of the various participants, and preparing her own testimony. During the actual "trial," Catherine gave her testimony, and the "judge" sentenced the perpetrator. Catherine asked for and received assurance that the "bad man" would no longer hurt her.

Let's explore certain rituals that have been used in the treatment of combat veterans. These rituals might suggest other ideas for your own healing rituals.

## NATIVE AMERICAN SWEAT LODGE AND PURIFICATION RITUAL

This ritual is richly symbolic. According to John Wilson and Benjamin Colodzin,[3] war is considered abnormal, and to return to the culture, individuals must be transformed and restored to balance. Thus, the returning warriors are ceremoniously cleansed before entering a dark, circular lodge. The warriors sit close together, cross-legged, in a circle surrounding a pit of extremely hot rocks. They are guided to their places by a medicine man, who speaks in a soothing, calm voice of welcome, hope, healing, and transition back to the community. Water is ladled over the hot rocks, producing steam, as the medicine man pronounces a song of prayer that participants repeat together. Each participant offers a personal prayer, beginning with thanksgiving and ending with an expression of unity with all others. The medicine man speaks additional words of wisdom and guidance. After about an hour or longer, the warriors leave the lodge and smoke the sacred pipe to close the ritual.

Now let's consider the symbolism. The ritual itself honors the warriors' contributions and demonstrates the desire to bring them back into the community. The medicine man, or shaman, represents healing and is a role model of spiritual strength. His guiding the warriors to their places in the dark symbolizes trust, goodness, and security, and opening the door flap periodically lets in wisdom and guidance. The circle symbolizes unity and shared suffering. In the total darkness, one confronts oneself, and a sense of inner strength emerges. The sweat literally and symbolically cleanses, and the emerging into the light and fresh air of nature symbolizes transition back to the community and rebirth. If the lodge is next to a running stream, this too symbolizes cleansing.

## REVISITING THE SITE OF THE TRAUMA

This special type of ritual permits one to confront the trauma from a perspective of experience and safety. Sometimes the survivor gains insights that were not afforded during the heat of the traumatic event. One of the most moving examples of this type of ritual is "Full Cycle," a University of Massachusetts project for Vietnam veterans who had been unsuccessfully treated for PTSD by conventional means.[4] Twelve veterans were taken by bus to My Lai, where American soldiers had massacred more than a hundred South Vietnamese civilians. One veteran related extreme fear as the bus approached, anticipating that the villagers would drag the veterans out of the bus and parade them as war criminals. As they walked through the peaceful village to the visitors' center, children smiled. They learned that five hundred and four civilians had been massacred, not a hundred, and many of these were pregnant women. A guide at the visitors' center greeted them graciously and asked them to sign a visitors' book. One veteran wrote, "Please forgive us." And then a healing miracle occurred. A woman serving tea said, "The past is past. We know the American people did not want this to happen. It is time to forget and become friends." A veteran wept, "Here the South hasn't forgiven the North for something that happened a hundred years ago, and these people forgive us for something that happened twenty years ago."

In the same project, two nurses with PTSD returned to a hospital, a scene of gore that intruded repeatedly into their consciousness. They assumed that they would encounter hatred. Instead, graciousness and love was shown by local citizens. One nurse went to the hospital and found that the citizens had dedicated a room to the nurses who had ministered to civilians. In fact, a plaque hung in the very room where her bed had been.

Another veteran placed a marigold from My Lai on a Vietnam War memorial atop a hill as a sign of respect for the enemy he had killed. He cried, prayed for forgiveness, and released years of pain. Still another visited a battle site where he had been wounded to "return" to his comrades who had been killed after he'd been evacuated. He shed a few tears and made peace with them. Each of these individuals found a meaningful way to come to terms with his or her trauma.

Healing rituals surround the event and the survivors with healing emotions as the facts and feelings of the traumatic event are acknowledged, confronted, and honored. In this sense, healing rituals are much like healing imagery. Notice the degree of closure that has taken place following a ritual. Do not be surprised, however, if additional processing is still needed.

# CHAPTER 28

# *Grieving Losses*

---

**We grieve what we value; we grieve in proportion to our affection.**[1]
**—*paraphrased from memorial to Jane Austen, Winchester Cathedral***

All the many complex issues involved in PTSD must be disentangled for recovery to proceed. Grief is one such issue. All events that are significant enough to cause PTSD involve loss, yet grief often gets buried in the struggle for survival. Perhaps you were too numbed to grieve. Perhaps you were too busy or were discouraged from grieving. Perhaps some aspects of the trauma still feel so overwhelming that you have avoided them. These reactions are all normal. However, continually avoiding the normal, healthy feelings of grief keeps unresolved memories of loss in active memory, emotionally charged, and likely to intrude.

Grief memories are processed much like other aspects of traumatic memories: at your own pace and when you are ready. Losses are confronted and processed so that meaningful adjustments and adaptations can be made in our lives. Of course, adjustments can only be made if we clearly acknowledge the nature of our losses. We can't adapt and find new ways to satisfy the void if losses are not confronted. Losses that are buried—not explored, experienced, and expressed—can erupt at inopportune times, resulting in a host of physical and emotional symptoms.[2] The more we fear facing the pain of loss, the more we remain in bondage to the past. So it is important to process our losses.

## WHAT ARE GRIEF AND MOURNING?

Grief is the suffering associated with loss. People typically think of grief as intense feelings of sadness and sorrow. However, the experience of grief can also include bodily changes, such as fatigue and troubled sleep, and behavioral changes, such as keeping busy or using drugs to escape the pain.

Mourning refers to the process by which we explore, experience, express, and integrate our grief and adjust to a world with the loss. Mourning derives from the Indo-European base *mer*, meaning to remember or think of. Mourning and grieving are often used interchangeably.

## WHAT WE GRIEVE

In trauma, we don't only lose *something*, we also lose our way. Hard-earned gains and dreams for the future seem irrevocably lost. Development is seriously impaired. Grieving is about finding our way again. So by grieving, we try to name and understand our losses. We attempt to see clearly where we presently are in regard to where we were before the loss, and where we wish to be.[3] Losses resulting from traumatic events might be tangible,[4] such as the loss of a loved one. However, there are also many intangible aspects of loss that typically need to be grieved. Thus, the death of a spouse means more than just the tangible loss of a body, which may itself have given great comfort and pleasure. Intangible losses include the deceased spouse's roles as helper, friend, adviser, protector, parent, or emotional supporter. Losing the status of being married, the surviving spouse might also find himself isolated from old social groups comprised solely of couples. Lost too are dreams for the future, perhaps involving creating a family, traveling, or sharing hobbies. Secondary losses—consequent to the initial loss—might include having to move from a cherished home and community due to loss of the spouse's income. Having to work causes the spouse to abandon for a time her dream of writing a book. Sometimes when we grieve, we discover a sense of loss for things that never were. For example, an adult survivor of incest realized that she never had a healthy, normal, loving relationship with her father. When we clearly see our losses, several outcomes are possible. We might

- Identify the need to mourn and find constructive ways to heal
- Find ways to cherish precious memories
- Accept what can't be replaced, while finding alternative ways to meet our needs
- Discover or affirm inner strengths
- Discover or affirm what is really important to our lives
- Begin again to develop in areas that were frozen at the time of the trauma

None of these positive outcomes can occur if we simply try to flee our pain. Conversely, when our losses become clear, we can take steps to get back on course. So there is a greater purpose to grieving than simply discharging sadness. When overwhelmed, we might naturally try to escape the pain. As we begin to break down the trauma and understand our losses, we are then in a better position to find our way. Specific, tangible losses might be irreplaceable, but many intangibles—what they mean—are recoverable, at least in part. Traumatic events understandably involve a sense of loss. Your trauma might include the loss of the following:

- Life (e.g., of a loved one, colleague, or fetal child)
- Home
- Property
- Pets
- Health status: physical capacities, body parts, appearance
- Lifestyle
- Community
- Job, income, promotions (might be due to inability to concentrate or interact with coworkers, absence, medical illness, etc.)
- Memories: mementos/keepsakes (photos, baby books)
- Dreams, opportunities, hopes ("I was learning to be such a good parent and spouse; now I feel useless to my family.")
- Normal, trusting relationships (e.g., a relationship with an abusive parent that never developed, a disrupted relationship with a loved one or friend, incest that causes the removal of a parent from the home, loss of ability to connect with people)
- Innocence, a normal childhood (sense of play, spontaneity, joyful memories, discovery, warmth, zest, creativity)
- Virginity, ability to choose first sexual partner, sense of control of body
- Sexual confidence, feelings of sacredness of body and wholesomeness of sexuality, ability to enjoy sensual experiences
- Trust in others or self
- Sense of safety, goodness, beauty, humor, self-confidence, enjoyment, peace, fairness
- Previous self-concept (e.g., "I no longer consider myself wise, prudent, a good protector, moral," etc.)
- Self-respect

- Reputation
- Spirituality (e.g., feelings of peace with God, sense of being protected and valued)
- Faith in institutions (police, doctors, military, legal profession)

## UNCOMPLICATED GRIEVING

Normal, uncomplicated mourning typically follows the six "R" processes of mourning outlined by renowned grief authority Dr. Therese Rando.[5] You might think of the death of a parent who died expectedly after a long, satisfying life, although these six Rs apply to other types of losses with obvious adjustments:

1. **Recognize the loss.** We intellectually acknowledge the loss and understand the reasons and circumstances. For example, we listen to the medical report, view the body, and participate in the funeral. All aspects of the loss, including intangible and secondary losses, are identified.
2. **React emotionally.** We experience and express all emotions surrounding the loss, positive and negative. Respites and distractions from the pain are normal, but eventually the hurt will be experienced.
3. **Recollect and reexperience the deceased and the relationship.** Here we review and remember realistically all aspects of the deceased to gain an accurate composite of the deceased. We cherish the good qualities while accepting the flaws of the loved one. Unfinished business with the deceased is recognized and completed.
4. **Relinquish old attachments to the deceased and to assumptions that no longer work.** Here we accept that the deceased will not return so we no longer expect her for dinner or expect him to call. We give up the notion that nothing bad will ever happen and accept the fact that the world is not perfect. This step does not mean that we forget the deceased, only that we accept the reality of her passing.
5. **Readjust to the world without forgetting the deceased.** We accept that our loved one will not be able to take care of us and realize that we will need to make some changes in order to continue living a satisfying life. We figure out ways to retain healthy connections to the deceased while accepting their passing. We might identify ways to memorialize the deceased or to remember their teachings or perspectives on decisions. We might find a support group to help us transition to our new world, learn new skills to

meet needs that the deceased used to take care of, or accept life without certain needs being met.

6. **Reinvest in life—love, work, and play.** We find ways to redirect our emotional energy that will yield satisfying returns. We might find new hobbies, causes, or relationships. Cherished memories can furnish energy for these pursuits.

Rando notes that mourning does not usually progress smoothly through these six steps. Often it is two steps forward and one back. Mourning usually takes longer than we expect, as well. It helps to realize that even in uncomplicated mourning, a full range of emotional, physical, and behavioral symptoms are common:[6]

- Initially shock, numbness, bewilderment, disbelief, and even denial can occur. Sometimes people can accept the loss intellectually but not emotionally. The denial can help the person get through the first few days. Denial might take these forms: "This can't be happening—it feels like a dream." "It is happening, but it isn't that bad." "Others are worse off than I am." Taking care of others, appearing strong, trying to reverse the loss, or keeping busy are other ways to temporarily avoid confronting painful feelings.
- After days, numbness turns to intense suffering as the loss is acknowledged. Expect the following:
    Feelings of emptiness
    Repeatedly being reminded of the deceased
    Waves of crying and/or sadness sweeping over the survivor with each reminder
    Longing
    Preoccupation with the deceased's memory
    Dreams and apparent visitations
    Physical changes including insomnia, loss of appetite, loss of sex drive
- Despair follows as the loss is accepted. Dominant feelings are sadness and the inability to feel pleasure. A tense, restless anxiety may alternate with lethargy and fatigue. Common physical symptoms include weakness, sleep disturbances, loss of appetite, headaches, back pain, indigestion, shortness of breath, throat tightness, heart palpitations, dizziness, and nausea. Sadness can be mixed with anger at the deceased for leaving or for other disappointments, relief at not having to care for the deceased any longer, or gratitude for being alive. Some people seek company, while others with-

draw. People might alternate between avoiding reminders and cultivating memories. Many wish they had treated the deceased better, and a significant minority (about 40 percent) think they are losing their minds.

- Sadness and emotional swings may last for years. Even after recovery, grief spasms, or waves of grief, may return on anniversaries or other significant dates.

## COMPLICATED MOURNING

Rando defines complicated mourning as a response to loss that does not progress normally through the six Rs. That is, there is a problem or "sticking point" at a stage or stages in the grieving process. Many forms of complicated mourning involve trauma. Complicated grief symptoms are similar to those of uncomplicated grief, except that they are more prolonged and intense. In addition, clinical depression, anxiety disorders, compulsive gambling, low self-esteem, guilt, fear of relationships, chronic grieving as attempts to keep the loved one alive, and other symptoms associated with PTSD are common.

The following is a list of factors that can complicate the mourning process:

1. Denial is excessive and persistent:
   - An incest survivor thinks, "I can't believe my father did that to me—he loved me."
   - A mother of a son who died in an automobile accident says, "I don't want to know what really happened. Don't tell me the details or show me the accident report."
2. Preoccupation with anger and rage might prevent one from acknowledging the underlying grief.
3. Ambivalent feelings toward the deceased are not acknowledged.
   - A woman only recalls her father as loving when he was sober and can't permit herself to feel anger for his violence when drunk. Thus, she does not complete her business with him by processing her anger.
   - Anger is displaced from the deceased person to others such as doctors or relatives as a way to avoid the primary source of anger. For example, a woman could not acknowledge her anger at her usually careful husband who died in a careless industrial accident. Instead, she raged at his managers for not preventing the accident.
4. Unresolved guilt ("If only I had . . . ") blocks processing of grief.

5. The traumatic events were too sudden and overwhelming to confront. Often multiple losses seem impossible to break down and grieve singly. Perhaps you were too preoccupied with survival or too numb to grieve.

6. Other people discourage grieving or are unavailable to support the bereaved.
   - Most cultures routinely sanction funeral rites for the deceased. However, most cultures do not routinely provide ways to grieve miscarriage, abortion, suicide, sexual abuse, rape, domestic violence, or family dysfunction from alcoholism.
   - When a child dies, spouses may be unable to support each other because of their own grief.

7. People may learn a variety of myths that discourage grieving (see page 255).

## TIPS FOR GRIEVING

1. **Go as slowly as you need to.** Look for all emotions.

2. **Use pre-trauma photos to help identify "losses."** As someone once said, "the child you once were, you still are." Although trauma seems to bury the beautiful qualities of an individual, those qualities still exist and may again be cultivated.

3. **Memorialize the loss.** Memorials like the Vietnam Veterans Memorial help to contain grief. It gives grief a place to reside, wrapped in dignity, respect, and love, and gives us a way to stay connected. It says, "I love you, I always will; this gives me a way to remember you while continuing on with my life. I will not forget you."

4. **View upsurges in grief as opportunities to resolve grief and heal emotionally.** Look for unresolved grief from previous losses that might make you more vulnerable to more recent losses.

5. **Be willing to give up guilt, shame, the desire to judge or punish yourself, and the hope to change the past.** Compassion, not judgment, heals.

6. **Consider how loss might lead to gains:**
   - Increased empathy and capacity to help others
   - Clearer understanding of what really matters; greater wisdom
   - Constructive changes; commitment to use time and life energies wisely
   - The knowledge that you can survive anything; recognition of inner strengths
   - Gratitude and appreciation for what you still have

# MYTHS THAT COMPLICATE MOURNING

**1. *Grief is a weakness.***
Grief is a normal, understandable human experience that happens because we deeply value what has been lost. Grief is part of what makes us human, but like guilt, it is not meant to last forever at an intensely painful level. The grieving process allows us to feel the pain, express it, then move on with fewer long-term negative effects.

**2. *If I start to grieve, I will lose control and cry forever.***
According to the research, losing control is unlikely. You will more likely feel sad for a time, but you will recover. Should you lose control and cry for awhile, so what? This is a normal way to express pain so that we can recover sooner and retain our humanity.

**3. *If I stop to grieve, I will lose the gains I have made in life.***
As a rule, the sooner one resolves grief, the more productive one is able to be. Conversely, unresolved grief will detract from performance and enjoyment. Grieving does not mean that life's progress will stop. Grief work does take time, but it is an investment of some, not all, of one's time.

**4. *If I recover and feel joy, I will show that I don't care.***
Some combat veterans think they must continually grieve as a memorial to their fallen comrades, and feel disloyal if they stop feeling intense pain. We might ask, "Are there better memorials to the deceased than prolonged pain? Are there better ways to stay close to them? Do you think they want you to go on grieving and stop living? Might they prefer that you memorialize them with happy memories and a fruitful life?"

Others think that no longer feeling intense pain over their mistakes indicates betrayal of their values. We might ask, "Can we commit to living well without being emotionally distraught? Can we motivate ourselves with a carrot rather than a stick?"

**5. *If I stop grieving, I will forget the loss.***
When memories are no longer numbed, we remember the loss more completely—but with more peace and less pain.

**6. *If I give up the loss, I give up a part of self.***
Is it really prolonged anguish that we wish to preserve, or cherished memories and a satisfying life course?

**7. *The deceased (or offender) is a saint or a sinner. I must either love or hate him.***
This idea makes it impossible to process normal ambivalent feelings. Every mortal is somewhere between the extremes of perfect saint or complete sinner. So it is normal for a child to grieve a parent who was loving at times, yet have great anger for the criminal things the parent did. Conversely, to be angry at a generally decent deceased person does not make the survivor a bad person or mean that she didn't love the deceased.

**8. *Grief shows a lack of spiritual faith.***
Faith may help people keep going, but it does not insulate one from human sadness. Certainly Job was no stranger to grief, while even Jesus wept.

- Awareness of personal vulnerabilities
- Recognition of the need to develop new skills to strengthen yourself
7. **Consider thoughts that might help you better deal with the losses:**
   - "My baby is safe with God."
   - "My deceased loved one is in a better place."[7]
   - "I'm a good person who went through a bad experience."
8. **Consider the possibility of forgiving loved ones or others who disappointed you.** This difficult process will be discussed in Chapter 34.

You might find the "journey of grief" exercise that follows very helpful.

## THE JOURNEY OF GRIEF EXERCISE

Once we have confronted our pain, there is nothing left to fear. The journey of grief is like a voyage into darkness and sadness. We keep traveling into this darkness and sadness until eventually the darkness gives way to light and gladness. Then we have seen the whole picture and no longer need to run from the dark.

We will not lose ground if we pause to grieve. Grieving is like restful sleep. Sleeping takes time, but we awake refreshed for the next day's journey. In the same way, grieving allows us ultimately to progress further.

Begin your journey of grief with a sense of discovery and the nonjudgmental attitude of a scientist. That is, do not judge your feelings or reactions as good or bad. Just allow them to be and observe them.

Below are a series of questions to respond to. It is suggested that you place each question at the top of a separate blank sheet of paper. Number the sheets and questions, and answer each question in turn. Keep a fairly steady pace. You can go as slowly or as fast as you want. For major traumas or traumas that were prolonged, you'll probably be wise to advance in small doses. Return to questions as often as you like until you feel that you have completed your journey.

The journey of grief exercise consists of three parts: damage assessment, broadening the perspective, and readjusting and reinventing.

### Damage Assessment

A military commander receives a casualty report. This permits the commander to see where the unit is in terms of capabilities and needs, and how best to proceed. At times, the commander might determine that time is needed to regroup and retrain. At other times, the commander will know that the unit is ready to advance with confidence. In the journey of grief exercise, you, of course, are both the unit and the commander, gathering accurate information in order to determine how best to proceed.

1. Briefly describe what happened. That is, list the traumatic event(s) and when it/they happened.
2. What did I seem to lose? Consider the obvious tangible losses, as well as intangible and secondary losses. Ask yourself, How am I different since the trauma? What does the loss mean to me? What gains had I made that were reversed?
3. What negative impacts have the losses had on me? What painful feelings have resulted?
4. Do the losses following the trauma remind me of earlier losses, such as death, abandonment, or neglect? What did those earlier losses cause me to feel?
5. What factors have prevented me from grieving my losses?

## Broadening the Perspective

Here we view the loss in its complete, realistic context. As we have noted previously, there is a tendency in PTSD to see only the negative aspects of our experience.

1. What hasn't been lost? (What do I still have, such as abilities, capacities, relationships, other tangibles, and intangibles?)
2. What has been gained from the loss?
3. What have I learned?
4. What positive benefits can still be derived?
5. What has helped me to cope and survive? Has there been some goodness in the world that has assisted me?
6. What inner strengths have emerged or have I discovered in myself? (What personal qualities got me through the loss? What beautiful aspects are still there? What did I do well to survive? What have I done since the trauma that is honorable or noteworthy?)
7. What do I still value?
8. What could have made things worse for me? For others?
9. What do I miss most about the losses?
10. What memories do I still cherish that perhaps were buried by the trauma?
11. What won't I miss about the losses?
12. What can I still enjoy?

## Readjusting and Reinvesting

The purpose of grief is not to remain in a hole of sadness but to find ways to go on living fruitfully.

1. What would I wish to say to the people involved in the losses, including myself, to help complete unfinished business?
2. What thoughts might help me to deal with the loss?
3. What do I still need?
4. What would help me heal?
5. What losses are replaceable? (Are my tangible losses irrevocable? If so, how else might I fill my needs?)
6. What will help me set a good life course? (How can I transition to a more satisfying way of life and go on without the things I've lost?)
7. If I were no longer mourning, what would I like to be doing now with my life?
8. Imagine yourself a year or two from now. You think of the loss and remember it, but the intense pain has ended. What has happened to enable you to do this?

Perhaps you are realizing that grief work can be challenging, which is why it is called *work*. Expect the process to take time. Seek help if you feel "stuck."

# CHAPTER 29

# Making Sense of Trauma

## Coming to Terms with Suffering

We ask, "Why? Why?! Why!!" Why did it have to happen? Why to such a good person? Why to my loved ones? Why to me? Why is there so much evil? Why did God let this happen?

Without resolution, these questions keep us stuck and powerless. On the other hand, responding to these questions can be very empowering and liberating, even if the answers are not totally satisfying. Some counselors feel it is best to not ask the questions since one cannot fully answer them. They correctly point out that those who continuously ask why are more likely to be depressed. Or angry demands for answers might deflect one from accepting losses and moving on. So they think it wise to accept that bad things happen, and move on. This is one option.

Another approach is to more fully address the questions, answer them as completely and as quickly as possible, accept the limitations to our understanding, and then move on.

When we ask why, we are really asking "Why do we suffer?" a question that has plagued philosophers throughout history. Let's tackle this question and resolve it as satisfactorily as we can. In short, we suffer because the world and its people are imperfect. More specifically, we suffer for four reasons:

## OUR IMPERFECTIONS

We sometimes suffer as a result of our own imperfections. If we drive loved ones away because of our anger, it is good to recognize our shortcoming and make adjustments. A traumatic event might catch us unprepared, unskilled, unable to function at our best under duress, or careless—in short, imperfect. If we accurately accept responsibility for our flaws and try our best to improve without self-condemnation, then suffering is not in vain.

## OTHERS' IMPERFECTIONS

We sometimes suffer as a result of the imperfections of others. We live in a world where each individual has free choice. Mother Teresa wisely observed, "Even God will not force us to do good. We must choose to do good." A world of free choice permits individuals to rise to the very noblest of heights. As Norman Cousins observed, "Man is fallible, but infinitely perfectible." History is full of noble individuals, and we need not look too hard to find people like Albert Schweitzer, Mother Teresa, Abraham Lincoln, Arthur Ashe, or the kind neighbor down the block. On the other hand, a world of free choice permits people to choose evil. It is difficult to comprehend why a person would choose evil over good or to know for certain what factors are operative in an individual's life. But we can consider and understand the possibilities.

- People tend to reenact what they see and learn. If a child grows up in a violent home, he is more likely to become a victimizer than one who grows up in a loving home. The encouraging news is that the majority of abused children do not grow up to be abusers. However, the bad news is that the vast majority of prison inmates have a history of abuse. Sometimes victimizers have been numbed to all feelings of conscience, guilt, and compassion by a history of brutality. Sometimes they have not learned to interact in loving ways, and they lash out in frustration and pain.
- Brain damage has been observed in victimizers to a greater degree than would be expected by chance. Shaking or battering a child can damage areas of the brain that help to regulate emotions. This might help to explain explosive, uncontrollable anger and/or lack of remorse in some victimizers.
- Certain biological abnormalities can lead to mental or medical illnesses that are sometimes associated with victimizing behavior. These include certain forms of epilepsy, schizophrenia, or bipolar disorder (manic depression). Similarly, brain tumors, viral infections such as encephalitis or rabies, strokes, multiple sclerosis, Huntington's chorea, some forms of mental retardation, and substance abuse might interfere with affect regulation.[1]

- The Chinese philosopher Lao Tzu observed that bad and good coexist in each individual. We each grow up in environments that can favor the cultivation of one or the other. Beyond the influence of family, risk factors for victimizing include media violence and media sexual exploitation. Feeling incompetent or insecure, some people attach to hate groups made up of like-minded individuals who seek to control others.

## CHANCE

Sometimes we suffer as a result of chance. Rabbi Harold Kushner[2] writes of a woman who lost her loved one in a plane crash and cries out, "What did I do to deserve this?" He responds that bad things sometimes happen randomly to good people. Not all bad things happen because we are bad and deserve them.

## PERSONAL GROWTH

Sometimes we suffer so that growth becomes possible. Orthodox Judaism's most illustrious philosopher, Rabbi Joseph B. Soloveitchik, stated, "God left an area of evil and chaos in the world so that man might make it good."[3] Thus, suffering confronts us with the possibility of elevating ourselves and others. We cannot control others or force them to choose good, but we can choose for ourselves what course to follow and perhaps influence others. Perhaps more important than why a traumatic event happened is what we will do to make the suffering meaningful.

A young widow, Ardis Whitman[4] writes of the loneliness she felt following her husband's death. In gratitude, she sees more clearly what a loving, complex, often tormented person he was and wonders how she might have listened more and tried to understand him better instead of being so petty. She realizes through her grief that she was overcoming her fear of being alone. She gained compassion as she realized she could no longer condemn the alcoholic who tried to escape his pain. In short, she realized that her suffering was more than pain, it was the shaping of her soul. Similarly, through his anguish, Sheldon Vanauken[5] came to view the loss of his beloved wife as "a severe mercy" because of his soul's enlargement that ensued.

Understanding suffering as clearly as possible and taking responsibility only for that which we can control can help us to come to terms with suffering.[6] We accept that the world is imperfect and that very bad things can happen. Accepting does not mean that we like or allow bad things to happen. It only means that we acknowledge that they do and move on with as little bitterness and cynicism as possible.

# CHAPTER 30

# Hypnosis

Because survivors of trauma have already learned how to dissociate, many therapists will enlist this skill as an aid to recovery. Hypnosis is one strategy that uses dissociation in a comfortable way. There is nothing mysterious or magical about this effective strategy. As we discuss it, you will realize that you are already familiar with many of its aspects from previous strategies we have discussed.

In hypnosis, one deeply relaxes and opens the mind to possibilities. We voluntarily loosen our grip on the way things normally are and redirect our minds in productive, often creative ways.

As we relax, we sharpen our concentration, perhaps focusing attention on these:[1]

- Forgotten details. For example, a firefighter remembered only the cries of the person he could not save. Watching the fire from an imaginary safe place under hypnosis, he recalls the people he did save and all that he did to save them. As a result, his guilt was reduced.
- A better future and solutions ("What would the solution look like, sound like, feel like?")
- Positive feelings, beliefs, or self-images ("Was there a time when you felt safe?" etc.)
- Ways to value previously dissociated parts of the self
- Lessons learned from the trauma
- Healing suggestions that are agreeable to you ("You'll most likely find yourself worrying less and focusing more on the enjoyable aspects of situations.")
- Pain management ("Give the pain a color, temperature, and shape; see the color changing and cooling.")

The American Psychological Association has stated:[2] "Contrary to some depictions of hypnosis in books, movies, or on television, people who have been hypnotized do not lose control over their behavior. They typically remain aware of who they are and where they are, and unless amnesia has been specifically suggested, they usually remember what transpired during hypnosis. Hypnosis makes it easier for people to experience suggestions, but it does not force them to have these experiences."

Peaceful imagery or other forms of induction are often used to obtain a relaxed hypnotic state. In a soothing, rhythmic voice, the therapist might say, "Imagine walking slowly down stairs"; "Imagine that your limbs are warm and heavy"; or "Imagine resting in your favorite sofa, pleasantly fatigued, perhaps after taking a walk on a spring day." Induction usually takes ten to twenty minutes or more but with practice, might be accomplished within seconds. Hypnosis ends with a simple suggestion.

Robert Schwarz[3] describes how hypnosis might be used to help a person integrate trauma material. Bill remembers his image in a photograph taken shortly after his traumatic event. In it he looks sad, anxious, and numb. Thoughts of this image, along with the negative feelings, often intrude into awareness. Disliking the intrusions, he tries unsuccessfully to dissociate from the memory.

The therapist starts by asking Bill to identify the opposite of sad, anxious, and numb—which Bill describes as safe and happy. After induction, Bill is asked to think of a time when he *strongly* felt safe and happy, and to go there *fully*. She stated that she was going to touch Bill lightly on the wrist as a cue to remember those feelings of safety and happiness. Thereafter, the therapist lightly touched Bill's wrist each time she wished to activate those feelings. She then guided Bill to view the traumatic memory on a movie screen from a safe projection room, much like the rewind technique taught in Chapter 23. Bill was guided to imagine visiting the younger self in the movie and to provide what that younger survivor needed. Bill decided that the younger person needed to know that he's not a bad person, that he only made the choice that made the most sense at the time—and that he is still a valuable person. Bill was guided to bring the younger survivor off the screen and to sit with that survivor, infusing him with feelings of acceptance, compassion, love, and safety, and to notice the sad photo that had troubled Bill changing. Counting to five, the therapist brought Bill comfortably and safely back to the present.

The jettison technique[4] can be used at the end of a hypnosis therapy session or for relief from difficult memory work. Instructions follow:

1. Make a fist, and you have all your fears and problems clasped there in your fist.
2. On the count of three, you will open your fist and all your anxieties will disappear, and you will feel happy, confident, and calm.

**Cautions**

- If you decide to use hypnosis, it is important that you feel safe and in control. You might first practice using it to increase calmness and self-esteem before experimenting with it for other uses. Discuss with your therapist how hypnosis will proceed and be sure that you are comfortable with the plan. Agree upon a signal, such as a raised hand, to stop if the process becomes too distressing.
- In many states, memories recovered under hypnosis are not allowed in court. Discuss this with your therapist before using hypnosis if litigation is planned. While most people will not create a memory that is suggested, the possibility exists that some might. Others might have a vague uncertainty as to whether or not a suggested memory occurred. Thus, it is crucial that the therapist not try to influence a client's memory. Again, the principle is that hypnosis should remain under the control of the client, with the therapist acting only as a collaborator and guide.
- Hypnosis is a procedure that can be useful within a broad treatment plan. It should only be used by therapists who are trained in its use and who also have sufficient training and experience in the treatment of PTSD.
- Some people are more prone to experience intrusive memories when they become very relaxed. So be sure that you and your therapist have worked on skills to cope with intrusions before trying hypnosis.

# CHAPTER 31

# Expressive Art Therapies

Because experiencing and expressing trauma material is so important to recovery, the expressive arts are being increasingly incorporated into PTSD treatment plans. The expressive arts help unlock rigidly held memory material in ways that normal conversation or thinking might not, especially those memory aspects that are nonverbal. Once expressed, the material can be processed, and healing proceeds. The expressive arts are particularly appealing for a number of reasons. Some people find it difficult to talk directly about their traumatic experiences. Perhaps the trauma happened to preverbal children or to children who were told by the perpetrator never to talk about the trauma. For some, the feelings seem simply too complex for words. Some self-conscious people find it difficult to talk directly about their feelings. The expressive arts shift the focus to the project. It becomes easier to describe the feelings the art project expresses.

The types of expressive arts useful in the treatment of PTSD include visual arts (drawing, painting, sculpture, collages); movement/dance; music; language arts (storytelling, essays, poetry); drama; and play/sand-tray therapy.

We shall briefly explore and sample some forms of the expressive arts—enough to gain a general understanding and appreciation for what they can bring to the recovery process. As you will see, the expressive arts do more than access traumatic memories. They put us in touch with who we really are, the parts of us that reside beyond the intellect. They also can tap wisdom and healing powers in ways that normal conversation might not.

Some mental health professionals have specialized training in art therapy. Sometimes art therapists will be part of a treatment team. They may work with individuals or groups.

## VISUAL ARTS THERAPY

As Dee Spring[1] notes, in the process of creating art, history and feelings surface in symbolic language. Once formed and expressed, art can be interpreted, processed, and transformed. Since we can physically handle art, we can gain a greater sense of control over inner states depicted by the art. And the simple act of creating rekindles the inner forces of hope and healing. For example, a person might depict these elements of trauma and healing:

- Safe places; places to contain painful emotions such as a big freezer for painful memories
- Life or self before the trauma to find "lost" characteristics one wants to recover
- Nightmares[2] and new endings to them
- What happened
- The worst moment or event
- The moment of survival
- Separate depictions of self and the event (moving them around helps to show that the two are not the same)
- Positive and negative feelings about a victimizer
- Strengths shown during the traumatic event
- Where I am now, how I have improved since the trauma (e.g., draw a picture of self before treatment and now[3])
- Feelings (that were numbed or lost, that I'd like to have, that I have after creating the art)
- What I'd like to become in the future
- A collage of positive and negative outcomes including what I've learned and strengths I've gained
- A memorial to honor losses
- How to be safer in the future
- Coping in the future
- Comforting a friend or a pet who survived the trauma or one similar to it
- Beauty for enjoyment's sake

An art therapist who specializes in PTSD typically assembles the art materials and assists the person throughout the creative process. The art therapist will emphasize that the value of art therapy is in the expressive process. Artistic talent and the quality of the product are not important. If possible, the creator will discuss the various aspects of the project with the art therapist since verbalizing helps integrate the various components of disintegrated memories.

## MOVEMENT/DANCE THERAPY

The mind and body are connected. The body accurately reflects what is going on in the mind and emotions, even if the intellect disguises this. As Gabrielle Roth observes, "The body is a reflection of all that is being felt and held inside."[4] In this regard, our bodies are rather like art, which can express, reveal, and teach. Conversely, even subtle bodily movements can exert positive effect on the mind. Movement and dance therapists are trained to use the mind-body relationships in the recovery process in a variety of ways:

- **Movement activities relax and strengthen the body.** Simple exercises like stretching and breathing can discharge tension, while more vigorous activity both strengthens and relaxes. As a result, the mind is also relaxed and strengthened. This helps to lift the mood and stabilize the sensitized nervous system.
- **If we pay attention to the body, we can learn if we are frightened or tense.** We notice areas of discomfort; we observe movements that are restrained or full of strong emotion. We gradually gain comfort with those emotions as we just notice them in a nonjudging manner.
- **Circle dances, ball tosses, or other group activities help to build a sense of community and counter feelings of isolation.** We can sometimes connect more readily with people on a physical level than a verbal level. Unspoken trust can build as people in groups synchronize movements to each other. A therapist might nonverbally mirror one's physical movements through dance to communicate empathy and trust.
- **Memories might contain rigidly stored emotions and physical aspects that might only be unlocked through movement.** Movement might allow the person to safely express anger and defensiveness. Once this is accomplished, the way might be cleared to allow other strong but hidden emotions to be expressed, such as inadequacy, guilt, shame, sadness, and loss.[5] Once unspeakable memories are unlocked, they can be released, processed, and eventually verbalized.
- **Abused persons may be disconnected from their bodies because they contain pain.** Movement can help to release that pain and detect emotional issues underlying the physical discomfort. The person can then learn to

use physical discomfort as cues to comfort one's self emotionally and physically. Eventually, through the joy of movement, the body becomes associated with pleasant sensations.

- **A person might be able to physically act out complex or confusing feelings that cannot be verbalized.** This not only permits discharge of strong feelings but also provides a sense of control and an opportunity to better understand and integrate those feelings.
- **Movement can activate self-protection and expression.** A person might have bodily memories of freezing during a traumatic event. Now, through movement, the person can unfreeze that memory and create a new bodily memory. She can symbolically push away an offender or enact other nonverbal ways of protecting herself. She might also symbolically enact ways to say yes to healthy situations. A firefighter might re-create a desired rescue response now that there is less danger and fear.
- **Movement and dance can be used for nurture and comfort.** For instance, cradling or rocking provides support. Bowing to people communicates respect.
- **In a safe setting, movement helps one experience joy and personal empowerment.** One only needs to watch a child at play to be reminded that movement is pleasurable.
- **Body movement reflects personality.** Fluid body movements can help the mind function in a less fragmented, more integrated way.
- **Like meditation, movement helps us simply to be ourselves.** Words are not so important.
- **Games like the childhood game Red Light/Green Light teach impulse control.** This is taught with a light touch, not with too much seriousness.
- **Physical activity raises endorphin levels.** This improves moods and lessens pain.

The many uses of movement and dance have prompted Roth to observe, "If you just set people in motion, they will heal themselves."[6] Sessions begin with an explanation of activities and boundaries. They end with a discussion of what happened to maximize processing and integration. Like art, the purpose of the therapy is not to perform but to learn through the process. So there is no requirement to be a good dancer nor is there pressure to perform in any set manner.

## MUSIC THERAPY

Like dance and movement, music helps us pass intellectual barriers to processing. Combined with relaxation, music can stimulate images, emotions, memories, and body sensations. Afterward, the stimulated material can be processed verbally as one explores the meaning of the stimulated material.[7]

Depending on the type, music can evoke a wide range of moods from anger or loss to calm, tenderness, and love. One type of music might elicit negative memories. Shifting to a different type of music might elicit long-buried feelings of empowerment and hope that can help to transform negative memories.[8] As noted music expert Helen Bonny observes, music can stimulate changes in mood and memory perceptions by its innate "tension/release mechanisms . . . instrumental color, melodic line, [or] cadences."[9] Soothing music at the end of a session might facilitate a feeling of safety.

Cyd Slotoroff has described how drumming can be used to help overcome feelings of powerlessness and anger and develop assertiveness in a victim of abuse. The client and music therapist each have a drum. The client begins to drum, but the therapist must ask permission to start playing. The client sometimes says "yes" and sometimes "no" and may tell the therapist to stop at any time. The therapist will sometimes support the beat and sometimes interfere. Afterward, they discuss what it felt like for the client to be supported or disrupted, to have a say in whether the therapist began or stopped, or to say nothing. Anger is described in imagery in order to understand gradations. The client explores the idea of saying "stop" as soon as she wants something to stop and is encouraged to stop the therapist's drumming on subsequent rounds with increasing comfort.[10]

## LANGUAGE ARTS THERAPY

Poetry therapy uses the written or spoken media in the healing and growth process. Poetry therapy uses not only poetry as a tool but also stories, autobiographies, literature, journals, letters, essays, and song lyrics. In this type of therapy, you might create, read, and discuss your own written pieces or study the creations of others. Written or spoken media provide a safe place to contain strong emotions—we can control and understand what we put into words.

The process of speaking or writing our own stories begins to stir our inner creative and problem-solving forces. As we examine what we have created, we become more aware and appreciative of who we are inside. We gain confidence over our emotions and a sense of competence.

As we read or listen to the stories of others, we gain a sense of connection, a realization that we are not alone, that others understand and share our burden. We can gain distraction from our own problems and inspiration as we learn from others. The discussion that is stimulated can lead to insights and greater understanding of our experience.

According to Tina Alston, stories help give order to chaos. That is, they help us understand what can be confusing and complex. Notice how Homer's legendary epic can be useful to war veterans:[11]

> Homer's *Odyssey* is the story of a warrior who returned home after being gone for twenty years. The battle for Troy lasted ten years and his return home took ten years. His wife Penelope struggled to keep her suitors from taking over the bed and home of her husband Odysseus, the warrior. The journey home was perhaps more costly than the long battle. Odysseus faced the perils of sea monsters, the alluring invitations of the Sirens who offered him knowledge, and the temptations of the Lotus Eaters who offered him mind-erasing drugs. When he wandered into their home, at first, Penelope didn't recognize him. Here we find parallels to the story of the Vietnam veterans, some of whom are still on the way home after more than twenty years. Like Odysseus, they have been facing demons in the psyche that are as threatening and alluring as the fantastic creatures in the ancient Greek story.
>
> When Odysseus finally returned, his wife Penelope thought he was yet another impostor trying to trick her. Finally she tested him by casually mentioning that she had moved their great bed. This would have been an impossible task because the bed that Odysseus had made for her was built around a great tree: it could not have been moved without destroying the tree. When she saw his outrage, she recognized him. She actually saw his great love for her in his anger at the apparent destruction of their beautiful marriage bed. Along with his father, son, and larger family, she bade him enter his own home and return to the life of the hearth and community. Such a story of war, alienation, and return is timeless and finds echoes in the stories of Vietnam veterans and their families.

Alston also relates Joseph Campell's[12] story of a woman who cannot relate to her traumatized and numbed husband and asks a healer for a potion to cure her husband. The healer instructs her to bring a whisker plucked from the face of a tiger. After six months of bringing a tiger food, gradually getting closer and closer, she tenderly snips a whisker as the tiger nestles its head in her lap. However, the healer tosses the whisker in the fire, explaining that a woman who can accomplish such a feat needs no potion. With little or no interpretation, the listener realizes the need to discover inner strength when magical cures do not exist. However, groups might also discuss various aspects of the story. For example, what might the wife have felt at various points of the story? The husband? The tiger? There are no "correct" answers; this approach allows one to develop a broader range of feelings.

Stories can be told randomly, around a fire, or after supper. Stories of heroes who coped or blessed your life create a hopeful tone and a sense of safety. Fanciful stories, such as Dr. Seuss's *Oh the Places You'll Go*, contain uplifting themes about coping. Any personal or entertaining story helps to create a sense of community. Stories can also memorialize the deceased or affirm that your experience mattered.

If poems are created, they need not rhyme. They just need to express your honest feelings. Some find the rhythm and pattern of poetry soothing. The ideal poem will relate to your negative feelings but also communicate hope. An uplifting poem can break the inertia of depression and anxiety, soothe, and heal. "Fear," by J. Ruth Gendler,[13] is an excellent example of this type of poem. Here fear is depicted as a little, loud man who scares people from the shadows. When confronted, he loses his power to frighten us inappropriately.

Some find writing letters to other survivors quite healing and comforting. Letters to the deceased can also help maintain a healthy connection or sense of closure.

Registered poetry therapists are trained in literature and psychotherapy. They can be very effective helpers in the healing process.

## DRAMA THERAPY[14]

Drama therapy uses drama/theater processes to let clients tell their stories. In the process, they express feelings safely and appropriately, gain new understanding and perspective, solve problems, and set goals. Integration is facilitated because the drama balances verbal with nonverbal processes. Dramas can range from improvised and informal reenactments to scripted theatrical productions with props, masks, and costumes.

In one form of drama, psychodrama, individuals reenact a traumatic event to gain insight and control. Group members take assigned roles. Action is slowed to facilitate processing. New reactions or endings can be tried. The group might devise ways to protect the survivor. The individual might assume different roles to gain new perspectives. Afterward, the drama is processed for insights and understanding.

## PLAY AND SAND-TRAY THERAPY

Play can be a very useful part of treatment for both adults and children. For example, Helen found it very difficult to talk about the abuse she experienced as a child. However, using a dollhouse to recount that experience, she could slow down the events and found it easier to talk about her thoughts and feelings. The dollhouse became a form of art that contained and gave distance to her distressing feelings. She could move the dollhouse closer or farther away or she could move figures in the house around to gain mastery—just as one does with visual art. Eventually, the gradual exposure of play permitted Helen to talk directly about her experiences. She was then able to progress to other treatment strategies described in this book. However, it was nonthreatening play that started her progress.

Dr. Wendy Miller, cofounder of Create Therapy Institute in Kensington, Maryland,[15] explains that listening to a person's language during play will often reveal the form of art that is best to try. For example, in sand-tray therapy, an adult is asked to express his story or the world he experiences on a sand tray containing sand, water, and miniature people, structures, and animals. A person who says, "I am sitting under a gray cloud," might resonate with visual arts, while one who says, "I'm running around," might be suited to movement/dance therapy.

The sand tray also becomes another form of art, allowing the individual to explore and further integrate his experience. Dr. Miller writes, for example, that:

> One child who kept trying to build a dam that would hold everything back was, in the therapist's mind, attempting to create a metaphor of absolute strength, an image of something that would unfailingly hold back his anger. After watching many failed attempts, the therapist guided the child toward a dam that let the water through in a steady, regulated way, allowing both flow and control. This child needed to see that rather than completely binding his anger, he could find a way to live with the anger by expressing it in nondestructive, controlled ways.

In this case, the metaphoric play helped the child explore a new way to deal with feelings.

## BLENDING THERAPIES

The expressive arts might be blended in various ways depending upon the creativity and skill of the therapist and the receptivity of the client. For example, music is readily blended with movement and dance or with visual arts. A therapist might direct your attention to your posture while you are creating art or discussing what you created. If the feelings that your body is communicating can't be verbalized, the therapist might ask you to use a form of movement to express them. The skillful therapist will also blend art therapy with other forms of treatment, thus forming a complete treatment plan.

# CHAPTER 32

# Life Review

We have observed that traumatic events are so intense that they capture more than their fair share of our attention. In the life review strategy, we recall our entire lives, not just the traumatic events. A number of positive outcomes occur from this strategy:

- **We gain perspective on our lives and ourselves.** We see more clearly that there is more to our lives than the traumatic event and more to us than what we did during the traumatic event. One elderly survivor chuckled sagely, "Well, I survived the war and lots of years since then. Surely that counts for something!"
- **We contradict core beliefs that were acquired in early life or from the traumatic event.** For example, we might identify evidence that challenges our belief that we are worthless, have never contributed to life, or have never experienced love or happiness.
- **We can put our lives in better balance.** Assessing our lives realistically, we might rediscover what is really important and how we want to live the rest of our lives. Paying attention to their lives, many say, makes their lives richer and renews cherished ideals.
- **We make better sense of our lives.** In examining our lives, we better understand why we are who we are. When we "get it all off our chest," we not only discharge emotions but gain a chance to make sense of the memories.
- **We find memory gaps.** Sometimes these gaps may indicate dissociated material.
- **We gain acceptance of ourselves and our shortcomings.** In reminiscing about her life, one woman gave herself a diagnosis of "extenuating circum-

stances" in crediting herself for doing her best and surviving, even if imperfectly. When done in a group, we also gain a "comfortable acceptance of the life cycle," as we see that all people go through ups and downs in their short lives.[1]

- **Reminiscing has been associated with less depression, psychological well-being, and seeing one's life as meaningful and satisfying.**[2] One only has to look at a scrapbook of an individual's life to realize that all lives have meaning.

Life review is simply reminiscing about one's life. It can be done by making an oral or written history. Some prefer talking into an audio recorder. Some prefer writing an autobiography and, perhaps, making a scrapbook of mementos. The point is to see one's life in its entirety.

An excellent structured approach to the life review has been developed by Dr. Benjamin Colodzin. His instructions follow.[3]

## THE LIFE REVIEW

The goal is to learn more about who you truly are. You will be looking for information that can help you develop "anchors" to help you weather stormy moments in your life. You will look for strengths that have gotten you through thus far. You will be on a reconnaissance mission for the available choices that can bring acceptance and peace more powerfully into your life. These choices will be found inside yourself. As you search, you will ask important questions that have meaning to you. How can you find your place in this world? How can you obtain a measure of peace in your life? Is it possible to make sense out of the ugly things that have happened? Such questions are more important than paying attention to what's wrong with you or the world.

There is more to us than we habitually notice. We are more than a worker or a survivor of a traumatic event. The purpose here is to reconnoiter the path of your life—the experiences you have lived through—to take a look at the happenings that helped form you into the person that lives here and now and to see if perhaps you can relocate some parts of yourself that you may have lost touch with over time. Some are parts that will be painful to remember; these are the places where you lost your balance, where you were knocked down somehow by life. Other parts will be very nourishing to recall; these are likely the places where you learned some of what you know about holding your balance.

It's important to begin with the basic rule that this reconnaissance is something you do for yourself and no one else. As you proceed, you will need to write down your recollections, which means you will create a written record that is just for you. It helps to be honest if we are not worried about the judgments of others. If you wish to share something that comes up, that is fine. But it is also fine not to.

Your mission is to pay attention to the terrain and report what you see accurately. Only in this case, the terrain is your life, and the only one you will report to is yourself. To begin, you will look through what has happened in your life, using a particular method I will explain shortly, scanning for the different important experiences that have happened. The reason for doing this is to help fill in missing pieces in the story of who you are.

The things that have happened that occupy your thoughts most often are not the whole story. If you are old enough to read this book, you've been alive a long time and have been through many experiences of different varieties. You have not only lived through some traumatic event(s), but you've also been through a lot of other experiences as well. *In paying attention to what you have known, you can become more clear about what you need to know.* Many survivors have stated that in the here and now of their lives, they do not know how to relax or to reach a place of peace. And because repeated exposure to this way of experiencing leads such individuals to tell themselves the story "that is who I am," you may tell yourself you cannot experience these things, that the experience of peace is not included in "who I am."

What I am going to request that you do here is to take a time-out from holding so tightly to the story you have been telling yourself—time out to make sure you've got the whole story about who you are, time out to go through your life with an open mind, time out to explore. The chances are that somewhere in your life you have been happy (if only for a short while). Somewhere in your life you've felt confident and proud of who you are. There was a tendril of strength. Somewhere in your life you've felt some kind of fear and found a way beyond it. There was a victory. Somewhere in your life you have played and been relaxed. Somewhere you have tasted a good taste and found a drink that quenched your thirst. It will be helpful to find where these places are. Not so you can share them with anybody else or so anyone else can judge you, but because it is helpful for you to remember that you already know that there is more to you than the story you've let yourself see. The experiences you have had point to the skills that you have used, skills that you may not yet recognize as something useful for your life now. *It's easier to relearn something you once knew than to learn something that you have never done before.*

One purpose of this exploration is to reclaim some of the territory of yourself that you may not be using now—to remember that it is also part of your identity—so that when you consider this idea of "me," you can tell yourself a bigger story than you were remembering before. Although I won't ask you to accept this just because I say so, I will tell you what I have observed again and again: as the story you tell yourself about who you are gets more and more filled in, you become able to make more choices about how you want to live now. Your job at this point is neither to accept nor reject this statement, only to try it and see for yourself if it is helpful.

## SEARCHING INSIDE YOURSELF: A BASIC METHOD

The writing method I will now describe can help you to regain pieces of your story. It is not a game; it is a serious psychological tool of considerable power. You are not ready to use it unless you are willing to listen to what you have to say.

In working with this kind of technique, you will have to use your imagination. You don't have to have a particularly good imagination; you just need at a minimum to know what a road looks like. Do you know what a road looks like? As long as you've got that one figured out, you can start using this method.

The first step is to imagine your life—made up of all your experiences—as if it were a road. First, you're born; that's the beginning of the road for you here on planet Earth. Each place you've been and each event you've known exists along the road you have traveled. There's more of the road, untraveled as yet, but we will not look that way now. You were born, and the road started there. It stretches all the way to right now. Your reconnaissance assignments will be along this stretch of the road.

You're going to look at some of the things that have happened along the road. It would be best if you got a paper and pencil ready at this point, because you will be writing down some information about what you observe along the road. You won't want to write down too much. When you observe some important scenery along the road, you'll want to write down just enough so that you'll have a record of it. Here's how it works:

First, imagine yourself sitting up in the distant hills, overlooking the road. The road of your life. You will not be on the road; you are removed from it, looking down at this road from higher ground. You will be looking along the road, checking the scenery, looking at the things that have happened in your life. At first, you will look for the things that really made a difference in shaping you as you are.

Before you begin, I will explain how you write down your observations along this reconnaissance mission.

Imagine, for example, that you suffered a serious loss when you were six years old—such as the loss of a family member. This might well be an important event in your life, something that made a difference. When you scan along your road, it might be a piece of the scenery that you would notice. Another possibility might be that when you were six years old, you met another child who became your friend and taught you important things. This could perhaps also be something that made a difference in your life.

*When it is your life, it is for you to decide.* These important events can happen at any age in your life. You do not need to follow any particular formula. You are requested here to give your mind free rein, to follow the scenery along the road, looking for the things that made a difference. As you tell yourself about your own story and reencounter some of your important scenery, you make a record of what you observe. You just need to write enough so that the key word or words that you write down will remind you of the scenery you are seeing on that piece of the road.

Going back to the examples, the road watcher who lost some family member when he was six might simply write "family"; he knows what experience that refers to. The one who made an important friend when he was six might write "friend" or the friend's name. *Write just enough so you'll know what you're talking about when you refer back to it later.* Since you're not writing this for anyone else, there is no need to be detailed.

Here's how to use this method. In your mind's eye, imagine a picture of the road. You are not on the road; you are up in the hills or other high ground, and the road appears in the distance. The road starts where you were born and stretches through all the territory up until now. You are not on any part of the road; you are reconnoitering it from a distance. You may see a flat and straight road, or it may be very curvy. It may have peaks, valleys, or just about anything.

To start your reconnaissance, you will lift your imaginary binoculars to the start of the road from your vantage point on high ground. At the same time, you say to yourself, "I was born there." Then begin to sweep along the road with your binoculars as you say to yourself, "and after that . . . " Look for whatever shows up along the road of your life that made a difference. Do not attempt to structure your thoughts; just look at what comes up. Do not force your thoughts, worrying, "I should probably include this or that." Just imagine yourself scanning along the road while you hold this thought about the important things that made a difference in shaping you as you are and see what shows up in your field of view.

Repeat this procedure along your entire road up to now. Try to limit yourself to ten key items or so on this first effort. This will help you focus on some really important events. Take twenty or thirty minutes and see what you come up with. One of the curious things about this reconnaissance is that even though you are looking in just one direction along the road—from the past toward the present— you do not always remember the things that made a difference in the order they happened. When you have read these instructions to this point, you have the information necessary to take your first scan. When you are ready, give it a try.

When you have finished, look at your key words: Do you identify some with positive feelings and beautiful scenery along your road? Do you identify some with negative feelings and ugly scenery along your road? Which ones recall experiences where you felt good about who you are? Which recall experiences where you felt the opposite?

The answers to these questions contain clues about what these experiences mean to you inside. As you have recorded these experiences, you see, you have been reclaiming parts of you, experiences that you are intimately familiar with because you were there. So as you look back and remember the friend that made a difference, or enemy, or loved one, or idea—or whatever else you came up with— you can ask yourself, "Do I want more of that in my life now? Do I want less?"

You might see if the key words you have identified form a mixture of experiences that you would judge from your present vantage point as "good" and "bad," "positive" and "negative," "beautiful" and "ugly." If they appear heavily weighted in one direction, you have gained information that the story you are telling yourself about your life is focused in that direction. This means it is possible that your individual "life tree," in adapting to your life circumstances, may have once needed to reach away from certain aspects of your story, aspects you may now be ready to reclaim. This type of scanning can give you clues about where you are paying attention and where you are not.

Your answers are a beginning. They are a way to start telling yourself what you are looking for and what you do not want to look at. If you have spent a great deal of your time with your attention focused on scenery that you don't want to look at, it is easy to feel like you have no control. As you begin to get some information and some insight about the kind of experiences you want more of now, you will be better able to steer your life in that direction, toward the things you need to maintain balance. As you do that, you gain more control.

## Unfinished Business

As you make your scans and find events that made a difference, you may notice that some of them have a particular quality associated with them that can be termed "unfinished business." Events that are related to "unfinished business" can stimulate some inner reaction that is unbalancing when you turn your attention their way. You may have listed many events that had a major impact on your life. If, when you remember them, it is easy to look, observe, and put those memories "back on the shelf" in your mind, chances are good that those events do not contain "unfinished business" and that you have made peace with whatever happened and have laid it to rest. Events related to "unfinished business," though, tend to evoke some kind of reaction: anger, fear, love, sadness, or some other feeling. Places where you locate this "unfinished business" can be very important clues as to where to direct your future peacemaking activities.

## SEARCHING FOR INNER PEACE

In this next reconnaissance exercise, which should last twenty to thirty minutes, you will again imagine yourself on high ground, looking at the road of your life. However, instead of looking for everything that happened that made a difference, you will be looking for a specific type of scenery that made a difference.

During this reconnaissance, I'd like you to scan for the places in your life where you have felt natural and at peace—places you were doing what you felt you were supposed to be doing, where your balance felt most firm and made a difference in who you are. You will be looking for those experiences that held some quality of nourishment, connectedness, or sacredness as you lived them.

Perhaps, for example, you observe yourself at three years of age playing with your favorite toy. If it truly made a difference, write it down. Nothing should be judged as too silly, too trivial, or too anything else. You alone will use this record; if you are engaged on this mission, then you have chosen to learn just what kind of story you are telling yourself about you. Any experiences that pop up while you are scanning along the road are part of the story. So if you find your scan hovering on an idyllic fishing vacation, a positive sexual experience, a good idea, work on some project, a flower in your garden, whatever—write it down. Again, take twenty to thirty minutes and try to limit yourself to items of particular strength.

When you have completed this exercise, you will remember that there have been moments in your life—even if they were a long time ago—when you felt good. If you came up with a blank sheet (i.e., nothing has ever felt good), then you have gained some basic information about the story you have been telling yourself, namely, that life never feels good. In this special case, you may need to do some special work to remember the best in your life. Try this exercise again—only instead of looking for high "peaks" or wonderful moments, just look for the time where there was the most calm and the least discomfort in your life. This can be a starting point in helping you find the places in your experience where you were most comfortable with yourself. For those who are experiencing post-traumatic distress, it can be very difficult to locate the places in one's experience that held nourishment, peace, or positive spiritual resonances. One person who tried this exercise remarked that their road looked like a concrete airport runway and nothing else. I asked that attention be turned to looking for any places where there might be cracks in the concrete and a blade of grass had sprung up. If one's life has been filled with "nonpeace," look for the places along the road where the "nonpeace" was a little less and made a difference.

If you did come up with some observations on this scan, take a moment to consider what is on your list. The chances are good that you would like to have these sorts of experiences in your life now. Even if they happened a long time ago, you see, you are telling yourself the story of the experiences you appreciate now. So the person who is doing the appreciating, the one who has chosen these particular memories out of all that has happened, is the you that is alive in the present.

You are beginning to get some clues about the sorts of experiences that might bring more meaning to your life. This does not mean that you need to try to relive the past. That is not possible. It simply means that you have located some experiences in your past that tell you what makes it feel good to be alive. As you remember those experiences, they may help you face decisions about how to live now. They give you a sort of homing beacon to take readings from when you are facing the tough choices. You can ask yourself, "If I choose to go in this direction, will it move me toward those good feelings?" I like to think of these places along the road as spiritual "anchors," places that are like safe havens within our minds. They have power to help us return to balance when we are afraid or otherwise paying attention to what is "not OK" in our experience.

Because the knowledge of your innermost needs and feelings come from inside you, and not from anyone else, they are authentic, legitimate, and to be trusted as arrows pointing the way along your healing path.

Even if you have not been able to get at this knowledge for a long time, it is still there. Focusing your attention on the scenery on your road where you experienced your own balance may make it easier to make choices that help you get back there.

If you remembered a time when you felt very relaxed, for example, and you have not been able to relax for a long time, then you can help yourself relax now by imagining that you are back in the experience where you once relaxed. This is a way to make good use of your prior experience. Your body responds to the relaxing image in your brain.

## SEARCHING FOR INNER WOUNDS

For the next reconnaissance, use extra caution. Follow the same basic method as before and limit yourself to a time frame of twenty to thirty minutes. This time, you will be looking at some of the ugly scenery along your road, the places where painful and frightening things have happened—the places where you most seriously lost your balance.

This type of reconnaissance is the one you are most likely to avoid because it is very uncomfortable to recognize and pay attention to our fear and pain. There is no need to push yourself; when you are ready, you will stop avoiding this scenery. When you are not ready, it is best to be honest with yourself.

To do this reconnaissance, scan along your road and stop to write key words where you find places where pain or other ugliness happened and made a difference.

Because of the special nature of this type of scenery, you may have some strong reactions. If this occurs, make a record of what you were thinking or feeling when the reaction occurred. This is another clue about what is important to you. When you are finished with this reconnaissance, use your "internal radar" and scan your muscles for signs of tension. It is common to tense up when doing this difficult work. If you find a high tension level, take the time to breathe back to balance before you move on to something else.

If you have an extremely strong reaction as you observe this scenery along your road, break off the exercise and return to it later. Try to be honest with yourself about what you were observing on your road when the reaction happened. If this exercise is too difficult for you to complete at this time, you may consider finding some outside help in paying attention to these parts of the story. The people you trust the most and the people with similar scenery in their lives are good places to start a search for the right kind of help.

Please understand that if you have lived through "unusual experiences" that were overwhelming, it may be very difficult for you to fill in the parts of your story that can be found in this exercise. You may experience a very detailed reconnaissance, or you may feel as though you cannot see the terrain clearly. Sometimes seeing this terrain clearly takes time, similar to peeling an onion one layer at a time, little by little.

This is not an easy or comfortable job. Almost every trauma survivor I have encountered who has done this type of work agrees that "it gets harder before it gets easier."

Though we might wish it were otherwise, this is an accurate statement. I know of no way to take the hurt out of that which is painful. Yet it is also true that it does get easier. Your healing pathway can lead through being stuck with uncomfortable feelings to a more balanced position. If there are hidden dark spots inside that are very painful, they may need to see the light of day in order for healing to occur.

## SEARCHING FOR THE OPEN HEART

Now for another type of reconnaissance. This should also not take you longer than twenty to thirty minutes. This time, you will be looking for the scenery where love occurred inside you. It may have turned out with a happy ending, and it may have been disastrous. How it turned out is not the central question here. Look for the places along your road where love happened and made a difference. It doesn't need to be sexual love—it could also be love of a parent, a friend, an animal, an idea, a place, or generalized compassion without an object, anything that fired up your heart in a way that really counted. Repeat the basic procedure: Start on the high ground and observe your road and scan forward in time, repeating: "I was born, and after that . . . " Sweep along the road and find the scenery where love happened in your life and made a difference.

You may have had a terrible childhood, and perhaps you can remember no loving scenery until after you left home. Scan on. Or you may remember love as a child but nothing since. Keep scanning. Something happened, somewhere. Even if it is not what happened along most of your road, there are places where you can find that scenery somewhere—some kind of love, or caring, that made a difference. Find those experiences and record key words. Again, take twenty to thirty minutes and limit yourself to the most important items.

## RECLAIMING OUR WHOLE SELVES

These exercises help people to reconnect all aspects of their lives. If you have been telling yourself that you have never known pleasant or loving moments, then perhaps this will stretch the story because you have examined for yourself your whole life story. *You are a human being with the ability to live many, many different ways.*

You may also choose to use this inward scanning method to fill in other parts of your story. Choose any subject that is important to you as the "filter" you place on your scan. If you are having a problem with anger, for example, you might want to look at the scenery along your road where anger has happened and made a difference. If you are working on a relationship, you might want to recheck the relationships along your road. You might need to take a look at what has happened along your road in relation to work, money, or your body. Your road belongs to you: you can retrieve what you need from it when you are ready.

# CHAPTER 33

# *Building Self-Esteem*

Two conclusions are apparent from the research: self-esteem helps protect people from anxiety and stress, and self-esteem is a most important predictor of happiness and life satisfaction. So investing time in building self-esteem is most worthwhile. The tendency following a traumatic event is to feel shattered, perhaps worthless. But self-esteem can be developed, regardless of one's history or circumstances. Although space will not permit an in-depth survey of this important topic, we can note the principles and develop important foundation skills. Further reading on this important topic is suggested in the Additional Resources section at the back of this book.

## WHAT IS SELF-ESTEEM?

Self-esteem is a *realistic, appreciative* opinion of oneself. *Realistic* means accurate and honest. *Appreciative* implies positive feelings and liking. Self-esteem involves a clear view of self and a quiet gladness to be yourself.

It should be apparent that self-esteem is not destructive pride that says we are better than another as a person or that we are more capable or self-reliant than we truly are. This would be arrogance and deception. Nor is self-esteem the shame that says one is worse as a person than another, totally incapable, and lacking in worth. Rather, people with self-esteem retain a healthy humility as they are aware of their strengths and weaknesses. Yet weaknesses are viewed as rough edges— not the totality of who they are. Deep inside at the core, they are quietly glad to be who they are. This deep satisfaction motivates them to grow and improve.

The person with self-esteem views people on a level playing field, each with different skills and talents, but no one more worthwhile as a person than any other. So a person with self-esteem will respect someone in authority but not be intimidated. The person in authority has certain well-developed skills and attributes. But that makes him different, not more valuable as a person. So the person with self-esteem is not driven to compete with another to prove his worth. He may be motivated to succeed by enjoyment and a sense of mastery but not to prove his worth as a person.

Having self-esteem is not the same as being selfish or self-centered. I think of Mother Teresa, who had a quiet inner gladness yet was enormously altruistic.

## HOW DOES SELF-ESTEEM DEVELOP?

Children are more likely to develop self-esteem if they have parents who model it and show the children that they are valued for who they are. They show interest in the children's friends and activities. They respect their opinions, although they care enough to enforce limits that are in the children's best interests. The parents' expectations are high—after all, they believe in the children. The standards are reasonable, however, and the parents give a lot of support. Rewards are favored over punishment.

The obvious question is, Can adults who lacked this kind of parenting develop self-esteem? The answer is yes, provided they learn ways to satisfy these unmet needs. Can adults who lose self-esteem regain it? Yes, the principles are the same. Think of self-esteem building as a skill that requires steady practice and reinforcement.

## HOW DO I BUILD SELF-ESTEEM?

To change self-esteem is to first understand the factors upon which it is built: (1) unconditional worth; (2) unconditional love; and (3) growing. (See Figure 33.1.)

While each building block is essential for development of sound self-esteem, the *sequence* is crucial. Let's briefly describe each building block.

### Unconditional Worth

*Unconditional worth* means that each person has infinite, unchanging worth *as a person*. This worth comes with a person's creation and cannot be earned or lost by poor behavior. This is not the same as market or social worth, which clearly are earned and lost. This core worth is not comparable. So you might be a better doctor and I might be a better teacher, but worth as a person is equal. In theological terms, worth as a person is a given; each and every soul is precious. We might conceptualize this worth as follows (see Figure 33.2):

**Figure 33.1**
THE FOUNDATIONS OF SELF-ESTEEM

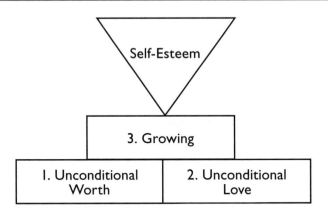

*From Schiraldi, G. R. 2001.* The Self-Esteem Workbook. *Oakland, CA: New Harbinger.*

**Figure 33.2**
THE CORE WORTH

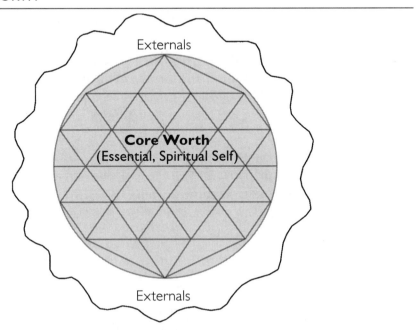

*From Schiraldi, G. R. 2001.* The Self-Esteem Workbook. *Oakland, CA: New Harbinger.*

The core self is like a crystal of great worth. Each facet represents a beautiful potential or attribute in embryo. Each person is *complete* in the sense that he or she has every attribute needed (such as the seeds of love, integrity, intelligence, and talents). However, no one is *completed* or perfect, since no one has developed all attributes fully. Yet the worth of the core is infinite. People sometimes ask, "But how can I have worth if I have never accomplished or produced anything noteworthy?" And I ask them to think why parents might spend two million dollars to save a two-year-old child who has fallen into a shaft in the earth.

Some externals (e.g., respectful treatment, making wise decisions) shine up the core and help us enjoy its beauty more. Other externals (e.g., criticism, abuse, unkind behaviors) can cover or camouflage the core like a dirty film. The basic core is still there, however, unchanged in worth as a person.

The goals of strengthening this building block are:

1. **Separate core worth from externals.** Externals include performance, appearance, health/disease, condition of the body, wealth, race, social status, gender, education, how we are treated, and traumatic events that happened.
2. **See clearly one's inner strengths.** The idea is not to see each strength as completely developed but to appreciate that the capacities are there, in embryo, to think rationally, to feel, to sacrifice, to love, to make responsible choices, to recognize truth and worth, to create, to beautify, to be gentle, patient, or firm. These capacities exist in each person, at different stages of development. What separates one person from another is the unique mix of strengths.

With these goals met, one is freed to find satisfaction and joy, even in poverty or fading health. This understanding permits us to experience value and worth amidst our imperfections. It gives us the perspective that there is more to us than what happened to us or what we did.

## Unconditional Love

Whereas unconditional worth refers to a thought process, *unconditional love* involves feelings and applies to the appreciative part of our definition of self-esteem. Many people understand with their minds that they have worth, but they do not *feel* a gladness, a joy inside. Each person has the capacity to love, although this capacity might be underdeveloped or buried at present. But love is like a seed and is capable of cultivation. Love is:

1. **A feeling that you experience.** Each one recognizes it and responds to it when one sees it.
2. **An attitude.** Love wants what's best for the loved one at each moment.[1]
3. **A decision** and a commitment that you make every day. Sometimes you "will it," even though this may be difficult at times.
4. **A skill** that is cultivated.

Can you recall television's Mr. Rogers telling children each day that it is *you* he likes? Not your clothes, your hairstyle, or other things that surround you, but you. This is a way of saying, "I love your core, the part that is deeper than the externals." Just as Hitler and other violent dictators learned hatred in their youth, the great lovers of the world *learned* to love. It is a skill, a talent, something that can be cultivated at any season of life. If you did not receive love from your parents, it is even more important to learn ways to provide this essential nutrient for yourself. Love is the *foundation* of growth. It is a way of feeling like a somebody of worth (i.e., not that it *gives* you worth but that it lets you *feel* it).

Self-love is similar to self-acceptance. *Accept* means to take in, to receive gladly. To self-accept, then, is to receive ourselves kindly, acknowledging our flaws and experiences.

### Growing

This is the process of moving toward our potential. It is a never-ending process where you develop your capacities and attributes at a pace that is suited to you, not someone else. I like many names for this factor in self-esteem: "coming to flower"; "elevating ourselves while we elevate others"; "love in action"; "developing"; and "reaching for excellence."

We feel more satisfied with ourselves and our lives when we know that we are on a satisfying course. This building block could involve many activities, including striving for competent and ethical behavior, developing talents or virtues, implementing healthy behaviors, or producing something meaningful.

Many people assume wrongly that if they can only do something noteworthy and achieve social acceptance then they will achieve inner peace and satisfaction. So they desperately and impatiently strive for quick results. This approach rarely succeeds if the first two building blocks, unconditional worth and unconditional love, are not securely in place. However, if these building blocks are in place, then people are free to grow because it is deeply satisfying, not to prove their worth. This produces happy achievers, not driven neurotics. Again, the sequence is crucial. A person who can separate competence and confidence from worth feels secure enough to patiently try just about anything.

## HOW DO I IMPLEMENT THESE PRINCIPLES?

Reasoning that self-esteem can be built systematically, I developed a college course based on the foregoing principles. The course significantly reduced anxiety and depression and raised self-esteem in the students who completed it. The skills are described in a separate work (*The Self-Esteem Workbook*; see Additional Resources). Space will permit us to include some of the skill-building exercises here along with two additional exercises.

---

## SKILL-BUILDING ACTIVITY: NEVERTHELESS I (SIX DAYS)

The following is a very simple and effective skill. It reminds you of your unchanging worth amidst stressful situations that can undermine that perception. It is based on these principles:

1. Feeling bad about events, behaviors, outcomes, or some other external can be appropriate (i.e., as in appropriate guilt or disappointment). This is different from the unhealthy tendency to feel bad about the core self (this has been described as "shame").

2. Saying "My skills are not quite adequate for the job yet" is quite different from saying "I'm no good *as a person*." Feeling bad about failing is very different from "I am a failure" at the core.

3. It's OK to judge the behaviors and skills but not the core, essential self.

In short, we want to acknowledge unpleasant external conditions without condemning the core self.

### Nevertheless Skill Concepts

People who dislike the self tend to use *"Because . . . therefore"* thoughts:

> *Because* of my mistakes (my lack of training, my weight, or some other external condition), *therefore* I am no good as a person.

Obviously, this thought will erode self-esteem or keep it from developing. So we want to avoid such thoughts.

The nevertheless skill provides a realistic, upbeat, immediate response to unpleasant externals—a response that reinforces one's sense of worth by separating worth from externals. Instead of a *"Because . . . therefore"* thought, we use an *"Even though . . . nevertheless"* thought. It looks like this:

**Even though** _____ , nevertheless _____

                 (some external)                      (some statement
                                                     of worth)

For example: Even though *I botched that project*, nevertheless *I'm still a worthwhile person.*

Here are some other nevertheless statements:

- I'm still of great worth.
- I'm still an important and valuable person.
- My worth is infinite and unchangeable.

Perhaps you can think of others that you like.

## Drill

Get a partner you feel very safe with. Ask your partner to say whatever negative things come to mind, be they true or false:

- You really blew it!
- You have a funny nose!
- You mumble when you talk!
- You bug me!
- You're a big dummy!

To each criticism, put your ego on the shelf and respond with an "Even though . . . nevertheless" statement. You'll probably want to use some of your cognitive therapy skills. For example, if someone labels you "a dummy," you could respond, "Even though I behave in dumb ways sometimes, nevertheless . . ."

## Steps for the Nevertheless Skill

1. For each of the next six days, select three events with the potential to erode self-esteem.
2. In response to each event, select an *"Even though . . . nevertheless"* statement. Then record on a sheet of paper the event or situation, the statement used, and the effect on your feelings of selecting this statement and saying it to yourself. Keeping a written record reinforces the skill. Set up your record like this:

| Date | Event/Situation | Statement Used | Effect |
|------|-----------------|----------------|--------|
|      |                 |                |        |

# SKILL-BUILDING ACTIVITY:
## COGNITIVE REHEARSAL (TEN DAYS)

Self-esteem can be cultivated by mindfully acknowledging what is presently "right" about one's self. For many people, this is difficult because habits of negative thinking make it easier to identify what's wrong. Although there is a time and benefit to acknowledging shortcomings and weaknesses, when these become the dominant focus—to the exclusion of strengths—self-esteem suffers.

This exercise, then, is designed for practice in acknowledging and reinforcing strengths with appreciation. Doing this is a way of loving. This skill is based on the research of three Canadians—Janel Gauthier, Denise Pellerin, and Pierre Renaud[2]—whose method enhanced the self-esteem of subjects in just a few weeks.

To warm up, place a check if you sometimes are, or have been, reasonably:

| | |
|---|---|
| _____ clean | _____ appreciative |
| _____ handy | _____ responsive to beauty or |
| _____ literate (come on—if you've | nature |
| read this far, check this) | _____ principled, ethical |
| _____ punctual | _____ industrious |
| _____ assured or self-confident | _____ responsible, reliable |
| _____ enthusiastic, spirited | _____ organized, orderly, or neat |
| _____ optimistic | _____ sharing |
| _____ humorous, mirthful, | _____ encouraging, |
| or amusing | complimentary |
| _____ friendly | _____ attractive |
| _____ gentle | _____ well-groomed |
| _____ loyal, committed | _____ physically fit |
| _____ trustworthy | _____ intelligent, perceptive |
| _____ trusting, seeing the best | _____ cooperative |
| in others | _____ respectful or polite |
| _____ loving | _____ forgiving or able to look |
| _____ strong, powerful, forceful | beyond "faux pas" |
| _____ determined, resolute, firm | (mistakes) |
| _____ conciliatory | _____ patient |

_____ rational, reasonable, logical

_____ intuitive or trusting of own instincts

_____ creative or imaginative

_____ compassionate, kind, or caring

_____ disciplined

_____ persuasive

_____ talented

_____ cheerful

_____ sensitive or considerate

_____ tranquil or serene

_____ successful

_____ open-minded

_____ tactful

_____ spontaneous

_____ flexible or adaptable

_____ energetic

_____ expressive

_____ affectionate

_____ graceful, dignified

_____ adventurous

Check if you are sometimes a reasonably good:

_____ socializer

_____ listener

_____ cook

_____ athlete

_____ cleaner

_____ worker

_____ friend

_____ musician or singer

_____ learner

_____ leader or coach

_____ organizer

_____ decision maker

_____ counselor

_____ helper

_____ "cheerleader," supporter

_____ planner

_____ follower

_____ mistake corrector

_____ smiler

_____ debater

_____ mediator

_____ storyteller

_____ letter writer

_____ thinker

_____ requester

_____ example

_____ mate

_____ taker of criticism

_____ risk taker

_____ enjoyer of hobbies

_____ financial manager or budgeter

_____ family member

Perfection was not required for you to check these items, since nobody does any of these all of the time—much less perfectly. However, if you checked a few of these and have managed to maintain reasonable sanity in a very complex world, give yourself a pat on the back. Remember, this was just a warm-up. The exercise that follows has been found to be very effective in building self-esteem.

## Cognitive Rehearsal

1. **Develop a list of ten positive statements about yourself that are meaningful and realistic/true.** You may develop the statements from the list on the preceding pages, generate your own statements, or do both. Examples might be: "I am a loyal, responsible member of my _____ (family, team, club, etc.)."; "I am clean, orderly, etc."; "I am a concerned listener." If you mention a role that you perform well, try to add specific personal characteristics that explain why. For example, instead of saying that one is a good football player, one might add that he sizes up situations quickly and reacts decisively. Roles can change (e.g., after an injury or with age), but character and personality traits can be expressed across many different roles. Write the ten statements on a sheet of paper.

2. **Find a place to relax for fifteen to twenty minutes.** Meditate upon one statement and the evidence for its accuracy for a minute or two. Repeat this for each statement.

3. **Repeat this exercise for ten days.** Add an additional statement each day.

4. **Several times each day, look at an item on the list.** For about two minutes, meditate on the evidence for its accuracy.

If you prefer, you can write the statements on index cards and carry them with you. Some find the cards easier to refer to during the day.

Notice how you feel after practicing this skill, which disputes the all-or-none distortion "I am no good" by substituting appreciative thoughts and feelings. Students especially enjoy this skill. Comments they have made over the years include these:

- Hey! I am not so bad after all.
- I got better with practice. I didn't believe the statements at first. Then I found myself smiling on the way to school.
- I feel motivated to act on them.
- I felt peaceful and calm.
- I learned I have a lot more good than I give myself credit for.

## A Variation of Cognitive Rehearsal

Integrating traumatic memories sometimes brings an unexpected benefit. As we clearly see the whole picture, we can often see ways in which our inner strengths were revealed and see beyond the negatives that previously felt so all-encompassing. As you consider each traumatic event—your motives, what you felt and did during and after—what inner strengths were shown? Consider what you did to survive and cope, what you did to protect yourself or others. What have you done since to carry on or lift people? Here we are simply recognizing the truth and not minimizing our limitations. Do any of the strengths you have recognized in yourself apply lately, at least in part, to the trauma? Consider also the possibility of seeing yourself as:

- Emotionally strong, courageous, determined, unwilling to give up the fight
- Having good motives and intents: caring, concerned, willing to help and try again
- Resourceful, quick thinking, clever (e.g., just to survive)
- Principled (e.g., to be troubled by this means I have a conscience; to change course, when appropriate, indicates integrity)
- Honest (e.g., to acknowledge the damage, pain, my limitations, the need for patience in healing)
- Physically strong
- Resilient
- Stronger now in some ways
- Others?

Try putting each strength on a separate index card. Refer to one at a time, several times a day. Consider the evidence for its accuracy, drawing from not only the trauma but from the rest of your life.

# SKILL-BUILDING ACTIVITY: NEVERTHELESS II (SIX DAYS)

Whereas the first nevertheless skill focused on unconditional worth (a cognition), this skill focuses on unconditional love (which involves feelings). Remember the premise that unconditional love is necessary for mental health and for growth. *Unconditional* means that we choose to love even though there are imperfections that we would wish were not there.

Let's take two people who are overweight. Jane thinks, "I am fat. I hate myself." Mary thinks, "I am really glad inside to be me. I'd feel better and enjoy life even more if I lost some of this fat." Notice the difference in emotional tones between Jane and Mary. Which one is more likely to adhere to an eating and exercise plan to lose weight? Which one is more likely to arrive at her desired weight without being emotionally distraught?

Let's review some of the key concepts of the first nevertheless skill:

1. We want to acknowledge unpleasant external conditions without condemning the core self.
2. People who dislike the self tend to use *"Because . . . therefore"* thoughts (e.g., "Because I am fat, therefore I hate myself"), which erode self-esteem.
3. The nevertheless skill provides a realistic, upbeat, immediate response to unpleasant externals, which reinforces one's sense of worth by separating worth from externals.

The second nevertheless skill uses this format:

**Even though** _____ , **nevertheless** _____
(some external)                          (some statement
                                          of love/appreciation)

For example: Even though *I am overweight*, nevertheless *I love myself*.
Consider these nevertheless statements:

- I sure love myself.
- Inside I am really glad to be me.
- Deep down, I really like and appreciate me.

Perhaps you can think of other statements you like. Try the second nevertheless skill over a six-day period, recording the results just as you did for the first one. Try to say the nevertheless statement with real feeling. You might try this at times in front of a mirror, looking into your eyes, and seeing beyond the imperfections into the core with the love you would have for a good friend.

A graduate student shared with me a wonderful experience she had with the nevertheless skill. She was driving with her six-year-old son, who happened to be upset with her. In response to his criticism, she said, "Nevertheless, I'm a worthwhile person." The boy retorted, "You're not worthwhile, Mommy." She calmly replied, "Yes, I am, and you are too, and I love you so much!" She said, "Michael looked at me so strange because he wanted to be mad at me—he was caught off guard." The anger quickly faded. I've since thought how fortunate that boy is to have seen his mother model a way to buffer criticism, and at the same time be reminded of her love for him.

# LOOKING AT YOURSELF THROUGH LOVING EYES

Developed by family therapist John Childers, this strategy combines the skill of dissociation with art to experience a loving self-image.[3]

## Step 1: Establish the Experience of Being an Artist

Each of us has within ourselves an artistic part of our personality. This artistic part is able to create new and wonderful drawings of the world around us. These drawings need not look exactly like a tree, house, or person. That is not important. What is important is your freedom to express your artistic self on paper. Imagine, for the time being, that you are an artist. In a few minutes, as an artist, you'll use crayons and paper to create a wonderful drawing. But for now, just imagine being an artist.

## Step 2: Identify Someone You Know Who Loves You

As an artist, you'll be drawing a picture of someone in your life who you know loves you (and has treated you respectfully). Take a moment to think about people in your life—perhaps Mom, Dad, Grandfather, or Grandmother; perhaps a brother or a sister, a classmate, teacher, or coach. Select one very special person. A person you know loves you.

## Step 3: Describe to Yourself the Characteristics That Make That Person Special

In a minute or two, you'll draw a picture of him or her, but first think about how to draw this special person. For example, how does this special person look? Is he or she tall, medium, or short in height? What color of hair does this special person have? What's the color of his or her eyes? Do the eyes sparkle? Does this person have a smiling face? Is this person reaching out with his or her arms? How does this person's voice sound? Does it sound soft? Loud? Strong? Kind? If voice sounds could be colors, what colors would this person's voice be? How would you describe this special person's feelings? Continue to think about this special person's qualities for a few more minutes—those things that make him or her so very special to you. As you think about this special person, who loves you, become aware of your own feelings. How are you feeling right now? Loving? Warm? Excited? Happy?

## Step 4: Draw a Picture of the Person Who Loves You

Now let the artist within you draw a picture of this special person—this special person who loves you. Feel free to begin drawing this person now, selecting just the right crayons to color this person as you see him or her. If you want to, you can use colors to describe this person's voice and feelings as well. You may want to write a few words on this drawing that also describe this person. Take your time and enjoy drawing this special person who loves you. As the artist, once you have completed your picture, you may want to give it a title.

## Step 5: Imagine Being This Special Person and Able to See Yourself Through His or Her Loving Eyes

Now, I would like you to imagine that you are this special person. Imagine being this special person you have drawn. Float outside of yourself and imagine becoming this special person who loves you. OK, as this special person, I would like you to think about how you see yourself. You see yourself through the eyes of someone who loves you. Look carefully at yourself through these loving eyes. In a few moments, I'll ask you to draw a picture of yourself through these loving eyes. But for now, please continue to see yourself through these loving eyes.

## Step 6: Describe and Draw What Is Loved and Seen Through Loving Eyes

Seeing yourself through the eyes of someone who loves you, you see yourself as someone to love. Describe to yourself what you love about the person you see. Continue seeing yourself through the eyes of someone who loves you. OK, please draw a picture of yourself as seen through the eyes of this special person who loves you. As you draw and color this picture, continue seeing yourself through loving eyes. Use colors and/or words that describe your looks, behaviors, and feelings as seen through loving eyes. Continue your drawing, seeing yourself through the eyes of someone who loves you. Your drawings may be lifelike, or abstractions or splashes of color. Whatever you choose to make them.

## Step 7: Re-Associate into Your Own Body, Bringing Back Lovable Feelings

Now, slowly come back into your own being. Looking at this picture of yourself, you see yourself as someone who is lovable. Seeing yourself as lovable, say silently to yourself, "I am lovable," and notice the warm, loving feeling growing within you.

# CHAPTER 34

# Unfinished Business

## Resolving Anger

---

He who pounds a pillow is in touch with
neither his anger nor the pillow.
—*Thich Nhat Hanh*[1]

Unresolved anger is a costly burden. It keeps traumatic material highly charged and in active memory. It keeps us chained to the past, in bondage to a heavy load that we carry around each day, a load that erodes peace, happiness, and eventually health. Whereas Chapter 13 suggested ways to *manage* anger, this chapter will explore ways to *resolve* it.

Resolving anger from a serious offense or trauma is not easy. It does not usually happen quickly or all at once. Rather, it is a process that may not progress until considerable healing has taken place. The complexities of the simple term *resolving anger* suggest why the process is not simple at all and why it takes time. Resolving anger involves five processes:

1. **Reexperience and express enough anger to get in touch with your feelings.** This does not necessarily mean raging and screaming. Chronic, uncontrolled anger can reinforce anger and actually prevent processing.[2] Conversely, those people who chronically bottle up their anger may need to let it out in order to loosen rigidly contained material. As the emotional pendulum swings, people discover a balance point, a place somewhere

between detached, intellectual control and uncontrolled emotions, where memories can be honestly and effectively processed.

2. **Gain understanding.**
   - We learn through anger to better understand ourselves. Anger following a traumatic event is usually accompanied by underlying grief, fear, disappointment, hurt, or insecurity. As we recognize these primary emotions, we can touch and soothe them so that the anger can subside.
   - We identify the true source of our anger and hurt. Perhaps we are upset at a loved one who died. Perhaps we are angry that loved ones did not protect us. Perhaps we are angry at ourselves. Directing our anger at the government, the media, or some other secondary source might deflect us from resolving the primary issues and putting them to rest.
   - We seek to understand the offender's viewpoint. As much as possible, we seek to replace hatred, revenge, and resentment with understanding and compassion.[3]

3. **We say what has needed to be said to gain a sense of closure.** Giving appropriate verbal expression to unresolved anger helps to integrate and neutralize traumatic memories.

4. **We seek outcomes that can help bring the event to completion.**
   - Sometimes an apology, the words "I hurt you, I was wrong, I am sorry," can be enormously healing. Sometimes to simply have one's pain respectfully acknowledged can be healing. Sometimes just knowing that the offender has gone as far as he is capable of toward recognizing the pain he caused is helpful.
   - At times seeking justice will seem appropriate. For example, incarceration of an offender can protect you and others. It may do the offender no favor to permit him to hurt others without being disciplined.[4] Compensation for damages might also be needed. If you hold the offender accountable, do so for the safety of yourself and your community, not as a personal matter. Recognize that confronting a childhood abuser in court or in person can prove traumatizing all over again.
   - Often we will not receive the things we wish for to set things right. Perhaps the offender is dead. People who were disturbed enough to commit serious offenses will likely be unable or unwilling to treat your pain respectfully now. The legal system often fails to find and punish offenders. So, instead, we discover ways to do what we can and accept these limitations.

5. **We release anger and resentment.** Chronic anger and resentment poisons the carrier. We can more readily release these as we learn other ways to protect ourselves.

## GESTALT CHAIRS TECHNIQUE

This technique is very effective to help resolve unresolved anger. Gestalt chairs can be used to process unfinished business with an offender who is dangerous, unavailable, or unable or unwilling to deal with your hurt.

1. **Arrange two chairs facing each other at an angle.** Sit in one.
2. **Take two easy, deep breaths.** Relax. Calm yourself as you prepare to get in touch honestly with your feelings. Remember that feelings are teachers. Exploring them in a secure environment is healthy.
3. **Imagine the offender sitting in the other chair.** Notice what it is like being with this person.
4. **Begin a dialogue.**
   - Start by saying a positive statement (e.g., "Years from now I want to have good feelings when I think about you, but right now I don't. My aim is to resolve this, not hurt you.")
   - Explain what you want (e.g., "I want you to hear and understand my hurt and not have you cut me off with 'I'm sorry' or 'I didn't mean it' before hearing me out.")
   - Tell the person what you are thinking and feeling. Describe what happened. Describe the impact of the offense, and especially your feelings (e.g., "I felt . . . ; Now I feel . . . ").
   - Remain seated. Think. Feel your feelings—the anger, the hurt, the sadness.
5. **Change seats.** Allow the offender to think and feel his feelings—his own hurts, disappointments, frustrations. Allow the offender to respond. Express the offender's perspective, including his view of what happened, his thoughts and feelings. Stay seated after talking. Think. Feel—as though you were the offender—all his feelings.
6. **Keep changing seats until both have fully expressed themselves.**

Look at the person in the other chair. Stay with your feelings until they are fully experienced and expressed. At some point, you'll probably want to:

- Check to ensure that what is said was understood. ("Do you understand why this was difficult for me? Are you hearing that?" Then let the other person respond. Both can pose this question.)
- Ask the offender, "I'm trying to understand—what were you feeling? Why did you do that?"
- Consider creating an opportunity for the offender to say those healing words: "I hurt you. I was wrong. I'm sorry."
- Consider if there were two angry or hurt people, or just one.

You might consider recording such a dialogue to better hear the feelings expressed and further process the dialogue. Gestalt chairs can be used for dialogues with "failed protectors," people who are deceased, or yourself. Here the older self can ask the younger self questions such as "What happened?" "What were you feeling?" "What do you need?" and "How would you like to see things change?"

The gestalt chairs technique helps overcome avoidance. Sometimes it leads us to the questions "What could the offender be teaching? Is it possible he is teaching me how to self-accept even when others don't?"

## FORGIVING

Originally a theological concept, forgiving has made its way into the psychological literature as an effective tool for resolving anger. To forgive is to release resentment, hatred, bitterness, and desires for revenge for offenses or wrongs done to us. It is a closing of the account book and a release of the debtor so that we don't allow him to set up camp in our homes. One rabbi who lost his family in the Holocaust said that he chose to forgive because he did not want to bring Hitler with him to America.[5] It is like opening the doors to our homes and taking out the garbage.

Forgiveness is something we choose to do whether or not the offender deserves it, asks for it, or apologizes. While it is *easier* to forgive when the offender acknowledges the hurt he caused and subsequently changes his ways, forgiveness is really about the offended, not the offender. We voluntarily forgive because we no longer wish to suffer, realizing that getting even does not heal.[6] We choose not to hate the offender, even though we hate what they did.

### What Forgiveness Is Not
Forgiving is made more difficult by some common misconceptions. Forgiving does not mean the following:

- **Minimizing the offense or its impact.** In fact, acknowledging the hurt is usually necessary to heal and move beyond it.
- **Forgetting the offense.** Indeed, it is wise to remember the offense so that we can avoid being hurt in that way again. The offense, if confronted, can furnish useful experience, wisdom, and empathy. However, it is possible to remember without bitterness.
- **Condoning the offense.** We can forgive while despising the offense and taking action to ensure that it doesn't recur.
- **Reconciling or trusting.** Trust, the firm belief in one's integrity, is necessary to rebuild a healthy relationship and must be earned over time. However, even if reconciliation is not possible, forgiveness can occur at any time.

## When Forgiving Is Needed

For many of us, forgiving when someone has hurt us has to be learned; it does not come naturally. Failure to forgive can lead to a wide range of symptoms, any of which might indicate the need to forgive.

- Sarcasm
- Rancor
- Anger
- Backbiting
- Criticism
- Grudges
- Suspicion
- Resentment
- Cynicism
- Mistrust of others
- Sensitivity to criticism
- Desires for revenge
- Demanding
- Anxiety
- Depression[7]
- Fatigue
- Tension
- Others are uncomfortable being around you
- Bristling when the offender's name is mentioned or you think about him or her
- Loss of peace, happiness

- Fear, expectation of disappointment
- Need to control others to prevent them from hurting you
- Hatred
- Mood swings
- Self-medication
- Difficulty trusting
- Difficulty tolerating flaws

Forgiving can help to lessen these symptoms, sometimes in unexpected ways. An interesting case was reported in the journal *Psychotherapy*. Tom was a critical father who could not hold a job because of his anger and sensitivity to criticism. Months of counseling unearthed the origin of his anger—an alcoholic, critical father. He acknowledged his pain, which he had buried. Tom also talked it over with his pastor. As a result, Tom visited his dad and said, in effect, "Dad, I prayed for help to forgive you. I think maybe it worked. I want you to know I love you and forgive you for your alcoholism and your criticism." To his surprise, Tom's father cried and embraced him. Although his relationship with his father didn't change much, *Tom* changed. He became a loving and gentler father, less sensitive to criticism, and able to hold down a job.[8]

Is forgiving a serious offense easy? No. Can it be done? Yes. Bill is one who rose above bitterness. After six years in a WWII concentration camp, he looked surprisingly vigorous, living a life of love and forgiveness. He had watched his wife and three children be machine-gunned to death, then pleaded for his captors to take him next. They said, "No, you speak six languages. We need you." About that terrible moment in his life, he said, "I had to decide then to hate or to love."[9] Again, forgiving is an act of will that we choose because we realize that we are more than the offense and no longer wish to carry it around with us.

### Ideas That Block Forgiveness

1. **That act is unforgivable. I can never forgive it.** There is a difference between a despicable act and an unforgivable one. The unforgivable act only requires our willingness to change it to a forgivable one.
2. **I should not be angry or hurt. I should be able to forgive.** These would be nice, but we are human and never perfect. We can only forgive as best as we can.
3. **The offender is all bad. He must pay.** The offender is weak, perhaps sick.[10] Anyone who knowingly hurts others has paid, is paying, and will pay a

price in terms of his own suffering. We can't fully know the painful history of others. But even the worst people can be our greatest teachers if they cause us to learn forgiveness.

4. **I must remain bitter to insure that it never happens again, until justice is secured.** Remembering and wisdom protect, not bitterness. Justice and protection can be sought with or without bitterness.

5. **Staying mad will get it out of my system.** Reliving and rehearsing anger keeps it in focus and causes us to be controlled by it.

6. **I'll betray myself or others if I drop the grudge.** We ask if there are better ways to show loyalty than infection with anger.

7. **I'll make myself so invulnerable and strong that no one can hurt me.** To be human is to love. To love is to be vulnerable. The only way to never be hurt is to avoid loving. It is possible to remain loving, but with greater wisdom regarding whom we choose to trust.

## Whom to Forgive

Anger and other symptoms can be a cue and an opportunity to forgive all parties involved in your hurt. We might explore our life history and notice people along the way. It is good to start our forgiveness work on people responsible for traumatic offenses. Then we might work on forgiving those less directly involved such as those who failed to protect or support us. We can forgive ourselves. The skills we'll discuss can also be applied to other offenses from critical teachers to prejudiced people.

## How to Forgive

1. **Ask yourself these questions:**
   - What percentage of the offender's behavior can be explained by a desire to hurt you personally? What percentage can be explained as a reflection of his own pain or frailties?
   - Am I prepared to condemn the offender's behavior but not the offender?
   - Am I open to learning ways to protect myself without bitterness?
   - Could I envision releasing some of my anger and shifting my focus more to life's loveliness?
   - Is it possible to relinquish some responsibility for settling the account? One person with a spiritual perspective found comfort in the suggestion that "The battle is not yours, but God's."[11]

2. **Decide to heal.** As Murray has noted, "The moment one definitely commits oneself, then Providence moves too."[12]

3. **Find constructive ways to identify and express all feelings.** The goal is not to rehearse the pain forever, but to release the infection and soothe the wound so that it can heal. Writing in journals, artistic expression, or confiding to another trusted person are some ways to do this.

4. **Rely on yourself to heal, not the offender.** You need not wait for the offender to change.

5. **Forgive as best you can.** Remember that forgiving is a difficult process that does not usually happen all at once or once and for all. Surges of negative feelings do not invalidate your progress. They may indicate the need for further healing. Do your best and go on living. Forgiveness may occur when we are not expecting it.

6. **After processing your feelings, try rituals to symbolize the release of your hurt.** For example, you might draw your pain on a balloon and release it into the sky.

7. **Discriminate.** Remember that not all offenders are unwilling or unable to respect you. Some people who hurt us are not willfully malicious. Many people will appreciate the chance to air differences and restore relationships.

### Forgiveness Imagery

1. **Identify a loving figure** (parent, relative, deity, etc.)—someone who loves you and makes you feel safe, like someone important.

2. **Think of a person who has offended you.** Reflect upon the offense, assigning responsibility for the wrong he or she did.

3. **Express your pain in the presence of the loving figure.** Physically locate your feelings of rejection, inferiority, violated trust, anger, or other forms of hurt. Give the pain a shape and color. Imagine the love of that loving figure surrounding you and infusing the places that hurt.

4. **Imagine the offender's real-life battles** (trials, challenges, difficulties). Imagine the adversity he or she is facing. What is it like to face it? Imagine the offender as a hurting child, perhaps a victim.

5. **Recall their strong points and shared good times** (such as joyful experiences or ways they supported you or made you feel good). Recalling these might help you view the offenders more realistically (and with more compassion) and can sometimes mitigate the difficulty of letting go.

6. **Accept responsibility for taking offense.** The effects of serious offenses committed against us are worsened when we fill our lives with agitation—blaming and judging the offender. Such reactions keep us feeling stuck and victimized. Put your ego on the shelf. Notice that the purpose of accepting responsibility for taking offense is not to condemn, but to free us.

7. **Send your forgiveness and healing to the offender.** Imagine something nice happening to him, such as filling the gaps and needs of his childhood. Imagine wishing him well. See him filled with and behaving with loving kindness.

8. **Scan your body for remaining hurt or heaviness.** Feel it lifting away from your body and taking shape in front of you. The loving figure pulls you through the hurt and heaviness, embraces you, and whispers kindly: "The hurting is healing. You are safe, loved, and protected now." You feel your entire body filled with peace.

## Forgive in Writing

Make a list of all the people you have not yet forgiven. For each person, complete this statement for each offense.

Dear _____ ,

I felt _____ when _____
      (hurt, angry, etc.)      (describe what happened)

because _____ . I still feel _____ .
    (why you felt as you did)     (describe present feelings)

If possible, add an empathic thought that reflects the other's emotional state or viewpoint at the time, such as "You were probably feeling pain/insecurity yourself at the time" or "I guess you thought harsh punishment was good discipline." Then, *"I want to forgive you."*

Signed _____

After completing the above statement for each person, finish this sentence:

Dear _____ ,

To the best of my ability, I now choose to forgive you for all these hurts. I release my burden of ill will toward you now and free you and me to live.

Signed _____

Some people find it useful to ritualistically burn their writings as a symbol of closure.

## Forgiving Self

We can't erase or change the past no matter how hard we fight. But we can acknowledge the past and forgive ourselves. Just as releasing resentments toward others frees us to live, so does letting go of resentments toward ourselves.

Steven Hayes[13] notes that forgiving means giving what went before the harm was done. Thus, forgiving self means to give back to oneself the life that went before the trauma. As an exercise, contemplate these questions suggested by Robyn Walser and Darrah Westrup[14]: "If you were to give to yourself the life that went before the trauma, what would that life look like? What actions would you take toward yourself?" You might record your reactions in your journal. In so doing, the actions needed to forgive will become clear.

# CHAPTER 35

# *Innovative Treatments*

Many new treatment approaches have been researched in recent years. This chapter covers some of the more promising ones.

## COUPLES AND FAMILY THERAPY

When a member of a family is traumatically wounded, all the members of the family system are affected. Consider these examples:

- When a combat vet returns home, the emotional numbing and avoidance caused by PTSD might leave the spouse wondering what she has done wrong or frustrated that she cannot help him or feel as close as they used to.
- Intensely angry outbursts by the trauma survivor can damage relationships with family members who do not understand the origin of the anger or how to cope with it.
- Family members might fear becoming traumatized by hearing the survivor's story. They might change the subject or tell the survivor to "get over it," causing the survivor to further withdraw.
- Members of the family might become exhausted and resentful from trying to protect the survivor from upset or from protecting other family members from the survivor.
- Parents might feel helpless and guilty for failing to protect a traumatized child. They might transmit their own excessive anxiety, rather than needed comfort and support, to the child.
- Children might feel fearful, resentful, and neglected by their emotionally wounded parent.

In addition, the support that a PTSD survivor gets from others is one of the strongest predictors of recovery. Thus, recent treatment efforts have attempted to involve family members. In general, couples and family therapies for PTSD help family members regulate strong emotions, comfort and empathize with each other, build intimacy, and process unresolved traumatic wounds that interfere with present relationships. As appropriate, treatment will usually combine sessions where family members meet together with sessions where individuals meet separately with the therapist.

Following are some ways that couples and family therapy can be effective in the treatment of PTSD:

- In a safe setting, a vet, who had maintained that nothing was wrong, was encouraged to tell his combat story. Although he started to relate the story without feeling, he began to weep at having to bear his losses alone. The wife, who had long resented his coldness, now reached for his hand compassionately. He learned that "what is sharable is bearable," while she learned how to become his ally.
- Family members can be instructed in how to support, and not interfere with, the survivor's therapy.
- Couples can learn to identify triggers and avoidance behaviors. Then they work together to engage in feared behaviors, such as going to a restaurant and experiencing the rewards of going out together and enjoying good food.

Additionally, EMDR has been tried in the context of couples and family therapy[1]

- **To resolve past issues that cause problems in present relationships**, such as anger or sexual dysfunction. Under certain conditions and only with mutual consent, a partner might be present while the other partner processes traumatic memories in order to build empathy and understanding.
- **To promote security in traumatized children.** A parent might hold a traumatized child, providing comfort while a traumatic memory is processed. The parent might even provide bilateral stimulation in the forms of alternate shoulder taps as the child does trauma work.
- **To help repair maternal-infant bonding failure.** This failure usually occurs for two reasons, neither of which is the mother's fault. Either the mother was emotionally absent around the time of birth (due to her being

highly distressed or traumatized), or the mother and child were physically separated at birth, even for a few hours (such as when the baby is placed in an incubator). After processing the distress or trauma, the mother is helped to imagine and experience a joyful, intimate birth (such as with the baby lying on the mother's chest right after the delivery). Typically, the mother's instinctual bonding feelings for the child return, which might be sufficient to improve the mother-child relationship. Older children can process feelings of feeling unloved by the mother, if needed.[2]

For help in locating a marriage and family therapist with expertise in treating PTSD, see Additional Resources at the end of this book. Ensure that such a therapist has needed trauma skills.

## HEALING THE WARRIOR'S SOUL[3]

In nearly every culture throughout history, people have honored the tradition of the honorable warrior soul. The warrior has stood for protecting loved ones and the highest ideals of civilization. The ideal warrior embodies virtue, strength, sacrifice, service, courage, discipline, and camaraderie. It is not cruelty and the taking of human life that are valued, but the protection of what is most precious. Thus, children "play at being warriors," and young people are rigorously trained for battle.

Then they go to war and witness unspeakable horrors. In disgust, they often renounce and disown the warrior part of them, hoping to distance themselves from war's ugliness. In so doing, they also distance themselves from many of their deepest strengths.

Warriors are not warriors simply because they have gone to war. Rather, they are those who return and use their acquired strength and wisdom to preserve peace and ensure that violence is restrained and never misused. Once the fighting is over, they build bridges of peace to all people and use their experience to benefit their communities and their world. They reconnect to their basic goodness, their capacity to love, and their spirituality.

Dr. Ed Tick has worked with returning veterans for decades. Using the above principles, he has developed treatment for returning combat veterans that reclaims the honorable warrior identity. Tick considers PTSD to be a soul wound, with moral pain[4] a prime symptom. Even in the absence of immoral behavior, war can leave survivors feeling dirty, guilty, shamed, and helpless—disconnected from others, self, and God. His nontraditional ways to heal the warrior's soul include the following:

- **Reconciliation visits return veterans to the lands of battle.** Many veterans returning to Vietnam are pleasantly surprised to learn that those who once fought against them so fiercely are now so welcoming and forgiving. Common physical and "heart" wounds are honored. Reconciliation is made with those slain in battle. Former enemies are now received as friends who share a common history. In reconnecting to the humanity of former enemies, we reconnect to our own.
- **Compassionate service is rendered to former enemies.** This includes building medical clinics, rebuilding schools and homes, sending medical supplies and aid, and supporting orphans.
- **Retreats of several days welcome returning veterans.** The veterans and those who care about them share stories, experience healing rituals and ceremonies, and learn healing principles.

Dr. Tick's therapy includes three principles. First, "Traumatic wounds shrink as the soul grows big enough to carry them."[5] Warriors learn to accept their combat experience and reaffirm their original commitment to goodness, meaningful living, and service to humanity.

Second, the society that sends young people to battle has the responsibility to welcome them home and help them to reintegrate. The entire society bears the warrior's wound. Ideally we all listen to and honor the warrior's story. Ideally, society will provide purification and cleansing rituals, where elders guide returning warriors back into normalcy, where stains and pain are removed. Native Americans have had such rituals. Catholic confession and Judaism's Ten Days of Repentance are other examples.

Third, the moral dilemma of killing in war is reduced. Killing that is authorized by a government is distinguished from murder, which is the malicious, unlawful taking of life, often for one's personal benefit. It is murder, not killing to protect one's civilization, that is proscribed by most religions.[6] A fair fight among warriors is also distinguished from the killing of innocent civilians. Spiritual healing for impulsive, unethical, or disagreeable acts is explored.

## INTENSIVE TRAUMA THERAPY

Several features make intensive trauma therapy (ITT) unique in the treatment of PTSD and related dissociative disorders. First, it skillfully blends hypnosis, art therapy, and video technology. Second, ITT is relatively rapid. Treatment is compressed into a one- to two-week period, depending on the complexity of the trauma. This is done in an outpatient setting, usually without a long stabilization period. Typically, treatment is seven hours a day, Monday through Friday. Third, ITT is directed by a multidisciplinary team of therapists. This tends to reduce dependence on any single therapist. Preliminary research indicates that this approach is well tolerated and effective.[7] ITT consists of four phases.

Phase I is *evaluation*. A thorough intake interview identifies symptoms and treatment goals. A trauma history is taken. As a general rule, the earliest trauma will be processed first, which may obviate the need to process repetitions of that trauma. The fear of processing the trauma usually diminishes when the survivor understands that symptoms abate as soon as the memory is processed and that processing does not require reliving of the trauma. If mental functioning is unstable, ITT is delayed until it is stabilized.[8]

The client watches a video recording outlining the seven phases of the *instinctual trauma response*: the startle, the thwarted intention to fight or flee, the freeze, the altered state of consciousness, the body sensations, automatic obedience, and self-repair. Understanding these phases normalizes the survivors' experiences and provides the structure and organization that will help them to process their own traumatic memories.

Phase II (narrative processing) and Phase III (reversal of dissociation) are applied to each trauma in turn, normally one trauma per day.

In *narrative processing*, the client, usually aided by hypnosis, watches and describes the traumatic event from the perspective of a hidden observer. The hidden observer just observes from a safe distance without feeling or judging. Telling the story, while paying attention to the seven phases of the instinctual trauma response, helps to put the memory fragments together in correct historical context and reinforces the sense that the trauma has a beginning and an end. The therapist recaps the story, infusing understanding, adding compassionate statements, and recognizing coping strengths in the client. The client in the waking state—if hypnosis is used for this phase—and the therapist then review the video recording of the narrative processing that has occurred thus far. The therapist stops the video recording as necessary to reinforce the seven phases of the instinctual trauma response, grounding the client as needed to prevent reexperiencing. This video review is done as soon after the hypnotic narrative as possible in order to minimize the buildup of anxiety, help the client assimilate the trauma, and avow the trauma as past history.

Creating a graphic narrative continues the narrative processing. Here the client, in the safe hidden observer mode, creates a picture story of the trauma. On separate sheets of paper, the client draws at least one scene depicting each of the seven phases of the instinctual trauma response. In addition, the person draws a safe place image, a "before the trauma" picture, and an "after the trauma" picture to indicate closure and containment. After the client describes the pictures to the therapist, the therapist posts them on a wall and then "re-presents" the story to the client, telling the story with drama, empathy, and resolution. Watching this "re-presentation" at a distance affords the client a sense of safety, while the therapist's compassion helps to neutralize the memory. This "re-presentation" is also video-recorded for later review. Both through artistic and verbal expression, narrative processing helps to reverse the motionless and nonverbal freeze state without causing the client to experience the overwhelming arousal that blocks processing.

Phase III (*reversal of dissociation*) is usually done at the end of the day. This phase helps to reverse any remaining splits in consciousness that tend to occur in the instinctual trauma response. This phase employs video-recorded externalized dialogue, which is used as follows (in each case watching the playback reinforces integration):

- The present self, looking into the camera, speaks to the self that was left behind due to the trauma. The aim is to bring the old self into the present. The video-recorded dialogue continues until all necessary communication has been completed.
- The video-recorded externalized dialogue procedure is also used to treat auditory hallucinations and dissociative identity disorder. The client addresses the voice or alter personality while looking into the camera. The client watches and listens to the playback on behalf of the voice or alter personality. Then the client responds into the camera "for" the voice or alter personality. The dialogue continues until the client resolves issues, such as the compulsion to hurt oneself (the dialogue might explore where the compulsion originated and how it could be resolved). The person with dissociative identity disorder directly negotiates with her various personalities, assuming responsibility for integration.

The externalized dialogue is also used toward the end of treatment (Phase IV) to confront and modify victim myths, which thwart recovery. In arguing against unreasonable, pessimistic thoughts, the client sharpens her thinking and persuades herself of more reasonable views. One approach to changing victim mythology is to construct a courtroom drama in front of the camera. Here the client enacts different roles. Donning one mask, the "prosecutor" argues for myths such as "I'm powerless, helpless, damaged goods, entitled to special treatment, unable to trust." Donning a different mask, the "defense" argues against these myths. After reviewing all the evidence, the "judge," wearing a different mask, renders a "verdict," sentencing the client to a life of compassion, meaning, and enjoyment, without unreasonable, punishing guilt.

Whereas all externalized dialogues are video-recorded in the clinic, the client can also conduct externalized dialogues on audio recordings, in a journal (perhaps using different colors), or via e-mail.

A valuable art therapy process used in ITT is working in clay. One might sculpt in clay the traumatic event and the self that was frozen then. As the client narrates, clay figures are healed and moved out of their frozen state. Soothing objects for grounding and depictions of safe places might also be sculpted.

In summary, the ITT approach processes memories relatively rapidly, usually without prolonged stabilization and time between treatment sessions. The intensive approach minimizes avoidance, forgetting, and the excessive buildup of anticipatory anxiety, while permitting processing without excessive emotional arousal. ITT might be useful for those who cannot access long-term treatment.

# CHAPTER 36

# *Complementary Approaches*

This chapter describes two types of programs that can aid the recovery process: action-based programs and the twelve-step recovery program. Although these are generally not used as stand-alone treatments, they might serve as useful adjuncts to a comprehensive treatment plan.

## ACTION-BASED PROGRAMS[1]

Contemplate the children who enter the world. They are enthused and full of adrenaline as they anticipate new adventures. They relish the world, which is full of things to discover, explore, and master. They take delight in new challenges and spontaneously play with them and with others. Trauma elicits a similar kind of physical arousal but with very negative feelings. Action-based programs re-create this type of physical arousal, but this time surrounded by some of the positive feelings and experiences that we just contemplated.

Many action-based programs trace back to Outward Bound. This program includes action experiences in nature such as hiking, mastering outdoor obstacles, and working together in teams in a safe emotional climate. Such emotionally positive experiences rekindle positive emotions that exist in pre-trauma memory or, in some cases, provide new positive emotional experiences. For example, an Outward Bound program for combat veterans leads small groups into the wilderness for several days where group members might engage in hiking, climbing, rappelling, negotiating rope obstacle courses, practicing survival skills, and white-water rafting. A variation might include a helicopter ride, this time with a sense of joy and safety, not fear. Throughout the experience, a trained leader creates a compassionate emotional climate and sense of camaraderie, where thoughts and feelings can be safely discussed among group members. Individuals are encouraged to participate in the activities, but no one is forced beyond his comfort zone. Leaders at some point might tactfully discuss participants' options, reasons for their choices, the effects of those choices, and how similar choices might affect everyday life. The program frequently results in favorable outcomes:[2]

- An openness to trust others again (This follows from the strong bonds that naturally form as, for example, group members help each other overcome physical obstacles.)
- A feeling of success, accomplishment, overcoming adversity, enhanced self-esteem, and empowerment
- A recapturing of the positive qualities of soldiering (courage, triumph, selflessness, self-confidence, dedication, determination, interdependence, compassion, responsibility, brotherhood, power, competence) without the horrors of war
- A sense of being energized by nature, physical activity, and camaraderie
- An awakened sense that one can grow and change one's life

Although action-based programs are not therapy or substitutes for therapy, they can be effective adjuncts to therapy. They might help to prepare some individuals for therapy or expedite the healing process. Groups exist that are customized for survivors of violence, sexual assault, incest, cancer, substance abuse, mild traumatic brain injury, and grief (see Additional Resources).

## TWELVE-STEP RECOVERY PROGRAM

Dr. Joel O. Brende, M.D., has developed a twelve-step recovery program as a support for those with a spiritual perspective. The program, in essence, invites God, as individually understood, into the recovery process. Participants explore the Twelve Spiritual Steps:[3]

1. Acknowledge traumas and seek God's help.
2. Seek meaning.
3. Seek healing in order to trust.
4. Seek self-understanding and openness to change.
5. Seek understanding and control of anger.
6. Seek understanding and control of fear and helplessness.
7. Seek resolution of guilt through forgiveness and love.
8. Seek healing in grief.

9. Seek to surrender self-destructive tendencies and commit to life.
10. Seek to replace revenge with justice and forgiveness.
11. Seek knowledge and direction in order to find a renewed purpose in life.
12. Seek to love.

Consistent with Alcoholics Anonymous (AA), participants are encouraged to make meaningful changes while turning over to their deity with an attitude of acceptance that which cannot be presently changed.

Many other twelve-step groups, tracing back to the AA model, can help survivors with specific problems related to PTSD such as substance abuse, gambling, or eating disorders. (See Additional Resources.)

**PART VI**

---

# Moving On

# CHAPTER 37

# Transitioning

---

**The life you have led doesn't need to be the only life you have.**
*—Anna Quindlen*

Ponder what you were like before the trauma. It might help to look at a photo taken before the trauma, if you have one. What interested you? What got you excited and curious? What made you laugh? Cry? What did you consider beautiful? What was your sense of spirituality like? What were some of the qualities that you liked about yourself? What were some that you'd wished to improve?

Then consider the trauma and the ways that it understandably affected you. Perhaps much of your growth and development seemed to be put on hold.

Now ponder your future. What would you wish to feel more of? What would you wish to be doing and thinking? What important aspects of your life do you wish to rekindle? On what new adventures do you wish to embark?

Trauma changes people. We are never quite the same afterward. On the other hand, in many ways, we are still the same people—older, wiser, able to pick ourselves up, dust ourselves off, and get back on our life's journey; able to overcome despair. Often we have learned better ways to cope in similar situations.

Trauma is but a detour over which the human spirit triumphs. As you continue to heal, the present and future will become increasingly important to you. Should distressing feelings recur, you now know that this might simply be a cue to process unprocessed material. Distressing feelings might also signal new opportunities for growth. This part of the book will explore ways to move beyond recovery. As you progress through the remaining chapters, you might consider how you will choose to recapture your dreams and create new ones. You might begin to create a time line from now into the future. As you read ahead, you might add goals and dreams to the time line as they occur to you. You might also consider starting a letter to a loved one, written a few years in the future, telling of the positive changes that have happened.

## TRAUMA'S OPPORTUNITIES

Interestingly, research[1] has shown that trauma cannot only be overcome but can actually have positive effects on one's life. In fact, people who experienced traumatic events reported more growth than those who did not.[2] Such positive effects include the following:

- **New possibilities** (discovery of meaning, interests, life path; desire to leave a legacy for children)
- **Personal strength** (inner strength discovered and developed, improved self-esteem, self-assurance, confidence to survive that generalizes to other situations, accepting the need to protect self, replacing simplistic or naive ways of thinking with more adaptive views)
- **Spiritual change** (stronger faith, greater insights, less attachment to material things)
- **Appreciation of life** (reordered priorities, living life to the fullest, slowing down, spending more time with family, seeing everyday hassles in perspective, seeing what's really important, finding joy in the simple things)
- **Relating to others** (greater compassion and desire to lift others, appreciation for others, relationships more valued, accepting the need to trust others and disclose, accepting the need to be assertive in relationships, fewer petty quarrels)

Contemplating the positive in the traumatic experience in no way minimizes one's suffering. Neither is simplistic positive thinking implied. What is suggested is that we see accurately all aspects of the trauma so that it might be better integrated. We deny neither negative nor positive aspects. Unfortunately, some victims see only the negatives. Scurfield[3] suggests how each negative aspect in combat can be balanced by a positive one. These examples are easily adapted to other forms of trauma (see Table 37.1).

In recalling traumatic events, people are not usually glad that they occurred. But they can be glad for what they have done with their lives in the aftermath. As R. Carl Sipprelle reported:[4]

**Table 37.1**
## THE NEGATIVE AND POSITIVE ASPECTS OF COMBAT

| Negative Aspect | Positive Aspect |
| --- | --- |
| Sense of loss, grief, hurt | The extraordinary sense of comradeship experienced in combat suggests that the veteran has already experienced deep friendship and therefore has the potential to do so again. |
| Confusion, questioning of values and life direction | Healthy questioning and reaffirmation of one's values |
| Difficulties in dealing with "everyday" stresses | Knowing that one can remain committed and proficient under very trying circumstances |
| Fall in self-esteem due to imperfect behavior and difficulty in adjusting to post-trauma life | Appreciation of the strength it took to survive both the war and the postwar recovery years |
| Disturbing loss of trust and faith in the country's institutions | Healthy questioning of those institutions, realizing that when government becomes immoral, everyone suffers |
| Intolerance for insensitive, impersonal authority figures and institutions | Strong convictions that one deserves to be treated with respect and dignity |
| Isolation and alienation from others, who are assumed incapable of understanding the trauma experience | Shared bonding among veterans that would not be possible without having the combat experience[5] |
| Loss of belief in God, religion, or faith in humanity | Marked positive changes in outlook, expansiveness of worldview, profound spiritual/religious insights; potential for religious rebirth |
| Dwelling on the fact that one should have died; resentment over suffering | Concept of "bonus time"—to consider survival extraordinary and to appreciate and take advantage of limited time on earth |
| Fear of risks or danger, or being an "adrenaline junkie" who is constantly exposed to dangerous, needless risk | Appreciation of thrilling and peak experiences that did occur in the war, and the willingness to experience healthy and safe stimulation today |
| Bemoaning and resenting one's postwar difficulties and deprivations | Profound appreciation of freedom and the ability to persevere despite pain |
| Painful memories | Appreciating the ability to remember lessons |
| Accepting total or exaggerated degree of responsibility for war zone trauma | Realization and appreciation that situations are often complex, with diverse influences to consider |

Fifty years after surviving the Bataan death march and a subsequent forty-two-month internment at slave labor in Japanese POW camps, a seventy-year-old veteran was interviewed. He stated that he would not repeat his experiences for a million dollars, but recalled them as the most enriching, ennobling experiences of his entire life.

We can ask ourselves, "What frame of mind would it take to view my trauma this way?" Some people figure out a way to change the trauma from a stumbling block to a building block.[6] Gradually, perhaps imperceptibly, a victim of trauma can transition to survivor and then thriver. A victim is one who merely undergoes a traumatic event. Surviving suggests a certain fighting spirit and determination to keep going. Thriving implies that one is living well. From the perspective of experience, thrivers have learned to appreciate themselves, others, and life. They have learned the art of being happy despite adversity. They have learned optimism. Optimism does not mean that one expects everything that happens to be wonderful. It means that one thinks, "No matter what happens, I can still find something to enjoy, to find satisfaction in." Optimists find and accept partial, imperfect solutions. Optimists, therefore, can examine negative events and accurately see their positive potential.

## CONSTRUING BENEFIT IN TRAUMA

Make three columns on a blank sheet of paper. In the first column, list the negative impacts trauma has had on your life. In the second column, list the positive impacts that have occurred as a result. In the third column, list the positive things that could still occur in your life. Keep this exercise in your journal. Refer to it often to reinforce your sense of optimism.

## THE ELDERLY CHILD REMEMBERS

Trauma therapist Beverly James uses this strategy to help victims of childhood trauma rehearse a happy future. This strategy, however, adapts well to survivors of any trauma. She explains that this dramatic strategy "playfully allows the [survivor] to imagine a future for herself in which she has integrated her traumatic experience into the fabric of her interesting life. It is best accomplished with a small group . . . joining the [survivor] in treatment in an individual session. It is helpful to have on hand some amount of dramatic play props for both [males and females], such as hats, masks, scarves, jewelry, dishes, building materials, makeup, etc." The strategy is explained as follows:[7]

Today we are going to imagine ourselves in a future time. You are going to be wonderful old ladies (or old guys) who are hanging out together having a good time. You have been successful in taking care of yourselves, in following your careers, and in raising your families. This is a time in your lives when you are very creative. There are many things you enjoy doing. You work part of the time and find your work interesting. Although you are old now, you have kept your bodies active and healthy. You have good friends that you enjoy spending time with, and today you are visiting with some of these good friends. You are in a restaurant [on a mountaintop, fishing, on an airplane . . . ] and are talking about your lives. You are going to talk about a long, long time ago when you were about [use current age] years old and feeling bad [worried, scared . . . ] about the [trauma, the future . . . ]. You are going to talk about how you felt way back then, how you got stronger, and then how you went on in your life to be successful. Talk about how it is for you now that you are an older person who is thinking back so long ago. And how does it feel when, as an older person, you think back to the (trauma) and remember that it was an important part, but just one part, of your very interesting life. First, let's get some props and costumes together. Should I be the waitress [friend, ranger, boat-cleaner]? Are we ready? Let's begin. Action!

# CHAPTER 38

# Intimacy and Sexuality

With sufficient healing, the areas of intimacy and sexuality can become increasingly meaningful in the lives of PTSD survivors. It is fitting, then, to explore these areas now.

## SNAPSHOT LENS

Following a traumatic event, victims tend to see the world through a new lens. They see themselves as worthless and undeserving. Others now seem untrustworthy, and relationships dangerous, while sex is confusingly different. It is as though a snapshot has been taken through a clouded lens. A moment in time determines the view that persists. To retain the old lens is to remain a victim. To carry on despite the clouded lens is to be a survivor. To clean off the lens and take a fresh look is to thrive.

We have talked about gaining an accurate view of self when we explored self-esteem building. We'll now separate intimacy and sexuality—two areas of conflict and confusion for PTSD survivors—so that we might see them clearly and be liberated to create new and satisfying experiences. Each new experience is an opportunity to create a new, positive memory. We want to scrub off our lenses on self, relationships, and sex—all of which interrelate. The thriver learns to view the self as capable, strong, good, worthy, and deserving of happiness. Relationships are seen as an opportunity to joyfully bond in a loving, committed, enduring relationship, and sex is seen as a beautiful aspect of a loving relationship.

## INTIMACY

Intimacy means that we share what we are really like, who we really are, and what we have been through. Two people are intimate when they truly know each other and, it is suggested, like and accept one another. Sharing thoughts, feelings, values, and sometimes sexual love are ways to be intimate. In addition to making life more joyful, intimacy is important in PTSD recovery. People who actively connect with others following a traumatic event seem to fare better. For example, Holocaust survivors who made an effort to get involved with others had better mental health than those who did not. These people formed social groups with friends, family, and neighbors. They self-disclosed or confided what was happening in their lives— their pains, concerns, even finances. They used the telephone, visits, and letters to stay in touch, and provided support for their comrades. They also accepted support from others. The researchers concluded that staying isolated is bad for your health. A positive finding in this research was that survivors were more likely to help out family and friends than those who did not endure trauma.[1]

Unfortunately, PTSD survivors seem to have more relationship difficulties such as divorce and avoidance of intimacy. Some appear to marry in hopes of re-creating their pre-trauma life[2] or escaping difficult circumstances before sufficient healing has taken place. For some, fear of intimacy interferes with connectedness. As one survivor said, "I heard that love casts out fear, but in my case, fear cast out love." Patricia Sheehan has identified five fears that interfere with intimacy and that must be neutralized in order for intimacy to grow. Otherwise, survivors will sabotage intimacy in ways that include workaholism, picking fights, abandoning their partner, and drinking. As you'll see, these fears make perfect sense for one who has survived trauma, so be understanding toward yourself. The fears are:[3]

1. **Loss of control.** In intimacy, we open ourselves up emotionally. This means that we are prone to emotional intrusions of unresolved memories. This can lead to avoidance or anger to prevent loss of control.[4] It is logical, then, to sufficiently heal so that intimacy might progress. In some cases, survivors fear being controlled by their partner. This follows logically from trauma where choice and control were taken away, especially when it was another human wresting control from the victim. The antidote is to find a trustworthy person, or persons, who can be viewed as an ally and teammate. In such a relationship, we gradually learn to relinquish or share some control.

2. **Abandonment.** We manifest this fear by never loving again, engaging in casual sex without emotional involvement, being distant or revengeful in relationships, or overreacting with clinging, jealous insecurity. This follows from being left by significant people or by the failure of significant people to protect the victim.

3. **Rejection.** To protect against this fear, the survivor might not let herself be fully known or will reject the other person first. This fear arises from the feeling of being damaged and unlovable and by the perception that people would reject her if they knew her secret.

4. **Attack.** In close relationships, people are more vulnerable to put-downs, teasing, or other abusive acts. Such behaviors seem like a betrayal of the unspoken pledge to support and protect one's loved one. One who has become sensitized to danger will have an even greater need for safety. Because of this vulnerability, survivors are likely to feel threatened by even small disagreements. A "you are with me or against me" mind-set might develop that makes communication difficult.

5. **One's own tendency to hurt others.** Survivors may not see their anger, disappointment, or hurt as normal feelings that can be constructively dealt with, or they may lack the skills to do so.

Intimacy is more likely to flourish if survivors do the following:

1. **Accept the fears.** View them as normal, understandable consequences of trauma without judging yourself. Normalizing fears is one way to neutralize them.

2. **Replace ideas that block intimacy:**
   - **All men/women are no-good.** This idea would lead one to either avoid all intimacy or to permit someone untrustworthy to enter one's boundaries since there is apparently no hope of finding someone decent. In truth, some people do not reject, abandon, attack, or take advantage of others' weaknesses. Some people respect and honor others, even with their imperfections. This is the essence of love.
   - **Nobody has gone through the terrible things I have gone through. Nobody can relate to me.** Even among young, apparently healthy college students you will typically find a wide range of severe traumas. No matter what you have gone through, many others have experienced similar traumatic events. People exist who will relate to you with compas-

sion. Some people have learned this compassion through the things they have suffered, while others have learned compassion by being raised in loving homes.

- **Nobody could accept me if they knew what I've been through.** Some people may not. When trusted with secrets, however, some people will accept and respect the survivor as much or more.
- **It is demeaning to be flawed, and foolish to reveal vulnerabilities.** Everyone is flawed, and sharing our true feelings is the essence of wholesome intimacy.
- **I can't burden others with my problems.** If people care about you, they will want to know about the bad times as well as the good. People in high-quality relationships create time for humor, play, and affection. And when discussion of difficult emotions is needed, they make time for that, too.

3. **Develop communication skills.** Visit your library or talk with your counselor. There are many, many effective skills for resolving differences peacefully, expressing affection verbally and nonverbally, expressing negative feelings constructively, complimenting, and standing up for yourself. (See the book *Fighting for Your Marriage* in Additional Resources.)

4. **Gradually risk and discern.** As wisely as possible, involve trusted people in your life. Allow them to help to meet your needs. With the right person, disclosing your true self can be pleasantly surprising. Hiding your true self creates barriers. As fears are permitted expression and are respected, trust builds. The climate of safety that develops also fosters the expression of positive emotions. It is possible to be known emotionally without disclosing details that are too uncomfortable to discuss. Test the waters and discern how the other person responds. Caution may indeed be wise if the other person is too defensive to reciprocate, is judgmental or abusive, or will not keep confidences. Heed those warnings. When you discern, however, that the other person is safe, begin to accept nurturing in the form of emotional support, listening, and compliments.

5. **Notice how conflicts are handled.** Conflict in relationships is normal and to be expected. However, it is the way conflict is handled, and not the presence of conflict, that has been found to predict marital success. Attacking verbally or physically, withdrawing, sulking, threatening, criticizing, raising the voice, manipulating, dishonesty, and jealousy are styles that create interpersonal distance. Approaches that favor intimacy include good listen-

ing skills, sticking to issues, kind humor, patience, calmness, emotional openness, sharing control, complimenting, empathy, and willingness to tolerate differences.

6. **Consider picking up where they left off before the trauma.** This could mean building the types of healthy relationships that were enjoyed before the trauma, or cultivating better ones. Ponder the kind of relationship that you'd enjoy. Try to create a vision of what it would be like.

## RESTORING WHOLESOME SENSUALITY AND SEXUALITY

Our bodies are part of the way we experience being alive, and sexuality is an important aspect of this experience. Bodies allow us to feel the wind through our hair and the joy of a warm embrace. Yet commonly, people with PTSD feel shamed emotionally. Because the mind and body are connected, they also feel physically and sexually shamed. Physical and sexual sensations that were once innocent and wonderful become conflicted and confusing. Understandably, sexual difficulties often arise.

Several studies have indicated that males and females with PTSD are more likely to experience sexual problems than those without PTSD. These problems include sexual disinterest, aversion, dissatisfaction, and performance difficulties (erectile problems, premature ejaculation, painful intercourse, impaired arousal or climax). For example, in one study, 80 percent of Vietnam veterans were found to have clinically relevant sexual problems.[5] It is common for survivors to feel anxiety, disgust, shame, and a devalued body image during sex.

Sexual difficulties are certainly likely if the traumatic event involved some form of sexual abuse, although other forms of trauma produce similar difficulties. For example, survivors who were abused in any way (sexually, emotionally, physically) commonly feel shamed emotionally and sexually. Beautiful women or handsome men might not feel attractive despite positive feedback from others. If bodies were treated as objects in the past, it is difficult to see them now as beautiful. They may be driven to have a perfect body. Yet despite successful exercise and dieting, they still feel ashamed, dirty, and ugly outside and in. Victims might find ways to avoid sexual relations by wearing unattractive or drab clothes, gaining weight, mutilating their bodies, or developing psychosomatic illnesses.

Following sexual assault, sex itself can become a trigger. It is now associated with humiliation, exploitation, danger, secretiveness, and shame. Even if the present partner is trusted, the smell of semen might trigger painful memories. Likewise, certain ways of being touched—even nonsexual touches—or certain positions taken by the partner during lovemaking might trigger traumatic memories. If the victim climaxed during rape, then climaxing becomes associated with shame. The victim may have dissociated from her body during the trauma and might again dissociate when her present partner becomes aroused. She may see the face of the rapist in her husband even though the rape occurred years ago and the husband is loving and devoted. So it is understandable that the victim might avoid sex, touch, and intimacy, and find it difficult to relax and enjoy sexual relations. Others may be drawn to sex in unhealthy relationships (a futile form of repetition compulsion) in an attempt to "make sex right" again. (It doesn't work, because the context is all wrong.) Some feel too shattered to resist manipulative lovers, as unhealthy sex in unhealthy relationships maintains the problem.

Emotional numbing, depression, and substance abuse also help to explain why sexual difficulties can arise in all forms of trauma. As with other areas in PTSD, we can pick up where we left off in our development as regards wholesome sensuality and sexuality. The transition period is an excellent time to do this.

## Understanding and Neutralizing Disgust

Along with fear, disgust is another emotion that is commonly fused with traumatic memory material. It is helpful to understand this emotion as a way to neutralize it.

Disgust is a strong emotion that, like other emotions, can serve a protective purpose—in this case, keeping something away that is harmful. With permission, we'll explore some essential concepts from William I. Miller's *Anatomy of Disgust*.[6]

Disgust conveys a "strong aversion to something perceived as dangerous because of its powers to contaminate, infect, or pollute by proximity, contact, or ingestion." Other words for disgusting are "repulsive," "revolting," and "abhorrent." Disgust is close to sentiments of contempt, loathing, hatred, horror, even fear. Disgust is often accompanied by feelings of uneasiness, panic, or incompetence—particularly if the disgusting object caused us to feel helpless in the past. The emotion of disgust may be accompanied with physical sensations of nausea, queasiness, or sick feeling: "it makes my skin crawl" or "it gives me the creeps."

It is normal to feel disgust. Disgust rules mark the boundaries of self; they keep out what is threatening. The relaxing of these rules marks privilege, intimacy, duty, and caring. Thus, the initial disgust with body functions or parts (e.g., menstruation, odors, or hair) is overcome as a "prelude to normal sexual behavior."

Certain objects, such as decaying garbage, pose obvious threats of contamination. Their odors, sights, or tastes might be described as "fetid, foul, stink, stench, rancid, vile, revolting, nauseating, sickening."

The fear of disgust is not just that the body will be contaminated, but also that the soul will become dirty inside. Thus defects of character can seem disgusting—vulgar. Think of sexual assailants in rape. It is not just that perpetrators "mock principles we feel should be better served; it is that they impose vices on us: distrustfulness, cynicism, and paranoia." This is why it is normal to feel disgusted following rape. It is not sex per se that disgusts, but sex in the context of exploitation. Sex is used to defile, and it is natural to assume that sex could do so again. Lost perhaps is the perception that sex in a different context and setting could also lift the individual. Sex out of place, without love, is disgusting. To say it another way, sex can be uplifting, wholesome, and enjoyable when experienced in a committed, loving, and responsible relationship. It is normal to be repulsed by sex that is misused for selfish pleasure, domination, power, or ego gratification.

**Disgust by Association.**  Like fear, disgust has a strong tendency to fuse with memories in confusing ways. For example, disgusting smells are associated with shame and immorality (e.g., "I stink"). Strong sexual smells that are disgusting in the context of rape might then also become fused with shame.

Disgust can become state-dependent. That is, any present situation that disgusts (defecation, present sex, disgusting entertainment) can trigger a full-blown disgust/shame reaction. It is natural, then, that sex will be aversive and avoided. Instead of being a source of satisfaction and beauty, it brings back uncomfortable feelings. Because of the proximity of the sex organs to the anus, sex can become confused with decay and its odors so that all parts of the body in the genital region become devalued.

Another infrequently mentioned aspect of disgust is that we tend to view our bodies as we view ourselves. If people view themselves badly (i.e., disgusting), then their orifices and secretions are viewed as disgusting and likely to repulse a lover. (This fear of repulsing is challenged by engaging in a sexual relationship in the context of love, trust, and dignity.)

**The Positive Side of Disgust.**  As Miller observes, disgust can benefit humans. Disgust can help us avoid what is harmful and seek what is elevating. "Morality, cleanliness, and loathing of cruelty depend on it." Indeed, we "recoil from the stench of sinful deeds." If we are disgusted by certain behaviors, it shows that we still have an appreciation of good behavior. Disgust with misused sex and bad character means we still have an appreciation for good character and sex used within a healthy context. In fact, walling off sexuality is a way to protect it until it is safe to experience in a safe context.

We note that disgust for certain things is not necessarily static. As we mentioned, initial disgust with the human body is overcome as a prelude to normal sexual behavior. Anything that was once beautiful and pure can become disgusting, and vice versa. A rose is beautiful and decaying garbage is not. But the beautiful rose eventually decays, and the decaying garbage can eventually become the soil used to grow a rose.[7] Disgust can be neutralized and modified, although the imprint of disgust might not change overnight. Miller notes that love enables people to overcome disgust.

## STRATEGIES FOR REBUILDING WHOLESOME SENSUALITY AND SEXUALITY[8]

Fortunately, a number of strategies aid the goal of rebuilding (or building) a sense of wholesome sensuality and sexuality. These are best tried as part of a comprehensive treatment plan and within the context of a balanced, wholesome lifestyle.

1. **Normalize the genital area.** Survivors need to relearn that the genitals are normal, matter-of-fact parts of their bodies. Beverly James approaches this process in a straightforward, playful way with her young clients. Following a discussion of appropriate names for body parts, James explains:[9]

   > First of all, let's take "butts." Do you realize that everyone in the world has a butt? What good is a butt? You're right, it's good for sitting on. What would it be like if people didn't have a butt? They couldn't sit down. There'd be no chairs in the world. Everyone would lie down a lot. What would cars look like? What else is the butt good for? What comes out of the butt? If we didn't have a butt, then poop would come out somewhere else. Where could that be? What would that be like? What would bathrooms be like?
   >
   > [A similar process would continue for "vagina" and "penis." The message to be left with the child is that all humans have these things, they are efficiently designed for their unique functions, and they are neither glorious nor shameful, that is, "Parts are parts."]

2. **Neutralize feelings of disgust.**
   - Realize that sexual abuse temporarily contaminates the body, but not the soul, unless we take in the message "I am only an object."
   - Consider disgust normal without judging yourself. Look at disgust and objectively examine what it is saying. Is something disgusting because it is presently dangerous, or does it just trigger memories of the past? Ask, "Will this really contaminate me, or is it just an unpleasant thought?"
   - Discriminate. Break down overwhelming feelings of disgust into parts to gain a sense of control over those feelings. What specifically is disgusting? Is it all aspects of sex or just certain behaviors? Is it all touch or just certain types? Distinguish disgust related to sex from disgust related to other body functions. You might try writing about this to gain a greater sense of control.
   - Separate disgust with sex from shame. Remember that shame is feeling bad for who we are at the core, rather than feeling bad for what we did or for what was done to us. Feeling polluted by your own or others' behavior signals a need for cleansing and healing, not a destruction of self. Regarding shame, a survivor of rape might ask, "Am I bearing the costs for another's crime?"
   - Neutralize disgust with love for self and others whom you choose to let in. Think, perhaps, of your affection for a newborn baby or a trusted lover.
   - Expand your focus. Don't focus exclusively on the negative, but also see the beauty. Ask yourself, "What else is there to notice?" Look for opportunities to appreciate the beauty of the human body. Tasteful art is one way to do this. Enjoy the curves and proportions of the body; notice how beautiful they are. Also notice nonsexual aspects of people. Just appreciate the wholesome beauty of people: enjoy the countenances, colors of dress, overall appearance, or personality. Wholesome sensuality is broader than sexuality. Sensuality applies to using all the senses to enjoy the pleasures of the world. Thus, we can enjoy a sunset, a flower, or a good meal, too.
   - Create a wholesome vision of sex within the context of a committed, loving relationship. What would that relationship be like? Would it be marked by mutual love, respect, trust, tenderness, laughter, admiration, and security? More simply, perhaps you would just treat each other well. Imagine that you and your partner know each other not just physically, but emotionally, philosophically, and creatively as well. You might view

sex as the culminating expression of a good relationship, one marked by hugs, good conversation, and play. You might envision comforting and pleasuring your mate, while receiving the same in return. If desired, you might envision sex for the purpose of creating babies who are loved, nurtured, and raised so that they grow into decent people who are good company. It might help to ponder the differences between unhealthy and healthy sexuality, as summarized in Table 38.1.

3. **Learn the paradoxes of satisfying sexuality, suggested by Beverly Engel:**[10]

The harder you try to make something happen sexually, the less will happen. [In other words, relax. Go slow. Allow whatever happens to happen. Have reasonable expectations. Take a moratorium on genital sex if you wish, and focus on other aspects of physical intimacy—touching, stroking, holding, hugging, kissing, fondling, and other expressions of affection that many people find just as satisfying as intercourse. This period of abstinence can allow other satisfying aspects of a relationship to grow without pressure to perform.]

The way to cure your sexual problem is to not try to cure it. [Tensing and trying too hard to fix a problem can worsen it. Allow healing to occur at its own rate.]

The way to be able to have sexual activity whenever you want is to learn to recognize when you do *not* want to have sex. [Recognize when sex does not feel right, and say so.]

The way to relax is to learn to recognize when you are anxious.

The way to learn to concentrate is to recognize when you are not concentrating.

The way to be able to please your partner is to learn what feels good for *you*.

4. **Sensate focus is useful for a wide range of sexual problems, and is especially useful for PTSD.** This technique enables partners to learn or relearn to enjoy the simple act of touch, without the expectation or pressure to perform sexually. *Sensate focus* is so-called because the person focuses only on the sensation of touch. Because the focus is in the present and grounded in physical reality, there is less tendency to dissociate. The directions follow:[11]

- As closely as possible, you'll focus on touching your partner's skin. You will focus just on the exact point of contact between your fingertips,

**Table 38.1**
UNHEALTHY VS. HEALTHY SEXUALITY

| Unhealthy Sexuality | Healthy Sexuality |
| --- | --- |
| Feels secretive and shameful | Feels good; is celebrative; adds to self-esteem |
| Is illicit, stolen, exploitive, abusive, and/or demeaning; the victim is used, then abandoned or dominated | Is healing; has no victims; loves, lifts, trusts, cares for, and protects the other person |
| Compromises values and spirituality | Deepens meaning and spirituality; adds to the feeling of closeness to God |
| Fear provides excitement | Shared vulnerability and regard provide excitement and deep satisfaction |
| Reenacts childhood abuses | Cultivates a sense of being an adult |
| Disconnects one from oneself | Adds to one's sense of self |
| Is self-destructive and dangerous | Enhances the sense of safety and security |
| Uses conquest, control, and power; an "I-It" relationship | Uses love; honors the partner; shares control in a meaningful way; an "I-Thou" relationship |
| Pain is covered, medicated, escaped, or killed in a sterile way | Pain is surrounded and infused with love and intimacy |
| Is dishonest | Is responsible to both parties; enhances integrity |
| Becomes routine, grim, joyless | Is stimulating, challenging, playful, and fun; becomes more interesting as feelings are honestly shared |
| Requires a double life | Integrates the most authentic parts of the self |
| Demands perfection | Accepts the imperfect |
| Is separate from intimacy and a loving relationship; sex is confused with caring | Exists within a loving, respectful relationship |
| Creates distance or enmeshment/engulfment | Creates comfortable intimacy |
| Overemphasizes superficiality (looks, talents, etc.) | Is more concerned with feeling comfortable with one's partner and the partner's goodness, kindness, and decency |
| Overemphasizes fears from the past | Focuses primarily on building the relationship |
| Is selfish, focused only on self-gratification | Also considers the partner's pleasure and well-being |

*Adapted with permission from Carnes, P., with J. M. Moriarity. 1997. Sexual Anorexia: Overcoming Sexual Self-Hatred. Center City, Minn.: Hazelden. Copyright © 1997 by Patrick Carnes.*

hand, and forearm and your partner's skin, noticing what it is like to touch and be touched by your partner's skin.

- With tender, caring, gentle movements, caress your partner. That is, using the flats of your fingertips, the flat of the hand or fingers, palms, wrist, or even the forearm, slowly stroke your partner's skin in long, sweeping strokes. The strokes are much lighter than a massage.
- This technique is intended for your pleasure as well as your partner's, so don't worry about doing it "right." Just focus on your own feelings and assume that your partner is OK. Your partner just relaxes passively and enjoys the experience, focusing only on the point of contact.
- Go very, very slowly. Then cut the speed in half. Focus only on the point of contact.
- Relax and be silent. There is no speaking, groans or moans, or sexual movements.
- Afterward, honestly discuss what the experience was like. Honestly discussing what was enjoyable and what was not increases trust and communication.

Eliminating the pressure to perform, this technique often helps partners to feel valued for things other than being a sexual partner.

5. **Distinguish sex from love, affection, and attention.** When we see the differences clearly, we can better choose how to experience sex in the context desired.

6. **Prepare for flashbacks during sex.**[12] First, ask your partner for help. Communicate to your partner what you have experienced and how it has affected you. Teach your partner how to recognize signs of flashbacks and to check it out if you appear to be experiencing one. Instruct him or her to gently bring you back to the present and comfort you with comments such as "It's me, you're safe now" and to wait until flashbacks stop to respond sexually. Should a flashback occur, open your eyes and notice where you are. Notice that your partner is not the perpetrator—notice specific differences between your partner and the perpetrator and between the present surroundings and the place where the sexual assault happened. Use easy, deep breaths and calming self-talk to relax, or focus on a symbol of safety or security.

7. **Discuss using the rewind technique with your therapist, rewinding to a point where sex was viewed positively.** Sex, here, could simply mean viewing someone as attractive or beautiful.

8. **Create a collage of wholesome sexuality and sensuality.** You might include images that remind you of your pre-trauma views, as well as images of what you wish to create. You might include pictures of a loving parent with child, someone of the opposite sex with a kind face, a person at home in nature, or beautiful art that celebrates the beauty of the body.

9. **Use eye movements to integrate the past and present.** Create a wholesome vision of sexuality—where sex is seen within the context of love. You might, for example, imagine a couple embracing warmly as they watch a sunset. Perhaps you'll use an image from your collage. Then pick or create a wholesome image of sexuality from a time before the trauma. Think of the first image, then think of the image from the past. Then do a set of eye movements to reinforce the connection.

10. **Several strategies of somatic trauma therapy can be useful for someone who froze during some form of sexual assault.** In one technique described by trauma specialist Babette Rothschild, an actual safe place with an actual safe person (or persons) is visualized. The client, usually seated, pictures running the route from the scene of the assault to that safe place. Once there, she imagines receiving the necessary support from the safe person(s). If tolerated, the feet and arms can replicate a running movement. This technique, first developed at the Bodynamic Institute in Copenhagen, tends to loosen the traumatic freezing, release anxiety, and infuse the memory with a feeling of connection to a safe person(s), rather than isolation.[13]

11. **When women experience painful intercourse, practicing Kegel exercises, which strengthen the pelvic floor muscles, is often helpful.** The pubococcygeal muscle tightens when the vagina and rectum are contracted, as when stopping the flow of urine or when going up in an elevator. The feeling of relaxing this muscle is similar to an elevator going down. Ten repetitions done two to three times daily over at least six weeks is recommended to increase muscle strength. During intercourse, it may be best if the female is on top of her partner in order to maintain the ability to stop if intercourse becomes painful. The female tenses those muscles and feels the sensation of contraction as she says to herself, "Up the elevator." She says to herself, "Down the elevator" as tension is released. A side benefit of the Kegel exercises is that they help to prevent incontinence with aging or pregnancy.[14]

12. **Consider trying healing sexual imagery or stories.** One imagery approach utilizes the assumption that confronting painful memories dissipates their control over the victim. This approach involves four steps:

a. Recall negative sexual experiences and their results.

b. String these negative experiences together and form an image that represents them.

c. Stay with the image. Let it settle. Go into it.

d. Notice what comes into your awareness.

For example, one survivor's negative sexual memories included experiences of abuse, being used and rejected by lovers, and seeking empty sexual liaisons to escape her pain of loneliness. The image that represented these experiences was a sense of darkness that enveloped her and settled over her. As she allowed the darkness to settle around her and went into the darkness, she noticed that her fear subsided. She felt at peace. In the midst of the darkness, she noticed an ember, a flame of brightness. To her, the light symbolized the love that she was seeking and had once experienced in the presence of her grandparents. She realized that it was love she wanted to cultivate and preserve. As she became aware of love, she no longer made choices in her relationships that were contrary to love.

Healing stories are another type of imagery. In a very relaxed state, simply imagine seeking the ear of a trusted, wise adult. You relate the negative experience to this adult, who listens with great love and compassion, then offers a soothing antidote. For example, a woman who was raped as a teenager hears, "I'm sorry that your first sexual experience wasn't a beautiful and tender one. That must have been so difficult for you. I want you to remember, though, that sex with someone you truly love and who truly loves you is beautiful and tender. You're smart. You'll find a relationship where there's love and commitment. And then sex will be wholesome and right." The people in the story give each other a warm hug, the young girl thanks the adult, and that ends the story.[15]

13. **Let go of all-or-none thinking.** Remember that even in healthy relationships where partners haven't experienced trauma, sexual relations can be very satisfying, disappointing, and everywhere in between. Remembering this takes some of the pressure off and helps one adapt a more relaxed attitude.

Like other aspects of post-traumatic healing and growth, building or rebuilding healthy intimacy and sexuality is a process. Don't be discouraged if the process is initially two steps forward and one step back. Instead, watch the process with kind interest, curiosity, and patience.

# CHAPTER 39

# Meaning and Purpose

**My legs you will chain—yes, but not my will—**
**no, not even Zeus can conquer that.**

*—Epictetus*

In the twentieth century, the famous psychotherapists Carl Jung, Rollo May, and Viktor Frankl described an anxiety that is associated with a lack of meaning and purpose. Perhaps the most profound thoughts on this subject have been written by Viktor Frankl. Frankl survived the horror of the World War II concentration camps. He noticed that those who had goals, a reason for living, and meaning and purpose in their lives withstood the suffering better. He marveled that some people in the most dire straits found joy in serving their comrades. He himself transcended the meaningless, miserable world of the concentration camps by envisioning his beloved wife's love and seeing himself at some future time lecturing to others on the lessons of the concentration camp. He also realized that one could take consummate pleasure in something as simple as watching the sun rise through the barbed wire. He reaffirmed that one might imprison your body, but no one can take away the last freedom, one's attitude toward suffering. He developed the school of psychotherapy called *logotherapy*, which helps people find meaning in their lives, and found great meaning in his own life by helping others find meaning and purpose. He has said, "What man actually needs is not a tensionless state but rather the striving and struggling for a worthwhile (freely chosen) goal."[1]

A psychological scale has been developed based on Frankl's work. Research with the *purpose-in-life scale* has shown that those with meaning and purpose are happier, less anxious, and freer of psychopathology in general. Raymond Scurfield poignantly exhorts survivors to give up vengeance as their purpose for living and replace it with love, peace, and joy again.[2]

## REDISCOVERING THE MEANING AND PURPOSE WITHIN

All individuals already have within them the seeds of great meaning and purpose that can be nourished and cultivated. Take a few moments to ponder and respond to these questions as a way to get in touch with these seeds:

- Why did you survive? For what purpose?
- Why didn't you commit suicide?
- Why have you kept going?
- What is it that makes my life worth living?[3]

Perhaps this exercise helped you get in touch with:

- A realization of what life has invested in you
- Hopes and dreams; anticipation of experiencing life's loveliness (One survivor said, "Life still holds adventure.")
- A realization of to whom you matter
- Faith in the future ("I had faith that my suffering would resolve.")
- Expectations of being useful (because of what you have learned and because of who you are)
- Hopes in and for others ("As bad as I feel, perhaps someone will help me find greater joy"; "I've seen others get through this—so can I.")
- Trust in your sense of discovery ("I believe I'll find greater meaning and more enjoyment.")
- Inner resources, sense of worth ("Deep down, I know I am worth something; I am not a quitter; I believe in myself; there's more to me than this trauma; I've been to the depths, and now I know I can survive anything.")

## FURTHER CULTIVATING MEANING AND PURPOSE

We might categorize methods of finding meaning and purpose into three groups.

1. Giving something meaningful to the world
2. Experiencing and enjoying the world's wholesome, beautiful pleasures
3. Developing personal strengths and attitudes

## FINDING MEANING AND PURPOSE

*Giving something meaningful to the world.* Contributing in ways that make the world a better place:

_____ establishing or joining a social or political cause (family, politics, science, church or synagogue, Mothers Against Drunk Driving, Parents of Murdered Children, etc.)

_____ creating art, poetry, writing; other creative expression that makes something new, beautiful, or useful

_____ giving money or material support to a worthy cause

_____ altruistic service, self-transcendence, building up or helping others

_____ giving in small ways (it needn't be grandiose) that are useful to others, like picking up trash by the road; beautifying your yard for your neighbor's benefit—not yours; giving a coworker, spouse, or neighbor a hand unexpectedly; lifting anyone in any small way (a smile, thank-you, listening ear, etc.)

_____ committing to doing your best at your job today

_____ simply observe what you do to meet others' needs

_____ sharing with others what you have discovered to reduce your own suffering

*Experiencing and enjoying life's pleasures/beauties*

_____ nature (e.g., get up early and watch the sunrise; gaze at the constellations at night)

_____ intimate love

_____ friends

_____ connecting with neighbors

_____ entertainment

_____ exercising your body

_____ notice what you appreciate in others; tell them

_____ cathedrals; majestic or beautiful buildings

_____ faces

_____ teamwork

*Developing personal strengths and attitudes*

_____ peace of mind

_____ personal growth, holiness, goodness of character, self-actualization

_____ courage, taking responsibility for my own life ("I can't" often means "I won't take responsibility for my own life," a form of avoidance.[4])

_____ refraining from criticizing, complaining, whining, backbiting, and other negatives

_____ improving the mind

_____ understanding, empathy, patience, compassion

_____ loyalty and honesty (survivors will not betray others, as they were)

The existential psychotherapist Irvin Yalom writes, "One begins with oneself in order to forget oneself and to immerse oneself into the world; one comprehends oneself in order not to be preoccupied with oneself."[5] In other words, self development is a means to engage further in the world in a meaningful way. Describing the most fulfilled people, psychologist Abraham Maslow observed, "Self-actualizing people are, without one single exception, involved in a cause outside their own skin, in something outside of themselves . . . and which they love."[6] Echoing this thought in *On the Meaning of Life*, historian Will Durant said, "Join a whole, work for it with all your body and mind. The meaning of life lies in the chance it gives us to produce, or to contribute to something greater than ourselves. It need not be a family (although that is the direct and broadest road which nature in her blind wisdom has provided for even the simplest soul); it can be any group that can call out all the latent nobility of the individual and give him a cause to work for that shall not be shattered by his death."[7]

## FINDING MORE MEANING AND PURPOSE

Frankl explained that there is no one road to meaning and purpose. Each person finds it in his or her own unique way, and on his or her own timetable. Page 342 lists some possible approaches. As an exercise, check an item if it seems like it might be of interest to you, either now or at some future time. Ask yourself as you go, "What do I really want from life?" A balance among all three areas is characteristic of many of the most fully developed and satisfied people.

# CHAPTER 40

# Spiritual and Religious Growth

Never shall I forget those moments that murdered my
God and my soul, and turned my dreams to dust.

—Elie Wiesel

Of course, the sovereign cure for worry is religious faith.

—William James, psychologist, philosopher

It has been frequently observed that trauma can shake one's religious faith or lead to its rebirth. Sometimes both occur following trauma. As healing occurs, survivors might discover the potential for greater religious faith, perhaps becoming more receptive to spiritual development after returning from "the valley of death."[1]

Sigmund Freud called religion the "universal neurosis." The famous modern-day psychologist Albert Ellis stated that religion creates irrational thinking.[2] However, the research presents a different picture.

Scientific polling among Americans reveals that the proportion of Americans who believe in God has remained remarkably constant over the last sixty years, exceeding 90 percent.[3] However, in predicting health outcomes, one's religious commitment is more important than the beliefs one professes.

Religious commitment means putting belief into practice, or action. It measures not affiliation or denomination but taps the depth of one's faith. Typically, it is defined in the research as prayer, reading sacred works, and attendance at church/synagogue/mosque/temple. It also includes a relationship with God, making beliefs an important part of one's life, and connection with others in the religious community. In reviewing the studies published in recent years, psychiatric epidemiologist David Larson concluded that "The impact of religious commitment on physical and mental health has been demonstrated to be overwhelmingly positive."[4] The religiously committed are more satisfied with life and marriage, are mentally and physically healthier, live longer, are less stressed, and are less likely to commit suicide or abuse drugs.

In a review of the scientific literature, John Gartner and colleagues observed: "The preponderance of evidence suggests that religion is associated with mental health benefits. Furthermore, the best religious predictors of mental health are not religious questionnaire responses (religious attitudes), but real-life religious behavior (such as frequency of church attendance). Behavior predicts behavior."[5]

## WHY IS RELIGIOUS COMMITMENT BENEFICIAL?

We might surmise why religious commitment is associated with positive health outcomes. The following are possible reasons.

### Heightened Self-Esteem

Self-esteem is fostered by knowing that one matters and is loved. As one religious man said, "I take comfort in knowing that I am a child of a loving God, with worth and potential." In one study, high self-esteem was associated with loving images of God.[6] An older person might see himself as more than just an aging body, thereby buffering the stress of aging.

### Greater Meaning and Purpose

Sometimes under the stress of living, it is easy for us to lose sight of the meaning and purpose that steadies us and sees us through the difficult times. One woman said, "I don't see the world purely in terms of pleasure and needs; religion helps define who I am and how I fit into the world." And considering his own mortality, a father wrote:[7]

> Help me
> To weave
> The threads of my life
> Into a tapestry that will
> Keep my children warm
> When I die.

Viktor Frankl acknowledged the relationship between psychological and spiritual health, and that the latter included a religious component. He noted that "If there is a meaning in life at all, then there must be a meaning in suffering [and in dying]."[8]

### Peace of Conscience

Among the world's religions, there is agreement on those moral values that lift humanity and promote happiness: fidelity, honesty, respect, fairness, forgiveness, and schooling of the appetites. Settling upon and living these values fosters a sense of inner security. Said one medical professional, "It is relaxing to know you are living a good life." Religious communities can support us in this difficult process. And when we stumble, religion provides a way toward personal forgiveness and reconciliation.

### Overcoming Aloneness

Said a friend since youth, one of the most quietly saintlike people I know, "It is comforting to know someone is looking down on me lovingly and generously and compassionately, who's trying to help me out." When asked if they were afraid, survivors of a California earthquake said: "I wasn't afraid—I knew God would take care of us." "I just trusted God. What else can you do?"

### Eternal Perspective

Seeing things from the eternal view, momentary stressors assume a smaller significance. Said one teenager, "I know I can't mess things up too bad. So the weight of the world is not on my shoulders." Cardiologist George Sheehan said that religion gives one the sense that there "is no final defeat."[9] Rather, there is hope beyond the present, even the grave. As Harvard's Herbert Benson says, there are "realities that the senses cannot detect."[10]

When we don't realize all the goals we impatiently expect, we can take solace in the comforting words that "all these things will be added" eventually if we seek first the godly life. So we need not feel the pressure of rushing to obtain all things immediately. A woman who discovered her spiritual side gained a perspective on her difficult challenges in life: "I understand trials as homework to grow from, not punishment."

### Reduced Death Anxiety

For many, death anxiety is significant. One might assume that dying is an awful experience. Religion can help one face death with greater peace.[11]

Dr. Claire Weekes writes that religious beliefs in the afterlife are an "inborn comfort."[12] She explains that most do not find dying disagreeable: "I speak as a doctor. I have rarely attended a person actually dying who realized that he or she was dying. A few do, but very few. Nature blunts the edge off her sword; even during the years before our death, nature helps us." As with birth, we will be the star performer, but we will likely be unaware of the drama. And for those who are aware, the famous physician William Hunter said, "If I had strength enough to hold a pen, I would write how easy and pleasant a thing it is to die."[13]

Some find going a relief as the tasks of living become more difficult. Some consider reunion with God and loved ones with anticipation and curiosity.

Dreading death takes away the joy of living. We can accept death but enjoy the precious moments of life as well. In fact, death denial takes energy. Releasing this energy allows us to focus more fully on life. If you fear for the loved ones who survive you, prepare them as best as you can, which is all you can do. Then don't fear. They might be hardier than you assume. They will grieve. If you let them know that grieving is permissible, they will eventually mourn and move beyond the grief. If judgment is fearful, take action. Focus on what you can do now and do it, which is all you can do.

Some people find a belief in the afterlife comforting in the death of loved ones. One Mother Against Drunk Driving dreamed that her deceased daughter returned, assured her that she was all right, and told her to keep doing what she was doing. The mother took great comfort in this dream, which seemed to affirm her belief in an afterlife.[14]

## Sharing and Surrender of Control

Religion teaches us to share control and to accept loss of control with greater peace. As one married couple explained, "God will give us ultimate answers, but not here on earth. Religion teaches you how to have faith and not understand everything. This is a good thing." Generally, an active coping style that seeks control favors health. However, there are inevitably areas of life that we can't control. Trusting that God will ensure that all things work out for our eventual good helps us to accept those things. As A. Dean Byrd and Mark Chamberlain observe, the Western approach to willpower places total reliance on the self. Religion shares control with God.[15] Dr. Martin Luther King, Jr., said, "My obligation is to do the right thing. The rest is in God's hands." A mother whose daughter was killed in a drunk-driving crash cried to God, "How big do you think these shoulders are?" Realizing she can share control, she now says, "I give to God what I can't deal with now."[16]

## Reduced Hostility

Hostility is associated with earlier death from a variety of causes. The world religions teach the principles of charity and forgiveness as antidotes. Interestingly, compassionate behavior increases as people become involved in religious communities.[17]

## Spiritual Support

Religious communities support the growth of religious commitment. While the religious community provides social support, the benefits are more complex.

Others who are striving to live the spiritual life can share insights, affirm values, inspire, encourage, and remind us to rise above the weaknesses of human nature. A father opined that his religious community afforded common goals and ideas: "I feel like I am not standing alone in my beliefs, morality, and devotion to a higher being." Said a mother of two, "We need to reach out to people who respect our beliefs in order to define and clarify what we believe. I don't think I'd have a very close relationship with God without sharing with others."

A teenager put it this way: "Church is a time to be friendly with people of all ages. I feel more secure with God, a part of God's family. Church makes my relationship with God stronger—it helps me think of God more; it's like having another friend."

Religious communities can often be a learning lab for values. Sometimes the most difficult people to love are those who worship beside us, and vice versa.

## Social Support

I don't know Ivan. I've only heard his name spoken with reverence for the way this quiet, elderly gentleman donated his time to help a dear relative cope in time of illness. Sometimes neighbors in religious communities bring meals, health care, or physical labor in times of need. Sometimes rituals, like funerals, help us share the burden of grief. Sometimes the religious community helps us rejoice. And people with severe psychiatric disorders are just as likely to seek help from clergy as from mental health professionals.[18] One interesting study found that religious content improved the effectiveness of psychotherapy for the depressed, even if the therapist was not religious.[19]

## A Time for Rest

The Sabbath, whether it be observed on Friday, Saturday, or Sunday, provides a respite from the cares of the world. However, the Sabbath today is less likely to be devoted to spiritual renewal and more likely used for work, shopping, or amusement than in years past.

## Family

Most religions promote family solidarity, which buffers stress. Most sacred writings, for example, encourage us to treat family members with love, kindness, and respect.

## IMPLICATIONS/CAUTIONS

Certain precautions might help prevent disappointment in religion. As William James noted, "the fruits of religion . . . are, like all human products, liable to corruption by excess."[20] Some members of any institution will be corrupt. Religion does not guarantee that people won't be prejudiced, judgmental, or immoral. It only appears to reduce the likelihood of such attributes or blunt their sharpness.

Religion does not guarantee that life will be problem-free, as Job's account reminds us, although it might help us to bear up a bit better.

Religious ideals can inspire us to be our best selves. However, we can also experience guilt when our behavior falls short of our ideals. Guilt can be a good thing if it causes us to change destructive behavior. Thereafter it serves little purpose and is best released.

Religion does not deal in the realm of scientific proof, which is why heated debates rarely change minds. I have heard people say, "Don't you know it's a sin to worry? Have greater faith." I think that a more wholesome way to look at it is that it is human to worry, although it is not usually in our best interest to do so. Instead of feeling guilty for worrying, just think, "Faith is like a seed. It probably won't flourish overnight." Then relax and cultivate it patiently.

Finally, Harvard psychology professor Gordon Allport stated that the intrinsically religious person lives according to her personal beliefs regardless of outside social pressure or consequences. For the externally religious person, religion is a means to social acceptance and personal safety. He reasoned that only intrinsic orientation facilitated mental health. Research has found that the intrinsically oriented are indeed mentally healthier, showing less anxiety, more openness to emotions, greater self-esteem, and a greater sense of control.[21]

# CHAPTER 41

# *Happiness, Pleasure, and Humor*

---

**What is human life's chief concern? . . . It is happiness.**

**How to gain, how to keep, how to recover happiness,**

**is in fact for most men at all times the secret motive of**

**all they do, and of all they are willing to endure.**

**—*William James***

As people recover from PTSD, the happiness that once appeared irrevocably taken begins to return. The capacity for pleasure and the ability to laugh begin to resurface. Thus, happiness, pleasure, and humor are signs that healing is taking place. They also help us to enjoy life and protect against distress. This chapter explores approaches to facilitating these positive aspects of life.

## HAPPINESS

The happier people are, the less distressed they feel. It is fitting, therefore, to begin with the topic of happiness. Two researchers have devoted considerable effort to summarizing the burgeoning research on this topic. They are psychologists David Myers and Michael Fordyce.[1]

According to Myers, most people are quite resilient and happy. Happiness levels remain consistently high across different levels of age, gender, race, education, and place of residence. Once people rise above the misery levels, wealth and health don't predict happiness either. On average, even those who are handicapped bounce back to previous levels after a period of adjustment. So if these outward circumstances do not predict happiness, what does?

The following factors correlate with happiness. Notice that many of these factors are the same as those that help treat or prevent PTSD and that most are things we can do something about.

- **Self-esteem, peace of mind, and religious commitment.** These are discussed in Chapters 20, 36, and 40.
- **Healthy habits** such as regular exercise, sufficient sleep, wise eating.
- **Rewarding social interaction.** Happy people are more involved with friends, family, and organizations. They reach out and invest themselves to form high-quality, supportive relationships. They are more outgoing and sociable.
- **Active involvement in life.** Viktor Frankl observed that happiness ensues from actively pursuing meaning. Happy people are more likely to immerse themselves in things they find meaningful or satisfying (family, work, pleasant activities, avocations). They seem to be energized by this activity and don't sit around passively waiting for life to happen to them. Enjoyable activities can be planned; many are spontaneous and inexpensive.
- **Mastery and control.** These can be characterized by the following:
    **An active coping style,** committed to problem solving and not passive or helpless, shows initiative.
    **Control** over time, organization, deliberate planning, moving/progressing toward meaningful goals, nonprocrastinating, efficiency, having both long-term and short-term plans.
    **Goals are somewhat modest, compared to the unhappy.** But they are realistic and achievable, thus providing more satisfaction. The unhappy tend to overcompensate for their feeling of inadequacy by shooting for grandiose goals and derive less satisfaction because they are achieved less often. Happy people don't seem to need success as badly as the unhappy. For them, success ensues from what they love to do; it is not directly pursued.
    **Present orientation.** Happy people have cultivated mindfulness, or the ability to become absorbed in and enjoy the present moment. This is considerably easier when one has made reasonable plans for the future—when one experiences the peace of preparation.
- **Optimism.** Optimism is not the naive expectation that everything will turn out rosy. Rather, it is the attitude that no matter what happens, I can find

*something* to enjoy; it is the choice to be happy despite obstacles. This is in direct opposition to the pessimistic distortions of overgeneralizing and fortune-telling. The happy person

Anticipates pleasure

Expects something good to happen or that some things will probably go well

Reasons that whatever happens will be for the best

Looks to the bright side

Believes that he plays an important role in shaping his own future

Considers how things could be worse and then how to salvage the most possible

Realizes that failure does not equal a character flaw or the end of the world

Overcomes failure with new strengths

Has a fighting spirit

The person with this mind-set does not make a career of suffering. She won't be defeated, but anticipates problems and is determined to make the best of things.

- **Lower need for success.** Like people with self-esteem, happy people don't seem driven by the need for success in order to prove themselves. Rather, they commit first to happiness, the great energizing motivator; success then follows. Fordyce counsels to do what you love, and productivity and success will follow. He says, "Success may not lead to happiness, but happiness leads to success."[2] He observes that less happy people complete the sentence stem, "I'll be happy when . . . " with answers like "I am successful, wealthy, married," etc. Happy people tend to answer with "I am happy now."
- **The absence of negative internal attitudes.** These include blame, bitterness, and helplessness.

Correlations between factors do not necessarily prove causality. However, Fordyce reasoned that acting like happy people would increase happiness and thereby reduce anxiety, depression, and stress. This assumption has been borne out by measuring happiness and mental health before and after people completed his happiness course. The tasks and skills include the following:

1. **Get involved.** Don't become passive or stop trying the steps that have been found to raise happiness levels.
2. **Socialize more** (say hello, ask people how they are doing, listen).

3. **Organize and plan.** Have a plan for reaching achievable, meaningful goals—then enjoy reaching them. The future is no more enjoyable than the present moment. So enjoy the process of throwing yourself into life, mindful of the joy that is experienced in each moment.

4. **Stop worrying.** Do what you can to combat fears now. In addition, try writing down your worries for a twenty-five-minute period—facts and feelings —at the same time and place each day. Then, instead of worrying during the day, tell yourself that you will postpone your worries until your designated worry period. This approach very effectively reduces worries.

5. **Develop optimism** (e.g., try saying for each bad outcome, "Well, at least . . ." Thus, after you don't get the promotion you'd wanted, you might say, "Well, at least I won't be away from home as much.").

6. **Cultivate a healthy personality.** Be yourself, be expressive, and be spontaneous. With self-esteem, this is easier.

---

### PLEASANT ACTIVITIES SCHEDULING*

We tend to feel balanced when we're doing both necessary and pleasant activities. Under periods of great stress and pressure, however, we might give up pleasant activities. We can lose balance, falling into the habit of doing only what is needed. If we do this long enough, sadly, we might even forget what used to give us pleasure or assume that it won't be fun anymore. Doing pleasant activities reverses this cycle. As we do things that are pleasant, we begin to feel happier. We feel more active, interested, and encouraged—and less distressed. Maintaining reasonable levels of pleasant activities also helps to prevent drops in mood.

The exercise that follows will both help you to discover (or rediscover) what is pleasant for you and to make a plan to do some of these things.

**STEP 1:** The "Pleasant Events Schedule" on the next page lists a wide range of activities. In Column 1, check those activities that you enjoyed in the past. Then rate from 1 to 10 how pleasant each checked item was. A score of 1 reflects little pleasure, and 10 reflects great pleasure. This rating goes in Column 1 also, beside each check mark. For example, if you moderately enjoyed being with happy people but didn't enjoy being with friends/relatives, your first two items would look like this:

____√ (5)____ _____ 1. Being with happy people

_____ _____ 2. Being with friends/relatives

---

# PLEASANT EVENTS SCHEDULE

I.  **Social Interactions.** These events occur with others. They tend to make us feel accepted, appreciated, liked, understood, etc.*

COL. I     COL. 2

|  |  |  |
|---|---|---|
| ___ | ___ | 1.  Being with happy people |
| ___ | ___ | 2.  Being with friends/relatives |
| ___ | ___ | 3.  Thinking about people I like |
| ___ | ___ | 4.  Planning an activity with people I care about |
| ___ | ___ | 5.  Meeting someone new of the same sex |
| ___ | ___ | 6.  Meeting someone new of the opposite sex |
| ___ | ___ | 7.  Going to a club, tavern, bar, etc. |
| ___ | ___ | 8.  Being at celebrations (birthdays, weddings, baptisms, parties, family get-togethers, etc.) |
| ___ | ___ | 9.  Meeting a friend for lunch or a drink |
| ___ | ___ | 10.  Talking openly and honestly (e.g., about your hopes, fears, what interests you, what makes you laugh, what saddens you) |
| ___ | ___ | 11.  Expressing true affection (verbal or physical) |
| ___ | ___ | 12.  Showing interest in others |
| ___ | ___ | 13.  Noticing successes and strengths in family and friends |
| ___ | ___ | 14.  Dating, courting (this one is for married people, too) |
| ___ | ___ | 15.  Having a lively conversation |
| ___ | ___ | 16.  Inviting friends over |
| ___ | ___ | 17.  Stopping in to visit friends |
| ___ | ___ | 18.  Calling up someone I enjoy |
| ___ | ___ | 19.  Apologizing |
| ___ | ___ | 20.  Smiling at people |
| ___ | ___ | 21.  Calmly talking over problems with people I live with |
| ___ | ___ | 22.  Giving compliments, back pats, or praise |
| ___ | ___ | 23.  Teasing/bantering |
| ___ | ___ | 24.  Amusing people or making them laugh |
| ___ | ___ | 25.  Playing with children |
| ___ | ___ | 26.  Others: _____ |

*You might feel that an activity belongs in another group. The grouping is not important.

## II. Activities That Make Us Feel Capable, Loving, Useful, Strong, or Adequate

_____ _____   1.  Starting a challenging job or doing one well
_____ _____   2.  Learning something new (e.g., fixing leaks, new hobby, new language)
_____ _____   3.  Helping someone (counseling, advising, listening)
_____ _____   4.  Contributing to religious, charitable, or other groups
_____ _____   5.  Driving skillfully
_____ _____   6.  Expressing myself clearly (out loud or in writing)
_____ _____   7.  Repairing something (sewing, fixing a car or bike, etc.)
_____ _____   8.  Solving a problem or puzzle
_____ _____   9.  Exercising
_____ _____  10.  Thinking
_____ _____  11.  Going to a meeting (convention, business, civic)
_____ _____  12.  Visiting the ill, homebound, or troubled
_____ _____  13.  Telling a child a story
_____ _____  14.  Writing a card, note, or letter
_____ _____  15.  Improving my appearance (e.g., seeking medical or dental help, improving my diet, going to a barber or beautician)
_____ _____  16.  Planning/budgeting time
_____ _____  17.  Discussing political issues
_____ _____  18.  Doing volunteer work, community service, etc.
_____ _____  19.  Planning a budget
_____ _____  20.  Protesting injustice, protecting someone, stopping fraud or abuse
_____ _____  21.  Being honest, moral, etc.
_____ _____  22.  Correcting mistakes
_____ _____  23.  Organizing a party
_____ _____  24.  Others: _____

## III. Intrinsically Pleasant Activities

_____ _____   1.  Laughing
_____ _____   2.  Relaxing, having peace and quiet
_____ _____   3.  Having a good meal
_____ _____   4.  A hobby (e.g., cooking, fishing, woodworking, photography, acting, gardening, collecting things)
_____ _____   5.  Listening to good music
_____ _____   6.  Seeing beautiful scenery
_____ _____   7.  Going to bed early, sleeping soundly, and awakening early

| | | | |
|---|---|---|---|
| ——— | ——— | 8. | Wearing attractive clothes |
| ——— | ——— | 9. | Wearing comfortable clothes |
| ——— | ——— | 10. | Going to a concert, opera, ballet, or play |
| ——— | ——— | 11. | Playing sports (e.g., tennis, softball, racquetball, golf, horseshoes, Frisbee) |
| ——— | ——— | 12. | Trips or vacations |
| ——— | ——— | 13. | Shopping/buying something I like for myself |
| ——— | ——— | 14. | Being outdoors (e.g., beach, country, mountains, kicking leaves, walking in the sand, floating in lakes) |
| ——— | ——— | 15. | Doing artwork (e.g., painting, sculpture, drawing) |
| ——— | ——— | 16. | Reading sacred works |
| ——— | ——— | 17. | Beautifying my home (redecorating, cleaning, yard work, etc.) |
| ——— | ——— | 18. | Going to a sports event |
| ——— | ——— | 19. | Reading (novels, poems, plays, newspapers, etc.) |
| ——— | ——— | 20. | Going to a lecture |
| ——— | ——— | 21. | Going for a drive |
| ——— | ——— | 22. | Sitting in the sun |
| ——— | ——— | 23. | Visiting a museum |
| ——— | ——— | 24. | Playing or singing music |
| ——— | ——— | 25. | Boating |
| ——— | ——— | 26. | Pleasing my family, friends, employer |
| ——— | ——— | 27. | Thinking about something good in the future |
| ——— | ——— | 28. | Watching TV |
| ——— | ——— | 29. | Camping, hunting |
| ——— | ——— | 30. | Grooming myself (e.g., bathing, combing hair, shaving) |
| ——— | ——— | 31. | Writing in my diary/journal |
| ——— | ——— | 32. | Taking a bike ride, hiking, or walking |
| ——— | ——— | 33. | Being with animals |
| ——— | ——— | 34. | Watching people |
| ——— | ——— | 35. | Taking a nap |
| ——— | ——— | 36. | Listening to nature sounds |
| ——— | ——— | 37. | Getting or giving a back rub |
| ——— | ——— | 38. | Watching a storm, clouds, the sky, etc. |
| ——— | ——— | 39. | Having spare time |
| ——— | ——— | 40. | Daydreaming |
| ——— | ——— | 41. | Feeling the presence of the Deity in my life; praying, worshipping, etc. |

| | | |
|---|---|---|
| _____ | _____ | 42. Smelling a flower |
| _____ | _____ | 43. Talking about old times or special interests |
| _____ | _____ | 44. Going to auctions, garage sales, etc. |
| _____ | _____ | 45. Traveling |
| _____ | _____ | 46. Others: _____ |

**STEP 2:** In Column 2, check if you've done the event in the last thirty days.

**STEP 3:** Circle the number of the events that you'd probably enjoy (when you're feeling good, on a good day).

**STEP 4:** Notice if there are many items you've enjoyed in the past that you are not doing very often (compare the first and second columns).

**STEP 5:** Using the completed "Pleasant Events Schedule" for ideas, make a list of the twenty-five activities that you feel you'd enjoy most.

**STEP 6:** Make a written plan to do more pleasant activities. Start with the simplest activities and the ones you are most likely to enjoy. When depressed or anxious, it is common to find that your old favorite activities are now the most difficult to enjoy, particularly if you tried them before when you were very upset and failed to enjoy them. You might say, "I can't even enjoy my favorite activity," making you feel even more stressed. These events will become pleasant again. For now, start with other simple activities. Gradually try your old favorites as your mood lifts. Do as many pleasant events as you reasonably can. We suggest doing at least one each day, perhaps more on weekends. *Write* your plan on a calendar, and carry out this written plan for at least two weeks. Each time you do an activity, rate it on a 1 to 5 scale for pleasure (5 being highly enjoyable). This tests the idea that *nothing* is enjoyable. Later, you can replace less enjoyable activities with others.

Certain blocks (such as negative thoughts, guilt, or a feeling that "I don't deserve pleasure") can interfere with your enjoyment. You know how to deal with distortions. If you feel guilty about the past or feel that you should be doing something "constructive," remind yourself that prolonged guilt serves no one and that work becomes more efficient after a period of recreation.

### Tips for Pleasant Events Scheduling

- **Tune into the physical world.** Pay less attention to your thoughts. Feel the wind, or the soapsuds as you wash the car. See and hear. This is living in the present.
- **Before doing an event, set yourself up to enjoy it.** Identify three things you will enjoy about it. Say, "I will enjoy _____ (the sunshine, the breeze, talking with brother Bill, etc.). Relax and imagine yourself enjoying each aspect of the event as you repeat each statement.
- **Ask yourself, "What will I do to make the activity enjoyable?"** Sometimes the answer is to just relax and enjoy it without trying to control it.
- **If you are concerned that you might not enjoy some activity that you'd like to attempt, try breaking it up into steps.** Think small, so you can be satisfied in reaching your goal. For example, start by only cleaning the house for ten minutes, then stop. Then reward yourself with a "Good job!" pat on the back.
- **Check your schedule for balance.** Can you spread out the "need-tos" to make room for some "want-tos"?
- **Time is limited, so use it wisely.** You needn't do activities you don't like just because they're convenient.

### Happiness Meditation

There is a very beautiful meditation practice. After having completed the skills up to this point, you are ready to enjoy it. The Vietnamese monk Thich Nhat Hanh, who was nominated for the Nobel Peace Prize, explains that joy, peace, and serenity can be found in simple moments—eating, walking, breathing, driving—if we are living in the present and receptive to its pleasures. He suggests this simple meditation exercise.[3] Simply recite these four lines silently as you breathe in and out:

> Breathing in, I calm my body.
> Breathing out, I smile.
> Dwelling in the present moment,
> I know this is a wonderful moment!

He teaches that breathing is a joyful, soothing experience. Smiling relaxes the many muscles of the face and signals mastery of your body. Practice many times throughout the day, in various situations. Relax your body as you breathe in, as if drinking a glass of cool lemonade on a hot day. Smile as you breathe out and enjoy the subtle shift in mood.

## Loving Kindness Meditation

Jack Cornfield teaches a beautiful way to meditate for fifteen to twenty minutes during the day.[4] Sit in a relaxed way. Let your heart be soft and your mind free of preoccupations. Recite inwardly these phrases:

> May I be filled with loving kindness.
> May I be well.
> May I be peaceful and at ease.
> May I be happy.

As you repeat these phrases silently, you might think of times when you were surrounded with love. Be patient and allow kind feelings to develop over time. When you feel that you have developed and experienced a sense of loving kindness, then expand this meditation to include others. First, select loved ones (May he be filled with loving kindness, etc.). Then expand this meditation to include others, even those you might not feel kindly toward. You can also use this meditation in traffic jams or other stressful situations.

## HUMOR

A combat veteran relates the following incident:[5]

> I was standing at the counter of our neighborhood dry cleaner, which had been recently bought by a Lebanese family. Suddenly a truck backfired nearby with two loud bangs.
>
> I instinctively hit the floor, face down. Embarrassed, I got to my knees and peered over the counter, only to see the owner also in a prone position.
>
> "Saigon '68," I said. We both laughed when she stood up and replied, "Beirut '79."

By now, the benefits of humor are well documented. Humor connects us to other humans, as we share a laugh over life's absurd moments. Like love, humor warmly surrounds and soothes pain, making it more bearable. When we can laugh at our problems, we gain distance, perspective, and a sense of mastery. Humor says, "Things might not be so great right now, but that's OK. I might not be perfect, but I'm a darn sight better than I look." A humor break can recharge creative batteries. In addition, laughter results in numerous beneficial effects on the body: relief from pain, cardiovascular conditioning, improved breathing, muscle relaxation, and improved immune system functioning.

Several cautions apply to humor, however—no kidding.

1. **The overuse of humor can be a form of avoidance.** Such overuse can prevent one from processing pain.
2. **Sarcasm or "put-down" humor is a thinly disguised form of hostility and is rarely appropriate.** Humor, like sex, works best when surrounded by love.
3. **Making light of someone's pain can seem insensitive and can undermine trust.** When in doubt, check it out. You might say, "I was just being humorous there. Was that all right?" Humor may require that a certain degree of healing has taken place. It may be premature to try to get someone to laugh at intense pain. Likewise, it may be premature to expect yourself to laugh too soon.
4. **Humor is not a panacea nor a substitute for therapy.** Humor can, however, support the healing process if it is suited to you.

Given these precautions, these principles might help to incorporate more humor into our lives.

1. **Be willing to "play the fool" at times.** This openness undermines the rigid need to be perfect, which, of course, no one is. Laughing at ourselves says, in effect, "Isn't it funny that a person of my caliber has such funny quirks." This is really practice in self-acceptance.
2. **Just be willing to play.** If we plan to have lightly structured time, light moments might spring up unexpectedly. Thus, planning a day at the zoo or time for stories with a child creates a place for humor to bubble up.
3. **Humor does not require that one be a joke teller or loud laugher.** A sense of humor includes simply appreciating a good joke. Humor can also mean simply noticing life's incongruities with a light heart.
4. **Humor is not an all-or-none skill.** A sense of humor is standard issue, and each person has the capacity to develop it over time.
5. **Don't be discouraged if not many things seem funny to you.** Trauma can bury anyone's sense of humor—it is hard to laugh when one is emotionally

numb. Instead, simply allow time for healing. With time, you'll probably become open to humor at your own pace and in your own way.

Think of humor as a skill or a hobby that becomes more enjoyable with time. You might create a humor file of things that make you laugh, or a humor bulletin board. You might also take some time to reflect on this. Have you ever been in a place where you laughed when humor "wasn't appropriate?"[6] For some reason, I think of musical solos in church services that were not intended to be funny. About fifteen minutes spent on this exercise might return some surprising, pleasurable dividends.

# CHAPTER 42

# *Relapse Prevention*

---

> A lapse is often part of a larger pattern of recovery
> and [some people] may have to cope with a future
> lapse in order to continue on [their] way.
>
> —*Dr. Francis Abueg and colleagues*[1]

Life is not linear. It is comprised of ups and downs. It would be nice if once we were headed on a good course at a good pace, no slips, setbacks, or falls were to occur. However, as you move ahead, you will undoubtedly have periods where some PTSD symptoms return. Such troubling periods are normal in PTSD and do not invalidate your recovery work or detract from your gains. They can actually be useful opportunities to overlearn previously encountered coping skills and to process unresolved memory material. This chapter deals with anticipating and preventing symptoms and situations before they occur. We'll also explore how to prevent the return of some symptoms from evolving into a full-blown relapse. Relapse prevention is a wonderful way to put your skills together and continue to practice them.

Relapse prevention consists of six parts:

1. Understand the dynamics of "failure."
2. Identify and anticipate high-risk situations or cues.
3. Develop a sound coping plan.
4. Rehearse the plan.
5. Try out the plan in real life.
6. Evaluate and make improvements if needed.

We'll now look at these six parts in turn.

## UNDERSTAND THE DYNAMICS OF "FAILURE"

Let's say that your PTSD symptoms have greatly lessened. For several months, you are noticeably less troubled by the past. Then you encounter a setback. Perhaps you encounter a feared situation. Maybe it's a place that reminds you of the traumatic event. Maybe it is a social situation that stirs up old feelings of not fitting in. You notice the return of intrusive thoughts and arousal. Perhaps you have a nightmare. Although these experiences are normal and to be expected, symptoms can be lessened or worsened, depending upon our actions and reactions to them. So let's understand how setbacks occur and how viewing them as failure can worsen symptoms.

Some setbacks are simply a part of the normal recovery process. Other setbacks are set up. That is, sometimes we do things along the way that will influence an outcome. For example, we are more prone to setbacks when we have not taken care of our health, practiced our coping skills, anticipated difficult challenges, or monitored our self-talk. Sometimes stressful situations pile up and set us up for more intense stress reactions. Let's say you've gotten less sleep lately because you have many things to do. During the day, you feel tired and let some of your needed chores slip. Your car has been acting up, but you don't bother to get it checked out. You like to spend time with your family, but you don't take the time to plan that enjoyable evening, and when that evening comes, you just feel too busy. Instead, you return home from work after the family is in bed and watch TV to unwind until quite late. You oversleep the next day and find that your car won't start. You are quite late for work and fall behind on an all-important project. At the end of the week, you blow up at your spouse and go to the company party angry. And then the symptoms hit. You feel out of touch and distant from your colleagues, like you don't fit in. Your anger and frustration begin to mount. You think, "Why bother?" as you start to think about drowning your troubles with alcohol. Here, managing time better—budgeting time for sleep, recreation, and chores—might have prevented stress from building to the breaking point.

The way you think about setbacks, or lapses, is also very important. You might think of the return of symptoms as failure, which might remind you of past failures. What kind of things go through your head when you fail at something? This exercise might shed light on what failure means to you:[2]

Relax. I'm going to ask you to close your eyes if you feel comfortable. Otherwise just look down at the floor and breathe regularly and deeply. I want you to see yourself as a young child. You may be five years old, ten years old; you may be a teenager. At the count of three, I'd like you to see yourself facing an important task or challenge. Unfortunately, it's a task that you are unable to do or complete. At the count of three (again, if you are comfortable, close your eyes): one, two, three. Good. See yourself facing this challenge. Where are you? What do you look like? Who is around, if anyone? Let the action unfold and notice your physical and emotional reaction. What does your face look like? How did it feel? Hold onto these impressions, remember them. What happens later? See the details as best you can. Good. Now let go of the image and return to regular, relaxed breathing. I'll count backward from twenty to one. You will become more and more alert as I count. Twenty, nineteen, eighteen . . .

What do you learn about why failure might be uncomfortable for you now? Perhaps you learned to associate failure with rejection, abandonment, or punishment.

Failure can be so painful that people try to explain it in a way that makes sense. Often the explanations are so negative that the fear of future failure becomes excessive. When failure recurs, the negative thoughts return with a vengeance, and the fear is reinforced. We will now learn how to stop the cycle of negativity as early as possible. This approach, described by Abueg and colleagues, has been found to reverse depression and pessimism. When you experience failure, Abueg continues:

1. **Immediately: Stop, look, and listen.** Take a minute, if you can to step out of the flow of events, and try to get as rational a view as possible. Look for your own cognitive distortions as they are developing.
2. **Keep as calm as you can** so you can function in the situation.
3. **After the crisis is past: Think of the situation as external, specific, and changeable.** *External* means that we focus on the event and do not condemn ourselves at the core. *Specific* means that we keep what is happening in the here and now. We do not assume that what is happening is a reflection of life in general. *Changeable* means that things can improve. The opposite of external, specific, and changeable is *internal*, *global*, and *unchangeable*.

   The pessimistic way to think of a setback is:

   | | |
   |---|---|
   | **Internal** | It's me. I am so incompetent. I have no willpower. |
   | **Global** | I do this all the time. |
   | **Unchangeable** | This failure is proof that I can't change. |

This way of explaining failure leads to further distress. It might set one up to find solace from the pain in drink or drugs. At any rate, it will likely depress one's mood and undermine the motivation to keep trying to improve. In short, it sets you up to fail in the future by creating the expectation of failure. Notice the difference when one looks at a setback more optimistically:

| | |
|---|---|
| **External** | This is a difficult situation. I was tired and overworked. |
| **Specific** | This isn't the way I always act. |
| **Changeable** | This isn't a signpost for the rest of my life. In a few days I'll probably be back in balance again. This is more changeable than I now think. This is a chance to learn a better coping style. |

Rather than focusing on judging the self, focus on the situation and what you did and what you would do in the future. For example, you might think, "I made the mistake of getting out of balance. In the future, I'll do better at being rested so that I can be more efficient during the day." Blaming and judging are eliminated, so one feels motivated to improve.

4. **Keep setbacks from getting worse by looking at other self-talk.** Many reactions get worse by self-defeating reactions such as shame, self-disgust, impatience, or discouragement. These emotions maintain arousal. They are preceded by negative self-talk. So learn constructive versus destructive reactions.

- **Cognitive dissonance.** This refers to the gap between seeing yourself as totally recovered and present reality. Filling the gap with negative self-talk, such as "I should be better by now," creates frustration. Instead, you could think, "It's too bad that symptoms return sometimes. But this is normal—not a catastrophe. They'll pass."

- **Replace the word *failure*.** Failure has a self-defeating all-or-nothing quality to it. Instead of failure, think of a return of symptoms as a setback, lapse, temporary detour, opportunity, normal and expected challenge, falling short of the ideal, or a wake-up call for needed attention.

- **Stand your ground and renew your commitment to recover.** Don't give in to "What's the use?" (fortune-telling) or "I've blown it" (all or nothing). Remind yourself that setbacks are normal. Remember the benefits of recovering.

## IDENTIFY AND ANTICIPATE HIGH-RISK SITUATIONS (CUES)

The most effective copers have been found to anticipate stressful times so that they can be better prepared for them. They form an action plan rather than avoiding thinking about stressful times or constantly worrying without making a plan. In order to make an action plan, we first identify high-risk situations, or cues. As you look ahead, what situations are likely to be challenging for you? Consider a variety of possible triggers, the return of PTSD symptoms, and new situations.

- Places
- Things
- People
- Symptoms (e.g., nightmares)
- Funerals
- Significant dates, such as the anniversary of the trauma, when a deceased child would have graduated, when you reach the age of a parent who died, a wedding that a deceased loved one doesn't attend, the birth of a child without the loved one being present, holidays without loved ones, Veterans Day
- Fatigue, illness, hormone swings
- Stressful times with negative emotions (Consider what increases the urge to drink. What situations contribute to depression, anxiety, anger, guilt, loneliness, or stress—such as financial problems, crime, work overload, or medical exams?)
- Interpersonal conflict
- Social situations: can't open up and express yourself, no confidence, feelings of hostility or intolerance, afraid of meeting people, feeling isolated from people, being reminded that you can't forget problems and relax, fear of being boring, fear of intrusive thoughts, fear of rejection, tension, nervousness about having sex
- Overconfidence: on top of the world; telling yourself that nothing can go wrong, you're permanently fixed and don't need to practice your skills or anticipate difficult situations
- Other triggers

Not all arousal, of course, is bad. It is comforting to realize that some arousal over new lifestyle choices is excitement or normal curiosity and concern. Try to distinguish the various forms of arousal.

To increase awareness of high-risk situations, list in the first column of Table 42.1 the high-risk situations that you thought of. In the second column, indicate the likelihood of encountering the situations, as a percentage. In the third column, indicate your expected reactions. Emotional reactions might be anger, sadness, or fear. Physical reactions might be difficulty breathing or tension. Behaviors might include leaving the situation early or using food for sedation. In the fourth column, see if you can connect the high-risk situation to a past trauma. It helps to understand this connection but then separate present fearful situations from past trauma. You might decide that the high-risk situation is just a new feared situation. If you think there is a connection to the past but the connection is not clear, just continue. (This might be a fruitful area to explore with your counselor.) The fifth column is a percentage rating of how much distress you anticipate. This helps to view the situation in the gray areas, the middle ground—and avoid extreme predictions. The last column indicates how much distress you actually experience, and will be completed after you make a coping plan and try it out. It can be motivating to find that distress was less than predicted.

**Table 42.1**
**HIGH-RISK SITUATION RECORD**

| High-Risk Situation | Likelihood of Encountering (%) | Expected Reactions (Emotional, Physical, Behavioral) | Connection to Past Trauma | Anticipated Distress (%) | Actual Distress (%) |
|---|---|---|---|---|---|
| | | | | | |

## DEVELOP A SOUND COPING PLAN

There is a certain amount of peace in preparation. The next step is to make a coping plan for each high-risk situation. The plan is made well in advance, perhaps two months before the high-risk situation occurs, to permit time to practice and gain confidence. The plan involves multiple elements or tools that will be used at the same time. For each situation, we consider the coping strategies that are available to us. Table 42.2 lists coping strategies that are usually adaptive versus those that are not.

Note that selective avoidance might be a wise coping approach at times. For example, in selecting intimate partners, it is wise to steer clear of people with tendencies to batter or abuse. The characteristics of potential batterers are well documented (tendency to control and isolate, jealousy, insecurity, criticism, anger, etc.). Discuss these with your therapist, and don't expect "love" to change this kind of person. (Love does not expect to change someone but accepts others as they are.) You might wish to avoid social situations that you find uninteresting, but ask yourself if you are depriving yourself of a potentially pleasant opportunity.

For each high-risk situation, write out a specific plan. Consider all the things you need to do to cope effectively. What would you do to cope? What will you do to ensure that a setback does not become a full-blown relapse? Who would you contact for help? What do you need to tell yourself? What would you do first? In what order would all these things occur?

Part of the coping plan involves preplanned, self-instructional statements.[3] Imagine confronting a difficult situation. Imagine eliminating unproductive thoughts, such as "Here we go again" (fortune-telling, all or nothing) and "I'll never be OK" (fortune-telling). Instead, you have a battery of thoughts planned for before, during, and after the situation (see Table 42.3).

One way to plan for high-risk situations is to break down the feared situation into parts. Make a written total hierarchy of the feared situation. Think of the situation as one pearl in a string of life pearls. Think of pleasant things that will occur after you encounter the feared situation. Think of pleasant events preceding the feared situation. Then break down the feared situation into chronological steps. Decide what is needed for each part of the feared situation. Anticipate unproductive thoughts and figure out replacement thoughts at each step.[4]

Also, make a plan for immediate recovery, should a setback be encountered. Review the skills in this book, and identify those that will help you return to balance after the setback. Write these down. The plan might include a booster session with your therapist.

**Table 42.2**
COPING OPTIONS

| Usually Unproductive | Usually Productive |
| --- | --- |
| Hostility (judge, take revenge, act out anger) | Empathize, show compassion, remain calm enough to be effective, use anger control techniques |
| Withdraw, freeze, avoid, give up, do nothing, be passive, wait to be rescued, be helpless | Gather facts, make a plan, problem solve, take rational action, ask for help, replace trigger with something constructive (such as read a pleasant book instead of watching news), learn needed skills |
| Isolate yourself, suffer alone | Make connections with mental health professionals, support groups, or individuals |
| Allow abusive treatment | Assert, negotiate, compromise |
| Placate | Acknowledge feelings constructively |
| Deny problems | Acknowledge problems, but don't stew |
| Sedation, escape | Take responsibility for coping; healthy distractions, relaxation; talk it over |
| Make excuses | Acknowledge external factors, improve behavior |
| Take total blame | Acknowledge all influences; accept rational responsibility with self-acceptance |
| Cynicism, fatalism, pessimism | Laughter, soft humor, optimism |
| Constant worry | Confine worry to a twenty-five-minute daily worry period; worry in writing, with an eye toward solutions, then do something else that's distracting/pleasant |
| Despair | See how far you've come, replace distortions (e.g., is this symptom actually occurring all the time, or is it actually less severe or frequent than it was?); normalize the symptoms |

**Table 42.3**
**PREPLANNED, SELF-INSTRUCTIONAL STATEMENTS**

| | |
|---|---|
| *Before* | Realistically, what are the odds that something bad will happen?<br>I've been through this before. I know what to expect.<br>I'm prepared. I know what to do. Just stay calm and think what you need to do.<br>Things might go well. If not, that's OK. I'll do my best and see what happens.<br>A good job is OK—no need for perfection.<br>Some upset is to be expected. It's normal. It will pass.<br>Be gentle. Relax into the symptoms.<br>I have better coping skills now.<br>I'm capable.<br>Challenges to grow are just a part of life. |
| *During* | No need to be too upset.<br>Just use arousal as a cue to cope.<br>This is just a moment. It will pass. I can handle this. I can ride this out.<br>It will end soon. I'm doing fine.<br>I am capable. I can figure out ways to calm myself down.<br>Just relax and breathe calmly.<br>I've survived all sorts of things—I'll survive this.<br>This is inconvenient, not the end of the world.<br>These are just harmless memories. No need to take them too seriously or pay attention to them now. |
| *After* | I did pretty well. Maybe not perfectly, but all in all pretty well.<br>Next time will probably be easier now.<br>*Some* symptoms do not mean total relapse.<br>It's normal to have upset. That's life. I know how to restore balance.<br>I just had a bad day. It's silly to expect perfect peace. I'll feel better again.<br>A setback means I made some progress.<br>What have I learned to help me cope in the future? |

## REHEARSE THE PLAN

This is an opportunity to put everything together and practice your plan, much like an actress or athlete would rehearse or practice in relatively low-stress situations. Rehearsing can be done in image or in role-playing.

In imagery, you imagine yourself encountering the feared situation and coping successfully. Abueg and colleagues instruct the individual as follows:

1. **Take two to three minutes to recall all your coping actions.** Think of all the elements of your coping plan, including what you will think and do.

2. **Begin to get comfortable in your chair, and slowly close your eyes.** Allow yourself to begin to feel relaxed and comfortable. Take a deep breath, hold it, and then release it, noticing yourself getting rid of tension and becoming more relaxed. Good. (Do a relaxation technique here such as progressive muscle relaxation.)

   Now, imagine a black screen in front of your eyes. You can't see a thing, just a dark black screen in front of your eyes. Just a deep black screen like you're looking out into deep space. As you look at the blackness, you begin to see your high-risk scene. Look around the scene and notice what you see, the colors, shapes, things in the room or on the ground. Notice what sounds you hear, and listen to the sounds. Notice what other people look like and what they're doing. Now, visualize yourself coping positively and effectively. Good. Now I'd like you to turn your attention back to this room and become aware of your surroundings here. When you're ready, open your eyes and return your focus to the present.

3. **Discuss.** How well did the coping routine work? Which parts seemed effective and not so effective? At what points did you notice strong emotions? What are the lessons learned? How would the imagined situation compare with the real situation?

4. **Practice a daily five-minute visualization of positive coping.** You can change the high-risk situation from day to day if you like.

This form of imagery is called *mastery imagery* because you imagine yourself mastering the situation. Some people find it more realistic to first imagine yourself being distressed but then rebounding and coping well.[5]

## TRY OUT THE PLAN IN REAL LIFE

When sufficiently confident, implement your plan with a scientist's eye. Without judging yourself, just see how well your plan works and how well you coped.

## EVALUATE AND MAKE IMPROVEMENTS IF NEEDED

If the plan worked well, or even partially, give yourself credit for making and executing it. If the plan needs improvements, identify what they would be and practice them.

# CHAPTER 43

# Summing Up

Having worked your way through this book, you are now familiar with an array of skills that can help you lessen your PTSD symptoms and cope with stress throughout life. Like most other skills, you will probably need to practice them to keep sharp. It will not be unusual to need to return to this book to review certain principles and skills.

Try to keep your life in balance. Remember to do things that keep you physically fit, nourished, and rested. It is also important to include pleasurable and satisfying activities in your life. Be kind to yourself when you are less than perfect, or when things don't go as smoothly as you'd like. And finally, remember that help is available when you need or want it (see Additional Resources for a variety of resources).

To summarize and reinforce what you have learned, please flip back through the pages of this book and list those ideas and skills that you most want to remember. Complete the following:

1. **The ideas that have had the most meaning to me are . . .**

_____

_____

_____

_____

_____

_____

2. **The skills that I most wish to return to and use again are** . . .

_____

_____

_____

_____

_____

_____

3. **What do I need right now? Are there skills that I would like to spend more time with? (If so, make a plan and take the time to do so.)**

_____

_____

_____

_____

_____

_____

I close with my earnest wishes for your healing, recovery, and growth.

# Appendix A

## The History of PTSD

It is instructive to review the history of PTSD and understand that people have experienced this and coped with it throughout history.

| | |
|---|---|
| 1900 B.C. | Egyptian physicians first report hysterical reactions. |
| 8th century B.C. | Homer's *Odyssey* describes the "travails of Odysseus," a veteran of Trojan Wars, including flashbacks and survivor's guilt. |
| 490 B.C. | Herodotus writes of a soldier going blind after witnessing the death of a comrade next to him. |
| 1597 | Shakespeare vividly describes war sequelae (Lady Percy in *King Henry IV*). |
| 1600 | Samuel Pepys describes symptoms in survivors of the Great Fire of London. |
| 1879 | Johannes Rigler coins term *compensation neurosis*. |
| 1880s | Pierre Janet studies and treats traumatic stress and eventually describes "hysterical and dissociative symptoms, inability to integrate memories, biphasic nature" of suppression and intrusion, and other symptoms often resulting from abuse. |

The interested reader will find an excellent historical overview in C. R. Figley's foreword in J. P. Wilson and B. Raphael, eds., *International Handbook of Traumatic Stress Syndromes* (New York: Plenum, 1993): xvii–xx, from which this is primarily adapted. Quotations are his.

| | |
|---|---|
| 1899 | Helmut Oppenheim coins term *traumatic neurosis*. |
| 1890s | Sigmund Freud believes patients' memories of abuse and develops seduction theory, which relates symptoms to traumatic sexual experience. Unfortunately, within a few years, he recants in favor of the theory that patients' accounts are just fantasized sexual desires. |
| World War I | The term *shell shock* is used to describe symptoms believed to be caused by artillery barrages. |
| World War II | The terms *battle fatigue*, *combat exhaustion*, and *traumatic neurosis* are used to describe symptoms thought to be caused primarily by the stress of combat. |
| | General George Patton slaps soldier nervously incapable of combat. |
| 1980 | PTSD becomes a diagnostic category in *DSM III*. |
| 1985 | Society for Traumatic Stress Studies formed (publishers of *Journal of Traumatic Stress*). |
| 1980s | The False Memory Foundation urges caution in some cases of trauma since memories can change over time. |
| 1991 | Dr. George Everly coins the term *psychotraumatology* to describe the study of traumatic experience and the prevention and treatment of symptoms. |
| Present | Thousands specialize worldwide in psychotraumatology. |

# Appendix B

## Assessing Abuse

Some people are uncertain whether or not what happened to them was abuse. The following questions from Francisco Cruz and Laura Essen might help.[1]

### SEXUAL ABUSE

Has anyone ever fondled you; touched, held, or kissed you inappropriately; forced you to look at or touch another person's private parts; forced you into a prone position; forced you to listen to off-color stories or look at pornography; forced you to go nude, touch, or masturbate yourself; raped you; required you to share a bed after toddlerhood; given enemas when unnecessary? Were you threatened or told to keep such actions secret? Did the other person's actions cause you to feel frightened, ashamed, or cause other negative reactions?

### PHYSICAL ABUSE

How were you disciplined? Were you hit, slapped, spanked? Where? Did it cause marks? Were you kicked, pinched, shoved, punched, bitten, scratched, choked, thrown? Did it cause broken bones? Were you restrained? Were your arms twisted? Were you forced to eat or drink bad food, or forced to eat or drink large quantities? Did your caretakers minimize or deny abuse? Were you hit with an object or threatened with a weapon?

### EMOTIONAL ABUSE

Were you frequently called names, put down, insulted, ridiculed, ignored, rejected, humiliated, teased, threatened with harm or abandonment, bullied, isolated, told you were no good or wrong? Did your caretakers demand all your attention? Did they fail to protect you from emotional attacks by others? Did others force you to depend on them and forbid you to form friendships with others?

Cruz and Essen suggest that old photographs might help you to assess abuse, revealing what you were like before, during, and after the abuse. Photographs might help one to see the impact of abuse at different stages of life. Photographs can also help you to rediscover disowned parts of yourself. What do you notice regarding your face, body, expression, and physical sensations? What did you like? What were you proud of? What were your beliefs about self, others, and the world—compared to now? What meaning does the photo have for you now? What do you learn about yourself and others? Sometimes a photo helps break denial (e.g., a man insisted that his childhood was idyllic, yet the picture tells a different story). Draw comparisons: What differences between the "before," "during," and "after" phases do you notice? Do you remember sights, sounds, smells, or tactile sensations? What feelings did you have then that you no longer have? Do you have any physiological reactions to those feelings? What feelings are still evident today? Are you able to soothe yourself? Keep a picture of your pre-trauma self, in a special frame, as a reminder of feelings you can again experience—such as love, acceptance, respect, and joy.

# Appendix C

## *The Brain and Memory*[1]

Neuroscientists are beginning to understand how the brain processes memories. The limbic system is the emotional center of the brain. The amygdala, part of the emotional center, begins processing emotional memories. It sits next to and communicates with the hippocampus, which helps integrate memories that are fragmented, emotional, and irrational. The hippocampus performs these critical roles in memory integration:

- Connects aspects of a single memory to each other
- Connects a single memory to other memories
- Locates a memory in time and space, permitting one to recall a memory in the context of one's life history (i.e., the memory is filed in an organized way alongside other memories)
- Gives memories "narrative coherence" by sending them to the prefrontal cortex for interpretation

A certain area of the left frontal cortex, Broca's area, generates names for emotions and verbally integrates memories. This gives a memory logic and understanding and allows it to make sense. This process allows strong emotions to settle so that the memory can be stored in long-term memory. We say that the hippocampus is emotionally cool—it permits us to recall memories without being overwhelmed by uncontrolled emotions.

The locus ceruleus is the brain's alarm, or stress center. Located in the brain stem near the limbic system, it communicates directly with the amygdala and hippocampus. In response to fear, the locus ceruleus fires, sending alarm messages throughout the brain and starting a cascade of changes in chemical messengers, or neurotransmitters, throughout the brain. Once sensitized, the locus ceruleus reacts to smaller stressors as if they were recurrences of the original trauma.

Traumatic memories seem to be processed and stored differently than normal memories. The hippocampus is (or becomes) smaller in traumatized individuals and appears to become less functional during subsequent stressful periods. Broca's area shuts off, and other prefrontal areas become less active. At the same time, the amygdala seems to become more active under stress or when reliving traumatic memories. Charged negative emotions seem to be "stuck" in the right hemisphere, split from the more logical left hemisphere. This accounts for the speechless terror of PTSD. As a result, trauma material remains fragmented, emotionally charged, nonverbal, and unstable. Now relatively harmless triggers can cause trauma memories or memory fragments to flood one's awareness. The material is emotionally distressing and does not make sense. It cannot be put away as just one memory in a file of memories. Rather, it seems as if the trauma memory is the only memory on file. Because the memory cannot be expressed verbally, it is often expressed as physical symptoms.

The brain is relatively plastic. That is, it heals and expands more than we'd previously thought. Critical areas that shrink following trauma appear to grow or be spared from shrinkage when exposed to certain antidepressants, regular aerobic exercise such as walking, and possibly other PTSD treatments and self-care strategies (such as sleep, sound nutrition, and social stimulation). Conversely, alcohol disrupts hippocampal processing of memories.

# Appendix D

## Psychiatric Disorders

The disorders described here[1] might result in response to trauma. They usually develop by early adulthood. However, there are other factors that can contribute, and not all victims of trauma develop these disorders.

### ANTISOCIAL PERSONALITY DISORDER (SOCIOPATHY/PSYCHOPATHY)

Think of Adolf Hitler or Saddam Hussein, and you will have an image of this disorder. Brutally abused as children, they became indifferent to the suffering or well-being of others. This disorder is defined as extreme disregard for, and violation of, the rights of others. It is marked by aggression to people or animals, destruction of property, deceit, manipulation or bullying, stealing or other criminal behavior, inability to keep a job or remain in relationships, anger, revenge, irresponsibility (failing to pay child support or debts), lack of compassion or remorse, and cockiness. The victim might become the victimizer, thinking, "I should do what I can get away with—push before I'm pushed; It's OK to lie; I'm entitled to what I want; I count, you don't."[2] This disorder prevents the bonding that would otherwise help heal. Note that people with this disorder can be charming on the surface.

### BORDERLINE PERSONALITY DISORDER

Think of a woman who was abused and abandoned in childhood. As an adult, she clings desperately to relationships, yet fears she will be abandoned. This personality disorder is characterized by extreme instability in relationships, mood, and self-image. It is seen frequently in people who come from homes marked by abuse (especially incest), abandonment, conflict, invalidation, or neglect. Interestingly, 70 percent of people diagnosed with dissociative identity disorder (DID) also share a diagnosis of borderline personality disorder, suggesting common roots.[3] Its diagnostic features include the following:

- Poor self-esteem that might lift when the person is in an intense relationship but falls with any threat of rejection or abandonment.
- A profound need to be in an intense relationship, coupled with a feeling of impending rejection. People with borderline personality disorder make unreasonable demands on lovers and caregivers, idealizing them when they are sufficiently devoted and demonizing them when they show insufficient attention (either the loved one is a devil or an angel). They rage at perceived slights (such as being kept waiting), which seem to confirm their lack of worth. They can become very angry and sarcastic when caregivers or lovers are not attentive enough.
- Rejection or being alone may lead to impulsive, self-destructive behavior: suicide, gambling, binge eating, drug abuse, unsafe sex, or deliberate self-injury.
- They are plagued by feelings of emptiness, boredom, inability to be alone, and neediness.

The psychological underpinnings—low self-esteem, fear of being unloved (a symptom of low self-esteem), and fear of being alone with dissociated material—all suggest antidotes to the disorder.

## NARCISSISTIC PERSONALITY DISORDER

An air of superiority and the need for admiring attention manifested in people with this disorder suggest an underlying lack of self-love. Their self-absorption does not permit empathy or love for others. Instead, the narcissist will exploit others in order to succeed. Narcissism may be viewed as compensation for uncertain self-worth and self-protection from vulnerability. [4]

## DISSOCIATIVE IDENTITY DISORDER (DID)[5]

Although not a personality disorder, this condition affects the personality. According to the International Society for the Study of Trauma and Dissociation, a person with DID is a single person who experiences having separate parts of the mind that function with some autonomy. The patient is not a collection of separate people sharing the same body. The terms *personality* and *alter* (short for alternate personality) refer to dissociated parts of the mind that alternately influence behavior. Some clinicians prefer terms such as *disaggregate self state*, *part of the mind*, or *part of the self*.

DID can be very effectively treated, which is important especially because people with DID often suffer from a wide range of resulting mental and medical disorders. Whenever possible, treatment should move the patient toward a sense of integrated functioning and connectedness among the different alternate personalities. Individual psychotherapy generally involves one to two sessions per week over a period of two to five years (or more in complex cases). Treatment modalities include psychodynamically oriented approaches, supplemented by cognitive-behavioral strategies, dialectical behavioral therapy, expressive art therapies, and hypnosis, which is most commonly for calming, soothing, containment, and ego strengthening. While some believe that hypnotic techniques are useful in memory retrieval, others believe that hypnotically facilitated memory processing increases the patient's chances of mislabeling fantasy as real memory and increases the patient's level of belief in "retrieved" imagery that may actually be fantasized. Therapists, therefore, should minimize the use of leading questions that may in some cases alter the details of what is recalled in hypnosis. Group psychotherapy is not a viable primary treatment modality and may prove destabilizing for some people with DID. However, carefully structured, time-limited groups can be a useful adjunct to promote a sense that survivors are not alone in coping with their symptoms.

Most with this disorder have a history of childhood abuse.

# Appendix E

## *72-Hour Emergency Preparedness*

An emergency kit that will sustain you for several days can provide a tremendous sense of security for a variety of emergencies, such as natural disasters, the need to flee an abuser, or civil unrest. As much as possible, store items in a single container (e.g., a suitcase, duffel, backpack) in a safe and accessible place. This inventory list can be kept with the container.

| ITEM | ON HAND (✔) | PURCHASE (✔) |
|---|---|---|
| Sleeping bag and pad | | |
| Light tent | | |
| Clothing (coat, change of clothes) | | |
| Underwear | | |
| Socks | | |
| Gloves | | |
| Hat | | |
| Footwear | | |
| Whistle | | |
| Money (credit cards, cash, coins for phone calls) | | |
| Important papers (notarized copies) | | |
|    Driver's license, car title | | |
|    Birth certificate, passport | | |
|    Will | | |

| ITEM | ON HAND (✔) | PURCHASE (✔) |
|---|---|---|
| Insurance (medical, home, etc.) | | |
| Important phone numbers & addresses | | |
| Assets (locations, amounts) | | |
| Military discharge | | |
| Food (ready-to-eat meals, tuna, peanut butter, etc.) | | |
| Candles and flares | | |
| Waterproof matches | | |
| Blanket | | |
| Poncho | | |
| Flashlight (rechargeable, batteries) | | |
| Can opener | | |
| Pocket knife | | |
| Toilet articles (soap, toothbrush, floss, toilet paper, towelettes, etc.) | | |
| Pencil, pen, paper | | |
| Sunscreen | | |
| Insect repellent | | |
| First aid | | |
| Tweezers | | |
| Aspirin | | |
| Adhesive tape | | |
| Gauze bandage | | |
| Medications | | |
| Canteen with water and additional water | | |
| Sewing kit | | |
| Entertainment (reading, games, etc.) | | |
| Other items to take (not stored with container) and their location: | | |

# Appendix F

## *Meditation*

In meditation, simply allow your mind to release and relax into our true, happy nature. When agitated water is allowed to settle, it becomes very clear. Likewise, your mind will become clearer as it settles beneath racing thoughts and fears. Approach this with a pleasant attitude, a spark of playfulness, and good humor.

### MEDITATION SCRIPT

1. Go to a quiet place where you will be free from distractions for fifteen to twenty minutes. Loosen clothing. Remove glasses/contacts and shoes if you wish.

2. Sit quietly and comfortably. Place both feet flat on the floor. Use the back of the chair to support your whole back so that your spine is comfortably erect. This frees the diaphragm and disinhibits energy flow through the spinal column. Think of a bamboo pole that goes from your head to the base of your spine. Two holes at the bottom release all tension from your body. Your chin is neither up nor down, but resting comfortably, perhaps slightly back to straighten the neck. Rest your hands in your lap. The shoulders, neck, and chest are very relaxed. Sit like a dignified mountain.

3. Gently close your eyes, if that is comfortable. (If not, keep them open at half-mast, looking at a spot in front of you on the floor.) Relax your entire body. Start at your feet and relax each part in turn. Especially warm and relax your abdomen. Let your facial muscles be smooth and relaxed in a pleasant, peaceful expression. Breathe gently and peacefully through your nose, if that is possible. Take regular, rhythmic, slow, abdominal breaths.

4. Notice the gentle coolness of the air going into your body and the pleasant, relaxing feeling as it leaves. As you concentrate on breathing, allow external stimuli to fade into the background. Much as the sound of the waves at the beach begin to fade into the distance until you barely notice them, so the sounds of the world around you gently fade until you hardly notice them. Notice that the simple act of breathing is pleasant. Just be aware of your breathing and enjoy its pleasant rhythm. Notice that in closing your eyes and paying attention, your breathing tends to slow down and become more regular on its own. Don't try to make this happen. Just notice whatever the breath does.

5. Imagine the breath to be like gentle waves on the shore. Ride the waves of the in-breath. Ride the waves of the out-breath.

6. Now begin to concentrate on the word "one." See it rolling in on the in-breath, and say it silently to yourself. See it roll out on the out-breath, and say it silently to yourself as you exhale. Let the word "one" fill your mind.

7. Should distracting thoughts or worries enter your mind, just greet them cordially and without judgment ("That's OK; that's life."). Watch them float into awareness, and then let them float out of awareness—like watching a cloud floating across the sky—and return to repeating the word "one" as you breathe in and as you breathe out. So, it's breathe in . . . "one." Breathe out . . . "one." Continue quietly and peacefully for the next few moments. Let the word "one" fill your awareness, reverberating peacefully in your mind. Eventually you, your breathing, and the word "one" become one. Most of your attention focuses on the peacefulness of resting in your true happy nature. In time, you might simply stop focusing on breathing and the word "one" and simply rest in your mind, noticing that it becomes whole and peaceful. (If your mind wanders to distracting thoughts, then simply return to the method of counting and focusing on the word "one.")

8. End your meditation rather slowly, allowing peaceful feelings to spread to the rest of your life.

## SUGGESTED COURSE OF PRACTICE

Practice meditation once or twice daily for at least a week. Initially, you might wish to practice for about five minutes each time, increasing gradually to about twenty minutes each time.

# Appendix G

## Rape and Sexual Assault Facts and Myths

*Rape* refers to criminal sexual assault. The legal definition of *criminal sexual assault* is: "any genital, anal, or oral penetration, by a part of the accused's body or by an object, using force or without the victim's consent." Lack of consent includes the inability to give consent due to being underage or due to impaired mental function caused by alcohol and/or drugs, sleep, or unconsciousness.

The American Medical Association has compiled common myths believed by rape victims. These myths can lead to inappropriate guilt:

1. **A woman who truly resists can't be raped. If she didn't fight back, she must have wanted it.** Some women are too afraid of physical harm to fight back. Particularly in acquaintance rape, the woman is often too shocked to believe that someone whom she knows and trusts would rape her. She is not mobilized to hurt the other person and hopes that he will come to his senses and stop.
2. **A woman who gets drunk deserves to be raped.** Getting drunk may reflect poor judgment but does not justify being assaulted.
3. **A woman who goes to a man's room after a party deserves it.** Consenting to go to someone's room to "see my new saltwater fish collection," or for any other reason, does not equate to consenting to have sex.

---

Source: American Medical Association. 1995. *Strategies for the Treatment and Prevention of Sexual Assault.* Chicago: American Medical Association. Copyright © 1995 by the AMA. Reprinted by permission.

4. **Agreeing to some degree of sexual intimacy means (s)he wants intercourse.** Consenting to some physical closeness is not the same as consenting to intercourse.

5. **A woman must want it if it has happened before and she allows it to happen again.** People who have been abused before often feel helpless to protect themselves. A condition called *learned helplessness* develops that probably includes biologically based changes.

6. **Women really want to be raped.** There is a difference between intimacy and rape.

7. **Women aren't physically hurt by rape, they'll get over it.** Physical trauma is possible. However, emotional wounds are often more debilitating than physical ones, and usually last longer.

8. **If the woman is not a virgin, it is not a big deal.** Any sexual assault can severely traumatize and impede interpersonal and intimate relationships for a very long time. Even prostitutes can be traumatized, although they rarely report it because they are seldom taken seriously.

9. **Sexual assault is only perpetrated by strange men against women.** Rape is just one type of sexual assault. Sexual assault can also be committed by women against men and men against men. Most sexual assault is committed by acquaintances, not strangers.

Other myths:

- **If the woman had an orgasm, she wanted to be raped.** Orgasm is a physiological response that can happen when the genital area is stimulated. It can happen without wanting it to happen. An orgasm does not mean that the victim wanted to be raped, or enjoyed it.
- **Something about the victim caused the rape.** Rape is a criminal act. The perpetrator is responsible for it, not the victim.

# Appendix H

## Medication Facts and Guidelines

**I've never seen anyone cured of PTSD with a pill.**

*—Dr. George Everly*

Psychotropic medication is sometimes used to lessen certain symptoms of PTSD. All have side effects of varying degrees, and none reduce all the symptoms. None seem to work well in reducing guilt, grief, interpersonal difficulties, or moral outrage. Although most people prefer psychological treatments to medication, medications might help to reduce reexperiencing (nightmares, recollections, flashbacks), physical arousal (insomnia, irritability, startle reactivity), avoidance/numbing, and other troubling symptoms. They can be useful when symptoms are so severe that therapy cannot proceed or one's safety or medical care is compromised. These medications are sometimes tried:

**Antidepressants** may reduce PTSD symptoms and may also lessen symptoms of depression, anxiety, and chronic pain, with little risk of dependence.

- The selective serotonin reuptake inhibitors (SSRIs), such as sertraline (Zoloft) and paroxetine (Paxil), have fewer side effects than older antidepressants and are currently the first line of treatment for PTSD. They might also help reduce anger and aggression. Fluoxetine (Prozac), fluvoxamine (Luvox), citalopram (Celexa), and escitalopram (Lexapro) are other SSRIs.
- Dual-action antidepressants that block serotonin and norepinephrine include venlafaxine (Effexor) and duloxetine (Cymbalta).

- Monoamine oxidase inhibitors (MAOIs). Phenelzine (Nardil) has been most studied. Extreme side effects occur with most formulations if dietary restrictions are not followed.
- Tricyclics. Imipramine (Tofranil) and amitriptyline (Elavil) are the most studied. Special precautions must be taken regarding overdosing and interactions with SSRIs.

**Mood stabilizers and atypical antipsychotic agents** are less commonly used but might be useful when antidepressants don't work or need augmentation. These may help to reduce mood swings, rage, violent impulses, aggression, irritability, hypervigilance, hyperarousal, hallucinations, and delusions.

- Newer atypical antipsychotics include risperidone (Risperdal), olanzapine (Zyprexa), and quetiapine (Seroquel). Quetiapine may also help with disordered sleep.
- Mood stabilizers include lithium (Eskalith), carbamazepine (Tegretol), and divalproex (Depakote).

**Antiadrenergic agents** are high blood pressure medications that block the actions of stress hormones throughout the body. They appear to dampen arousal centers in the brain, while enhancing the brain's prefrontal cortical function.

- Beta-blockers block the stress hormones that help to implant traumatic memories with strong emotional charge. Propranolol (Inderal) might help to prevent PTSD if given before, or a within a few hours after, a traumatic event. Researchers suggest that taking propranolol after an old traumatic memory is recalled might reduce the memory's emotional intensity.
- The alpha-blocker prazosin (Minipres) might reduce nightmares and insomnia and promote restorative sleep in some.
- Clonidine (Catapres) might also reduce arousal, intrusions, and angry outbursts.

**D-cycloserine** (Seromycin) is used to treat tuberculosis, but this medication might also reduce PTSD and anxiety symptoms, with few side effects. Thus, it might augment prolonged exposure.

**Benzodiazepines** (antianxiety drugs or minor tranquilizers) can quickly lessen symptoms of anxiety, but their use is controversial and generally not recommended. They can be quite addictive, and rapidly discontinuing their use can cause complicated withdrawal symptoms. Rebound anxiety can follow discontinuation, especially when discontinuation is too abrupt. The use of benzodiazepines can induce depressive symptoms, which should be monitored. The benzodiazepines include diazepam (Valium), lorazepam (Ativan), and alprazolam (Xanax). Clonazepam (Klonopin) has somewhat less abuse potential and is sometimes used to treat anxiety symptoms for the initial several weeks required for SSRI therapy to become effective.

**Buspirone** (BuSpar), an antianxiety medication that is not a benzodiazepine, also helps reduce arousal but causes less dependence and withdrawal symptoms.

Other medications are being developed to prevent or reverse damage to hippocampal neurons (antidepressants appear to reverse such damage), reduce dissociation, and promote positive brain functioning.

## SPECIAL CONSIDERATIONS

Several points are important to keep in mind when taking medication:

- Medications have side effects (such as dry mouth, constipation, dizziness, sleepiness, and nervousness). These are generally mild and tend to lessen with treatment.
- It takes awhile for antidepressants and other medications to work. During the first few weeks, you may experience side effects but little relief from PTSD symptoms. Therefore, your doctor may ask you to stick with a medication six to twelve weeks. If no improvement is then noticed, your doctor may try a different medication or combination of medications. Careful adjustment of dosage and monitoring for side effects require that you work closely with your doctor.
- Maintenance periods might last a year or longer, or until recovery is stabilized.
- Before taking any medication, give your doctor a complete history of *all* drugs you use, including alcohol, marijuana, caffeine, and cocaine. Even one drink a day can interfere with the effects of antidepressant medication. Some drugs can trigger anxiety symptoms. Some can react with antianxiety drugs, causing severe side effects.
- It is important to consult a physician who is familiar both with diagnosing PTSD and with properly prescribing medication. As a rule, a psychiatrist

(or a team with one) is preferable to a family physician in prescribing drugs for PTSD. A psychiatrist is usually more experienced in recognizing symptoms of mental disturbance and is usually more knowledgeable about the medications used. If you wish reassurance that a medication is properly prescribed, consult a current edition of *Drug Facts and Comparisons* or *Physicians' Desk Reference* (check your library or a medical school library) or get a second opinion.

- After prolonged use, do not stop taking medication all at once. Abrupt withdrawal of medication might cause confusion, nausea, sleep disruption, or relapse. The likelihood of keeping symptoms manageable is greatest if you have learned sound coping skills and if discontinuation is tapered over the course of several weeks or months. The return of symptoms is likely after discontinuation if medication is not combined with psychotherapy until symptoms resolve. In some cases, prolonged use of medications is recommended. Discuss *any* changes in medication with your doctor. And do not miss doses.

- Be sure you completely understand instructions for taking your medications. Prescriptions can be confusing. If you are at all confused, ask your doctor to help you. Reasonable questions to ask:

    "What is the name of the drug, and what is it supposed to do?"

    "How and when do I take it, and when do I stop taking it?" (For example, some medications are stimulating and interfere with sleep if taken near bedtime.)

    "What are the side effects, and what should I do if they occur?"

    "Is this drug addictive?"

    "How long does it take to be effective?"

    "What foods, drinks, drugs, or activities should I avoid while taking the drug?"

    "What should I do if I forget to take a dose?"

    "Is there any written information about the drug?"

- Ask your pharmacist for information. He or she can often give you information about side effects, medications, food to avoid, etc.

- Some antidepressants (Prozac and other serotonin enhancers) do not work well if there is inadequate intake of protein, so make sure that you are eating balanced meals.

- Medication is usually not as effective as psychotherapy and has a greater risk of relapse when stopped. Medication plus psychotherapy is generally more effective than using medication alone.

# Appendix I

## Victim, Survivor, Thriver

Although the terms *victim* and *survivor* are often used interchangeably, the terms *victim*, *survivor*, and *thriver* can reflect important attitudinal distinctions as shown in Table 1.

**Table 1**
POST-TRAUMA MIND-SETS

| Victim | Survivor | Thriver |
|---|---|---|
| Helpless | Satisfying sense of having gotten through intact or mostly intact | Committed to move forward |
| Out of control | | Planning for the future |
| Angry | Beginning to feel strong | Active |
| Hoping to be rescued | Perception that one has resources and choices | Self-determined |
| Perception of lacking choices | | Feels joy day to day |
| Self-pity | Recognition of one's potential to change and grow | Achieving mastery |
| Passive | | Self-esteem; sees self as more than a victim—a valuable person |
| Payoffs (secondary gains) persuade one to remain in victim role | Living one day at a time; coping from day to day; present life is primary focus | |
| | | Reaching out to others; finding meaning and purpose |
| Identity as a victim | Beginning to take control | |
| In pain or numb | Beginning to "thaw out" or heal | Ennobled by the experience; has grown from the trauma |
| Defeated | Living moderately well | |
| Avoidance of feelings | Suffering beginning to lessen | Living well |

| Victim | Survivor | Thriver |
|---|---|---|
| "I'm still in the trauma" | Neutral about life—not depressed, but not happy | Can endure remaining PTSD symptoms with relative comfort or acceptance |
| Controlled by memories | Realization that one is outside of the trauma; one has gotten through it | Guilt has been resolved |
| Controlled by depression, anxiety, hatred, bitterness, revenge, physical complaints | Extricated self from abuse (either in actuality or at least mentally) | Generally satisfied with life |
| Has not yet learned from the experience, likely to repeat trauma, victimization | Confronting trauma | Perception that one has moved beyond the trauma |
| Shame, self-dislike | Beginning to integrate | Acquiring peace, happiness, renewal, commitment to life, optimism despite scars, empowerment |
| Self-destructive, addictions | Guilt beginning to be resolved | Committed to physical health |
| Hiding | Committed to healing, trusting, and restoring boundaries | Committed to loving again |
| Feeling fragile, vulnerable, defenseless | Influenced, but not controlled, by past | Feeling strong, compassionate—able to connect with others who are suffering and imperfect without a need to hide |
| Sense of no future, preoccupation with the past | Mostly back to normal | Resilient, renewed |
| Discouraged, immobilized | | Has learned coping skills that did not exist before the trauma |
| | | Sense of humor |
| | | "Beginner's mind"—openness to possibilities |
| | | Finds ordinary life interesting—does not need "adrenaline fix" |

Thrivers keep their dreams alive. They set goals, which communicate hope of life beyond the trauma, and make plans to reach them. In writing, try these exercises to nourish your dreams:

- List your goals under the following seven categories: *personal development, mental and physical health, relationships, career, recreation, meaningful causes to better the world,* and *possessions.* Don't limit your thinking. Sincerely consider what would help to make you happier. Ask yourself what really matters most.

- For each goal, indicate what you'll do to reach it and when you will start. The principle is to start taking a few steps each year to advance your goals.
- Establish a monthly calendar with your goals in mind.
- Construct a typical weekly work and recreation schedule. First block out time for the essentials (sleep, eating, exercise, sanity breaks, time with loved ones, etc.). Do what you can, and don't overload yourself.
- Make a daily "to do" list. List items in priority order, and do the highest priority items first. Place unfinished items on tomorrow's list. You might make tomorrow's list before bedtime and review it at the start of the next day. Keep all of your written planning sheets together so that you can refer to them often.

# Endnotes

## INTRODUCTION

1. G. R. Schiraldi, *Conquer Anxiety, Worry and Nervous Fatigue: A Guide to Greater Peace* (Ellicott City, MD: Chevron, 1997), from the foreword.

## CHAPTER 1

1. C. R. Figley, ed., *Trauma and Its Wake: The Study and Treatment of Post-Traumatic Stress Disorder* (New York: Brunner/Mazel, 1985).
2. PTSD patients have higher scores than psychiatric or normal controls on all scales of the MMPI, a widely used inventory of psychological disturbance. (P. A. Saigh, "History, Current Nosology, and Epidemiology," in *Post-traumatic Stress Disorder: A Behavioral Approach to Assessment and Treatment*, ed. P. A. Saigh [Boston: Allyn and Bacon, 1992], 1–27.) Especially noteworthy is that PTSD patients are higher in anxiety, depression, and hostility. (J. C. Jones and D. H. Barlow, "A New Model of Post-traumatic Stress Disorder: Implications for the Future," in Saigh, *Post-traumatic Stress Disorder*, 147–65.) To further appreciate the ubiquitous nature of PTSD, see Appendix A.
3. M. J. Scott and S. G. Stradling, *Counselling for Post-Traumatic Stress Disorder* (London: Sage, 1992), 28.
4. As Schopenhauer observed, "Suffering which falls to our lot in the course of nature, or by chance, or fate, does not seem so painful as suffering which is inflicted on us by the arbitrary will of another." (Quoted by M. A. Simpson, "Bitter Waters: Effects on Children of the Stresses of Unrest and Oppression," in *International Handbook of Traumatic Stress Syndromes*, ed. J. P. Wilson and B. Raphael [New York: Plenum, 1993], 613.)
5. Some experts think that emotional abuse alone is not sufficient to cause PTSD but it must occur in combination with other forms of abuse. See Appendix B for help in determining whether abuse has occurred.
6. This example was described by M. Crocq, J. Macher, J. Barros-Beck, S. J. Rosenberg, and F. Duval, "Posttraumatic Stress Disorder in World War II Prisoners of War from Alsace-Lorraine Who Survived Captivity in the USSR," in Wilson and Raphael, *International Handbook*, 253–61.

7. K. C. Peterson, M. F. Prout, and R. A. Schwarz, *Post-Traumatic Stress Disorder: A Clinician's Guide* (New York: Plenum, 1991).

8. Ibid.

9. Dr. George S. Everly, Jr., "Short-Term Psychotherapy of Post-Traumatic Stress: A Neurocognitive Perspective." Second World Congress on Stress, Trauma and Coping in the Emergency Services Professions, International Critical Incident Stress Foundation, Baltimore, MD, April 1993.

10. Saigh, *Post-traumatic Stress Disorder.*

11. For example, catecholamines and thyroxin are elevated, while cortisol, which may be depleted, is lowered.

12. For example, the constant "partyer" may be denying that wounding has occurred.

13. H. Krystal, "Beyond the DSM-III-R: Therapeutic Considerations in Posttraumatic Stress Disorder," in Wilson and Raphael, *International Handbook*, 848.

## CHAPTER 2

1. J. G. Allen, *Coping with Trauma: A Guide to Self-Understanding* (Washington, D.C.: American Psychiatric Press, 1995); R. B. Flannery, Jr., *Post-Traumatic Stress Disorder: The Victim's Guide to Healing and Recovery* (New York: Crossroad, 1992).

2. Krystal, "Beyond the DSM-III-R."

3. Example provided by C. R. Hartman and A. W. Burgess, "Treatment of Victims of Rape Trauma," in Wilson and Raphael, *International Handbook*, 507–16.

4. The olfactory nerves are proximate to the amygdala and hippocampal areas of the brain. Odor memories are closely connected to emotions and resist decay.

5. B. A. van der Kolk and J. Saporta, "Biological Response to Psychic Trauma," in Wilson and Raphael, *International Handbook*, 25–34.

6. The amygdala is the part of the brain that arouses state-dependent memories.

7. T. M. Keane, J. A. Fairbank, J. M. Caddell, R. T. Zimering, and M. E. Bender, "A Behavioral Approach to Assessing and Treating Post-Traumatic Stress Disorder in Vietnam Veterans," in Figley, *Trauma and Its Wake*, 257–94.

8. Flannery, *Victim's Guide.*

9. A similar case was reported in T. M. Keane et al., "A Behavioral Approach."

## CHAPTER 3

1. While associated features are not included in the formal diagnostic criteria for PTSD, they are observed so frequently that they warrant discussion here. Indeed, some experts feel that a number of associated features should be added to the DSM diagnostic criteria.

2. R. Janoff-Bulman, "The Aftermath of Victimization: Rebuilding Shattered Assumptions," in Figley, *Trauma and Its Wake*, 15–35; S. Epstein, "The Self-Concept, the Traumatic Neurosis, and the Structure of Personality," in *Perspectives on Personality*, vol. 3, ed. D. Ozer, J. M. Healy, Jr., and R. A. J. Stewart (Greenwich, CT: JAI, 1991); R. M. Scurfield, "War-Related Trauma: An Integrative Experiential, Cognitive, and Spiritual Approach," in *Handbook of Post-Traumatic Therapy*, ed. M. B. Williams and J. F. Sommer, Jr. (Westport, CT: Greenwood Press, 1994), 179–204; J. D. Lindy, "Focal Psychoanalytic Psychotherapy of Posttraumatic Stress Disorder," in Wilson and Raphael, *International Handbook*, 803–9; M. Crocq, J. Macher, J. Barros-Beck, S. J. Rosenberg, and F. Duval, "Posttraumatic Stress Disorder in World War II Prisoners of War from Alsace-Lorraine Who Survived Captivity in the USSR," in Wilson and Raphael, *International Handbook*, 253–61.

3. Peterson et al., *A Clinician's Guide*, 36.

4. Ibid.; Flannery, *Victim's Guide*; J. R. Davidson, D. Hughes, D. G. Blazer, and L. K. George, "Post-traumatic Stress Disorder in the Community: An Epidemiological Study," *Psychological Medicine* 2 (1991): 713–21.

5. Indeed, Op den Veld and colleagues feel that exhaustion should be a diagnostic criterion for PTSD. (W. Op den Veld et al., "Posttraumatic Stress Disorder in Dutch Resistance Veterans from WWII," in Wilson and Raphael, *International Handbook*, 219–30.)

6. Dr. R. Bruce Lydiard, Medical Director and Director of Psychopharmocology Unit, Anxiety Disorders Research, Medical University of South Carolina, explains the relationship between anxiety and the gut. Some parts of the brain regulate both anxiety states and gut function. For example, locus ceruleus activation inhibits the stomach and small intestine while increasing motility contractions in the lower colon and rectum. This explains why antianxiety drugs help irritable bowel syndrome. Stimulating the gut in turn activates the locus ceruleus. Unlike other cells outside the brain, the enteric nervous system, the "little brain," shows properties of the brain. "Gut hormones," such as cholecystokinin and vasoactive intestinal peptide, are also found in the brain. Gut sensors lead to the brain, which in turn regulates acid secretion, contractions, and hormone secretions. It is common to find a history of sexual and physical assault in irritable bowel syndrome patients. (R. B. Lydiard, "Anxiety and the Gastrointestinal System," *ADAA Reporter* 7, no. 3 [fall 1996]: 1–25.)

7. K. A. Lee, G. E. Vaillant, W. C. Torrey, and G. H. Elder, "A 50-year Prospective Study of the Psychological Sequelae of World War II Combat," *American Journal of Psychiatry* 152, no. 4 (1995): 141–48.

8. B. G. Braun, "Multiple Personality Disorder and Posttraumatic Stress Disorder," in Wilson and Raphael, *International Handbook*, 35–47.

9. L. R. Daniels and R. M. Scurfield, "War-Related PTSD: Chemical Addictions and Nonchemical Habituating Behaviors," in Williams and Sommer, *Handbook*, 205–18.

10. A. Matsakis, *Post-Traumatic Stress Disorder: A Complete Treatment Guide* (Oakland, CA: New Harbinger, 1994), 93–95. Dr. Matsakis has cogently explained a number of the reasons underlying self-mutilation, from which the discussion below is primarily adapted.

11. van der Kolk and Saporta, "Biological Response."

12. Friedman points out that Vietnam vets show higher pain thresholds after watching the movie *Platoon*, due to sudden increases in opioid levels (M. J. Friedman, "Psychobiological and Pharmacological Approaches to Treatment," in Wilson and Raphael, *International Handbook*, 785–94). Van der Kolk uses the term "addiction to trauma," which might also help explain repetition compulsion and risk-taking behavior.

13. Krystal, "Beyond the DSM-III-R."

14. Simpson, "Bitter Waters."

15. Flannery, *Victim's Guide*.

16. Flannery estimates that half of bulimics are victims of past abuse.

17. Neurological changes may interfere with the victim's ability to recognize danger, read and interpret facial expressions, and so forth.

18. J. G. Allen provides these cogent insights and the term "shred of affection" (Allen, *Coping with Trauma*, 158).

19. A discussion of alexithymia in PTSD may be found in Krystal, "Beyond the DSM-III-R." See also N. Milgram, "War-related Trauma and Victimization: Principles of Traumatic Stress Prevention in Israel," in Wilson and Raphael, *International Handbook*, 811–20; and J. P. Wilson, "The Need for an Integrative Theory of Post-Traumatic Stress Disorder," in Williams and Sommer, *Handbook*, 3–18.

## CHAPTER 4

1. Some people exhibit PTSD symptoms in response to so-called stressors of normal living (e.g., divorce, being fired, business loss, chronic illness, death from natural causes). This response is usually characterized as an adjustment disorder, rather than PTSD, although sometimes the distinction is blurry.

2. Some argue that expected events can also be traumatic, such as repeated incest. However, at least the first occurrence is usually not expected, nor completely prepared for.

3. D. W. Foy, S. S. Osato, B. M. Houskamp, and D. A. Neumann, "Etiology of Post Traumatic Stress Disorder," in Saigh, *Post-traumatic Stress Disorder*, 28–49.

4. F. Flach, "The Resilience Hypothesis and Posttraumatic Stress Disorder," in *Post-Traumatic Stress Disorder: Etiology, Phenomenology, and Treatment,* ed. M. E. Wolf and A. D. Mosnaim (Washington, D.C.: American Psychiatric Press, 1990), 36–45. Cited in Allen, *Coping with Trauma*, 187. See also J. N. Lam and F. K. Grossman, "Resilience and Adult Adaptation in Women with and without Self-reported Histories of Childhood Sexual Abuse," *Journal of Traumatic Stress* 10, no. 2 (1997): 175–96.

5. See, for instance, T. Ali, E. Dunmore, D. Clark, and A. Ehlers, "The Role of Negative Beliefs in Posttraumatic Stress Disorder: A Comparison of Assault Victims and Non Victims," *Behavioural and Cognitive Psychotherapy* 30 (2002): 249–57.

6. L. L. Harkness, "Transgenerational Transmission of War-related Trauma," in Wilson and Raphael, *International Handbook*, 635–43.

7. A. A. Feinstein, "Prospective Study of Victims of Physical Trauma," in Wilson and Raphael, *International Handbook*, 157–64. See review by A. Y. Shalev, "Stress Versus Traumatic Stress: From Acute Homeostatic Reactions to Chronic Psychopathology," in *Traumatic Stress: The Effects of Overwhelming Experience on Mind, Body, and Society,* ed. B. A. van der Kolk, A. C. McFarlane, and L. Weisaeth (New York: Guilford, 1996), 77–101. Also see J. D. Bremner and E. Brett, "Trauma-Related Dissociative States and Long-Term Psychopathology in Posttraumatic Stress Disorder," *Journal of Traumatic Stress* 10, no. 1 (1997): 37–49.

8. Troops returned from the Gulf War to nationally televised victory parades; our troops who served in Vietnam received no such welcoming ritual. Dr. Jim Reese, of the International Critical Incident Stress Foundation, relates that he got off the plane in San Francisco following his tour in Vietnam. He was emaciated and exhausted. The customs inspector said, "You don't have any contraband, do you? Welcome home, son." One wishes for such support for all survivors.

9. M. J. Horowitz, "Stress-Response Syndromes: A Review of Posttraumatic Stress and Adjustment Disorders," in Wilson and Raphael, *International Handbook*, 49–60.

10. This oft-stated estimate is somewhat misleading. Children, particularly those who are traumatized prior to personality integration (i.e., eight to ten years of age), fare much worse. About half of WWII survivors (armed forces and concentration camp survivors) have been found to suffer PTSD forty years after the war. This estimate generally applies to adults experiencing criminal assault, rape, natural disasters, and other events of relatively limited duration.

11. Long-term studies are instructive: 84 percent of Dutch resistance fighters had PTSD at some time after WWII, 55 percent had it more than forty years after the war, and many got worse after retirement (Op den Veld et al., "Dutch Resistance Veterans").

12. Figley, *Trauma and Its Wake*.

13. Wilson, "Need for an Integrative Theory."

14. S. Berglas, "Why Did This Happen to Me?" *Psychology Today* (February 1985): 44–48.

15. This term is used by R. P. Kluft, "Multiple Personality Disorder," in *Review of Psychiatry*, ed. A. Tasman and S. Goldfinge (Washington, D.C.: American Psychiatric Press, 1991), 375–84.

16. J. H. Albeck, "Intergenerational Consequences of Trauma: Reframing Traps in Treatment Theory—A Second-Generation Perspective," in Williams and Sommer, *Handbook*, 106–25.

17. Foy et al., "Etiology."

18. M. A. Donaldson, and R. Gardner, Jr., "Diagnosis and Treatment of Traumatic Stress among Women After Childhood Incest," in Figley, *Trauma and Its Wake*, 356–77.

19. A. Matsakis, "Dual, Triple and Quadruple Trauma Couples: Dynamics and Treatment Issues," in Williams and Sommer, *Handbook*, 78–105.

20. Op den Veld et al., "Dutch Resistance Veterans."

21. See, for example, J. J. Sherman, "Effects of Psychotherapeutic Treatments for PTSD: A Meta-Analysis of Controlled Clinical Trials," *Journal of Traumatic Stress* 11, no. 3 (1998): 413–35. This study indicates that cognitive-behavioral therapies substantially reduce symptoms of PTSD, anxiety, and depression by the end of treatment, and these effects are maintained at follow-up three to twelve months later.

22. Allen, *Coping with Trauma*. Van der Kolk concurs that dissociation may cause distortions (B. A. van der Kolk, "Trauma and Memory," in van der Kolk et al., *Traumatic Stress*, 279–302). Everstine and Everstine echo the fact that extreme emotions interfere with the hippocampus's ability to store memories accurately in time (D. S. Everstine and L. Everstine, *The Trauma Response: Treatment for Emotional Injury* [New York: Norton, 1993]).

## CHAPTER 5

1. D. Meichenbaum, *A Clinical Handbook/Practical Therapist Manual for Assessing and Treating Adults with Post-Traumatic Stress Disorder* (Waterloo, Ontario: Institute Press, 1994), 14.

2. Adapted from Cambridge Hospital Victims of Violence program resolution criteria by psychologist Mary Harvey. In M. P. Koss, "Date Rape," *Harvard Mental Health Letter* 9, no. 3 (September 1992): 6.

3. Cited in Allen, *Coping with Trauma*, 213.

4. B. James, *Treating Traumatized Children: New Insights and Creative Interventions* (Lexington, Mass.: Lexington, 1989), 58.

5. A well-written book on boundaries from a Biblical perspective is H. Cloud and J. Townsend, *Boundaries: When to Say Yes, When to Say No, To Take Control of Your Life* (Grand Rapids, MI: Zondervan Publishing, 1992). I am grateful for the ideas it suggests as regards PTSD.

6. From *Peace Is Every Step* by Thich Nhat Hanh. Copyright © 1991 by Thich Nhat Hanh. Used by permission of Bantam Books, a division of Random House, Inc., 51–56.

## CHAPTER 6

1. Everstine and Everstine, *Trauma Response*.

2. Items 3, 4, and 6 are adapted from Scurfield, "War-Related Trauma."

3. Adapted with permission from F. Shapiro, *Eye Movement Desensitization and Reprocessing: Basic Principles, Protocols, and Procedures* (New York: Guilford, 1995).

4. Consider soldiers in combat. They drink to bond and deaden the pain. The bonding is superficial, and the anesthesia soon wears off. They deny danger and put on a brave, self-sufficient front. The thrilling violence of combat provides a temporary distraction from emotional pain, which must be deadened to survive. The trauma survivor might repeat retraumatizing behaviors for their temporary gains.

5. This quote is suggested by K. Olness and D. P. Kohen, *Hypnosis and Hypnotherapy with Children*, 3rd ed. (New York: Guilford, 1996).

6. Shapiro presents a cogent discussion of secondary gains, from which these examples and questions are adapted. See Shapiro, *Eye Movement*.

7. Flannery, *Victim's Guide*, 159.
8. Matsakis, *Complete Treatment Guide*, 224.
9. F. Ochberg, "Posttraumatic Therapy," in Wilson and Raphael, *International Handbook*, 773–84.
10. L. A. Pearlman and I. L. McCann, "Integrating Structured and Unstructured Approaches to Taking a Trauma History," in Williams and Sommer, *Handbook*, 42.
11. An excellent overview of assessment issues may be found in B. T. Litz and F. W. Weathers, "The Diagnosis and Assessment of Post-Traumatic Stress Disorder in Adults," in Williams and Sommer, *Handbook*, 19–37.
12. This list is slightly adapted and reprinted with permission from Matsakis, *Complete Treatment Guide*. Copyright © 1994 Aphrodite Matsakis.
13. F. R. Abueg and J. A. Fairbank, "Behavioral Treatment of PTSD and Co-occurring Substance Abuse," in Saigh, *Post-traumatic Stress Disorder*, 111–46; K. S. Calhoun and P. A. Resick, "Post-Traumatic Stress Disorder," in *Clinical Handbook of Psychological Disorders: A Step-by-Step Treatment Manual*, 2nd ed., ed. D. H. Barlow (New York: Guilford, 1993), 48–98.
14. Survivors can be damaged by groups that are poorly managed; thus, caution is advised. Esther Giller, Executive Director, Sidran Institute, adds that group members often dump trauma material into a group in a graphic and triggering manner, causing other group members to react problematically. Flashbacks are contagious. Therefore, she suggests these ground rules: Members should not describe traumatic events graphically, nor should they compare war stories to see which is more horrible. The focus of communication should be on the present, and leaders should vigilantly monitor members for grounding versus dissociation.

## CHAPTER 7

1. In some cases, the even more sensitive TRH stimulation test might be used. PTSD might cause elevated levels of blood thyroxine, with a normal TRH stimulation test. M. J. Friedman, "Biological and Pharmacological Aspects of the Treatment of PTSD," in Williams and Sommer, *Handbook*, 496–509.

## CHAPTER 8

1. With CPAP, or other positive airway pressure devices, a mask is placed over the nose (and sometimes mouth). Air is pumped with enough pressure to ensure that the airway stays open. Ask about other treatments for apnea.
2. Get as much calcium as you can from foods, especially dairy products. Most of your calcium requirements will be met if you follow the USDA Food Guide Pyramid. Calcium supplements, such as calcium carbonate, can supply the remaining needs.

## CHAPTER 9

1. D. R. Catherall, *Back from the Brink: A Family Guide to Overcoming Traumatic Stress* (New York: Bantam, 1992), 160.

## CHAPTER 10

1. C. Weekes, *More Help for Your Nerves* (New York: Bantam, 1984), 23.
2. Ibid., 27.
3. Some clinicians also train panic disorder patients to distract from their symptoms when they need to function (e.g., when driving). This can be done, for example, by sensing colors around

you, noticing sounds in the environment, feeling the floor supporting you, counting backward, and so forth, until the symptoms subside. This counters the tendency to catastrophize about the symptoms and helps the person instead focus on functioning.

# CHAPTER 11

1. C. Patel, cited in B. H. Timmons and R. Ley, eds., *Behavioral and Psychological Approaches to Breathing Disorders* (New York: Plenum, 1994), ix. British chest physician Claude Lum calls hyperventilation the "great mimic."

2. Technically, "overbreathing" means that you expel carbon dioxide faster than the rate required by the metabolic demand for oxygen (i.e., faster than the cells are using oxygen). It is like smoke clearing the chimney faster than the fire is burning (Dr. Ronald Ley, personal communication, 22 January 1996). Some experts theorize that hyperventilation can be triggered by initial elevations in blood $CO_2$ levels, which eventually drop below normal.

3. Perhaps 10 percent of patients visiting general internists complain of signs and symptoms associated with hyperventilation, according to G. J. Magarian, "Hyperventilation Syndromes: Infrequently Recognized Common Expressions of Anxiety and Stress," *Medicine* 61 (1982): 219–36. Hyperventilation appears to be seen in a majority of those with anxiety disorders. In 60 percent of patients with anxiety neurosis or anxiety hysteria at Lahey Clinic, hyperventilation was a significant cause of symptoms (W. I. Tucker, "Hyperventilation and Differential Diagnosis," *Medical Clinics of North America* 47 [1963]: 491–97). Also, 50 to 60 percent of phobics seen in the Department of Clinical Psychology, University of Amsterdam, showed signs of hyperventilation syndrome. (H. Van Dis, "Hyperventilation in Phobic Patients," in *Stress and Anxiety*, Vol. 5, ed. C. D. Spielberger and I. G. Sarason [New York: Hemisphere, 1978]). Prevalence ranges from 10 to 25 percent of the population. It accounts for 60 percent of ambulance calls (R. Fried, *The Breath Connection* [New York: Plenum, 1990]).

4. Dr. Richard Gevirtz uses the metaphor of a milk wagon that brings milk to the house but can't drop it off at the door. In the same way, blood cannot release oxygen that it delivers to the cells when the blood becomes alkaline.

5. For example, calcium and phosphorous enter muscles and/or nerves, making them more active.

6. Barelli explains that breathing during sleep is unilateral, shifting from one nostril to another, and causing the body to turn during sleep, preventing various symptoms. Impaired nasal functioning may disturb sleep. A good overview of nasopulmonary problems is provided by P. A. Barelli, "Nasopulmonary Physiology," in Timmons and Ley, *Breathing Disorders*, 47–57.

7. Rosenman and Friedman observed this in type As, as reported by D. Boadella, "Styles of Breathing in Reichian Therapy," in Timmons and Ley, *Breathing Disorders*, 233–42.

8. To restore the acid-base balance, the kidney excretes bicarbonate, an important biochemical buffer. The next episode of hyperventilation will then induce rapid changes in pH and ionic balance.

9. L. C. Lum, "The Syndrome of Habitual Chronic Hyperventilation," in *Modern Trends in Psychosomatic Medicine*, 3 vols., ed. O. Hill (London: Butterworth, 1976), 196–230.

10. Magarian, "Hyperventilation Syndromes."

11. A capnograph compares the resting end-tidal $PCO_2$ with levels following the provocation test. This test is sometimes the only way to be certain that one is hyperventilating. Capnographs are found in research settings and some clinics.

12. For this reason, some psychotherapists use this test as a cognitive-behavioral strategy. Others avoid this, however, fearing that the provocation test might trigger adverse cardiovascular

symptoms (angina, arrhythmias, spasms of coronary arteries, etc.). If cardiovascular disorders are suspected, it is essential that this test be conducted under proper medical supervision.

13. P. G. F. Nixon and L. J. Freeman, "The 'Think Test': A Further Technique to Elicit Hyperventilation," *Journal of the Royal Society of Medicine* 81 (1988): 277–79.

14. This section incorporates the ideas of E. A. Holloway, "The Role of the Physiotherapist in the Treatment of Hyperventilation," in Timmons and Ley, *Breathing Disorders*, 157–75. The writings of D. H. Barlow and J. Ross have also been helpful.

15. Explains Dr. Michael Johnson, Anxiety Disorders Clinic, Medical School, University of South Carolina: "My own experience is that the addition of mental counting to the breathing practice helps the individual stay focused and has the added benefit of distracting him/her from other worries. I will have people count at the end of their inhalation and think 'relax' at the end of their exhalation. The idea of pausing (slightly) at the end of inhalation and at the end of exhalation is very useful in helping people to slow their breathing rate" (Personal communication, 1 November 1995).

16. J. H. Weiss "Behavioral Management of Asthma," in Timmons and Ley, *Breathing Disorders*, 205–19.

## CHAPTER 12

1. H. Benson, *Beyond the Relaxation Response* (New York: Berkley, 1984).

2. J. S. Brooks and T. Scarano, "Transcendental Meditation in the Treatment of Post-Vietnam Adjustment," *Journal of Counseling and Development* 64 (1985): 212–15. Transcendental meditation (TM) trains people to attain inner calm awareness devoid of thought. Since meditation had been found to reduce many symptoms found in PTSD, including insomnia, depression, anger, anxiety, substance abuse, emotional numbness, and job and relationship problems, this small study randomly assigned Vietnam veterans to three months of TM vs. three months of psychotherapy. TM was practiced twice daily, twenty minutes each time. The TM group showed significant improvements in PTSD symptoms, emotional numbness, anxiety, depression, alcohol consumption, insomnia, job problems, and family problems, and a trend toward a faster recovery from stressful stimuli. A richer, more complete discussion of meditation may be found in S. Rinpoche, *The Tibetan Book of Living and Dying* (San Francisco: Harper, 1993).

## CHAPTER 13

1. "Visitor From the Future" by Ron Klein is adapted and reprinted with permission. Copyright © 1989–1991 by Ron Klein, American Hypnosis Training Academy, Inc. The exercise is adapted from the original work of Steve Andreas, Richard Bandler, and Neurolinguistic Programming, Division of Training and Research. The client's role is to stop if there is discomfort in doing this exercise and to tell the therapist if images on the screen are difficult to "hold on to." More mundane images may be practiced if this occurs.

2. At any time during this procedure, if the client feels overwhelmed by negative feelings or "pulled into" the earlier experience, either the client or the therapist may interrupt the procedure to restore a sense of safety, security, and separateness from the earlier experience. The procedure may be started again when the client feels ready.

3. R. DiGiuseppe, "Developing the Therapeutic Alliance with Angry Clients," in *Anger Disorders: Definition, Diagnosis and Treatment*, ed. H. Kassinove (Washington, D.C.: Taylor and Francis, 1995), 131–49.

# CHAPTER 14

1. This technique was developed by Dr. Larry D. Smyth, Sheppard and Enoch Pratt Hospital, as a useful modification of Dr. Francine Shapiro's eye movement desensitization and reprocessing. Detailed instructions may be found in L. D. Smyth, *Treating Anxiety Disorders with a Cognitive-Behavioral Exposure Based Approach and the Eye-Movement Technique: Video and Viewer's Guide* (Havre de Grace, MD: RTR Publishing, 1996). Copyright © 1996 by Larry Smyth, Ph.D., from which this chapter is adapted with permission.

# CHAPTER 15

1. I am grateful to Dr. Bethany Brand, Trauma Disorders Unit, Sheppard and Enoch Pratt Hospital, for articulating most of these approaches. B. Brand and N. N. Funk, "The Basics of Treating Dissociative Patients," Maryland Psychological Association/MPAF Annual Convention, 6 June 1997.
2. Adapted with permission from *Trauma Practice* by A. Baranowsky, J. E. Gentry, and D. F. Schultz, ISBN 978-0-88937-289-4, copyright © 2005 by Hogrefe & Huber Publishers.
3. For flashbacks occurring in therapy, the therapist says loudly, "_____ (say name), I know you are having a flashback. You are here now. Come toward my voice. 1. Coming closer. 2. Almost here. 3. Here now." When the therapist detects the first signs of dissociation, she might ask, "I wonder where you went just now."
4. Adapted with permission from *Trauma Practice* by A. Baranowsky, J. E. Gentry, and D. F. Schultz, ISBN 978-0-88937-289-4, copyright © 2005 by Hogrefe & Huber Publishers.
5. This technique is adapted primarily from Shapiro, *Eye Movement*.
6. Williams suggests that the safe place might be the place where one went in imagination during abuse. (M. B. Williams, "Establishing Safety in Survivors of Severe Sexual Abuse," in Williams and Sommer, *Handbook*, 162–78.) Some people find it helpful to look through magazines to find a soothing place to use, then hang up the picture as a reminder of safety.
7. Dr. Bethany Brand adds that an adult with PTSD can use safe place imagery before sexual activity and remind herself that "I'm thirty years old now; that was long ago. I'm in a safe place now; my partner is safe," and so on. An adult with dissociative identity disorder can metaphorically bring the abused, frightened child to a safe place during the adult's sexual activity.
8. Adapted with permission from *Trauma Practice* by A. Baranowsky, J. E. Gentry, and D. F. Schultz, ISBN 978-0-88937-289-4, copyright © 2005 by Hogrefe & Huber Publishers.
9. The freezing and dirty laundry strategies are adapted with permission from undated handout, "Containment Techniques," courtesy of Dr. Bethany Brand.

# CHAPTER 16

1. Not uncommonly, those with PTSD report chronic pain (e.g., head, back, pelvic), cardiovascular disease, fibromyalgia, diabetes, gastrointestinal disease, and chronic fatigue syndrome.
2. Abuse emphasizes the harmful consequences of substance use, such as domestic violence, failure to show up for work, and social withdrawal. Technically, SUD also includes dependence, with its tolerance, withdrawal, and compulsive drug use despite the problems such use causes.
3. This is especially likely to occur in women with a history of childhood sexual or physical abuse. Men with a dual diagnosis are more likely to have experienced crime or war trauma.
4. This section mainly summarizes L. M. Najavits, *Seeking Safety: A Treatment Manual for PTSD and Substance Abuse* (New York: Guilford, 2002).

5. V. M. Follette and J. I. Ruzek, eds., *Cognitive-Behavioral Therapies for Trauma*, 2nd ed. (New York: Guilford, 2006).

6. Some may choose to begin processing prior to the completion of all topics, or while topics are being covered.

7. R. T. Murphy and C. S. Rosen, "Addressing Readiness to Change PTSD with a Brief Intervention," in *Trauma Treatment Techniques: Innovative Trends*, ed. J. Garrick and M. B. Williams (New York: Haworth, 2006) 7–28.

8. Mindfulness was tested among incarcerated individuals, typically a highly traumatized group. It was well tolerated and reduced substance use and psychiatric symptoms, suggesting that mindfulness might be useful for people with PTSD and SUD. See T. L. Simpson, D. Kaysen, S. Bowen, N. Chawla, A. Blume, G. A. Marlatt, and M. Larimer, "PTSD Symptoms, Substance Use, and Vipassana Meditation among Incarcerated Individuals," *Journal of Traumatic Stress* 20, no. 3 (2007): 239–49. See also F. C. Breslin, M. Zack, and S. McMain, "An Information-Processing Analysis of Mindfulness: Implications for Relapse Prevention in the Treatment of Substance Abuse," *Clinical Psychology: Science and Practice* 9, no. 3 (2002): 275–99.

9. If you feel that you don't deserve compassion, can you see yourself giving compassion to the child you once were?

10. If bringing awareness to traumatized regions of the body is too uncomfortable, try the body scan with the feet and hands only.

11. Mindfulness-based cognitive therapy utilizes this principle and can be a powerful complement to the cognitive therapy described later in the book.

12. Ultimately, mindfulness teaches one to sit with unpleasant emotions, fully embracing, and thus neutralizing, them with compassion and acceptance. The feelings are experienced in the body. The attitude is "Whatever I feel is OK; let me feel it." The image is that the wisdom mind is like a vast ocean, vast enough to hold even this emotion.

13. Putting feelings into words without judging them downtunes the amygdala and activates the prefrontal cortex of the brain. See M. D. Lieberman, N. I. Eisenberger, M. J. T. Crockett, S. M. Tom, J. H. Pfeifer, and B. M. Way, "Putting Feelings into Words: Affect Labeling Disrupts Amygdala Activity in Response to Affective Stimuli," *Psychological Science* 18, no. 5 (2007): 421–28. And J. D. Creswell, B. M. Way, N. I. Eisenberger, and M. D. Lieberman, "Neural Correlates of Dispositional Mindfulness During Affect Labeling," *Psychosomatic Medicine* 69, no. 6 (2007): 560–65.

14. This involves chronic neglect, disrespect, and/or abuse.

15. The major dialectic is acceptance and change. A DBT therapist might say, "Of course you are angry with your abusive father. That makes sense." Thus, one feels validated that she is not crazy. Later she might learn how to regulate the anger.

16. This section is adapted mainly from S. C. Hayes, with S. Smith, *Get Out of Your Mind and Into Your Life: The New Acceptance and Commitment Therapy* (Oakland, CA: New Harbinger, 2005). Also, S. C. Hayes, K. D. Strosahl, with K. G. Wilson, *ACT: An Experiential Approach to Behavior Change* (New York: Guilford Press, 1999). This discussion could also suitably be placed in Part V, because memories are gently confronted and issues of transitioning to a meaningful life are considered. ACT might be suitable for people who are not willing to try prolonged exposure.

17. Usually the battle we are locked into is with the words we use to describe the memory, not so much the memory itself. Defusion separates the words from the memory and then separates our self from the words and/or broadens our response to the words. For example, in the defusion strategy that follows, one can repeat the representative word quickly or slowly, in a high or low pitch, or in a playful way. Soon the word becomes just a word.

## CHAPTER 17

1. M. B. Williams, "Interventions with Child Victims of Trauma in the School Setting," in Williams and Sommer, *Handbook*, 69–77.
2. R. M. Scurfield, "Treatment of Posttraumatic Stress Disorder among Vietnam Veterans," in Wilson and Raphael, *International Handbook*, 879–88.
3. Beverly James uses the metaphor of a photograph album of an event with children. B. James, "Long-Term Treatment for Children with Severe Trauma History," in Williams and Sommer, *Handbook*, 52–68.

## CHAPTER 18

1. T. Beck, G. Emery, and R. L. Greenberg, *Anxiety Disorders and Phobias* (New York: Basic Books, 1985).
2. Emery uses this term in Beck et al., *Anxiety Disorders and Phobias*, 206.
3. Your concern probably indicates that you will not be violent. If it truly seems likely that you might hurt someone, discuss this completely and immediately with your therapist.
4. The "exception to the rule" rebuttal was suggested by G. S. Everly, Jr., "Short-Term Psychotherapy of Acute Adult Onset Post-Traumatic Stress: The Role of Weltanschauung," *Stress Medicine* 10 (1994): 191–96.
5. G. S. Everly, Jr., and J. T. Mitchell, "Advanced Critical Incident Stress Debriefing," Third World Congress on Stress, Trauma and Coping, Baltimore, MD, April 1995.
6. Dr. Aaron Beck originated the process of questioning to uncover the core beliefs. David Burns popularized the technique in *Feeling Good* (New York: New American Library, 1980), calling it "the downward arrow technique."

## CHAPTER 19

1. Act iv, scene 3, line 208.
2. Confronting the trauma is not the same as confronting an abuser, which is often counterproductive.
3. B. W. Zeigarnik, "Aber das behalten von erledigten und unerledigten handlungen," *Psychologische Forschung*, 1927; K. Lewin, *A Dynamic Theory of Personality* (New York: McGraw-Hill, 1935). Both cited in J. W. Pennebaker, *Opening Up: The Healing Power of Expressing Emotion* (New York: Guilford, 1997).
4. J. Murray, A. D. Lamnin, and C. S. Carver, "Emotional Expression in Written Essays and Psychotherapy," *Journal of Social and Clinical Psychology* 8 (1989): 414–29. Emotional expression plus cognitive reappraisal was superior to simple affective discharge.
5. Dr. Judith Herman of Harvard asserts that retelling should involve all the senses—sights, smells, feelings, thoughts, bodily sensations (racing heart, tension, weakness in the legs, etc.)—and the meaning of the event to the survivor and important people in his/her life to facilitate the association of memory fragments. J. Herman, *Trauma and Recovery* (New York: Basic Books, 1997).
6. D. A. Donnelly, and E. J. Murray, "Cognitive and Emotional Changes in Written Essays and Therapy Interviews," *Journal of Social and Clinical Psychology* 10 (1991): 334–50. See also D. L. Segal and E. J. Murray, "Emotional Processing in Cognitive Therapy and Vocal Expression of Feeling," *Journal of Social and Clinical Psychology* 13 (1994): 189–206. Also, E. J. Murray and D. L. Segal, "Emotional Processing in Vocal and Written Expression of Feelings About Traumatic Experiences," *Journal of Traumatic Stress* 7 (1994): 391–405.

7. Dr. A. Dean Byrd offers this helpful point: "Dealing with the past is useful insofar as there are intrusions into the present. Bringing the past forward often provides more benefits than taking the person back into the past." (Personal communication, 23 January 1996).

8. B. Bettelheim, afterword to C. Vegh, *I Didn't Say Goodbye*, trans. R. Schwartz (New York: E. P. Dutton, 1984), 166.

9. James, "Children with Severe Trauma History."

10. Matsakis, *Complete Treatment Guide*, 230.

11. State-dependent memories are dissociated memories that are only recalled when the individual is feeling an emotion similar to that associated with the original event.

12. Dr. Patricia Resick developed cognitive processing therapy (CPT). See, for example, P. A. Resick, C. M. Monson, and K. M. Chard, *Cognitive Processing Therapy: Veteran/Military Version* (Washington, D.C.: Department of Veterans' Affairs, 2007).

13. Quoted in van der Kolk, et al., *Traumatic Stress*, 551.

14. van der Kolk and Saporta, "Biological Response," 30.

## CHAPTER 20

1. C. R. Figley, *Helping Traumatized Families* (San Francisco: Jossey-Bass, 1989).

2. Reprinted with permission from Scurfield, "War-Related Trauma."

3. This personal experience was related by Jim Reese of the Critical Incident Stress Foundation.

4. A. Matsakis, *I Can't Get Over It: A Handbook for Trauma Survivors* (Oakland, CA: New Harbinger, 1992).

5. Everstine and Everstine, *Trauma Response*.

6. N. S. Jacobson, J. M. Gottman, J. Waltz, R. Rushe, J. Babcock, and A. Holtzworth-Monroe, "Affect, Verbal Content, and Psychophysiology in the Arguments of Couples with a Violent Husband," *Journal of Consulting and Clinical Psychology* 62 (1994): 982–88. Other reasons can make the decision to leave an abusive relationship more difficult: good memories, wanting to support a troubled partner, believing that marriage is forever, not wanting to fail at marriage, not wanting to break marriage vows (even though the abuser has broken his), and feeling responsible to make the marriage work (even as the abuser is destroying it). See E. S. Kubany, M. A. McCaig, and J. R. Laconsay, *Healing the Trauma of Domestic Violence* (Oakland, CA: New Harbinger, 2003).

7. Donaldson and Gardner, "Women after Childhood Incest."

8. Matsakis, *Complete Treatment Guide*, 181.

9. M. A. Simpson, "Traumatic Stress and the Bruising of the Soul: The Effects of Torture and Coercive Interrogation," in Wilson and Raphael, *International Handbook*, 667–84.

10. Ibid.

11. L. D. Smyth, *Clinician's Manual for the Cognitive-Behavioral Treatment of Post Traumatic Stress Disorder* (Havre de Grace, Md.: RTR Publishing, 1994), 77.

12. Janoff-Bulman, "Aftermath of Victimization."

13. Rinpoche, *Tibetan Book*.

14. This contemplation is adapted from the Tibetan *phowa* practice, which is beautifully and completely described in Rinpoche, *Tibetan Book*.

15. A variation is to approach the presence and feel embraced by that loving being.

## CHAPTER 21

1. This chapter is summarized with permission primarily from Shapiro, *Eye Movement*. Copyright © 1995 by Francine Shapiro; also F. Shapiro and M. S. Forrest, *EMDR: The Breakthrough*

*Therapy for Overcoming Anxiety, Stress and Trauma* (New York: Basic Books, 1997). Copyright © 1997 by Francine Shapiro.

2. For example, a meta-analysis of sixty-one studies found EMDR produced effects similar to those produced by conventional behavioral and cognitive-behavioral therapy for PTSD (M. L. Van Etten and S. Taylor, "Comparative Efficacy of Treatments for Posttraumatic Stress Disorder: A Meta-analysis," *Clinical Psychology and Psychotherapy* 5 (1998): 126–44. Thus, EMDR has been recommended by the American Psychiatric Association, the Department of Veterans Affairs, the Department of Defense, and other organizations around the world.

3. van der Kolk, et al., "A General Approach to Treatment of Posttraumatic Stress Disorder," in van der Kolk et al., *Traumatic Stress*, 435. Figley has called EMDR one of the most significant developments in psychotherapy (C. Figley, "Adult Traumatization" Paper presented at the National Conference on Loss and Transition: Finding Hope in Broken Places. 14–16 May 1997).

4. The combination of elements in EMDR from the major psychological modalities can be effective even without eye movements. If eye movements are inappropriate (e.g., the client has visual problems or a child cannot follow the fingers), other forms of rhythmical stimulation can also be effective. Various clinicians have effectively used alternating hand taps, tones, or finger snaps. The clients can tap their own legs with their fingers. A handheld instrument can also provide alternating pulses of varying length or rate.

5. Throughout the desensitization process, the clinician interactively determines the next focus of attention and does unblocking procedures as needed.

6. This can be particularly important for individuals such as veterans, who can find it difficult to discuss traumatic memories. That EMDR does not require sustained exposure might also make it more tolerable for the highly anxious, bereaved, or suicidal.

7. Thus, EMDR might be used on consecutive days. Promising research suggests that EMDR might be useful for mass trauma situations, including natural disasters and terrorism, and the front lines of combat.

8. Research suggests that EMDR might also simultaneously treat pain and sleep disturbances.

9. Ways in which EMDR is combined with couples and family therapies are discussed in F. Shapiro, F. W. Kaslow, and L. Maxfield, eds., *Handbook of EMDR and Family Therapy Processes* (New York: John Wiley, 2007).

## CHAPTER 22

1. This is roughly equivalent to the rewind technique presented in the next chapter.

## CHAPTER 23

1. In slightly modified form, this is called *visual-kinesthetic* (VK) dissociation. The dissociation refers to seeing yourself separated from the trauma. The term *visual-kinesthetic* refers to seeing yourself moving away from and then into the film, experiencing all sensations.

2. D. C. Muss, "A New Technique for Treating Post-Traumatic Stress Disorder," *British Journal of Clinical Psychology* 30 (1991): 91–92.

3. D. C. Muss, *The Trauma Trap* (London: Doubleday, 1991), 132.

## CHAPTER 24

1. Scott and Stradling, *Counselling*.

2. E. M. Carroll and D. W. Foy, "Assessment and Treatment of Combat-Related Post-Traumatic Stress Disorder in a Medical Center Setting," in D. W. Foy, ed., *Treating PTSD: Cognitive-Behavioral Strategies* (New York: Guilford, 1992), 39–68; E. B. Foa, D. E. Hearst-Ikeda, and C. V. Dancu,

*Cognitive Therapy and Prolonged Exposure (CT/PE) Manual* (Philadelphia: Allegheny University of the Health Sciences/Eastern Pennsylvania Psychiatric Institute, 1994); Smyth, *Clinician's Manual.*

3. Prolonged exposure can also be effectively applied to hierarchies for nightmares.
4. H. S. Resnick and T. Newton, "Assessment and Treatment of Post-Traumatic Stress Disorder in Adult Survivors of Sexual Assault," in Foy, *Treating PTSD*, 99–126.
5. Scott and Stradling, *Counselling.*
6. S. Taylor, *Clinician's Guide to PTSD: A Cognitive-Behavioral Approach* (New York: Guilford, 2006).

## CHAPTER 25

1. From D. Barrett, ed., *Trauma and Dreams* (Cambridge, MA: Harvard University Press, 1996), 3. Copyright © 1996 by the President and Fellows of Harvard College. Reprinted by permission of Harvard University Press, in which book Canetti's quotation also appears.
2. Compiled from Barrett, *Trauma and Dreams.*
3. L. Zadra, "Recurrent Dreams: Their Relation to Life Events," in Barrett, *Trauma and Dreams*, 231–47.
4. J. A. Lipovsky, "Assessment and Treatment of Post-Traumatic Stress Disorder in Child Survivors of Sexual Assault," in Foy, *Treating PTSD.*
5. J. King and J. R. Sheehan, "The Use of Dreams with Incest Survivors," in Barrett, *Trauma and Dreams*, 62.

## CHAPTER 26

1. Some people can be verbally logical, yet still quite distressed. Healing images can be more profoundly emotionally soothing. It is thought that the images in the right hemisphere are more closely linked to the limbic system, or emotional center of the brain.
2. A number of great teachers have influenced the development of this exercise, including the skilled psychologist Arnold Lazarus, who taught time tripping at the First Annual Eastern Regional Conference in Advances in Cognitive Therapies: Helping People Change, Washington, D.C., 21–23 October 1988. The dialogue is a gestalt technique for finishing uncompleted business. Dr. A. Dean Byrd has provided invaluable instruction in touching the past with love.
3. Adapted and reprinted with permission of the publisher, Health Communications, Inc., Deerfield Beach, Florida, from John Bradshaw, *Healing the Shame That Binds You* (Deerfield Beach, FL: Health Communications, Inc., 1988). The corrective experience was adapted from what first appeared in P. Levin, *Cycles of Power* (Deerfield Beach, FL: Health Communications, Inc., 1988).
4. The Menninger Clinic, *Imagery and Grief Work: Healing the Memory* video (Topeka, KS: The Menninger Clinic, 1989).

## CHAPTER 27

1. One Vietnam vet said, "This is what our country meant to give us, and would have if the politics had been different then. I'm pretending this parade is for me, too."
2. Catherall, *Back from the Brink.*
3. From J. P. Wilson, "Treating the Vietnam Veteran," in *Post-Traumatic Therapy and Victims of Violence*, ed. F. M. Ochberg (New York: Brunner/Mazel, 1988), 254–77; B. Colodzin, *How to*

*Survive Trauma: A Program for War Veterans and Survivors of Rape, Assault, Abuse or Environmental Disaster* (Barrytown, NY: Station Hill, 1993).

4. G. C. Wilson, "Vietnam Revisited: Veterans Go Back to Battlefields to Lay Their Nightmares to Rest," *Washington Post Health Journal* (6 February 1990): 12–15.

## CHAPTER 28

1. A memorial to Jane Austen, Winchester Cathedral, reads, "Their grief is in proportion to their affection; they know their loss to be irreparable, but in their deepest affliction they are consoled by a firm though humble hope that her charity, devotion, faith and purity have rendered her soul acceptable in the sight of her Redeemer."

2. The grief literature suggests that symptoms of unresolved grief parallel PTSD symptoms. Survivors often increase the use of alcohol, tobacco, or drugs to medicate the pain. Visits to physicians often increase. Anniversaries, meaningful dates, and other triggers can cause grief spasms.

3. For instance, long after a fetal death, a couple realized that they had stopped developing as parents, spouses, and lovers. It was as if they had been frozen in many regards at the time of the trauma. For them it was useful to affirm, "We are parents of a dead child." This permitted them to acknowledge their loss and begin to develop again.

4. Rando discusses the concepts of tangible, intangible, and secondary losses, on which this discussion is based, in T. A. Rando, *Treatment of Complicated Mourning* (Champaign, IL: Research Press, 1993).

5. The discussion of uncomplicated and complicated mourning are adapted from Rando, *Complicated Mourning*.

6. "Bereavement and Grief—Part I," excerpted from the March 1987 issue of the *Harvard Mental Health Letter*. Copyright © 1987 by the President and Fellows of Harvard College.

7. Shapiro, *Eye Movement*, suggests this thought.

## CHAPTER 29

1. Flannery, *Victim's Guide.*

2. H. S. Kushner, *When Bad Things Happen to Good People* (New York: Avon, 1981).

3. Quoted in R. N. Ostling and M. Levin, "U.S. Judaism's Man of Paradox," *Time* (8 October 1984), 66.

4. A. Whitman, "Secret Joys of Solitude," *Reader's Digest* (April 1983): 128–32.

5. S. Vanauken, *A Severe Mercy* (New York: Bantam, 1977).

6. The suggestion to be responsible for one's suffering does not blame victims or minimize their suffering. Rather, it empowers by providing tools to understand and process suffering.

## CHAPTER 30

1. R. A. Schwarz, "Hypnotic Approaches in Treating PTSD: An Ericksonian Framework," in Williams and Sommer, *Handbook*, 401–17.

2. Executive Committee of the American Psychological Association, Division of Psychological Hypnosis.

3. R. A. Schwarz, "Hypnotic Approaches."

4. G. Ambrose, "Hypnosis in the Treatment of Children," *American Journal of Clinical Hypnosis* 11 (1968): 1–5, as described in Olness and Kohen, *Hypnosis with Children.*

## CHAPTER 31

1. D. Spring, "Art Therapy as a Visual Dialogue," in Williams and Sommer, *Handbook*, 337–51.
2. A pilot study by Charles Morgan and David Johnson at the National Center for PTSD in West Haven, Connecticut, which appeared in the December 1995 issue of the journal *Art Therapy*, found that drawing pictures of nightmares decreased the frequency and intensity of the nightmares, while writing about the nightmares led to increases. Perhaps drawing more directly discharges imagery aspects of memory, which are stored in the right brain.
3. Shapiro, *Eye Movement*, suggests reinforcing the positive images with sets of eye movements.
4. G. Roth, *Maps to Ecstasy* (San Rafael, Calif.: New World Library, 1987).
5. R. Milliken, "Dance/Movement Therapy with the Substance Abuser," *The Arts in Psychotherapy* 17 (1990): 309–17.
6. Roth, *Maps to Ecstasy*.
7. R. L. Blake and S. R. Bishop, "The Bonny Method of Guided Imagery and Music (GIM) in the Treatment of Post-Traumatic Stress Disorder (PTSD) with Adults in the Psychiatric Setting," in B. L. Wilson and M. A. Scovel, eds., "Psychiatric Music Therapy (special issue)," *Music Therapy Perspectives* 12, no. 2 (1994): 125–29.
8. Ibid.
9. H. L. Bonny, "Twenty-One Years Later: A GIM Update," in Wilson and Scovel, "Psychiatric Music Therapy," 73.
10. C. Slotoroff, "Drumming Technique for Assertiveness and Anger Management in the Short-Term Psychiatric Setting for Adult and Adolescent Survivors of Trauma," in Wilson and Scovel, "Psychiatric Music Therapy," 111–16.
11. T. Alston, "Storytelling: A Tool for Vietnam Veterans and Their Families," in *The Legacy of Vietnam Veterans and Their Families: Papers from the 1994 National Symposium*, ed. D. K. Rhoades, M. R. Leaveck, and J. C. Hudson (Washington, D.C.: Agent Orange Class Assistance Program, 1995), 384–95, quote 385. Reprinted with permission.
12. J. Campbell, *The Hero with a Thousand Faces*, 3rd ed. (New York: Meridian, 1975); J. Campbell and W. Moyers, *The Power of Myth*, edited by B. S. Flowers (New York: Doubleday, 1988).
13. J. Ruth Gendler, "Fear," in *The Book of Qualities* (New York: HarperCollins Publishers, Inc., 1987).
14. With gratitude for information provided by the National Association for Drama Therapy.
15. Create Therapy Institute, 10225 Montgomery Avenue, Kensington, MD 20895 (301-652-7183). Dr. Miller and cofounder Rebecca Milliken can often provide referrals to expressive art therapists around the country. Sand-tray example is excerpted from the institute newsletter, 1, no. 2 (August 1997): 4. Appreciation also to art therapist Dr. Eliana Gil of Rockville, MD, for assistance with this section.

## CHAPTER 32

1. Both examples are from M. I. Lewis and R. N. Butler, "Life-Review Therapy: Putting Memories to Work in Individual and Group Psychotherapy," *Geriatrics* 29, no. 11 (1974): 165–73.
2. For a review, see: L. B. Taft and M. F. Nehrke, "Reminiscence, Life Review, and Ego Integrity in Nursing Home Residents," *International Journal of Aging and Human Development* 30, no. 3 (1990): 189–96.
3. Reprinted with slight adaptation with permission from Colodzin, *How to Survive Trauma*. Copyright © 1993 by Olympia Institute.

# CHAPTER 33

1. Love for others and love for self are not mutually exclusive. Ideally, the attitude of loving encircles both.
2. J. Gauthier, D. Pellerin, and P. Renaud, "The Enhancement of Self-Esteem: A Comparison of Two Cognitive Strategies," *Cognitive Therapy and Research* 7 (1983): 389–98.
3. Reprinted with permission from J. H. Childers, Jr., "Looking at Yourself Through Loving Eyes," *Elementary School Guidance and Counseling* 23 (1989): 204–9. Copyright © 1989 by The American Counseling Association. No further reproduction authorized without written permission of the American Counseling Association.

# CHAPTER 34

1. Paraphrased from Nhat Hanh, *Peace Is Every Step*, 59.
2. Anger might suppress fear and other primary emotions locked in the traumatic memory material. Thus, the real pain does not get addressed or processed.
3. The word "resentment" derives from words meaning "to feel again" and suggests indignation for a past offense. If you can't feel positive toward the offender because he hasn't earned it, you might try to let your feelings toward him "go to neutral" (feel nothing at all toward him).
4. This is itself a very complex issue. Some people's hearts are softened by compassion, by those who refuse to retaliate and instead express forgiveness and hope for the offender. For example, on "The Donahue Show," Reginald Denny expressed compassion for the offender who severely injured him in the Los Angeles riots. He said, "It doesn't mean I'm not angry. But I truly love him." The offender's mother said that Denny was the first person to soften her son's anger. On the other hand, some hardened individuals repeatedly inflict severe suffering on others, despite repeated jailings. Perhaps stricter discipline rather than leniency is called for in such cases.
5. Quoted by Mary Grunte in D. Hales, "Three Words That Heal," *McCall's* (June 1994).
6. Dr. Judith Herman explains that mourning is not completed until we give up the hope of getting even. Revenge does not compensate for or change the harm that was done. Acts of revenge make the victim feel as bad as the offender, and waiting for compensation from the offender (e.g., an apology, acknowledgment of wrongdoing, public humiliation, or shame) holds the victim hostage to the offender's whim. Herman suggests instead that the survivor think in terms of holding the offender accountable for the crime. The survivor joins with society in bringing the offender to justice, not as a personal vendetta, but for the safety of self and the community. Even if the survivor loses the legal case, she knows she did all she could. See Herman, *Trauma and Recovery*.
7. Drs. Robert Enright and Suzanne Freedman found that incest survivors who attended forgiveness workshops had far less anxiety and depression than those who did not ("Forgiveness: Serious Stuff or Fluff?," *Psychology Today* [July/August 1996]: 12).
8. D. Hope, "The Healing Paradox of Forgiveness," *Psychotherapy* 24, no. 2 (1987): 240–44.
9. Related in *Fight For Your Life*, dir. M. Mears and J. Distel-Schwartz, The Fight for Your Life Co., videocassette. The Fight for Your Life Co., c/o Varied Directions, Camden, Maine, 1-800-888-5236.
10. It is helpful to remember that someone who is hostile toward you is like a dog with a leg in a trap buried under leaves. The pain is why he snarls and strikes out. (Suggested by W. D. Morgan and S. T. Morgan, "Cultivating Attention and Empathy," in *Mindfulness and Psychotherapy*, ed. C. K. Germer, R. D. Siegel, and P. R. Fulton [New York: Guilford, 2005, 73–90].)
11. 2 Chron. 20:15.

12. W. H. Murray, *The Himalayan Expedition* (London: J. M. Dent and Son, 1951, 7).
13. Hayes, *ACT*.
14. R. D. Walser and D. Westrup, *Acceptance and Commitment Therapy for the Treatment of Post-Traumatic Stress Disorder and Trauma-related Problems* (Oakland, CA: New Harbinger, 2007).

## CHAPTER 35

1. These points are discussed in Shapiro, *Handbook of EMDR*.
2. See A. Madrid, "Repairing Maternal-Infant Bonding Failures," in the above work, pp. 131–45.
3. This section is adapted primarily from E. Tick, *War and the Soul: Healing Our Nation's Veterans from Post-Traumatic Stress Disorder* (Wheaton, IL: Quest, 2005).
4. Moral pain can be a consequence of confusing killing with murder, committing atrocities, fighting for an unjust cause, or following immoral orders. War is not normal. Even after lawfully authorized killing, warriors can feel unclean and ashamed. Tick notes that they commonly ask, "Am I good, did I murder, will God love and forgive me, have I become indifferent to human suffering?"
5. E. Tick, *War and the Soul*, p. 198.
6. For an excellent discussion on spiritual considerations of killing vs. murder, see D. Grossman, with L. W. Christensen, *On Combat* (PPCT Research Publications, 2004). Grossman indicates that "thou shalt not kill" is more correctly translated as "thou shalt not murder." He adds that it is normal for warriors to feel initial exhilaration upon defeating an enemy, followed by remorse for feeling that exhilaration, before acceptance of the necessary work of war is reached.
7. L. Gantt and L. W. Tinnin, "Intensive Trauma Therapy of PTSD and Dissociation: An Outcome Study," *The Arts in Psychotherapy* 34 (2007): 69–80.
8. In ITT, the delay for stabilization is usually not prolonged. Stabilization strategies include prohibiting substance abuse; clay sculpting in a group setting and creating safe place images to soothe and overcome isolation; a regular daily schedule regarding sleep and meals; and ego strengthening (contour drawing of the client's body, creating an art life history, and learning to self-ground).

## CHAPTER 36

1. Scurfield, "Treatment among Vietnam Veterans"; C. M. Stuhlmiller, "Action-Based Therapy for PTSD," in Williams and Sommer, *Handbook*, 386–400.
2. Adapted from Stuhlmiller, "Action-Based Therapy."
3. J. O. Brende, *Trauma Recovery for Victims and Survivors* (Sparta, GA: Trauma Recovery, 1994).

## CHAPTER 37

1. R. G. Tedeschi and L. G. Calhoun, "The Posttraumatic Growth Inventory: Measuring the Positive Legacy of Trauma," *Journal of Traumatic Stress* 9, no. 3 (1996): 455–71. Growth was positively correlated with optimism, religiosity, extroversion, openness, agreeableness, and conscientiousness. Spiritual change was correlated with being more optimistic, religious, and extroverted.
2. For example, van der Kolk writes, "In the Grant Study, a 50-year study of Harvard men from the 1940s to the 1990s, the men who developed PTSD after World War II were much more likely to be listed in *Who's Who in America* than their nontraumatized peers." (van der Kolk et al., *Traumatic Stress*, 28. The original study is Lee et al., "A 50-Year Prospective Study.")
3. Adapted slightly and reprinted with permission from Scurfield, "Treatment among Vietnam Veterans," 886.

4. R. C. Sipprelle, "A Vet Center Experience: Multievent Trauma, Delayed Treatment Type," in Foy, *Treating PTSD*, 13–38, quote 36.

5. Bonding can occur even when the traumatic events are dissimilar. I am reminded of two young women in my class who formed a special friendship. One had survived a recent rape; the other, deaths of eleven family members and close friends over a period of months. As they heard each other disclose their suffering, they were drawn closer by a sense of compassion, respect, and the bond of shared suffering.

6. I am grateful to Suzanne Kobasa for this concept.

7. Reprinted with the permission of the Free Press, a Division of Simon and Schuster, Inc., from James, *Treating Traumatized Children*, 173–74. Copyright © 1989 by Lexington Books.

## CHAPTER 38

1. Z. Harel, B. Kahana, and E. Kahana, "Social Resources and the Mental Health of Aging Nazi Holocaust Survivors and Immigrants," in Wilson and Raphael, *International Handbook*, 241–52.

2. Y. Danieli, "The Treatment and Prevention of Long-Term Effects and Intergenerational Transmission of Victimization: A Lesson from Holocaust Survivors and Their Children," in Figley, *Trauma and Its Wake*, 295–313.

3. Adapted with permission from P. L. Sheehan, "Treating Intimacy Issues of Traumatized People," in Williams and Sommer, *Handbook*, 94–105.

4. F. R. Abueg and J. Fairbank, "A Behavioral Treatment of PTSD and Co-Occurring Substance Abuse," in Saigh, *Post-Traumatic Stress Disorder*, 111–46.

5. E. J. Letourneau, P. A. Schewe, and B. C. Frueh, "Preliminary Evaluation of Sexual Problems in Combat Veterans with PTSD," *Journal of Traumatic Stress* 10 (1997): 125–32.

6. W. I. Miller, *The Anatomy of Disgust* (Cambridge, MA: Harvard University Press, 1997).

7. This principle is from Nhat Hanh, *Peace Is Every Step*.

8. I am grateful to Allison Grad, whose research assisted in the compilation of this section.

9. Reprinted with the permission of the Free Press, a Division of Simon and Schuster, Inc. from James, *Treating Traumatized Children*, 90–91. Copyright © 1989 by Lexington Books.

10. B. Engel, *Raising Your Sexual Self-Esteem* (New York: Fawcett Columbine, 1995), 242. Published by Ballantine Books, a division of Random House, Inc.

11. Ibid., 217.

12. Y. M. Dolan, *Resolving Sexual Abuse: Solution-Focused Therapy and Ericksonian Hypnosis for Adult Survivors* (New York: Norton, 1991), 176; and Engle, *Sexual Self-Esteem*.

13. This technique is used only with caution. It is practiced within the context of a comprehensive treatment plan. The technique can be useful when one is stable and integrated enough to realize that this exercise is not a reenactment of the original trauma and, thus, not a trigger for it. B. Rothschild, personal communication, September 18, 2008; B. Rothschild, "A Trauma Case History: Somatic Trauma Therapy," (www.trauma.cc). See also B. Rothschild, "An Annotated Trauma Case History: Somatic Trauma Therapy, Part I," *Somatics* 11 (1), (Fall/Winter 1996/1997): 48–53. For further reading, see B. Rothschild, *The Body Remembers Casebook* (New York: W.W. Norton, 2003).

14. S. H. Spence, *Psychosexual Therapy: A Cognitive-Behavioral Approach* (London: Chapman and Hall, 1991).

15. The interested reader is referred to L. Wallas, *Stories That Heal: Reparenting Adult Children of Dysfunctional Families Using Hypnotic Stories in Psychotherapy* (New York: Norton, 1991).

## CHAPTER 39

1. V. Frankl, *Man's Search for Meaning* (Boston: Beacon, 1959), 110.
2. Scurfield, "Treatment among Vietnam Veterans."
3. I am grateful to Brian Richmond for suggesting this question.
4. I. Yalom suggests this on page 216 of his *Existential Psychotherapy* (New York: Basic Books, 1980).
5. I. Yalom, *Existential Psychotherapy*, 439.
6. A. Maslow, "Self-actualizing and Beyond," in D. Goleman and D. Heller, eds., *The Pleasures of Psychology* (New York: New American Library, 1986), 299.
7. W. Durant, *On the Meaning of Life* (New York: Ray Long and Richard R. Smith, 1932), 128–29.

## CHAPTER 40

1. Mother Teresa's life is instructive here. Though she was born into wealth, the untimely death of her father (some feel it was a politically motivated murder) plunged her quickly into poverty before she began her odyssey of service and faith.
2. A. Ellis, "Psychotherapy and Atheistic Values: A Response to A. Bergin's 'Psychotherapy and Religious Values,' " *Journal of Consulting and Clinical Psychology* 48 (1980): 635–39.
3. Princeton Religious Research Center, *Religion in America 1992–1993* (Princeton, N.J.: Princeton Religious Research Center, 1993). Recent polls by Gallup, *Newsweek*, Opinion Dynamics Corporation, and the Pew Forum on Religion and Public Life all concluded that the percentage of Americans who believe in God exceeds 90 percent.
4. D. B. Larson and S. S. Larson, *The Forgotten Factor in Physical and Mental Health: What Does the Research Show?* (Rockville, MD: National Institute for Healthcare Research, 1994), 35. Larson, a psychiatrist and former senior researcher for the National Institutes of Health, presided over the National Institute for Healthcare Research. This volume contains the summary of the religious research that follows.
5. J. Gartner, D. B. Larson, and G. Allen, "Religious Commitment and Mental Health: A Review of the Empirical Literature," *Journal of Psychology and Theology* 19, no. 1 (1991): 6–25. Cited in Larson and Larson, *Forgotten Factor*.
6. P. L. Benson and B. P. Spilka, "God-Image as a Function of Self-Esteem and Locus of Control," in *Current Perspectives in the Psychology of Religion*, ed. H. N. Maloney (Grand Rapids, Mich.: Eerdmans, 1977), 209–24.
7. D. Lowenstein, untitled poem in *Wounded Healers*, ed. R. N. Remen (Bolinas, CA: Wounded Healer Press, 1994), 59. Copyright © 1994 by Rachel Naomi Remen, M.D. Used by permission.
8. Frankl, *Man's Search*, 76.
9. Personal communication (1981).
10. Benson, *Relaxation Response*, 10.
11. K. Alvarado, D. Templer, C. Bresler, and S. Thomas-Dobson, "The Relationship of Religious Variables to Death Depression and Death Anxiety," *Journal of Clinical Psychology* 51, no. 2 (1995): 202–4.
12. Weekes, *More Help*, 78. Quote following, 76.
13. Cited in J. Hinton, *Dying* (London: Pelican, 1967).
14. Shared by Karolyn Nunnallee, Mothers Against Drunk Driving.
15. A. D. Byrd and M. D. Chamberlain, *Willpower Is Not Enough* (Salt Lake City, Utah: Deseret, 1995).
16. Shared by Millie Webb, Mothers Against Drunk Driving.

17. Gallup poll analyzed by Robert Wuthnow, Princeton University sociologist, in R. Wuthnow, "Evangelicals, Liberals, and the Perils of Individualism," *Perspectives* (May 1991): 10–13.

18. The National Institute of Mental Health's Epidemiological Catchment Area Survey, cited in Larson and Larson, *The Forgotten Factor*, 11.

19. L. R. Propst, R. Ostrom, P. Watkins, T. Dean, and D. Mashburn, "Comparative Efficacy of Religious and Nonreligious Cognitive-Behavioral Therapy for the Treatment of Clinical Depression in Religious Individuals," *Journal of Consulting and Clinical Psychology* 60, no. 1 (1992): 94–103. I had a very memorable experience with this in a graduate class. I asked my class if anyone wished to demonstrate how cognitive restructuring is used in modifying anger. One volunteered and chose as the stressor the death of her brother, who had fallen to his death from a building. Her anger centered on his careless supervisors, on her brother for not being careful, and on God for letting the accident happen. It was the latter she chose to work with. Among her self-talk was the idea "How could a loving God allow such a good twenty-nine-year-old man to die as he did?" As we pondered this question, this idea came to my mind, which I shared, knowing her religious orientation: "How could a loving God allow a perfect thirty-three-year-old man die as He did?" She reported later that that idea helped her dispel her anger in a profound and peaceful way, for the first time in the year since his death. Often, a single question can cause cognitive restructuring at several levels simultaneously, with considerable shifts in the emotional consequences.

20. W. James, *The Varieties of Religious Experience* (New York: Mentor, 1958), 288.

21. See Larson, *Forgotten Factor*, 88–93.

## CHAPTER 41

1. D. G. Myers, *The Pursuit of Happiness: Who Is Happy—and Why* (New York: Morrow, 1992). Also, M. W. Fordyce, *Human Happiness: Its Nature and Its Attainment*, 2 vols. (Ft. Myers, FL: Cypress Lake Media, n.d.).

2. Fordyce, *Human Happiness*, 171.

3. From Nhat Hanh, *Peace Is Every Step*, 10. Copyright © 1991 by Thich Nhat Hanh. Used by permission of Bantam Books, a division of Random House, Inc.

4. J. Cornfield, *Buddha's Little Instruction Book* (New York: Bantam, 1994), 137.

5. George B. Sellarole. Contributed to *Readers Digest* (January 1997).

6. I'm grateful to Brian Richmond for this simple question that caused me such pleasure.

## CHAPTER 42

1. I am grateful to Dr. Francis Abueg for the many helpful ideas in this chapter, which are adapted from F. R. Abueg, A. J. Lang, K. D. Drescher, J. I. Ruzek, N. Sullivan, and J. F. Aboudarham, *Trauma Relevant Relapse Prevention Training (TRRPT): A Group Psychotherapy Protocol for PTSD and Alcoholism* (Menlo Park, CA: National Center for PTSD, 1993). Available from F. R. Abueg at Trauma Resource Consulting, Suite 115, 4966 El Camino Real, Los Altos, CA 94022.

2. From Abueg et al., *TRRPT*.

3. The psychologist Donald Meichenbaum is recognized for developing this approach.

4. Clinicians familiar with EMDR might also process any disturbance that arises at each step. Some disturbance might be new aspects of past trauma, or it might be related to fears of failure or fears that successful recovery will lead to abandonment by the therapist.

5. EMDR practitioners will use eye movements to reinforce the image of coping successfully and positive feelings, once negative material has been processed and ceases to come up.

## APPENDIX B

1. Reprinted with permission from F. G. Cruz and L. Essen, *Adult Survivors of Childhood Emotional, Physical, and Sexual Abuse: Dynamics and Treatment* (Northvale, NJ: Jason Aronson, 1994), 125–27. Their ideas are supplemented with those of M. A. Dutton, "Post-Traumatic Therapy with Domestic Violence Survivors," in Williams and Sommer, *Handbook*, 146–61.

## APPENDIX C

1. This appendix is a synthesis of many sources, including:

   Colcombe, S. J., K. I. Erickson, P. E. Scalf, J. S. Kim, R. Prakash, E. McAuley, S. Elavsky, D. X. Marquez, L. Hu, and A. F. Kramer. "Aerobic Exercise Training Increases Brain Volume in Aging Humans." *The Journals of Gerontology Series A: Biological Sciences and Medical Sciences* 61 (2006): 1166–70.

   Everly, G. S., Jr., and J. M. Lating, eds. *Psychotraumatology: Key Papers and Core Concepts in Post-Traumatic Stress*. New York: Plenum, 1995.

   van der Kolk, B. A., A. C. McFarlane, and L. Weisaeth, eds. *Traumatic Stress: The Effects of Overwhelming Experience on Mind, Body, and Society*. New York: Guilford, 1996.

   van der Kolk, B. A., and J. Saporta. "Biological Response to Psychic Trauma," in J. P. Wilson and B. Raphael, eds. *International Handbook of Traumatic Stress Syndromes*. New York: Plenum, 1993, 25–34.

## APPENDIX D

1. The descriptions are adapted from the American Psychiatric Association, 2000: *DSM-IV-TR*.
2. Scott and Stradling, *Counselling*, 23.
3. Braun, "Multiple Personality Disorder."
4. E. R. Parson, "Posttraumatic Narcissism: Healing Traumatic Alterations in the Self Through Curvilinear Group Psychotherapy," in Wilson and Raphael, *International Handbook*, 821–40.
5. This section is adapted from International Society for the Study of Trauma and Dissociation. *Guidelines for Treating Dissociative Identity Disorder in Adults*, copyright © 2005. International Society for the Study of Trauma and Dissociation, 8400 West Park Drive, 2nd Floor, McLean, VA 22102.

# Bibliography

Abueg, F. R., A. J. Lang, K. D. Drescher, J. I. Ruzek, N. Sullivan, and J. F. Aboudarham. *Trauma Relevant Relapse Prevention Training (TRRPT): A Group Psychotherapy Protocol for PTSD and Alcoholism.* Menlo Park, CA: National Center for PTSD, 1993.

Ali, T., E. Dunmore, D. Clark, and A. Ehlers. "The Role of Negative Beliefs in Posttraumatic Stress Disorder. A Comparison of Assault Victims and Non Victims." *Behavioural and Cognitive Psychotherapy* 30 (2002): 249–57.

Allen, J. G. *Coping with Trauma: A Guide to Self-Understanding.* Washington, D.C.: American Psychiatric Press, 1995.

Alvarado, K., D. Templer, C. Bresler, and S. Thomas-Dobson. "The Relationship of Religious Variables to Death Depression and Death Anxiety." *Journal of Clinical Psychology* 51, no. 2 (1995): 202–4.

American Psychiatric Association. *Diagnostic and Statistical Manual of Mental Disorders.* 4th ed. Washington, D.C.: American Psychiatric Association, 1994.

———. *Diagnostic and Statistical Manual of Mental Disorders.* 4th ed. text revision. Washington, D.C.: American Psychiatric Association, 2000.

Baranowsky, A. B., J. E. Gentry, and D. F. Schultz. *Trauma Practice: Tools for Stabilization and Recovery.* Cambridge, MA: Hogrefe & Huber, 2005.

Barlow, D. H., and M. Craske. *Mastery of Your Anxiety and Panic.* Albany, NY: Graywind Publications, 1989.

Barlow, D. H., ed. *Clinical Handbook of Psychological Disorders: A Step-by-Step Treatment Manual.* 2nd ed. New York: Guilford, 1993.

Barrett, D., ed. *Trauma and Dreams.* Cambridge, MA: Harvard University Press, 1996.

Beck, A. T., G. Emery, and R. L. Greenberg. *Anxiety Disorders and Phobias.* New York: Basic Books, 1985.

Benson, H. *Beyond the Relaxation Response.* New York: Berkley, 1984.

Benson, P. L., and B. P. Spilka. "God-Image as a Function of Self-Esteem and Locus of Control." In *Current Perspectives in the Psychology of Religion,* edited by H. N. Maloney, 209–24. Grand Rapids, MI: Eerdmans, 1977.

Borkovec, T. D., L. Wilkinson, R. Folensbee, and C. Lerman. "Stimulus Control Applications to the Treatment of Worry." *Behavior Research and Therapy* 21 (1983): 247–51.

Bremner, J. D., and E. Brett. "Trauma-Related Dissociative States and Long-Term Psychopathology in Posttraumatic Stress Disorder." *Journal of Traumatic Stress* 10, no. 1 (1997): 37–49.

Brende, J. O. *Trauma Recovery for Victims and Survivors*. Sparta, GA: Trauma Recovery, 1994.

Breslin, F. C., M. Zack, and S. McMain. "An Information-Processing Analysis of Mindfulness: Implications for Relapse Prevention in the Treatment of Substance Abuse." *Clinical Psychology: Science and Practice* 9, no. 3 (2002): 275–99.

Brooks, J. S., and T. Scarano. "Transcendental Meditation in the Treatment of Post-Vietnam Adjustment." *Journal of Counseling and Development* 64 (1985): 212–15.

Byrd, A. D., and M. D. Chamberlain. *Willpower Is Not Enough*. Salt Lake City, Utah: Deseret, 1995.

Campbell, J. *The Hero with a Thousand Faces*. 3rd ed. New York: Meridian, 1975.

Campbell, J., and W. Moyers. *The Power of Myth*, edited by B. S. Flowers. New York: Doubleday, 1988.

Carnes, P., and J. M. Moriarity. *Sexual Anorexia: Overcoming Sexual Self-Hatred*. Center City, MN: Hazelden, 1997.

Catherall, D. R. *Back from the Brink: A Family Guide to Overcoming Traumatic Stress*. New York: Bantam, 1992.

Cloud, H., and J. Townsend. *Boundaries: When to Say Yes, When to Say No, To Take Control of Your Life*. Grand Rapids, MI: Zondervan Publishing, 1992.

Cohen, B. M., M. Barnes, and A. B. Rankin. *Managing Traumatic Stress Through Art*. Lutherville, MD: Sidran, 1995.

Colcombe, S. J., K. I. Erickson, P. E. Scalf, J. S. Kim, R. Prakash, E. McAuley, S. Elavsky, D. X. Marquez, L. Hu and A. F. Kramer. "Aerobic Exercise Training Increases Brain Volume in Aging Humans." *The Journals of Gerontology Series A: Biological Sciences and Medical Sciences* 61 (2006): 1166–70.

Coleman, V. D., and P. M. Farris-Dufrene. *Art Therapy and Psychotherapy: Blending Two Therapeutic Approaches*. New York: Taylor and Francis, 1996.

Colodzin, B. *How to Survive Trauma: A Program for War Veterans and Survivors of Rape, Assault, Abuse or Environmental Disaster*. Barrytown, NY: Station Hill, 1993.

Cornfield, J. *Buddha's Little Instruction Book*. New York: Bantam, 1994.

Creswell, J. D., B. M. Way, N. I. Eisenberger, and M. D. Lieberman. "Neural Correlates of Dispositional Mindfulness During Affect Labeling." *Psychosomatic Medicine* 69, no. 6 (2007): 560–65.

Cruz, F. G., and L. Essen. *Adult Survivors of Childhood Emotional, Physical, and Sexual Abuse: Dynamics and Treatment*. Northvale, NJ: Jason Aronson, 1994.

Davidson, J. R. T., and E. B. Foa, eds. *Posttraumatic Stress Disorder: DSM-IV and Beyond*. Washington, D.C.: American Psychiatric Press, 1993.

Dolan, Y. M. *Resolving Sexual Abuse: Solution-Focused Therapy and Ericksonian Hypnosis for Adult Survivors*. New York: Norton, 1991.

Durant, W. *On the Meaning of Life*. New York: Ray Long and Richard R. Smith, 1932.

Engel, B. *Raising Your Sexual Self-Esteem*. New York: Fawcett Columbine, 1995.

Everly, G. S., Jr. "Short-Term Psychotherapy of Acute Adult Onset Post-Traumatic Stress: The Role of Weltanschauung." *Stress Medicine* 10 (1994): 191–96.

Everly, G. S., Jr., and J. M. Lating, eds. *Psychotraumatology: Key Papers and Core Concepts in Post-Traumatic Stress*. New York: Plenum, 1995.

Everstine, D. S., and L. Everstine. *The Trauma Response: Treatment for Emotional Injury*. New York: Norton, 1993.

Figley, C. R., ed. *Trauma and Its Wake: The Study and Treatment of Post-Traumatic Stress Disorder*. New York: Brunner/Mazel, 1985.

Figley, C. R. *Helping Traumatized Families*. San Francisco: Jossey-Bass, 1989.

Figley, C. R., B. E. Bride, and N. Mazza, eds. *Death and Trauma: The Traumatology of Grieving*. Washington, D.C.: Taylor and Francis, 1997.

Flannery, R. B., Jr. *Post-Traumatic Stress Disorder: The Victim's Guide to Healing and Recovery*. New York: Crossroad, 1992.

——— . *Violence in the Workplace*. New York: Crossroad, 1995.

Foa, E. B., D. E. Hearst-Ikeda, and C. V. Dancu. *Cognitive Therapy and Prolonged Exposure (CT/PE) Manual*. Philadelphia: Allegheny University of the Health Sciences/Eastern Pennsylvania Psychiatric Institute, 1994.

Follette, V. M., and J. I. Ruzek, eds. *Cognitive-Behavioral Therapies for Trauma*. 2nd ed. New York: Guilford, 2006.

Fontana, A., and R. Rosenheck. "A Causal Model of the Etiology of War-Related PTSD." *Journal of Traumatic Stress* 6 (1993): 475–500.

Fordyce, M. W. *Human Happiness: Its Nature and Its Attainment*. 2 vols. Ft. Myers, FL: Cypress Lake Media, n.d.

Foy, D. W., ed. *Treating PTSD: Cognitive-Behavioral Strategies*. New York: Guilford, 1992.

Frankl, V. *Man's Search for Meaning*. Boston: Beacon, 1959.

Friedman, M. J., T. M. Keane, and P. A. Resick, eds. *Handbook of PTSD: Science and Practice*. New York: Guilford, 2007.

Gantt, L., and L. W. Tinnin. "Intensive Trauma Therapy of PTSD and Dissociation: An Outcome Study." *The Arts in Psychotherapy* 34 (2007): 69–80.

Garrick, J., and M. B. Williams, eds. *Trauma Treatment Techniques: Innovative Trends*. New York: Haworth, 2006.

Gauthier, J., D. Pellerin, and P. Renaud. "The Enhancement of Self-Esteem: A Comparison of Two Cognitive Strategies." *Cognitive Therapy and Research* 7 (1983): 389–98.

Germer, C. K., R. D. Siegel, and P. R. Fulton, eds. *Mindfulness and Psychotherapy*. New York: Guilford, 2005.

Gil, E. *The Healing Power of Play: Working with Abused Children*. New York: Guilford, 1991.

Goleman, D., and D. Heller, eds. *The Pleasures of Psychology*. New York: New American Library, 1986.

Green, B. L., and J. Wolfe. "Traumatic Memory Research." *Journal of Traumatic Stress* 8, no. 4 (1995).

Grossman, D., with L. W. Christensen. *On Combat*. PPCT Research Publications, 2004.

Harvey, M. R. "An Ecological View of Psychological Trauma and Trauma Recovery." *Journal of Traumatic Stress* 9, no. 1 (1996): 3–23.

Hayes, S. C., with S. Smith. *Get Out of Your Mind and Into Your Life: The New Acceptance and Commitment Therapy*. Oakland, CA: New Harbinger, 2005.

Hayes, S. C., and K. D. Strosahl, with K. G. Wilson. *ACT: An Experiential Approach to Behavior Change*. New York: Guilford, 1999.

Herman, J. *Trauma and Recovery*. New York: Basic, 1997.

Hinton, J. *Dying*. London: Pelican, 1967.

Horowitz, M. J. "Psychological Response to Serious Life Events." In *Human Stress and Cognition*, edited by V. Hamilton and D. M. Warburton. New York: Wiley, 1979.

———. *Stress Response Syndromes*. 2nd ed. New York: Jason Aronson, 1986.

Hossack, A. and R. P. Bentall. "Elimination of Posttraumatic Symptomatology by Relaxation and Visual-Kinesthetic Dissociation." *Journal of Traumatic Stress* 9, no. 1 (1996): 99–110.

Jacobson, N. S., J. M. Gottman, J. Waltz, R. Rushe, J. Babcock, and A. Holtzworth-Munroe. "Affect, Verbal Content, and Psychophysiology in the Arguments of Couples with a Violent Husband." *Journal of Consulting and Clinical Psychology* 62 (1994): 982–88.

James, B. *Treating Traumatized Children: New Insights and Creative Interventions*. Lexington, MA: Lexington, 1989.

James, W. *The Varieties of Religious Experience*. New York: Mentor, 1958.

Kassinove, H., ed. *Anger Disorders: Definition, Diagnosis and Treatment*. Washington, D.C.: Taylor and Francis, 1995.

Kessler R. C., K. A. McGonagle, S. Zhao, C. B. Nelson, M. Hughes, S. Eshleman, H. U. Wittchen, and K. S. Kendler. "Lifetime and 12-month Prevalence of DSM-III-R Psychiatric Disorders in the United States." *Archives of General Psychiatry* 51 (1994): 8–19.

Kluft, R. P. "Multiple Personality Disorder." In *Review of Psychiatry*, edited by A. Tasman and S. Goldfinge, 375–84. Washington, D.C.: American Psychiatric Press, 1991.

Kubany, E. S., M. A. McCaig, and J. R. Laconsay. *Healing the Trauma of Domestic Violence*. Oakland, CA: New Harbinger, 2003.

Kulka, R. A., W. E. Schlenger, J. A. Fairbank, R. L. Hough, B. K. Jordan, C. R. Marmar, and D. S. Weiss. *Trauma and the Vietnam War Generation: Report of Findings from the National Vietnam Veterans Readjustment Study*. New York: Brunner/Mazel, 1990.

Kushner, H. S. *When Bad Things Happen to Good People*. New York: Schocken, 1981.

Larson, D. B., and S. S. Larson. *The Forgotten Factor in Physical and Mental Health: What Does the Research Show?* Rockville, MD: National Institute for Healthcare Research, 1994.

Lee, K. A., G. E. Vaillant, W. C. Torrey, and G. H. Elder. "A 50-year Prospective Study of the Psychological Sequelae of World War II Combat." *American Journal of Psychiatry* 152, no. 4 (1995): 141–48.

Letourneau, E. J., P. A. Schewe, and B. C. Frueh. "Preliminary Evaluation of Sexual Problems in Combat Veterans with PTSD." *Journal of Traumatic Stress* 10, no. 1 (1997): 125–32.

Lewinsohn, P., R. Munoz, M. Youngren, and A. Zeiss. *Control Your Depression*. New York: Prentice Hall, 1986.

Lewis, M. I., and R. N. Butler. "Life-Review Therapy: Putting Memories to Work in Individual and Group Psychotherapy." *Geriatrics* 29, no. 11 (1974): 165–73.

Lieberman, M. D., N. I. Eisenberger, M. J. Crockett, S. M. Tom, J. H. Pfeifer, and B. M. Way. "Putting Feelings into Words: Affect Labeling Disrupts Amygdala Activity in Response to Affective Stimuli." *Psychological Science* 18, no. 5 (2007): 421–28.

Lowenstein, D. Untitled poem. In *Wounded Healers*, edited by R. N. Remen. Bolinas, CA: Wounded Healer Press, 1994.

Marlatt, G. A., and J. R. Gordon, eds. *Relapse Prevention*. New York: Guilford, 1985.

Maslow, A. "Self-Actualizing and Beyond." In *The Pleasures of Psychology*, edited by D. Goleman and D. Heller, 299. New York: New American Library, 1986.

Matsakis, A. *I Can't Get Over It: A Handbook for Trauma Survivors*. Oakland, CA: New Harbinger, 1992.

———. *Post-Traumatic Stress Disorder: A Complete Treatment Guide*. Oakland, CA: New Harbinger, 1994.

Mayo, B. *Jefferson Himself: The Personal Narrative of a Many-Sided American*. Charlottesville, VA: University Press of Virginia, 1942.

Meichenbaum, D. *A Clinical Handbook/Practical Therapist Manual for Assessing and Treating Adults with Post-Traumatic Stress Disorder*. Waterloo, Ontario: Institute Press, 1994.

Miller, W. I. *The Anatomy of Disgust*. Cambridge, MA: Harvard University Press, 1997.

Milliken, R. "Dance/Movement Therapy with the Substance Abuser." *The Arts in Psychotherapy* 17 (1990): 309–17.

Moore, T. *Care of the Soul*. New York: Harper Perennial, 1994.

Mother Teresa. *Total Surrender*. Edited by A. Devananda. Ann Arbor, MI: Servant, 1985.

Murray, E. J., A. D. Lamnin, and C. S. Carver. "Emotional Expression in Written Essays and Psychotherapy." *Journal of Social and Clinical Psychology* 8 (1989): 414–29.

Murray, E. J., and D. L. Segal. "Emotional Processing in Vocal and Written Expression of Feelings About Traumatic Experiences." *Journal of Traumatic Stress* 7 (1994): 391–405.

Murray, W. H. *The Himalayan Expedition*. London: J. M. Dent and Son, 1951, 7.

Muss, D. *The Trauma Trap*. London: Doubleday, 1991.

Myers, D. G. *The Pursuit of Happiness: Who Is Happy—and Why*. New York: Morrow, 1992.

Najavits, L. M. *Seeking Safety: A Treatment Manual for PTSD and Substance Abuse.* New York: Guilford, 2002.

Nhat Hanh, T. *Peace Is Every Step: The Path of Mindfulness in Everyday Life.* New York: Bantam, 1991.

Olness, K., and D. P. Kohen. *Hypnosis and Hypnotherapy with Children.* 3rd ed. New York: Guilford, 1996.

Ozer, D., J. M. Healy, Jr., and R. A. J. Stewart, eds. *Perspectives on Personality.* Vol. 3. Greenwich, CT: JAI, 1991.

Ozer, E. J., S. R. Best, T. L. Lipsey, and D. S. Weiss. "Predictors of Posttraumatic Stress Disorder and Symptoms in Adults: A Meta-Analysis." *Psychological Bulletin* 129 (2003): 52–73.

Pennebaker, J. W. *Opening Up: The Healing Power of Expressing Emotion.* New York: Guilford, 1997.

Peterson, K. C., M. F. Prout, and R. A. Schwarz. *Post-Traumatic Stress Disorder: A Clinician's Guide.* New York: Plenum, 1991.

"Post-Traumatic Stress Disorder—Part II." *The Harvard Mental Health Letter* 13, no. 1 (July 1996): 1–5.

Princeton Religious Research Center. *Religion in America 1992–1993.* Princeton, NJ: Princeton Religious Research Center, 1993.

Propst, L. R., R. Ostrom, P. Watkins, T. Dean, and D. Mashburn. "Comparative Efficacy of Religious and Nonreligious Cognitive-Behavioral Therapy for the Treatment of Clinical Depression in Religious Individuals." *Journal of Consulting and Clinical Psychology* 60, no. 1 (1992): 94–103.

Rando, T. A. *Treatment of Complicated Mourning.* Champaign, IL: Research Press, 1993.

Reiger, D., W. Narrow, D. Rae, R. W. Manderscheid, B. Z. Locke, and F. K. Goodwin. "The De Facto U.S. Mental and Addictive Disorders Service System: Epidemiologic Catchment Area Prospective 1-year Prevalence Rates of Disorders and Services." *Archives of General Psychiatry* 50 (1993): 85–94.

Resick, P. A., C. M. Monson, and K. M. Chard. *Cognitive Processing Therapy: Veteran/Military Version.* Washington, D.C.: Department of Veterans' Affairs, 2007.

Rhoades, D. K., M. R. Leaveck, and J. C. Hudson, eds. *The Legacy of Vietnam Veterans and Their Families: Survivors of War, Catalysts for Change.* Papers from the May 1994 National Symposium. Washington, D.C.: Agent Orange Class Assistance Program, 1995.

Rinpoche, S. *The Tibetan Book of Living and Dying.* San Francisco: Harper, 1993.

Ross, J. *Triumph over Fear: A Book of Help and Hope for People with Anxiety, Panic Attacks, and Phobias.* New York: Bantam, 1994.

Saigh, P. A., ed. *Post-traumatic Stress Disorder: A Behavioral Approach to Assessment and Treatment.* Boston: Allyn and Bacon, 1992.

Schiraldi, G. *Stress Management Strategies.* Dubuque, IA: Kendall/Hunt, 1994.

———. *Conquer Anxiety, Worry and Nervous Fatigue: A Guide to Greater Peace.* Ellicott City, MD: Chevron, 1997.

———. *The Self-Esteem Workbook.* Oakland, CA: New Harbinger, 2001.

Scott, M. J., and S. G. Stradling. *Counseling for Post-Traumatic Stress Disorder.* London: Sage, 1992.

Scurfield, R. M. "Treatment of Posttraumatic Stress Disorder among Vietnam Veterans." In *International Handbook of Traumatic Stress Syndromes,* edited by J. P. Wilson and B. Raphael, 879–88. New York: Plenum, 1993.

———. "War-Related Trauma: An Integrative Experiential, Cognitive, and Spiritual Approach." In *Handbook of Post-traumatic Therapy,* edited by M. B. Williams and J. F. Sommer, Jr., 179–204. Westport, CT: Greenwood Press, 1994.

Segal, D. L., and E. J. Murray. "Emotional Processing in Cognitive Therapy and Vocal Expression of Feeling." *Journal of Social and Clinical Psychology* 13 (1994): 189–206.

Shapiro, F. *Eye Movement Desensitization and Reprocessing: Basic Principles, Protocols, and Procedures.* New York: Guilford, 1995.

Shapiro, F., F. W. Kaslow, and L. Maxfield, eds. *Handbook of EMDR and Family Therapy Processes.* New York: John Wiley, 2007.

Simon, S., and S. Simon. *Forgiveness: How to Make Peace with Your Past and Get on with Your Life*. New York: Warner, 1990.

Simpson, T. L., D. Kaysen, S. Bowen, N. Chawla, A. Blume, G. A. Marlatt, and M. Larimer. "PTSD Symptoms, Substance Use, and Vipassana Meditation among Incarcerated Individuals." *Journal of Traumatic Stress* 20, no. 3 (2007): 239–49.

Smyth, L. D. *Clinician's Manual for the Cognitive-Behavioral Treatment of Post Traumatic Stress Disorder*. Havre de Grace, MD: RTR Publishing, 1994.

——— . *Treating Anxiety Disorders with a Cognitive-Behavioral Exposure Based Approach and the Eye-Movement Technique*. Havre de Grace, MD: RTR Publishing, 1996. Videocassette.

——— . *Treating Anxiety Disorders with a Cognitive-Behavioral Exposure Based Approach and the Eye-Movement Technique, Viewer's Guide*. Havre de Grace, MD: RTR Publishing, 1996.

Solomon, S. D., E. T. Gerrity, and A. M. Muff. "Efficacy of Treatments for Posttraumatic Stress Disorder." *Journal of the American Medical Association* 268, no. 5 (1992): 633–38.

Spence, S. H. *Psychosexual Therapy: A Cognitive-Behavioral Approach*. London: Chapman and Hall, 1991.

Taft, L. B., and M. F. Nehrke. "Reminiscence, Life Review, and Ego Integrity in Nursing Home Residents." *International Journal of Aging and Human Development* 30, no. 3 (1990): 189–96.

Taylor, S. *Clinician's Guide to PTSD: A Cognitive-Behavioral Approach*. New York: Guilford, 2006.

Tedeschi, R. G., and L. G. Calhoun. "The Posttraumatic Growth Inventory: Measuring the Positive Legacy of Trauma." *Journal of Traumatic Stress* 9, no. 3 (1996): 455–71.

Tick, E. *War and the Soul: Healing Our Nation's Veterans from Post-Traumatic Stress Disorder*. Wheaton, IL: Quest, 2005.

Timmons, B. H., and R. Ley, eds. *Behavioral and Psychological Approaches to Breathing Disorders*. New York: Plenum, 1994.

Vanauken, S. *A Severe Mercy*. New York: Bantam, 1977.

van der Kolk, B. A., A. C. McFarlane, and L. Weisaeth, eds. *Traumatic Stress: The Effects of Overwhelming Experience on Mind, Body, and Society*. New York: Guilford, 1996.

Van Dis, H. "Hyperventilation in Phobic Patients." In *Stress and Anxiety*, Vol. 5., edited by C. D. Spielberger and I. G. Sarason. New York: Hemisphere, 1978.

Walser, R. D., and D. Westrup. *Acceptance and Commitment Therapy for the Treatment of Post-Traumatic Stress Disorder and Trauma-related Problems*. Oakland, CA: New Harbinger, 2007.

Weekes, C. *More Help for Your Nerves*. New York: Bantam, 1984.

Wells, K. B., G. Goldberg, R. H. Brook, and B. Leake. "Quality of Care for Psychotropic Drug Use in Internal Medicine Group Practices." *Western Journal of Medicine* 145 (1986): 710–14.

Williams, M. B., and J. F. Sommer, Jr., eds. *Handbook of Post-traumatic Therapy*. Westport, CT: Greenwood Press, 1994.

Wilson, B. L., and M. A. Scovel, eds. "Psychiatric Music Therapy." *Music Therapy Perspectives* 12, no. 2 (1994).

Wilson, J. P., and B. Raphael, eds. *International Handbook of Traumatic Stress Syndromes*. New York: Plenum, 1993.

Wolf, M. E., and A. D. Mosnaim, eds. *Posttraumatic Stress Disorder: Etiology, Phenomenology, and Treatment*. Washington, D.C.: American Psychiatric Press, 1990.

Yalom, I. *Existential Psychotherapy*. New York: Basic Books, 1980.

# Additional Resources

## REFERRALS FOR FINDING MENTAL HEALTH PROFESSIONALS

In addition to the following resources, check with police, rape crisis hotlines, women's shelters, and crisis/sexual assault centers for referrals.

**Sidran Institute**, Baltimore, MD 21286 (410-825-8888; www.sidran.org). Locate psychotherapists specializing in PTSD, readings, and other resources.

**EMDR Institute**, Watsonville, CA 95077 (831-761-1040; www.emdr.com). Find clinicians trained in eye movement densensitization and reprocessing.

**Association for Contextual Behavioral Science** (www.contextualpsychology.org). Find an acceptance and commitment therapy (ACT) therapist.

**Behavioral Tech** (www.behavioraltech.com) provides information on dialectical behavior therapy, with link to clinical resource directory.

**Intensive Trauma Therapy**, Morgantown, WV 26508 (304-291-2912; www.traumatherapy.us). Masterfully blends hypnosis, video technology, and art therapy into one- to two-week intensives to facilitate processing of traumatic memories, with excellent results, without the need for a prolonged period of stabilization. Also trains providers.

**Seeking Safety.** To view research and locate Seeking Safety treatment for dual diagnosis of PTSD and substance abuse, go to www.seekingsafety.org.

**Virtually Better** (404-634-3400; www.virtuallybetter.com) lists virtual reality exposure (VRE) treatment centers.

**Childhelp USA**, Scottsdale, AZ 85260 (800-422-4453; www.childhelp.org). In addition to referrals to therapists, crisis centers, and child protective services, they provide a crisis counseling hotline for children, troubled parents, and adult survivors. Free literature on child abuse, parenting, and recovery.

**TIR Association**, Ann Arbor, MI 48105 (800-499-2751; www.tir.org; info@tir.org). Referrals to clinicians offering traumatic incident reduction (TIR).

**American Art Therapy Association**, Reston, VA 20191 (888-290-0878; www.arttherapy.org; info@arttherapy.org) refers to registered art therapists through local chapters.

**American Dance Therapy Association**, Columbia, MD 21044 (410-997-4040; www.adta.org; info@adta.org). Obtain referrals to registered dance therapists.

**American Music Therapy Association**, Silver Spring, MD 20910 (301-589-3300; www.musictherapy.org). Locate board-certified music therapists.

**Association for Play Therapy**, Clovis, CA 93612 (559-294-2128; www.a4pt.org; info@a4pt.org). Referrals to registered play therapists.

**National Association for Drama Therapy** (www.nadt.org) refers to registered drama therapists, specialists who are trained in drama and psychotherapy.

**Association for Poetry Therapy**, Delray Beach , FL 33483 (561-498-8334; www.poetrytherapy.org). Maintains registry of registered poetry therapists, who use the language arts in therapy.

**Anxiety Disorders Association of America**, Silver Spring, MD 20910 (240-485-1001; www.adaa.org). Provides a list of professionals who specialize in the treatment of anxiety disorders. Also provides information on self-help and support groups in your area. Has a catalog of available brochures, books, and audiocassettes, as well as a newsletter. Sponsors annual national conference.

**Mental Health America**, Alexandria, VA 22311 (703-684-7722 or 800-969-NMHA; www.nmha.org). Provides list of affiliate mental health organizations in your area who can provide resources and information about self-help groups, treatment professionals, and community clinics. Crisis line: 1-800-273-TALK.

**National Mental Health Information Center**, Washington, DC 20015 (800-789-2647; www.mentalhealth.samhsa.gov/cmhs). Lists local community mental health centers and family service agencies, both of which provide mental services on a sliding fee scale. Also provides information on mental health agencies, support groups, and clearinghouses.

**American Psychiatric Association**, Arlington, VA 22209 (703-907-7300 or 888-35-PSYCH; www.psych.org; apa@psych.org). Obtain referrals to psychiatrists in your area.

**American Psychological Association**, Washington DC 20002 (202-336-5500 or 5800; 800-964-2000; www.apa.org). Call or write for referrals to psychologists in your area.

**Association for Behavioral and Cognitive Therapies**, New York, NY 10001 (212-647-1890; www.abct.org/members/Directory/Find_A_Therapist.cfm). Find a cognitive-behavioral therapist in your area and receive complimentary brochure "Guidelines for Choosing a Behavior Therapist." You can ask for individual, group, or couples therapy.

**American Academy of Child and Adolescent Psychiatry**, Washington, DC 20016 (202-966-7300 or 800-333-7636; www.aacap.org). Locate child and adolescent psychiatrists in your area.

**National Board for Certified Counselors**, Greensboro, NC 27403 (336-547-0607; www.nbcc.org). Can refer you to certified clinical mental health counselors.

**National Association of Social Workers**, Washington, DC 20002 (800-638-8799 or 202-408-8600; www.naswdc.org). Refers to qualified clinical social workers in your area.

**Alliance for Children and Families**, Milwaukee, WI 53224 (414-359-1040; www.alliance1.org). Referrals to family/social service agencies, which accept payments on a sliding scale.

**American Association for Marriage and Family Therapy**, Alexandria, VA 22314 (703-838-9808; www.aamft.org). Find marriage or family therapists.

**American Association of Pastoral Counselors**, Fairfax, VA 22031 (703-385-6967; www.aapc.org). Many who seek help in times of need turn first to a clergyperson. This association provides referrals to certified pastoral counselors who consider both spiritual and psychological needs.

**American Psychiatric Nurses Association**, Arlington, VA 22209 (866-243-2443; www.apna.org). Locate a psychiatric nurse.

**S.A.F.E. Alternatives** (800-DONTCUT; www.selfinjury.com). Find therapists for trauma-related self-injury.

# SURVIVOR AND SUPPORT GROUPS

In addition to the following, check your local newspaper, white pages, library, police, hospitals, mental health professionals, or mental health agencies.

## Information Clearinghouses

These organizations collect and distribute information on diverse trauma-related concerns and support groups.

**American Self-Help Clearinghouse**, Dover, NJ 07801 (973-989-1122; 800-367-6274 in NJ; www .selfhelpgroups.org). Directs callers to diverse self-help groups. Inexpensive sourcebook lists national and model self-help groups, guidelines for forming self-help groups, and other clearinghouses.

**National Self-Help Clearinghouse**, c/o CUNY Graduate Center, New York, NY 10016 (212-817-1822; www.selfhelpweb.org). Refers to self-help and support groups. Also trains facilitators.

**National Clearinghouse for Alcohol and Drug Information** (800-662-HELP; www.findtreatment. samhsa.gov for referrals; www.samhsa.gov/shin for publications). Provides referrals to detoxification and rehabilitation programs, as well as alcohol and drug support groups and various publications on alcohol and substances.

**National Mental Health Consumers' Self-Help Clearinghouse**, Philadelphia, PA 19107 (800-553-4539; www.mhselfhelp.org). Technical assistance for self-help groups as well as help in locating self-help groups. Free informational packets and information for individuals.

## Recommended Self-Help/Support Groups

Below is a sampling of self-help/support groups, whose numbers may be obtained from the above clearinghouses/helplines. Many are based on the AA 12-step model.

Alcoholics Anonymous

Adult Children of Alcoholics

Al-Anon Family Groups and Alateen. For those whose lives have been affected by the drinking of a family member.

Incest Survivors Anonymous

Survivors of Incest Anonymous. Provides a hotline and bimonthly bulletins.

Narcotics Anonymous

Nar-Anon. Support groups for families of users of illegal drugs.

Overeaters Anonymous

Gamblers Anonymous

Sex Addicts Anonymous

Debtors Anonymous

Cocaine Anonymous

Parents Anonymous. For parents who batter and wish to learn effective parenting. Professionally facilitated and peer led. Not a 12-step program.

---

## SECULAR RECOVERY FROM ADDICTIONS

These focus on thinking; there is no spiritual component:
- SMART Recovery (www.smartrecovery.org) provides face-to-face or online mutual help groups.
- Rational Recovery (www.rational.org) guides one in self-recovery.
- Secular Organizations for Sobriety/Save Our Selves (SOS) (www.secularsobriety.org) provides autonomous groups that are not lead by professionals.

---

Theos (They Help Each Other Spiritually). Helps widowed persons move successfully through grief. Non-denominational.

The Compassionate Friends. Information and referrals to support groups for bereaved parents, siblings, and grandparents who grieve the death of a child.

Widowed Persons Service, American Association of Retired Persons. Referrals for widows and widowers to information and support programs.

Parents of Murdered Children. Support groups for anyone who has lost someone to homicide. Also court accompaniment, antiviolence advocacy, questions related to unsolved cases of suicide/homicide, and training for support groups and sensitivity to violence.

Survivors of Suicide. For families and friends of suicide victims.

SIDS Alliance. Provides advocacy and information about SIDS (sudden infant death syndrome).

Parents United International. For victims of all ages, offenders, and support persons (spouses, parents, and others).

Society of Military Widows

National Amputation Foundation

National Burn Victim Foundation

National Head Injury Foundation

Sex Workers Anonymous

**The Society for the Advancement of Sexual Health**, Atlanta, GA 31139 (770-541-9912; www.sash.net). Helps individuals find a 12-step program for sexual addiction and counselors with interest in treating this condition.

**National Council on Alcoholism and Drug Dependence**, New York, NY 10022 (212-269-7797 or 800-622-2255; www.ncadd.org). Referrals to self-help groups and low-cost treatment facilities.

**National SHARE Office**, St. Joseph Health Center, St. Charles, MO 63301 (800-821-6819/636-947-6164; www.nationalshareoffice.com; share@nationalshareoffice.com). Support for families who have suffered perinatal loss.

## AGENCIES/ORGANIZATIONS/VICTIMS' SERVICES

Check the Internet or telephone directory for violence shelters, counseling and support groups, hotlines, legal services, welfare, etc., under: *crises intervention, domestic abuse information and treatment centers, social services, human services, shelters, women's organizations,* or *family services.*

**International Critical Incident Stress Foundation**, Ellicott City, MD 21042 (410-750-9600; www.icisf.org). Develops and disseminates crisis intervention, stress education, and recovery programs for all those affected by work-related stress, disasters, and other traumatic events. Sponsors annual conference and publishes newsletter. Known for developing *critical incident stress debriefing.*

**Sidran Institute**, Baltimore, MD 21286 (410-825-8888 or 888-825-8249; www.sidran.org). National nonprofit organization devoted to education and information in support of survivors of traumatic experiences. Publishes books on PTSD and DID. Maintains a computerized information database of educational resources, therapists, organizations, conferences, training, and treatment facilities.

**National Domestic Violence Hotline.** (800-799-SAFE; TTY 800-787-3224; www.ndvh.org). Provides a 24-hour hotline with multilingual and deaf capabilities. Serves victims, including those of dating violence, and concerned family and friends. Helps victims with issues of safety, shelter, counseling, and legal advice. Also helps batterers get help. Offers printed information.

**National Organization for Victim Assistance** (NOVA), Alexandria, VA 22314 (703-535-NOVA or 800-TRY-NOVA; www.trynova.org). Provides support and advocacy for crime victims. Referrals to victim-assistance programs (battered women's programs, support groups, rape crisis centers, legal and medical advice, etc.). Crisis Response Team Project formed to deal with community crisis. Training and education for helpers.

**National Center for Victims of Crime**, Washington, DC 20036 (800-FYI-CALL; www.ncvc.org). Refers victims of any crime (sexual abuse, domestic violence, stalking, hate crimes, and others) to shelters, support groups, and legal advocacy programs. Also puts out information bulletins on these topics.

**Mothers Against Drunk Driving** (MADD), Irving, TX 75062 (800-GET-MADD; 24-hour helpline 877-623-3435; www.madd.org). Support services can include support groups, diverse publications (on crash victims, mourning, legal issues, etc.), court accompaniment, help with navigating the criminal justice system, training, and referrals for counseling and financial assistance.

---

## CRIME

- All states have a crime victims compensation/assistance program for violent crimes (including domestic violence) that are reported within specified periods. Benefits usually apply to medical and certain legal expenses, counseling, lost income, funerals, and shelter. Assistance programs advise victims of rights, help victims through the legal system, and help them secure protection. If local authorities do not direct you, call the Office for Victims of Crime, Washington, D.C. The OVC Resource Center/Clearinghouse (800-851-3420; www.ovc.gov) refers callers to the appropriate state or other helpful agencies. The Clearinghouse also offers a wide range of printed and audiovisual information, most of which is free.

- Contact police, social service agencies, or the local bar association or legal aid society to find victim-assistance centers that provides information about legal, financial, and psychological help. Sometimes pro bono (free) legal assistance is available.

- Your state's department of social services or state worker's compensation board will discuss worker's compensation for victims of violence on the job.

- Contact the Social Security Administration to apply for disability benefits if you are disabled due to crime.

**Rape, Abuse & Incest National Network** (RAINN), Washington, DC 20036 (www.rainn.org). Calling 800-656-HOPE (ext. 1) will automatically connect a victim of sexual assault to the nearest sexual assault center. These centers provide confidential 24-hour crisis hotlines for free advice and support; they also offer free or sliding scale private counseling and/or groups treatment.

**Prevent Child Abuse America**, Chicago, IL 60611 (312-663-3520 or 800-CHILDREN; www.preventchildabuse.org). Extensive printed material. Healthy Families America is a home-visiting service for parents that teaches parenting skills, links parents to resources, and provides a helping hand.

**Child Welfare Information Gateway**, Washington, DC 20024 (800-394-3366; 703-385-7565; info@childwelfare.gov; www.childwelfare.gov). Information available on all aspects of child mistreatment for the public and professionals. Find help for a personal situation.

**American Foundation for Suicide Prevention**, New York, NY 10005 (888-333-AFSP; www.afsp.org). Support groups for suicide survivors. Also referral to crisis hotline (800-273-TALK). Free materials on coping.

**Group Project for Holocaust Survivors and Their Children**, New York, NY 10075 (212-737-8524). Referrals, training for therapists and others working with all types of trauma survivors. Literature and bibliographies may be purchased. Counseling and intergenerational community meetings. Dr. Y. Danieli, Director.

---

## POST ABORTION STRESS

The Elliot Institute's website, www.afterabortion.org, lists various healing principles and resources, many with a spiritual orientation, such as:

- National Office of Post-Abortion Reconciliation & Healing, Milwaukee WI 53207 (800-5WE-CARE; www.noparh.org). Support services directory, audiovisual materials, annual conference. Directs Project Rachel, a Catholic counseling project that is for people of all faiths. In consortium with Reclaiming Fatherhood (www.menandabortion.info).

---

**Gift from Within**, Camden, ME 04843 (207-236-8858; www.giftfromwithin.org). Educational material. Roster of trauma and victimization survivors for peer support by telephone and letters.

**National Mental Health Information Center**, Washington, DC 20015 (800-789-2647; www.mentalhealth.samhsa.gov). Provides information on mental health, including disaster and emergency assistance, via publications, videos, website, electronic bulletin board, and telephone services. Referrals to mental health associations, clearinghouses, and advocacy organizations.

**Grief Recovery Helpline** (800-334-7606). Trained grief counselors handle calls from 9 A.M. to 5 P.M. Pacific time. Sponsored by Grief Recovery Institute Educational Foundation Inc. (GRIEF).

**Outward Bound** (888-837-5210; www.outwardboundwilderness.org/groups.html). A range of challenging wilderness environments coupled with emotional support to inspire self-respect and care for others, community, and environment. Since 1941. Groups customized for survivors of violence, war, sexual assault, incest, cancer, substance use disorders, mild traumatic brain injury, and grief.

## MILITARY/VETERANS SERVICES

**Military OneSource** (800-342-9647, www.militaryonesource.com). For active duty, Guard, and Reserve members and families. Get a real voice, usually a licensed counselor, 24 hours a day. Initial assessment, then referrals to private practice paid for by the Department of Defense, up to six sessions; then referral to Tricare for additional sessions. Also offers resources for crisis, deployment, injury, and more.

---

### VETERANS AFFAIRS FACILITIES AND SERVICES

The U.S. Department of Veterans Affairs (DVA) is the acknowledged expert in treating war-related trauma. DVA offers various treatment options:

- Outpatient clinics, mental health clinics, day hospitals, and day treatment centers provide a full range of services, including individual psychotherapy, medication, and group and family therapy. Located at DVA Medical Centers or independent sites.
- Over 200 vet centers provide individual, family, and group counseling services. Vets who are not close to a vet center may receive referrals to non-DVA providers. Also provides assistance with employment and benefits.
- Inpatient treatments upon admission to DVA hospitals include general psychiatry units and specialized inpatient PTSD units (currently there are several PTSD/substance use projects).

For compensation, educational, housing, medical, job training, or other benefits for PTSD, call or write your local DVA facility (e.g., vet center, regional office). If unable to locate one, call **Department of Veterans Affairs**, Washington, DC 20420 (800-827-1000; www.va.gov).

- **Women Veterans Health** (800-827-1000; www1.va.gov/wvhp). Programs for sexual trauma, PTSD, substance abuse, homelessness, victims of domestic violence, and vocational rehabilitation. Assistance with benefits claims.
- **Traumatic Brain Injury (TBI)** (www.va.gov/vhi). The Veterans Health Initiative offers an online course on TBI, including an excellent section on help for families. The course is available to civilians as well.

---

**Coalition of Iraq and Afghanistan Veterans** (www.coalitionforveterans.org). Partnership of organizations working to provide support and services to OIF/OEF veterans and their families for many needs, including: pain, physical/brain injuries, financial difficulties, clothes, legal, grief, building homes for injured vets, resources for kids, help lines, workshops, and online chats.

**National Center for PTSD**, Department of Veteran Affairs, VA Medical Center, White River Junction, VT 05009 (802-296-6300; www.ncptsd.va.gov). Research and information, including the *PTSD Research Quarterly* and fact sheets for vets or anyone else. PILOTS database locates published PTSD research.

**Veterans of the Vietnam War and the Veterans Coalition**, Inc., Pittston, PA 18640 (570-603-9740 or 800-VIETNAM; www.theveteranscoalition.org). Supporting veterans of all wars and families in need, including case management, education, interim housing for homeless vets, and help for incarcerated vets.

**Vietnam Veterans of America**, Silver Spring, MD 20910 (301-585-4000; 800-882-1316; www.vva .org). Congressionally chartered. Helps veterans and families. Referrals to all services (legal, medical, vet centers, etc.). Assists vets with processing disability claims.

**Veterans Hotline** (800-273-8255, press 1). Veterans can call for any crisis, including suicide.

**Disabled American Veterans**, Washington, D.C. 20024 (202-554-3501; www.dav.org). Free assistance in gaining benefits and referrals to mostly VA rehabilitation services.

**National Military Family Association**, Alexandria, VA 22302 (800-260-0218; www.nmfa.org). Information to support families of deployed, wounded, and fallen on topics including deployment and return stress and spouse education.

**Operation Purple.** Free summer camps for military kids enduring deployment of parents, with special help for kids of wounded parents. Run by the National Military Family Association (www.nmfa .org).

**Soldier's Heart**, Troy, NY 12180 (518-274-0501; www.soldiersheart.net; info@soldiersheart.net). A veterans' return and healing project addressing the emotional and spiritual needs of veterans, their families, and their communities. Nurtures a positive warrior identity. Veterans' return retreats are open to everyone, especially families and professionals. Sponsors reconciliation visits to old battlefields and countries, individual and family therapy at little or no cost, support for community-based services through regional contacts, help for vets to mentor new returnees, service to war-ravaged countries, benefits advisement, and free e-newsletter.

**United States Welcome Home Foundation**, Dallas, TX 75204 (214-559-4040; www.uswelcomehome .org; info@uswelcomehome.org). Nationwide organization; welcome home centers function as outreach and networking to develop and provide community-based health and wellness professionals to support veterans and their families. Seven-day reintegration retreats for couples, individuals, and families to help returning combat vets and service members reintegrate with families and communities (ceremonies, discussion groups, outdoor recreation—all at no cost). Focuses on wounds of the heart and soul using traditional and complementary and alternative medicine.

**The Coming Home Project**, San Francisco, CA 94109 (415-353-5363; www.cominghomeproject.net). Care, support, and stress management for military personnel and families involved in recent/current wars. Free and confidential workshops, retreats (includes airfare), counseling (in San Francisco area, referrals outside of that area), training for care providers, community forums. Dr. Joseph Bobrow, Director.

**Outward Bound** (888-837-5211 ext. 1; www.outwardboundwilderness.org/veterans.html) aids veterans of recent wars in readjustment (strongly advised that vets be using some form of veterans support system); full funding for veterans of recent wars; enrollment of individuals or intact groups with counselors are options. Also couples programs help build trust, mutual reliance, fun, and couples skills.

**Department of Defense Helpline** (800-796-9699). Any military service member, active or not, or their families can call with questions about medical or psychological care.

**Military Aid Societies.** Emergency financial assistance for personal or family crises. Funds for emergency mental health, welfare, travel, auto repair, and medical needs, including food and shelter. For active, retired, and family. Or call the American Red Cross (877-272-7337; www.redcross.org), which coordinates with these societies:

- **Armed Forces Relief Trust** (www.afrtrust.org)
- **Army Emergency Relief** (www.aerhq.org)
- **Navy-Marine Corps Relief Society** (www.nmcrs.org)
- **Air Force Aid Society** (www.afas.org)
- **Coast Guard Mutual Assistance** (www.cgmahq.org)

There are also American Legion, U.S. Department of Labor (Disabled Veteran's Outreach Programs for employment; local vets employment representatives), and veterans associations for Jewish, blinded, disabled, and paralyzed veterans.

## Printed Resources for Military

Grossman, D., with L. W. Christensen. 2004. *On Combat*. PPCT Research Publications. Helps warriors come to peace with war and survivor guilt.

Mason, P. H. C. 1990. *Recovering from War: A Woman's Guide to Helping Your Vietnam Veteran, Your Family, and Yourself*. New York: Viking.

*Taking Care of the Families of America's Armed Forces*. Very useful Department of Defense booklet for Reserve and Guard individuals and families. Google "Taking Care of the Families of America's Armed Forces."

Tick, E. 2005. *War and the Soul: Healing Our Nation's Veterans from Post-Traumatic Stress Disorder*. Wheaton, IL: Quest. Tick argues that PTSD is best understood as an identity disorder and soul wound, and moral pain is a root cause. How the honorable warrior soul is healed and reclaimed.

## RECOMMENDED BOOKS

Cohen, B. M., M. Barnes, and A. B. Rankin. 1995. *Managing Traumatic Stress Through Art*. Lutherville, MD: Sidran. An excellent, practical workbook for survivors.

Dr. Seuss. 1990. *Oh, the Places You'll Go*. NY: Random House. A clever, humorous treatise on human growth and fallibility. Written for kids. Or is it?

Frankl, V. 1963. *Man's Search for Meaning*. New York: Pocket Books. The classic work on discovering meaning in one's life out of suffering. Written by the Holocaust survivor who founded logotherapy. Republished by Simon & Schuster.

Kubany, E. S., M. A. McCaig, and J. R. Laconsay. 2003. *Healing the Trauma of Domestic Violence*. Oakland, CA: New Harbinger. A particularly useful aid for reducing the guilt that is typically found in survivors of domestic violence who have left the relationship.

Kushner, H. S. 1981. *When Bad Things Happen To Good People*. New York: Schocken Books. A compassionate treatise on suffering that happens to the good, and how to cope with it.

Markman, H., S. Stanley, and S. L. Blumberg. 1994. *Fighting for Your Marriage: Positive Steps for Preventing Divorce and Preserving A Lasting Love*. San Francisco: Jossey-Bass. Research at the University of Denver found that the program described in this book increased marital satisfaction and decreased divorce. This practical and down-to-earth guide shows how to discuss difficult issues safely and clearly, manage and resolve conflict, and enhance fun and intimacy.

Nhat Hanh, T. 1991. *Peace Is Every Step: The Path of Mindfulness in Everyday Life*. New York: Bantam Books. Nominated for the Nobel Peace Prize by Martin Luther King, Jr., this peaceful monk describes many practical ways to cultivate inner peace, joy, serenity, and balance. Useful while you are healing or after. Highly recommended.

Prevention and Relationship Enhancement Program: Resources for a Loving Relationship, Denver, Colorado, 800-366-0166. *Fighting for Your Marriage* and other books. Four excellent videos to help develop communication skills, solve problems, and promote intimacy. The PREP program is well researched and respected.

Pennebaker, J. W. 1990. *Opening Up: The Healing Power of Confiding in Others*. New York: W. Morrow. Explains why verbalizing grief and upsetting events from the past reduces distress.

Schiraldi, G. R. 1995. *Facts to Relax By: A Guide To Relaxation and Stress Reduction*. Detailed instructions for five relaxation exercises, plus exercise and nutrition guidelines, assertiveness, time management, changing stressful attitudes, and other ways to reduce stress. Order by telephone from Chevron Publishing, Ellicott City, MD (410-418-8002).

——— . 1997. *Conquer Anxiety, Worry and Nervous Fatigue: A Guide to Greater Peace.* Ellicott City, MD 21042: Chevron. Order by telephone (410-418-8002). Step-by-step instructions for recognizing, reducing, and preventing anxiety and its troubling symptoms. From hyperventilation to worrisome thought patterns. Extensive resource list. Also explains how to find professional help, if it is needed. "Dr. Schiraldi has brought together information from a variety of mental health disciplines, translated them into language that is easily understood, and sprinkled it all with the wisdom of some of the greatest minds known to man. A great job." (Robert J. Hedaya, M.D., biopsychiatrist)

——— . 2001. *The Self-Esteem Workbook.* Oakland, CA: New Harbinger. A clear, effective guide to understanding and improving self-esteem. Based upon the Stress and the Healthy Mind course, University of Maryland. Sound principles. Many effective skills. Self-esteem usually needs to be restored in PTSD.

——— . 2007. *Ten Simple Solutions for Building Self-Esteem.* Oakland, CA: New Harbinger. Combines mindfulness, acceptance and commitment therapy, and traditional psychological strategies for raising self-esteem in a way that might be particularly useful for trauma survivors.

——— . 2007. *World War II Survivors: Lessons in Resilience.* Ellicott City, MD: Chevron. Order by telephone (410-418-8002). Powerful lessons in preserving sanity and the ability to function under many forms of extreme duress. Resilience also includes the strengths that help people rebound from intense duress.

Schiraldi, G. R., and M. H. Kerr. 2002. *The Anger Management Sourcebook.* New York: McGraw-Hill. Anger can block healing and interfere with relationships.

---

## MINDFULNESS

- You can find CDs and books on meditations by Dr. Jon Kabat-Zinn at www.mindfulnesstapes.com. I especially like *Full Catastrophe Living*.
- Visit psychologist Jim Hopper's website www.jimhopper.com/mindfulness for an overview of the concept of mindfulness and resources.
- Schiraldi, G. R. 2007. *Ten Simple Solutions for Building Self-Esteem.* Oakland, CA: New Harbinger. Mindfulness basics, with instructions.

---

## FOR PROFESSIONALS

**International Society for Traumatic Stress Studies**, Deerfield, IL 60015 (847-480-9028; www.istss .org; istss@istss.org). Shares research, clinical strategies, and theoretical and policy concerns. Publishes *Journal of Traumatic Stress* and an electronic newsletter. Sponsors annual conference.

**International Society for the Study of Trauma and Dissociation**, McLean, VA 22102 (703-610-9037, www.isst-d.org). Sponsors conferences. Publishes the journal *Dissociation* and *ISSD News.* Offers referral listings.

**Association of Traumatic Stress Specialists**, Verona, NJ 07044 (973-559-9200; www.atss.info). Certifies trauma counselors and other helpers. Offers training conferences and quarterly *Trauma Lines* newsletter.

# Index

# *About the Author*

**Glenn R. Schiraldi**, Ph.D., has served on the stress management faculties at the Pentagon, the International Critical Incident Stress Foundation, and the University of Maryland, where he received the Outstanding Teaching Award in the college of Health and Human Performance. His other books on stress-related topics include: *World War II Survivors: Lessons in Resilience*, *The Self-Esteem Workbook*, *Conquer Anxiety, Worry & Nervous Fatigue*, *The Anger Management Sourcebook*, *Ten Simple Solutions for Building Self-Esteem*, *Hope and Help for Depression*, and *Facts to Relax By*. Dr. Schiraldi's writing has been recognized by various scholarly and popular sources, including the *Washington Post*, *American Journal of Health Promotion*, the *Mind/Body Health Review*, and the *International Stress and Tension Control Society Newsletter*.

While serving at the Pentagon, he helped to design and implement a series of prototype courses in stress management for the Department of the Army, including hostility/anger management and communication skills. For the International Critical Incident Stress Foundation, he designed and presents resilience training to prevent post-traumatic stress disorder (PTSD) in high-risk groups (such as military, police, and firefighters). Having taught at the University of Maryland since 1980, he has pioneered a number of mind/body courses, which have taught skills to a wide range of adults to prevent stress-related mental and physical illness. His recent research indicates that multiple mental health indicators can be favorably impacted by semester courses. He has also trained clinicians in the United States and Canada on treating PTSD and teaching self-esteem skills.

He has served on the board of directors for the Depression and Related Affective Disorders Association, founded as a Johns Hopkins University Department of Psychiatry cooperative, on the editorial board of the *International Journal of Emergency Mental Health*, and on the ABC News post-traumatic stress disorder working group.

He is a graduate of the U.S. Military Academy at West Point and holds graduate degrees from Brigham Young University (summa cum laude) and the University of Maryland. His research interests at the University of Maryland center on personality and stress, including post-traumatic stress, resilience, anger/hostility, self-esteem, depression, and anxiety.